Equality

on the

Oregon Frontier

Equality

on the

Oregon Frontier

JASON LEE AND THE METHODIST MISSION

1834–43

Robert J. Loewenberg

UNIVERSITY OF WASHINGTON PRESS

SEATTLE AND LONDON

This book was published with the assistance of a grant from the
Andrew W. Mellon Foundation.

Library of Congress Cataloging in Publication Data

Loewenberg, Robert J   1938–
    Equality on the Oregon frontier.

    Bibliography: p.
    Includes index.
        1. Oregon—History—to 1859.   2. Lee, Jason, 1803–
1845.   3. Chinook Indians—Missions.   4. Methodist
Episcopal Church in Oregon.   5. Missions—Oregon.
I. Title.
F880.L84   979.5   75-40876
ISBN 0-295-95491-4

FOR MY FATHER, A MAN OF VIRTUE,
IN MEMORIAM

Preface

*N*O STUDY, and certainly not this one, could even be attempted without the assistance of libraries and librarians. I acknowledge with pleasure and sincere appreciation the aid of some of the individuals and institutions who made my work possible: Desmond Taylor, library director, University of Puget Sound, Tacoma, Washington; Priscilla Knuth, managing editor, *Oregon Historical Quarterly;* Thomas Vaughan, director, Oregon Historical Society; James D. Cleaver, manuscripts librarian, Oregon Historical Society, Portland; Wyman W. Parker, librarian, Olin Library, Wesleyan University, Middletown, Connecticut; Martin Schmitt, Special Collections librarian, University of Oregon, Eugene; Charles H. Kemp, Reader's Services librarian, Pacific University, Forest Grove, Oregon; the Philip H. & A. S. W. Rosenbach Foundation Museum, Philadelphia, Pennsylvania; David C. Duniway, former state archivist, Oregon State Archives, Salem, Oregon; Miss Miriam Parsell, librarian, United Mission Library, New York; John H. Ness, Jr., executive secretary, Commission on Archives and History, United Methodist Church, Lake Junaluska, North Carolina; Mrs. Elizabeth Smith, Archives of the Archdiocese of Portland, Oregon; Les Archives de l'archidiocèse de Québec, Quebec; Mrs. Ruth Gates, assistant curator, Washington County Historical Society, Hillsboro, Oregon; Mrs. Donald Menefee, Lane County Historical Society, Eugene, Oregon; Lela Goodell, assistant librarian, Hawaiian Mission Children's Society Library, Honolulu; Kenneth E. Rose, Methodist librarian, Drew University, Madison, New Jersey; Dwight L. Cart, Congregational Library, Boston, Massachusetts; Anson Huang, assistant director, Missionary Research Library, New York.

I am especially indebted to Richard Horn of the University of Oregon, to Miss Dace Pedecis of the University of Puget Sound, and to Miss Janice Duncan of the University of Portland whose efforts on my behalf were remarkable for fidelity as well as for thoroughness. John Green of the Washington State Historical Society is well informed about Methodists and he was a very great help to me, as were Bruce LeRoy, director of the society, Raymond Morris of the Yale Divinity School, and Archibald Hanna of the Beinecke Library.

Because some of the materials I used come from uncatalogued depositories, for example, University of Puget Sound (UPS), Pacific University, and the Methodist archives in New York City, the location for each reference is usually given. Also, since the materials from UPS are new to the literature, I have quoted from them liberally not only because they contain relevant information, but because they are fascinating documents in their own right.

As for secondary accounts, a word or two should be said concerning them. This book touches several separable areas of scholarly concern. I have made no effort in the text or bibliography to use any but the most immediately relevant materials which have appeared as this book has made its way to press. For example, the excellent study of Oregon diplomacy by David M. Pletcher, which has an obvious place in a work such as the present one, has been added for use in chapter 2. On the other hand, more general intellectual studies such as Rush Welter's new book, *The Mind of America, 1820–1860* (New York: Columbia University Press, 1975), have not been included.

For the many hours in the offices of Yale historians Sydney Ahlstrom, the late Alexander Bickel, and Edmund Morgan, who gave me liberty to think out loud, and for their truly wise counsel, I am grateful beyond measuring. Howard Roberts Lamar, my dissertation director, shepherded me through my graduate years as adviser, critic, and friend with a kindliness and a devotion to scholarly achievement which only those who know him can fully appreciate. It has been a delight and an honor to study with him. Although he read the manuscript several times with an attentiveness, alacrity, and patience that will always astonish me, any errors of fact or judgment in this study are of course not his but my own. I should like also to thank Earl Pomeroy, a kind man and a scholar whose wide learning is matched by his willingness to share it with others. The extent to which all these men are teachers and scholars in the truest meaning of the words is easily gauged by noting that all of them hold views fundamentally at variance with my own. To my friends at Arizona State University, Tom Karnes especially, I am also most grateful.

R. J. L.

Seattle, Washington

Abbreviations

ABCFM	American Board of Commissioners for Foreign Missions
AHR	*American Historical Review*
AMQ	*American Quarterly Review*
CCH	*Clark County History*
CH	*Church History*
CHR	*Canadian Historical Review*
HBC	Hudson's Bay Company
HBS	Hudson's Bay Company Series
HMPEC	*Historical Magazine of the Protestant Episcopal Church*
JAH	*Journal of American History*
JSH	*Journal of Southern History*
MCH	*Marion County History*
MWQ	*Midwest Quarterly*
MVHR	*Mississippi Valley Historical Review*
NAM	National Archives Microfilm
OHQ	*Oregon Historical Quarterly*
OHS	Oregon Historical Society
OSL	Oregon State Library
PAA	Portland, Archdiocesan Archives
PHR	*Pacific Historical Review*
PNQ	*Pacific Northwest Quarterly*
TOPA	*Transactions of the Oregon Pioneer Association*
UPS	University of Puget Sound
WHQ	*Washington Historical Quarterly*
WMQ	*William and Mary Quarterly*
WPQ	*Western Political Quarterly*
WSHS	Washington State Historical Society

Contents

Equality

on the

Oregon Frontier

CHAPTER I

Introduction

Young thinkers always find refutation easy, and old
doctrines not hard to transcend; and yet what if the soul
of the old doctrines should be true just because the new
doctrines seemingly oppose but actually complete
them.
—JOSIAH ROYCE, *The Spirit of Modern Philosophy*

EW WHO write history nowadays wish to be criticized for keeping their subjects within narrow bounds. Not infrequently there is an inverse relation between the empirical size and the conceptual size of historical works. Thus the smaller the factual area explored by the historian, the larger the conceptual perimeter in which the study is set. Like the proverbial American novelist, historians seem more devoted than ever to finding the riddle of America by factoring out what symbolism they can find impacted in the Brooklyn Bridge, in the wilderness, or in the American eagle.

The case study approach, like so much of social studies analysis, assumes a uniformity that does not reflect demonstrable fact quite so much as it reflects a view of human behavior and human ideals. The Methodists of this study have not been chosen because they represent other Methodists or other contemporary Americans. Rather they appear to signify what seems most important and most true of certain ideas and values, specifically of the value equality in both its historical and philosophical dimensions. This is not a symbolist interpretation. No effort is made here to transcend disciplines and disciplinary modalities. Quite the reverse. I have undertaken to suggest a small sewing up of Clio's garment. It appears not to be seamless. Instead of looking upon human activities, and hence the study of them, as ultimately fluid, each part reducible to every other, I have sought to untangle the political from the economic, the social from the psychic. Social scientists have long since yielded to the

[3]

temptation to blend the categories of one area with those of other areas in the belief that such procedures will uncover new and expanded perspectives. Less comprehensive approaches, by contrast, often seem narrow and "academic," or simply irrelevant, perhaps even dangerous. The methodological concerns of this study are openly, but it is hoped not obtrusively, a part of the historical analysis, but the Methodist missionaries who settled Oregon in the 1830s and 1840s are my real subjects.

Americans have freely generalized about Methodists and about Oregonians too. Both, we seem to believe, are typically American. An essayist has only recently reaffirmed the suspicion that Methodism is America in miniature, and some years ago an Oregon old-timer told a group of aging pioneers: "You are representative men and women. You impersonate the history of the country for nearly half a century." [1] Although historians are not likely to be the ones to refute or confirm such wide-angled Hegelian generalizations, there is no doubt that the history of Oregon is important, and the Methodists who settled the area were often colorful.

The Methodist church arose in England in the late 1730s during a period of religious revival. John Wesley and his younger brother Charles, along with the once equally famous George Whitefield, were the early leaders of the movement. John Wesley lived a long and remarkably active life which included a ministry to the Indians of Georgia in 1736–37. A dismal failure, this trip, like so much of Wesley's life, suggests a fascinating counterpoint to the particular history of Methodism traced out in this book. The beginnings of the church as distinguished from the movement are usually dated from the day of Wesley's spiritual rebirth on May 24, 1738. Methodists did not become officially organized until 1744, when the first conference was held. Theologically Methodism does not differ from Anglicanism. In the crucial area of soteriology, or doctrines concerning salvation, Methodists are Arminian. They believe that all men, not merely a preelected few, can be saved. Thus Wesley was no Calvinist. He broke with Whitefield on just this point. A saved man was said to be jus-

---

1. Charles W. Ferguson, *Organizing to Beat the Devil: Methodists and the Making of America* (Garden City, 1971); George H. Williams, "Annual Address," *TOPA* (Salem, 1886), p. 32. Professional historians have been much less impressed with Oregon mission than with the Methodists. The mission of Jason Lee has only recently been called "insignificant from the viewpoint of Indian missionary history," a judgment I hope to reverse (see Robert F. Berkhofer, Jr., *Salvation and the Savage: An Analysis of Protestant Missions and American Indian Response, 1787–1862* [New York, 1972], p. 176).

tified by faith, that is, by acceptance of Christ. With his sins forgiven, the justified man endeavored to lead a sanctified life. While churchmen, Wesley preeminent among them, were often at pains to refine these difficult and elusive terms, one fact at least was not in doubt. Methodists believed that men have souls and that the primary religious relationship was that of a man to God.

American Methodism first took root in New York and in the upper South. Above all, Methodism was an evangelistic, revivalist creed, and it tended to flourish wherever enthusiastic lay preachers and exhorters could be found. But it was not until the arrival of Francis Asbury from England in 1771 that Methodism in America was truly launched. He was at the spiritual center of the American movement until his death in 1816.

The growth of the American church was not without grave problems in the colonial period. A serious stumbling block was Wesley's unwillingness to embrace the American cause against England. Difficult too was the factor of physical distance between Wesley and his missionaries in America. The Revolution brought decisive changes. American Methodists became a separate administrative body when they established their own church at the famous Christmas Conference of December 24, 1784. The history of the American church in its first decades is one of rapid institutional growth and inspired leadership. The efforts of Francis Asbury were supported by hosts of preachers and circuit riders of whom Jesse Lee, Freeborn Garrettson, and William McKendree are among the most famous. As the first native-born American to be elected a bishop in 1808, McKendree exemplified the distinctively American ideal of a Methodist minister. A Virginian by birth, McKendree became a frontier preacher. He traveled the hills of Kentucky and Tennessee in search of souls. His fierce and near fanatical energy was tempered by a sobriety bred of the unshakable conviction that he was performing the work of the Almighty. By the first decade of the nineteenth century cis-Atlantic Methodism was fast becoming a definitively American institution.

As Methodism adapted to the contours of American life, the church assumed the problems of American society. Slavery particularly troubled the Methodists. Churchmen were especially sensitive to the problem of slavery not only because they generally found the idea of slavery repulsive, but also because the institution itself provoked severe tension between church doctrine and ministerial practice. But while the idea of slavery may have bothered Methodists rather more than it did other people, the slavery

{5}

question touched all American institutions. The Methodist church was not better equipped than the federal system to resolve the problems of authority and sovereignty raised by the slavery controversy. For Methodists as for other Americans, slavery proved disruptive and finally led to a schism. Just as important as slavery itself were the organizational changes and dislocations brought in its train. What was true of the federal system was also true of the church. Ideas and institutions of authority were tested and deeply affected by the slavery controversy. With these changes came other even more important alterations of belief. In 1844, when the Methodist church divided, a southern wing called the Methodist Episcopal Church South was formed. Although John Wesley had proscribed slavery, the American Methodists were less able to do so. The Methodist *Discipline,* a catechism issued quadrennially, tells the story of compromise. In 1808, the year of McKendree's election as bishop, an attempt was made to excise all mention of slavery from the *Discipline.* Although this effort failed, each conference (ecclesiastical district) was to be permitted to make its own regulations concerning what might be said concerning slavery. "This gave rise," in the words of a recent student, "to a wide and confusing diversity of practice." [2] Actually the troublesome problem of local diversities and their relationship to general principles was at least as much responsible for the schism of 1844 as slavery. And indeed localism would prove to be a vital and thoroughly ambiguous aspect of the Methodist mission in Oregon as well.

The Oregon country, in the beginning at least, was something less than hospitable to Methodists, or to Americans generally. It would take more than fur trappers, who were the first whites to open the area, to bring about the kind of society in which New England Methodists could flourish. But before either the fur traders or the Methodists came to Oregon to stay, the huge wilderness of the Pacific Northwest was the private paradise of 180,000 Indians, divided into some 125 groups. The tribal designation suggests too much. Unlike the Indians of the East, the Iroquois or the Algonquin, for example, Indians of the Pacific regions were organized in units smaller than tribes, usually in family-centered villages. The Chinook Indians of the coast are the ones Jason Lee, leader of the Methodist mission, would later try to convert. These Indians, a seden-

---

2. Richard M. Cameron, "The Church Divides," in Emory S. Bucke, ed., *The History of American Methodism* (3 vols.; New York, 1964), II, 13.

tary people, were traders and fishermen. Fishing was a year-round vocation. The men dipped nets into the Columbia River in the spring for smelts. In the late fall and early winter they fished for salmon. Like the plainsmen for whom the buffalo fulfilled many needs, the Chinook made the salmon a source of lotions and perfumes as well as food. The fish had religious uses as well. The Indian supplemented his diet with camas and wapatoo roots which he and his squaw could gather in meadows. Life for the Indians was not sumptuous, but neither was it uncomfortable.

The Chinook economy, like that of other Indian groups in the region, was based upon simple bartering, although slaves and shells, called *higua,* were often used as currency. Each autumn the Chinook trader would meet with Indians from the interior at The Dalles or Kettle Falls and swap goods. From present Montana and Washington the Nez Percé and Cayuse brought horses, while others, the fierce Klikitats for example, offered weaponry, their specialty, in trade. These gatherings were no less riotous and licentious than the later more famous rendezvous of the American trappers and mountain men. The Indians' habits would later exasperate and offend the missionaries, as would the Chinook practice of "flattening" the heads of their young from forehead to crown. In fact it was just this procedure, or rather the sight of its effects, which set the Oregon missionary adventure in motion.

The story of the Indians who came to Saint Louis in 1831 is one of the best known of far-western sagas. In that year three Nez Percé and a Flathead—the latter from a tribe of that name whose members did not flatten their heads—journeyed eastward to Missouri. Exactly what they were seeking is still the subject of scholarly dispute. But as a consequence of their trip a drawing of an Indian with a flattened head appeared in several newspapers in the East; it was no doubt responsible for setting "off a chain reaction of events which added the Pacific Northwest to the United States." [3] Naturally the course of empire was not so direct as that and missionaries had been interested in the Pacific area before this time. But

3. Ray Allen Billington, "A Letter to the Editor That Got Unexpected Results," *Together* (November 1959), quoted in Clifford M. Drury, *Marcus and Narcissa Whitman and the Opening of Old Oregon* (2 vols.; Glendale, Calif., 1973), I, 49. Of course, it was the great captains, Lewis and Clark, who laid the foundation for American penetration. A fine account of their experiences in Oregon, with comments upon the Chinook, is Verne F. Ray, "The Chinook Indians in the Early 1800s," in Thomas Vaughan, ed., *The Western Shore: Oregon Country Essays* (Portland: Durham and Downey, 1975), pp. 121–50.

the "flathead" letter written by Methodist William Walker, the famous white chief of the Wyandot Indians, does mark the starting point of American entry into the Oregon country.

The story of Lee's settlement on the eastern side of the Willamette River and his experiences with Chief Factor John McLoughlin of the Hudson's Bay Company are told in the body of this work. These matters are perhaps less clearly a part of international affairs, also described in the text, than historical accounts have usually made them seem. But the so-called Americanization of Oregon, like the Americanization of Texas or California, is an important part of American history. The political history of Oregon divides neatly into periods based upon the source of government authority or, in the earliest years, upon the absence of such authority. From 1818 to 1846 the Oregon country was held jointly by the United States and England. In the latter year a treaty was signed setting the boundary line at 49°, from east of the Rockies all the way to the Pacific. Three years earlier, in 1843, the settlers had formed a government. This organization, called the provisional government, lasted quite serviceably until 1849. Oregon was made a United States territory in 1848 and a territorial government began to function a year later. The territorial period, a stormy and exciting one, was brought to a close when Oregon became the thirty-third state in 1859.

Readers familiar with the topics treated in this study will recognize that many of the "old doctrines," as Royce called them, have been "refuted" by completion. For example, the view that Jason Lee became "secular," that he played fast and loose with the Chief Factor of the Hudson's Bay Company, John McLoughlin, is not contradicted here, although my account might be considered more favorable to Lee than ones that claim he "ran in the world." Jason Lee's involvement in secular matters was not a retreat from his calling but an impassioned and single-minded fulfillment of it. In the words of one of his most extravagant admirers, Lee, "better than any other man of his day, comprehended the true missionary idea." [4] And yet what made him special was not only his comprehension or understanding of the missionary idea but rather the way he contained within himself, unsorted, the elements and the contradictions of the idea. "Rev.

---

4. Harvey K. Hines, *Missionary History of the Pacific Northwest* (Portland, 1899), p. 327.

Jason Lee was a *good* man," said one of his contemporaries and a co-worker; he "possessed the true missionary spirit." [5]

Experienced students of nineteenth-century missionary methods will recognize that Methodist uses of marriage resemble techniques used by Protestant groups and by Catholics as well. But here, too, the line of inquiry pursued leads to a set of generalizations about missionary motives somewhat at variance with standard anthropological or sociological views. Thus it is not cultural arrogance, paternalism, or even hypocrisy that Jason Lee's missionary methods imply, but more basic issues.

The beginning of the provisional government on July 5, 1843, is an important part of the narrative. It brings the several planes of the story into focus. Frances Fuller Victor, who wrote the Oregon volumes (XXIX and XXX) of H. H. Bancroft's *Works,* has done more than anyone else to mold historians' views about the genesis of Oregon's first formal government and the role of the Methodists. [6] Her version of events has held sway for almost a century. The wealth of new evidence, however, from the archives of the University of Puget Sound, from the Washington State Historical Society, and from other depositories, most of which has not been published before, substantially, and I believe conclusively, reorients the persuasive context Frances Victor established so many years ago. It is pertinent to observe that any revision of mine owes more to previous scholarship than to originality. It is especially important to make this point for the general reader, who has perhaps come to understand that historians regard revisionism as an indication of daring if not as a sign of superior virtue. In fact, most practitioners in their role as craftsmen (as distinguished from their role as members of the intelligentsia) recognize that the revisionist mode is most often mere polemics, tolerated, or in some quarters encouraged, on the lazy but general view that revision is per se a salutary undertaking. Indeed there is bitter irony in the assumption that a diversity of interpretations signifies professional healthfulness and conceptual rigor. It is likely that the opposite inference is true. The diverse in-

5. Margaret Jewett Bailey, *The Grains, or Passages in the Life of Ruth Rover* (2 vols.; Portland, 1854), I, 76. The only known extant copy of Volume I is in the Western Americana Collection, Beinecke Library, Yale University.

6. H. H. Bancroft, *History of Oregon,* Vols. XXIX–XXX of *Works* (San Francisco, 1886–88). Throughout these pages Mrs. Victor, not Bancroft, is discussed in the text, although her work is cited in the notes as Bancroft.

terpretations with which historians are familiar are in reality little more than products, often brilliant to be sure, of conceptual free association, spun off a few basic themes that are themselves seldom examined or may even be fallacious. Such themes (they can hardly be called hypotheses) as the labor theory of value or the tabula rasa, for example, continue to inform whole systems of analysis which in turn spawn numberless variants or interpretations, even though both ideas have been exploded for more than a century.

Students who have looked upon the forming of the provisional government in 1843 as an American movement or as a Methodist one will perhaps find my treatment of these matters revisionist enough. Typically, the present view of this as of other events in this period of Oregon's history continues to reflect the research of Frances Victor, albeit later commentators have refined and modified her interpretation. Francis Philbrick's observation that "the process of historical writing is compilatory" [7] certainly applies to the subjects considered in this book.

Finally, while I have tried to follow the advice of the editors of the *American Historical Review* concerning philosophical questions, namely, that they are "most effectively demonstrated through . . . scholarly application to particular subjects . . . ," [8] I have nevertheless been at some pains to make clear several philosophical matters which seem to me fundamental to the exposition of the historical subject matter. In this connection it is perhaps best, in a book dealing with equality to be read by historians, to avow with all frankness at the outset that the assumptions informing this study do not often square with prevailing ones. I make this avowal in no stiff-necked, arrogant way but rather in the spirit of scholarship with which I expect it and the book will be received. As for those critics who will insist, as they surely will, that Jason Lee and the settlement of Oregon should be kept separate from highfalutin discourses on equality, I suppose there is nothing for it but to say we disagree.

Historians, it is true, are liberals in the broadest sense—pluralist and democratic in political terms, monists and naturalists in philosophical ones.[9] Studies falling beyond the perimeter of these views are very

7. Francis Philbrick, *The Rise of the West, 1754–1830* (New York, 1965), p. 361.

8. "Articles for the *AHR:* An Editorial," *American Historical Review* 75 (1970): 1579.

9. American historians have made this clear not only in their work but in their comments on it and on themselves. See, e.g., Arthur Mann, "The Progressive Tradition," in John Higham, ed., *The Reconstruction of American History* (New York, 1962), p. 158;

frequently considered, at the very least, suspect at the level of scholarship as in other ways (although in saying so I wish not to be misunderstood as one who, repeating a familiar ploy, plays upon his reader's willingness, or guilt, to indulge a "new" or radically dissenting voice). The modern theist or moral nonrelativist, for example, is as fully prohibited from invoking theological categories in historical studies as effectively as ever the scholastic democrat was enjoined from keeping such things out of his. And yet the most significant difference here is that while the schoolmen were expected to concern themselves with God's involvement in human affairs because other views were thought wrong as well as immoral, the modern democrat and secularist leaves God out because theological views, and all ethical matters, are presumed a priori to be relative at best, at worst simply wrong, on the grounds that all "value judgments" are unprovable including, presumably, even this one. The very thing a learned man never asks, writes C. S. Lewis, when "presented with any statement in an ancient author . . . is whether it is true. . . . To regard the ancient writer as a possible source of knowledge . . . would be regarded as utterly simple-minded." [10] By modern lights a far-ranging tolerance on the part of the individual historian and a social order to match—the open society—are the measures of morality, although it is clear that the meanings of morality, as of society, have been altogether reversed in this view as compared with the ideas of the schoolmen or indeed with all pre-Enlightenment thinking.[11]

David Brion Davis, "Ante-Bellum Reform," in Frank Otto Gatell and Allen Weinstein, eds., *American Themes: Essays in Historiography* (New York, 1968), p. 26. As for the differences between "liberal" and "radical," Christopher Lasch underscores the obvious by pointing to the "underlying similarity" between them. See his *The New Radicalism in America, 1899–1963* (New York, 1965). More to the point is Isaac Deutscher's endorsement, as fundamental to radical belief, of naturalism, monism, and relativism. See Isaac Deutscher, *The Non-Jewish Jew and Other Essays* (London, 1963), pp. 35–36. I have stressed these connections in " 'Value-Free' versus 'Value-Laden' History: A Distinction without a Difference," *Historian,* in press.

10. C. S. Lewis, *The Screwtape Letters* (New York, 1959), p. 139.

11. Although I clearly think it is essential to bring these issues out into the open, my experiences with papers, articles, and symposiums promotes the fear that I shall be needlessly misunderstood. I do not wish to be thought an opponent of tolerance any more than I wish to be seen as opposed to the pioneering efforts of the early settlers of Oregon. Neither is true. One does not reject tolerance as virtuous, and certainly not the intellectual tolerance so richly and rightly praised by Alfred North Whitehead, for example, by rejecting a philosophy which raises it to the ontological level. By the same reasoning one is not to be supposed an enemy of the Oregon pioneers or of American community building if he

The connections between modern relativist and naturalist assumptions, and the democratic, egalitarian predilections of social scientists are explored in chapter 3. I mention these matters here to prepare the reader and to beg his indulgence if not his assent. The questions I hope to raise concerning equality and Methodism concern not only their functional and structural aspects, and hence their historical validity, but also their validity, and their connections, in wider contexts. Of course I am aware that social science recognizes no wider contexts.

A word or two about the structural and functional aspects of equality are in order. The problem of equality is not complex, at least at the theoretical level, even though the variations, practical and hypothetical, which may be wrung from egalitarian premises are admittedly great. One may suppose equality to involve either sameness or diversity, or indeed, both diversity and sameness may be conceived as reciprocal parts one of the other. It would be tedious to run through the various views these assumptions entail or have actually brought into being in America or elsewhere. It is enough to point out here that all modern views of equality rest upon the fundamental assumption, as outwardly fictional as is said to be the natural law assumption it supplanted, that there exist, somehow, a state of nature and a social state with a social contract between them. This view, wholly alien to pre-Enlightenment thinking, was as much the property of the liberal triumvirate Hobbes, Locke, and Rousseau, as of Burke and Alexis de Tocqueville. What this history of Jason Lee asks, no less, certainly, than any historical study might ask, is if this view and views related to it are true: true functionally, structurally, historically, or true in other ways. I have tried to present the data in such a way as to raise for consideration the possibility that such questions are properly to be asked of historical materials. One cannot discuss either equality or American history, I am convinced, without opening these long-closed areas.

To doubt the prevailing understanding which contends that "all metaphysical and ethical views can be assumed to be, strictly speaking, untenable, that is, untenable as regards their claim to be simply true . . . ," is to doubt historical methods as well as present philosophies. Thus if it is true that all metaphysical and ethical views cannot claim to be simply true, "their historical fate necessarily appears to be deserved. It

---

doubts the traditional and presumably pure example of it which is thought to have taken place in the Willamette Valley.

then becomes a plausible, although not very important, task to trace the prevalence, at different times, of different metaphysical and ethical views." [12] I assume, on the contrary, that the study of historical subjects is important historically because it is important philosophically.

12. Leo Strauss, *Natural Right and History* (Chicago, 1953), p. 19. John W. Gough, *The Social Contract: A Critical Study of Its Development* (2d ed.; Oxford, 1957), tracing the course of contract theory, broadly considered, shows how certain conventionalists—Stoics and others—developed doctrines concerning the artificiality of government. He does not wish to say, as I understand him, that even such conventionalists as Lucretius ever claimed that politics and social order as such were considered unnatural to man. This latter view and variations of it constitute the essence of the modern position from Hobbes onward. Ernst Cassirer and, more directly influential among historians, Peter Gay have done a great deal to promote an altogether different, more benign, and as I think, disastrously wrong view of the change from ancient to modern noted here. See especially Gay's *The Party of Humanity: Essays in the French Enlightenment* (New York, 1964), in which he undertakes, as the title suggests, to celebrate Enlightenment "philosophy." Charmed by the *philosophes,* Gay argues that they "did not draw the kind of ultimate conclusion that would subvert the humanism of their purpose" (p. 284). Like the modern naturalist and social scientist, Gay is untroubled by the nihilism resident in Enlightenment premises if only it can be shown how witty, how tolerant, how dogmatically undogmatic were the *philosophes* and how dull, how clerical, how localist were their opponents.

Gay's ideological purpose is plain throughout, and is carried through to his second book: ". . . the amiable caricature drawn by liberal and radical admirers of the Enlightenment has been innocuous: the naivete of the Left has been far outweighed by the malice of the Right" (Peter Gay, *The Enlightenment: An Interpretation: The Rise of Modern Paganism* [New York, 1968], p. ix). As a matter of simple influence, which is what Gay claims to be talking about, the amiable caricatures of the Left have far outweighed any efforts of the Right. The Left's effect has surely not been innocuous. But then the Right is the equivalent of malice in Gay's view: "Would it not be far more reasonable to see the paternity of modern totalitarianism in Christianity . . . than to seek it in the Enlightenment . . . ?" (Gay, *The Party of Humanity,* p. 281). Leo Strauss and others more rigorous than Jacob Talmon (whom Gay disputes in his texts) have answered such remarkable comments. Gay, however, dismisses Strauss as "idiosyncratic" (*The Enlightenment,* p. 532). Gay's views here are not, it seems, unconnected to his indulgent historicism toward Voltaire's anti-Judaism which, Gay claims, can be explained in context. Since Voltaire's views are substantially the same as Arnold Toynbee's, one is led to doubt Gay's approach. (See *The Party of Humanity,* pp. x–xi, 97–110.)

CHAPTER 2

The Hudson's Bay Company
in the Oregon Country, 1824-49

. . . it is a matter worthy of much consideration
whether it would not be more to the interest of the Coy.
to come to some understanding in respect to the division of the Trade than risk . . . opposition.
—GEORGE SIMPSON to the governor and committee,
August 10, 1824

*T*HE REVEREND Jason Lee was sent to Oregon by the Missionary
Society of the Methodist Episcopal church in 1834 to Christianize the Indians. He spent ten years in the attempt and
failed. The Missionary Society in New York City disapproved of Lee's
methods and dismissed him from his position as mission superintendent.
Even before Lee left Oregon in 1843 to return east, there were two views
about him and the mission. Both views continue to attract interest and
adherents among students of Methodism and of Oregon history. One view
is that Jason Lee's missionary spirit gave way to a more worldly interest in
the obvious commercial prospects offered in Oregon. According to this interpretation his famous trip to the East in 1838 and his return two years
later with thirty-three new mission members and their children is seen as
part of a covert program of colonization. Lee is sometimes thought to have
been an advocate of Manifest Destiny whose intention was to make sure
Oregon would be annexed to the United States and not lost to England. A
second view of Lee contends that he was a great missionary, a man completely committed to converting sinners, the work of a Methodist minister. One of my purposes is to assess these judgments and, more important, to explore their historical as well as their philosophical setting. A
rudimentary first step is to provide a sketch of Oregon at the time of Lee's
arrival.

In 1834, when Jason Lee arrived in Oregon to make the first American
settlement, the Hudson's Bay Company was firmly established, having

begun trapping the region a decade before. Actually the company had been hunting beaver in North America from the time its charter was granted in 1670, long before the advent of Methodism. It was one of the most successful monopolies in British commercial history. Trapping operations were underway in the Pacific Northwest in 1824 after the company had absorbed its most aggressive competitor, the North West Company. But as the Hudson's Bay Company reached out for new territories and profits, the English nation, after four centuries of imperial adventure, began turning inward.

The story of the Hudson's Bay Company and American settlement in Oregon cannot be understood unless England's imperial policy is taken into the account. Simply put, the Hudson's Bay Company was made an agent of empire by a nation losing its taste for imperialism. The company was at best reluctant to assume such a role and indeed, although Britain was eager to give the company imperial duties, she was not disposed to grant imperial power to go with them. The company was obliged to take on governmental functions which became in certain respects the price of its charter.

Parliament controlled the fate of the company's charter which it reviewed periodically. By 1824 parliamentary hostility to the Hudson's Bay Company was a factor of importance, one that the company could not safely overlook. As Englishmen lost their appetite for empire, they also became much less tolerant of monopolies. Further cause for worry lay in the fact that the company did not even have charter privileges in the Pacific Northwest, but merely a license. The license, granted in 1821, was to run for twenty years, and then Parliament must again be petitioned for a new one. One last difficulty, the most serious of all, was that international boundaries between the United States and Britain had not yet been determined in the Oregon country. Under the terms of a convention signed by the United States and Britain in London on August 6, 1827, the area from 42° to 54°40′ north latitude was to be "free and open" to the citizens of both countries. The convention, a continuation of an earlier one of 1818, provided that either country might terminate the agreement by giving the other party a year's notice. The Hudson's Bay Company would have much preferred a stable boundary to a few degrees of territory held in an uneasy partnership. But until a settlement could be made, the company had no choice but to stand its ground.

The position of the company in Oregon came increasingly to depend on the attitudes of the British government. Accordingly company projects began to take political considerations into ever greater account. Ironically, as John S. Galbraith has noted, "the Hudson's Bay Company could depend upon British national pride, but not upon British recognition of the importance of Oregon." [1] Moreover, the Oregon territory in dispute was never worth as much to the company as it might have been to imperial Britain. As a monopoly, the company instinctively sought stability. The absence of political certitude forced company managers to seek the protection of the government.

The Hudson's Bay Company could not leave the disputed territory without loss. It could not stay in the area profitably without exploiting it, thereby deepening its commitment and consequently increasing its need for government protection. Because the British government lacked any discernible policy for Oregon, company projects were conceived and executed in ambiguity. Motives were invariably mixed and many operations bore the stamp of haste and indecision. In spite of the valuable commercial and military factors at stake in the Pacific Northwest, the Oregon dispute became, in the end, a conflict between rival foreign offices. The effects of the disputes on the company are registered in the lives of all the settlers in the Willamette Valley, most of whom knew almost nothing of company affairs beyond their dealings with Dr. John McLoughlin, the company's number one man in Oregon.

The Hudson's Bay Company had faced difficult situations before and survived, a fact that owed largely to the ingenuity and cunning of its managers. The company's charter, resembling those used to settle Virginia, New York, and New Jersey, stipulated a governor and a deputy governor, together with a committee of seven members who were to direct company affairs. These officials, although not required to do so, remained in London. The chartered territories of North America (1.4 million square

1. John S. Galbraith, *The Hudson's Bay Company as an Imperial Factor, 1821–1869* (Berkeley and Los Angeles, 1957), p. 218. This chapter rests upon research in published primary materials and upon secondary writers. It should be noted that my suggestion, elaborated in this chapter, that George Simpson and the company were prepared to give up the disputed territory in exchange for stability is an inference of mine and is not the view of the secondary writers upon whom I have drawn. As for my characterization of Oregon diplomacy as a dispute between rival foreign offices, this would also appear to be the view of the most recent and careful student of the question, David Pletcher, in his *The Diplomacy of Annexation: Texas, Oregon, and the Mexican War* (Columbia, 1973).

miles, called Rupert's Land) were under the direction of a governor of North America after 1822. During the years of settlement in Oregon the company was run by four remarkable men.[2] At the head of the group was John Henry Pelly, governor of the company from 1822 to 1852. He was succeeded by Andrew Colville, who as deputy governor after 1839 had been Pelly's second-in-command. It was Colville who backed the appointment of George Simpson, the third member of the ruling group, as governor of North America, a post he held from 1826 to 1860. Edward "Bear" Ellice, formerly of the North West Company, was the fourth man in the group.

The company divided North America into four geographical units. The Columbia department was one of these. Company headquarters west of the Rockies were located at Fort Vancouver, 100 miles inland from the Pacific Ocean on the north shore of the Columbia River. The fort stood just slightly east of the junction of the Columbia with the Willamette River, flowing in from the south. Fort Vancouver, the "de facto capital of all the Oregon country," [3] served the settlers as a market from the time of the first settlements in the early 1830s until the 1850s.

The economic role of the Hudson's Bay Company was a vital one up to 1849, when the California gold rush brought much needed American capital into Oregon and stimulated trade. The most decisive economic factor in Oregon during the years from 1834 to 1849 was the inadequacy of markets for the export of wheat, the chief crop grown by Willamette Valley farmers. The Hudson's Bay Company monopolized the wheat trade with the Russian outposts in Alaska; trade with the Hawaiian Islands was never extensive. Until California became populous after 1849, providing Oregon with an import-export trade, competition with the Hudson's Bay Company was minimal.[4] The single most important man associated with the Columbia department was Governor George Simpson. But the company man every settler knew was the Chief Factor of the Columbia department, the legendary John McLoughlin. McLoughlin was at the center of local affairs in the Oregon country for the quarter century from 1824 to

2. *Ibid.*, p. 16.

3. Frederick Merk, *Fur Trade and Empire: George Simpson's Journal* (rev. ed.; Cambridge, 1968), p. xxvii.

4. Arthur L. Throckmorton, *Oregon Argonauts: Merchant Adventurers on the Western Frontier* (Portland, 1961), p. 54.

1856, when he died at his home in Oregon City.[5] He helped American immigrants with goods, cattle, and food. They liked him for his acts of kindness as well as for himself. For many years after his death he was affectionately remembered by Oregonians, and especially by Democrats, as a victim of the so-called Mission Party.[6]

The story of McLoughlin's controversy with the Methodist missionaries who contested his land claim is part of the folklore of American settlement in Oregon. The controversy began in 1828 when Governor Simpson instructed McLoughlin to take possession of the mill site at Willamette Falls, now Oregon City, the most valuable industrial location south of the Columbia. In 1841 Jason Lee set up a counterclaim on behalf of the mission, and, like Governor Simpson, he did not claim the site for himself or in the mission's name. Instead he had a member of the mission, the Reverend Alvan Waller, stake the claim. Years of wrangling and vexation ensued. After his somewhat ignominious discharge from the Hudson's Bay Company in 1845, McLoughlin moved to Oregon City where he took up residence on a part of his land claim, eventually becoming an American citizen.

Since the provisional government (1843–1849) was "provisional" in the sense that people were awaiting the extension of American laws, it was not competent to adjudicate the disputed claim. Lee had made his counterclaim on the assumption that an American government, applying American statutes, could decide whose claim was best. His strategy proved to be a better one than McLoughlin's, although the Chief Factor actually lost his claim because of a special provision in the federal Donation Land Law of 1850 written five years after Lee's death. As Oregon's first territorial delegate to Congress, Samuel Royal Thurston, a New Englander and a Mission Party man, took a hand in writing the Donation Law and he saw to it that the old controversy between the mission and McLoughlin was settled in favor of Methodist interests. Indeed, he managed to have McLoughlin's claim sold by the territory and the revenue

5. Dorothy O. Johansen and Charles M. Gates, *Empire of the Columbia* (2d ed.; New York, 1967), p. 124.

6. A term of derision coined by the Democrats in the late 1840s and applied to their opponents, many of whom were Methodists or New Englanders. See Walter C. Woodward, *The Rise and Early History of Political Parties in Oregon, 1843–1868* (Portland, 1913); Priscilla Knuth, "Nativism in Oregon," *Reed College Bulletin* (January, 1946); Robert W. Johannsen, *Frontier Politics and the Sectional Conflict: The Pacific Northwest on the Eve of the Civil War* (Seattle, 1955).

"donated" to the building of a university. This peculiar "preemption" of McLoughlin's claim assured him a martyr's reputation among Democrats and at the same time solidified the view that the American missionaries were, and had been from the start, worldly and conniving men.

The famous controversy about the Willamette Falls claim became an important part of Oregon's political lore. Partisans sought to establish their own reputations by claiming philosophical descent from either McLoughlin or Lee, and the two protagonists, with their old feud, have taken on something more than human stature. When Congress invited Oregon to nominate its most illustrious citizens to represent the state in Statuary Hall at Washington, Lee and McLoughlin were inevitable choices. As if feuding still, Lee's statue stands inside the hall, McLoughlin's outside it. Statues of both heroes have also been erected at Salem, the state capital, where they face each other on the northeast lawn of the capitol building grounds. Neither man was what his statue implies. Lee was not the prophet of Oregon, nor was McLoughlin the father of Oregon. Lee's activities are meaningless until they are set in the context of the Methodist church that sent him to the Northwest. McLoughlin's behavior is incomprehensible unless something is known of George Simpson and the company's political maneuverings at Whitehall. It was Governor Simpson, not Chief Factor McLoughlin, who shaped the large outlines of policy in the Columbia department and the early history of Oregon as well.

George Simpson was the overseas member of the quadrumvirate that directed company policy.[7] In 1822 he was made governor of the northern department; in 1826 he was appointed governor of all four departments in British North America. He remained the governor of North America until his death in 1860. Simpson was a brilliant man. His special talent for putting things in order was matched by a creative intellect continually suggesting new ideas and wider patterns of operations. "I am of the opinion," Simpson once remarked, "that every pursuit tending to leighten the trade is a branch thereof." [8] For his assiduous attention to company business he was knighted in 1842.

Since Simpson and McLoughlin have usually been seen as opposites, their more obvious differences have been overemphasized. Thus it is often

7. Galbraith, *Imperial Factor*, pp. 16, 18–19.
8. Merk, *Fur Trade and Empire*, p. 50.

pointed out that McLoughlin was a big man compared with Simpson, who was not. And whereas McLoughlin was warm and open, Simpson, by contrast, seems cold and calculating. Yet, though the two men may have been unlike each other, McLoughlin was not without guile nor was Simpson lacking in warmth. George Simpson was an aggressive and sometimes an impulsive man. He made his share of mistakes, including the fathering of two illegitimate daughters.

Simpson, an illegitimate child himself, was the only member of the company's ruling group who started life without the advantages of wealth and good family. Like others who have succeeded with the same social liability, Simpson learned quickly to adopt a diffident attitude with the truly influential while he used his wit to bypass his peers. Simpson was never diffident where McLoughlin was concerned. McLoughlin, polite but never unassertive when dealing with his superiors, was not Simpson's idea of the perfect subordinate. Their personal relationship was only one of the sources of discord between them.

Governor Simpson's relationship with Chief Factor McLoughlin turned on a number of elements, including the technical but by no means unimportant ones of company organization and monopoly enterprise. The continuing disagreements that mark their correspondence were, however, rooted in Simpson's approach to the Columbia department as a whole. As Simpson avidly pursued all possible means to lighten the trade by adjusting and readjusting its branches, McLoughlin had difficulty keeping up with him. Unraveling Simpson's plans and his logic, a task McLoughlin seldom undertook, is essential to understanding the political as well as the economic life of the Willamette Valley in the days of early settlement.

When Simpson first visited Oregon in 1824 no one in the company had much hope that the area would prove valuable. "We are not sanguine," observed the governor and committee, ". . . but if by any improved arrangement . . . loss[es] can be reduced to a small sum, it is worth a serious consideration, whether it may not be good policy to hold possession of that country, with the view of protecting the more valuable districts to the North of it." [9] Simpson made his own misgivings clear in a

9. Governor and committee to Simpson, London, February 27, 1822, H[udson's] B[ay Company] S[eries], III, 302 (R. Harvey Fleming, ed., *Minutes of Council Northern Department of Rupert's Land, 1821–31* [Toronto: Champlain Society, 1940; London: Hudson's Bay Record Society, 1940]). All company mail bound for London is referred to in the text as directed to the governor and committee. A useful summary of McLoughlin's rela-

letter to Governor Pelly just five days before leaving York, on Hudson's Bay, for his first visit to the Northwest. The absence of international boundaries north and south, he feared, might soon turn the company's ambiguous position into a precarious one.

Simpson suggested that the company would be better off with a well-defined international boundary than without one. As to trapping operations and strategy, he confessed, he was "at a loss how to act or advise in regard to the [Columbia department's] further management, no final arrangement having been determined on." Any extension of the trade would have to await "further information as to Territorial rights." Although reports over the preceding three years gave him reason to suppose a small profit could be realized in the department, "undisturbed possession" would have to be guaranteed to the company before any investment could be made. But without a boundary settlement, undisturbed possession could come only at the price of eliminating competition. It would be far better, thought Simpson, and "more to the interest of the Coy. to come to some understanding in respect to a division of the Trade" than to risk the evils of "entering the lists of opposition." [10]

Simpson's views about the Oregon country changed after he actually saw it. Shocked to find how wastefully the trade was being run, he realized that efficient management could not fail to bring marked changes for the better. Moreover, the youthful and ambitious Simpson was eager to exercise and display his managerial skills, for he knew how little the directors in London expected from the Columbia department. Here was the perfect opportunity for the newly appointed governor to show his worth. His enthusiasm got the better of him. In time he would sour on the

---

tionship with Simpson may be found in the introduction to William R. Sampson, ed., *John McLoughlin's Business Correspondence, 1847–1848* (Seattle and London, 1973).

10. Simpson to governor and committee, York Factory, August 10, 1824, HBS, X, 151 (E. E. Rich, ed., *Simpson's 1828 Journey to the Columbia: Part of Dispatch from George Simpson Esqr. Governor of Rupert's Land to the Governor and Company of the Hudson's Bay Company London, March 1, 1829, Continued and Completed March 24 and June 5, 1829* [Toronto, 1947]). Merk (*Fur Trade and Empire*, p. 1) contends that it "must have been profound discouragement that induced the directors of the . . . Company to consider a step so grave as withdrawal from . . . the lower Columbia. For here lay the core of the Oregon boundary dispute." Merk does not explain why the company should have thought it desirable to remain in disputed territory. The boundary dispute was hardly an attraction, and Simpson explains why the company would consider leaving the contested areas. The response of American fur traders is outlined in Dale L. Morgan, *Jedediah Smith and the Opening of the West* (Lincoln, Neb., 1964).

Columbia department, to McLoughlin's sorrow and confusion, but in 1824 his active mind was filled with plans for Oregon's future. "This point [Fort Vancouver]," said Simpson, indulging in playful exaggeration, "if situated within one Hundred Miles of London would be more valuable to the proprietor than the Columbian Trade." [11] The governor and committee were neither so playful nor so sanguine. Speaking of Fort Vancouver later on, Governor Pelly averred it is "unhealthy. . . . Its distance from the sea renders it by no means well adapted for the main depot of the West Side of the Mountains." [12]

Simpson's conception of the Columbia department envisaged the inclusion of New Caledonia (present British Columbia), the area that the original Columbia department was supposed to protect from competitors. [13] Oriented seaward and coastward, Simpson looked for a way to carry on the "Coasting trade . . . in conjunction with the inland business." [14] Though he brewed a typical batch of proposals, his plan was to concentrate on the coastal trade and to provide a land base for it at some location "two or three degrees . . . north [of Fort Vancouver] at the Mouth of Frazers . . . River . . . [a point] more central both for the Coast and interior Trade." [15] His underlying objective was to hinge the rich northern trade of New Caledonia to the Pacific Coast so as to gain access from the west by way of the Fraser River, as against the eastern route via the Saskatchewan River. Simpson did not know, as he should have known, that the Fraser River was not navigable, but even when he discovered in 1828 that canoeing on the Fraser was "certain Death, in nine attempts out of Ten," he still did not relinquish his basic plan for Columbia department trade. [16] Moreover, although admitting that his earlier hopes for river access to the coast north of the Columbia had been too optimistic,

11. Merk, *Fur Trade and Empire*, p. 124.

12. Governor and committee to Simpson, London, March 5, 1830, paraphrased *ibid.*, p. 322.

13. *Ibid.*, p. 72. That is, the southern area was to act as a buffer for the northern zone.

14. *Ibid.*

15. *Ibid.*, p. 73.

16. HBS, X, 39. Morgan, *Jedediah Smith*, pp. 280–82, urges the opposite, more familiar view that Simpson decided to make a stand at Fort Vancouver following his trip down the Fraser. Although this issue cannot be argued here, it seems fair to say that a correct view of the matter requires a choice among several possible perspectives. Emphasizing, as Morgan does, the local, fur-trading aspects of Simpson's thinking in 1827–28, instead of, as here, the political impingements acting upon him, it is plausible, if not entirely accurate in my opinion, to derive a view such as Morgan's.

Simpson thought the company needed only the "right of navigating the Columbia." [17] He expressed no concern about the possibility that the land north of the Columbia might be lost to England and thus to the company. Simpson went further. He said that even the right of navigation on the Columbia might not be essential if a settlement on the Babine and a depot at the mouth of the Nass River could be established. Both locations are well north of 49°.

Obviously Simpson had backed away from his earlier views of the Oregon country formed in 1824. Obvious, too, is that Simpson's attitude toward the area from the Columbia River to 49° did not in the least resemble a picture of unrelenting commitment to England's retention of it, the picture so often met with in studies of the Oregon question.[18] In the 1840s Simpson urged his superiors in London to consider several possible ways of resolving the boundary dispute, including suggestions that a line be drawn south of 49°. But his comments were based on political considerations, and not, as in the 1820s, on the comparatively simple facts of fur trading. The distinction is fundamental. Had McLoughlin been aware of it, he would have understood why he and Simpson could agree on so little after Simpson's second trip to Oregon in 1828–29.

By 1825 the company had all the things Simpson later said were essential to its survival in Oregon. In that year Britain and Russia signed a treaty making 54°40' the boundary between the two nations. (The Russians had signed a similar treaty with the United States in 1824.) To be sure, the United States was still legally entitled to access up to 54°40' along with England, but except for American coastal traders, the company had little to fear from competitors that far north.[19] The treaty of 1825 assured the company a clear division of the trade between itself and the Russian American Company and guaranteed entrée via the Pacific to the profitable fur preserves of the McKenzie River system. In fact, the Russian treaty met all Simpson's requirements for the Columbia department. Significantly, the lands from the Columbia River north to 49° were not part of the plan.

Because Simpson's ideas for trading in the Northwest were geared

17. HBS, X, 35.

18. *Ibid.*, p. 82.

19. Galbraith, *Imperial Factor*, p. 127; E. E. Rich, *Hudson's Bay Company, 1670–1870* (3 vols.; New York, 1961), III, 621; HBS, X, 81–85; Samuel Flagg Bemis, *John Quincy Adams and the Foundations of American Foreign Policy* (New York, 1949), p. 482.

especially to exploiting the coastal fur trade, his assessment of the company's political position and his calculations about trading possibilities on the Pacific Coast led him to see the trade in terms of its maritime potential,[20] as he demonstrated when he turned his attention to taking advantage of the Russian treaty. He told the governor and committee that the best way "of obtaining for the Honble. Coy. the valuable Trade of that Coast and Country, will be to establish a strong Post in the Harbour of Nass, at the Mouth of Simpsons River, in Lat. 54 falling from the Northern parts of New Caledonia." [21] Since this proposal, like all Simpson's plans, was "dependent on the operations of our Shipping," it was first necessary to rid the northern seacoast of American vessels trading for inland furs. Controlling the onshore trade by establishing trading posts, the company got most of the pelts that maritime traders had previously taken. By 1833 the Americans had not quit, but they were losing.[22] While Simpson was busy mastering the coastal trade, he was also pressing the Russians hard in the interior. Candidly, and with notable lack of anxiety, Simpson commented that Nass would do very well "in the event of the Columbia being given up to the Americans." [23] Once again it is difficult to see anything in Simpson's acts which suggests that he was tied by either sentiment or policy to the more southerly parts of the Oregon country.

Simpson's views about the Columbia department are not so difficult to understand once the Oregon dispute, with its sharp emphases on national pride and ethnic rivalry, is diminished as a major factor in his thinking. Simpson, an eminently rational man, was undoubtedly aware, as many economic historians have since pointed out, that the only workable alternative to stability for monopoly enterprise is instability that can be exploited. When it became clear in 1827 that England was not going to press for a boundary settlement with the United States, Simpson set about to make the most of the situation. He did his best to see that each activity undertaken in Oregon was put to as many uses as he could find. The Columbia department gave Simpson ample opportunity to develop new

20. Merk, *Fur Trade and Empire*, p. 72. Simpson's idea in 1824 was to use the English East India Company to help sell furs in Canton. The plan does not appear to have been naïve, as Merk claims; rather, it was not remunerative (*ibid.*, p. 73 n. 130; Galbraith, *Imperial Factor*, p. 124).

21. HBS, X, 81–82.

22. Galbraith, *Imperial Factor*, p. 140; Rich, *Hudson's Bay Company*, III, 638.

23. HBS, X, 82. For an opposing point of view see Galbraith, *Imperial Factor*, p. 180.

ways to "leighten the trade," now heavily freighted with unwonted political difficulties in London.

An excellent example of Simpson's ability to get the most out of Oregon is the famous expeditions of Peter Skene Ogden into the southeastern part of Oregon in the period 1823–1829. These trapping expeditions into the Snake country served several purposes. Ogden, one of the most daring and colorful of Hudson's Bay Company trappers, was instructed to take every pelt in the area, a standard method for dealing with oncoming competitors.[24] The strategy was to keep the periphery of company territory destitute of beaver and thereby to discourage penetration into the more valuable fur preserves in the interior. Ogden's pelts were sent to London where they took up the slack in the market created by the company's conservationist practices in Rupert's Land. Thus the peripheral Columbia department played a role in protecting the valuable and more secure fur areas of Rupert's Land. What is more, the strategy of protecting the company's fur supply was made to accommodate the marketing end of the business.

Most important of all, political uses were found for Oregon. For example, the company took advantage of the desire of English reformers to see the Indians civilized. Missionaries were sent to company forts in British North America for the benefit of English Christians as well as of Indians. In 1836 the Reverend Herbert Beaver went to Fort Vancouver to care for the Indians, although disagreements with Chief Factor McLoughlin forced his rather hasty return to England in 1838. In recognition that temperance was a matter of deep concern to English as well as American reformers, the company gave liquor to Indian trappers in trade for furs only when its competitors did so. The monopoly genuinely opposed the liquor traffic because it had adverse effects on the Indians and therefore on the fur trade. Company officials, quick to point out their stand on alcohol, observed that Britons could best ensure temperance among the Indians by supporting and protecting the company's monopoly of the British North American trade. But company policy could not always be so conveniently fitted to moral principles. The sign that the company had an uncertain future in Oregon came in the summer of 1827.

On August 6, 1827, when British plenipotentiaries agreed to a continuation of the convention of 1818, there was no mistaking that England

---

24. Galbraith, *Imperial Factor,* pp. 11–12.

cared little for the Northwest and even less about the interests of the Hudson's Bay Company. August 6th was a bleak day in the lives of Governor Pelly, Andrew Colville, and the rest. It was made bleaker still by the death of the foreign secretary, George Canning, a vigorous advocate of company rights and empire alike. Canning had guided the Russians into signing a treaty favorable to the Hudson's Bay Company in 1825. Almost alone among British statesmen, he saw mercantile advantages in the British possessions on the west coast of North America.[25]

With Canning gone the company was left at the mercy of politicians who cared nothing about the fur trade and who disliked monopoly on principle. Their overseas interests were limited to projects of benevolence and moral uplift. Despite the best efforts of Simpson and Pelly to convince the government's negotiators that a boundary settlement ought to be made, in the end the company counted itself lucky that England held to the terms of the 1818 convention.[26] Albert Gallatin, the American representative at the negotiations, thought he discerned in the British position a willingness "to let the Country gradually and silently slide into the hands of the United States," when "national pride" allowed for a "relinquishment of . . . pretentions." [27] In the end Gallatin's analysis proved correct. What is more, it is highly unlikely that the men of the Hudson's Bay Company, whose sensitivity to governments, competitors, and settlers rose at times to paranoia, saw the negotiations of 1827 as in any way propitious.

After 1827 the company had to protect itself not only against competitors but against the apathy of British politicians and a growing antipathy in British public opinion as well. Accordingly its efforts to possess and occupy strategic locations in the southern Oregon country—Willamette Falls, for example—were motivated not simply, as has frequently been suggested, by a desire to provide Britain with bargaining power in future American negotiations. Just as important, the company wanted to make sure that no British government could avoid negotiations altogether. Besides calculating the effects of competition and settlement on the fur trade, company planners now had to consider the uncertain variable of British opinion. In such circumstances it was obviously good business to

25. *Ibid.*, p. 189.
26. *Ibid.*, p. 219.
27. W. R. Manning, ed., *Diplomatic Correspondence of the United States: Canadian Relations, 1784–1860* (Washington, 1940–45), II, 613–14.

fly the Union Jack from company forts abroad as long as the company's commercial interests failed to inspire patriotism at home. Specifically, the company hoped to protect itself by looking northward for a new depot as a possible replacement for Fort Vancouver while solidifying its position in the south. The company's motives, and hence the clue to its behavior, should be sought not only in the United States but in England also. After 1827 the complexity of affairs in the Columbia department intensified. The Hudson's Bay Company pursued no single policy because there were too many imponderables. Trying to get all it could, the company strove equally to ensure losing as little as possible.

Company plans for southern Oregon as for all of the Pacific Northwest were made with the British as well as the Americans in mind. In January 1828 Simpson was instructed "to acquire as ample an occupation of the Country and Trade as possible, on the South as well as on the North side of the Columbia River, looking always to the Northern side falling to our Share on a division, and to secure this, it may be as well to have something to give up on the South, when the final arrangement comes to be made." [28] Historians have perhaps overstressed this assertion, supposing location and not simply a boundary line was uppermost in company minds. Certainly the two matters were distinct. In any event, the instructions fitted Simpson's plans to "push the Trade south of the Columbia and improve our Establishments in that quarter." [29] In fact, Simpson had urged McLoughlin to follow just this course before the convention adjourned. Simpson and the London planners both wanted to keep Britain from deserting the company. Their assumption was that no ministry would cede private property rights without indemnification and that any British government would find it unpopular and politically inexpedient to cede British property to the likes of American settlers. [30]

Company thinking maintained that American settlers were instinctively hostile toward Englishmen, monopolists especially. Company

28. Governor and committee to Simpson, January 16, 1828, HBS, X, 157.

29. Simpson to McLoughlin, York Factory, July 9, 1827, HBS, X, 156.

30. See, for example, Simpson to governor and committee, York Factory, August 10, 1824, HBS, X, 150. By 1845 President Polk's effect upon the anti-Americans in Peel's government, which was otherwise quite inclined to be pacific, had vindicated the company's reliance upon public dislike for Americans, especially Americans such as Polk who struck Englishmen as bellicose and impudent. Wellington and others were ready to go to war with the United States at this time for reasons of national pride. Pletcher, *The Diplomacy of Annexation*, pp. 222–26.

leaders were not absolutely sure, of course, that Englishmen could be counted on to overcome their own prejudices against monopolies should the property of the Hudson's Bay Company be subjected to American depredations. The company was unwilling to rely completely upon the plan of pushing the trade in the south or upon taking possession of southerly locations. A month after Simpson was told to pursue a holding strategy in the south, he was instructed to get "a firm footing in the Coast trade and in all the country on the West of the Mountains before the Americans arrive there in greater force." [31]

Harnessed to political shifts at home, to competitors and settlers in the field, and not least of all to a market and a product both approaching relative exhaustion, policy making was extraordinarily difficult. As a result it is not easy to determine just when the directors were eager to have a boundary established and when they were content to exploit the uncertainty about the boundary. But it is clear that efforts were made, after the convention of 1827, to get the boundary settled, with rather more than a hint that a line north of the Columbia River would be quite acceptable.

Predictably, company spokesmen made their appeal to the heart, not to the head, of the government, then under Wellington, the hero of Waterloo. Arguing that popular reforms, especially among uncivilized peoples, as well as national pride would suffer if a boundary was not drawn in Oregon, company officials waged a skillful propaganda offensive. A vital element in their approach was a certain company document, ostensibly private, but in fact intended for a wider audience. The document is Simpson's dispatch of 1829 from North America to the governor and committee in London. Although Simpson routinely sent an annual report to London, outlining developments in North America, the one he sent in 1829 was quite evidently intended to impress government officials as well as inform company directors.

The dispatch, three copies of which were prepared at different times in the busy spring of 1829, was apparently written in considerable haste. On September 2, 1829, the first copy arrived in London. Governor Pelly sent Sir George Murray, secretary for the colonies, "that part of dispatch just received" on the 18th. Pelly also enclosed a "Map of North America" promised to Sir George earlier.[32] Pelly, considering the map and the

---

31. Governor and committee to Simpson, London, February 27, 1828, Merk, *Fur Trade and Empire*, p. 295.

32. HBS, X, ix, 186. Rich does not indicate whether the three copies of this dispatch

dispatch to be complementary, as well as timely, was evidently eager to see some lines drawn on the map. Parts of the dispatch are straightforward; others, manifestly contrived, suggest propagandist purposes. For example, Simpson expressed an unfamiliar solicitude for Indian slaves. He complained bitterly that the American traders had made slaves "the principal circulating medium on this Coast." The "inhuman traffic," he said, "seems to call loudly for the interference of the British and American Governments." [33] The indignant, moralizing tone was not in character; on other occasions Simpson could speak lightly of the "marketable" prospects of an Indian woman he no longer had use for. [34] Furthermore, Simpson, ordinarily precise, recklessly exaggerated the extent of the traffic in Indian slaves, which he knew of largely by hearsay. His proposal for an Anglo-American moral consortium to rid the Northwest of the slave trade was, at the very least, out of place in a document meant only for a private company. Simpson mentioned slavery because he had in mind a broader audience than the governor and committee. He knew that few issues touched the reformer's heart more closely than the antislavery crusade and the plight of aborigines in distant lands. Some years later, when George Pelly was trying to persuade Parliament to renew the company's trading license for the Oregon country, he too stressed the philanthropic role the company could play among the less favored races of British North America. [35]

But Simpson did not stop with sentimental flourishes. His real message was that British honor was on the line in Oregon. The Hudson's Bay Company was all there was of England in the Northwest, and Simpson declared that any American presence must be seen as part of an aggressive effort by the United States to push the British out of Oregon altogether. Simpson said he was convinced that American penetration into Oregon would be minimal "unless the all grasping policy of the American Government, should induce . . . [a capitalist opposition] to embark . . . in

---

are identical. The published manuscript is not the one Governor Pelly sent to Sir George Murray in his first letter to the secretary for the colonies on September 18, 1829 (HBS, X, 186), since the printed manuscript did not arrive in England until October 22. Pelly's second letter to Murray (*ibid.*, p. 187), dated December 4, 1829, included yet another "part" of Simpson's dispatch, presumably a part or all of the copy that arrived on October 22. Pelly's two letters to Murray suggest that the documents are not identical. All three copies are evidently different. The map was probably Arrowsmith's of 1824.

33. HBS, X, 80.

34. Simpson to John George McTavish (private), Isle A La Crosse, November 12, 1822, HBS, III, 424.

35. Galbraith, *Imperial Factor,* p. 196.

furtherance" [36] of either settlement or trade. He supported his view by reporting a conversation he had had with the American fur trapper, Jedediah Smith. Smith had told him that private American citizens were not equipped to come all the way to Oregon. Whether or not Simpson believed Smith is immaterial; the fact is he made good use of the trapper's assertion by appearing to accept it. He drew the obvious conclusion that any American immigration would have to mean that the United States government was behind it. [37]

Whatever Simpson believed or did not believe about the views of the American and British governments is less important than what he wanted British officials to think. Simpson wished to show that the United States government was necessary to any American immigration into Oregon. His suggestion to the Wellington government was that future difficulties could be avoided by putting an end to the boundary dispute. If as a result the company would have to move out of southern Oregon, Simpson was ready to go. His fear was that American settlers would make it necessary for the company to move north in any event. He and the company both hoped that the government would see the Oregon question as a choice between negotiation and expropriation. Negotiations and a boundary settlement were ardently desired by Simpson and Governor Pelly in December 1829, and Simpson prepared for the eventuality of exclusion from the Columbia. He looked to "being firmly established on a navigable communication between the Coast and the Interior" [38] should the Columbia be closed to the company. The publication of a congressional report on the fur trade in March 1829 was the signal for Pelly to press for a settlement. [39]

Senator Thomas Hart Benton, of Missouri, was interested in Oregon, just as he was interested in all western and southwestern areas supplied from his state. Although Benton was an anglophobe he did not advocate extending America's claim to Oregon beyond 49°, as some others did.

36. HBS, X, 67.

37. Some historians believe Smith purposely misled Simpson about American intentions in order to put the Hudson's Bay Company off guard. Whether or not deception was Smith's purpose, his comments suited Simpson's objectives at the time. See, for example, Johansen and Gates, *Empire of the Columbia*, pp. 139–40.

38. Simpson to William Smith, Fort Vancouver, November 17, 1828 (Merk, *Fur Trade and Empire*, p. 300).

39. U.S. Congress, Senate, Committee on Indian Affairs, *Report from H. L. White*, 20th Cong., 2d sess., 1829.

Nevertheless, the report of his Committee on Indian Affairs made it plain that Americans were not going to accept any boundary line south of 49°. Benton's position in 1829 amounted to saying that 49° was already the American line, and an Englishman's suggestion of a boundary to the south of it was very nearly aggression. In his report Benton underscored his views by quoting from a British book on the Oregon country—Alexander McKenzie's *Voyages from Montreal to the Frozen and Pacific Oceans in . . . 1789–1793, With a Preliminary Account of the . . . fur trade of that country* (1801)—which strongly urged that England demand the Columbia River as the dividing line between Britain and the United States west of the Rockies. Since 1818 the British had wanted this boundary line, and Simpson had hoped his country's negotiators would insist upon it at the convention discussions in 1827. Benton apparently inserted the McKenzie quotation as an introduction to his own inflammatory comment that the Britisher's view "is the origin of all the British claims in the Columbia— of all the robberies and murders now going on there—of the 500 men killed and the $500,000 worth of property plundered from them, in the last 20 years." [40]

Another interesting feature of Benton's report was a proposed bill to protect American fur traders against furs imported by non-American companies. This protectionist bill, which Benton said was "in the spirit of the times," [41] was also calculated to give Hudson's Bay Company officials something to worry about. The bill would not affect the company's marketing operations, since the company sold no furs in the United States; but it might very well result in increased competition in the field. Protection was precisely the kind of "inducement" to American capitalists which Simpson cautioned Englishmen to regard as a clear sign of American intervention in the Oregon country. With protection for American trappers, American trading enterprises would grow larger and more aggressive. Without a boundary line, the only result for the company would be real competition. In his dispatch of 1829 Simpson argued that American intervention would bring settlers and colonization. Threats to the company's physical security would follow, and Englishmen would be forced to defend their fellow countrymen. All these difficulties could be avoided, Simpson insisted, if a boundary line were drawn.

40. *Ibid.,* pp. 18–19.
41. *Ibid.,* p. 3.

Senator Benton left no doubt as to his anti-British feelings: his report demanded the "exclusion of all British traders from our territories." Furthermore, the "project of joint occupancy by the British and Americans should be terminated and a line of demarcation amicably established with as little delay as possible, and the citizens and subjects of the two powers for all purposes of trade and intercourse with the Indians confined to their respective sides of it." [42] John Henry Pelly saw Senator Benton's point. On December 4, 1829, he wrote to the secretary for the colonies, calling "attention to the proceedings in the last Congress of the United States; a printed Copy of the part to which Mr. P[elly] alludes he has likewise enclosed, and respectfully submits, whether, as it is therein proposed amicably to establish a Line of Demarcation, the Subject might not now be discussed." [43] Pelly offered George Simpson's services as the company's expert in northwestern affairs.

Unfortunately, the archives of the Hudson's Bay Company apparently provide little information about Simpson's journey in 1828–29, particularly in regard to international diplomacy. [44] It seems, however, that Sir George Murray did not respond to Governor Pelly's letter for several months. The company's secretary, William Smith, wrote Simpson on March 6, 1830, to advise that Murray had "a desire to see" [45] him. Already on his way to York from Liverpool, Simpson was unable to comply. He directed Smith to put the 1825 correspondence between company officials and the government negotiators at Murray's disposal.

Whether Simpson was simply too busy to respond more enthusiastically or whether his recent hopes for a boundary settlement had collapsed is unknown. In any event, Murray certainly did not leap at Pelly's suggestion to begin negotiations on a line of demarcation. Murray's response to Pelly had probably arrived on or before March 5, since Simpson received a letter of that date from the governor and committee which indicated company knowledge of the government's position. This letter is a somber document whose contents clarify Simpson's comments to Smith. Reciting the hard-won successes in the Columbia department, the committee urged that a new depot be opened on Puget Sound to take advan-

42. *Ibid.*, p. 2.
43. Governor Pelly to Sir George Murray, London, December 4, 1829, HBS, X, 187.
44. HBS, X, x.
45. Governor Simpson to William Smith, York Factory, August 20, 1830 (Merk, *Fur Trade and Empire,* p. 300).

tage of "good harbors, fine timber, and opportunities for agriculture."
Subsequently it was decided to send an Episcopal clergyman to Oregon, as
"we consider it a duty both owing to ourselves and the natives, in a serious
point of view, and a highly expedient measure under existing circumstances in a Political light." [46]

The meaning of this note from the governor and committee of the Hudson's Bay Company to Simpson is not difficult to grasp. The government
had made it clear that it would not press for a settlement of the Oregon
boundary with the United States. The company had acknowledged that
its Oregon policies must be conceived with an eye to satisfying members
of Parliament. The plan to dispatch a clergyman was "highly expedient"
because many members of Parliament who did not like the company did
like the idea of sending missionaries to work among the aborigines.

More important than the opinion of Parliament, however, is the fact
that the Hudson's Bay Company, in seeking a boundary in 1829, was
willing to settle for a line "two or three degrees" north of Fort Vancouver.
To understand the Oregon question, one must look at the relationship between the Hudson's Bay Company and England. Company affairs in
Oregon, as well as British diplomacy in Washington, must be considered.
By 1830 the company's existence in the Northwest clearly depended, not
on American settlers or the American government, but on the policies and
the sentiments of British members of Parliament.

When Simpson arrived at Fort Vancouver in 1842 for his first visit
since 1828, he realized immediately that a boundary would have to be
agreed upon very soon. If existing conditions were allowed to continue,
Simpson feared, the company would surely come under attack from un-
ruly American settlers. James Douglas, McLoughlin's second-in-command and later his replacement, told Simpson in 1843 that the rights of
England in the Northwest would be lost by default "if the country remains open a few years longer." [47]

In the end the Hudson's Bay Company in Oregon was forced to func-

---

46. Governor and committee to Simpson, London, March 5, 1830 (Merk, *Fur Trade
and Empire,* p. 322).

47. James Douglas to Simpson (private), October 23, 1843 (Galbraith, *Imperial Factor,*
p. 227). See also Douglas to Simpson, March 5, 1845, HBS, VII, 185 (E. E. Rich, ed.,
The Letters of John McLoughlin from Fort Vancouver to the Governor and Committee, 3d ser.
[Toronto, 1944]): ". . . the long contemplated plan [of moving north] is now forced
upon us."

tion in ways that were alien to its nature and in conflict with standard commercial procedures. Thus Simpson, not McLoughlin, is the pivotal figure in any effort to see the total picture of Oregon's early history. That the company functioned at all was owing to Simpson's ability to think and rethink company plans hastily, and certainly to the company's undisturbed possession of the Oregon country for all but five or six of the twenty-eight years of joint access. As the position of the company at Fort Vancouver became increasingly political, McLoughlin was called upon to be more than a Chief Factor. Wanting only to excel at his job of buying and trapping furs and operating the Columbia department, and having little real interest in political questions, McLoughlin was ill equipped for a political role. He was no diplomat, and, in the words of one commentator, he was "never a particularly clear thinker," [48] at least in matters removed from the fur trade. The company would have been glad to have him stick to that trade, but the unresolved boundary question and Britain's unwillingness or inability to settle it poisoned the relationship between McLoughlin and company officials in London.[49]

To make matters worse, Simpson seems to have made a fine point of telling McLoughlin less than he needed to know. In several instances Simpson withheld information that would have helped McLoughlin cope with the difficulties of his position. In 1827, for example, when McLoughlin tried to get involved in the diplomatic issues surrounding the boundary negotiations, Simpson brushed him off with undisguised annoyance. "The Governor and Committee are . . . possessed of every information in regard to the claims of the British Government," he told McLoughlin, and it would be "unnecessary to urge their Honors further on this head." [50] Moreover, McLoughlin's land claim at Willamette Falls became a source of anxiety, mainly because Simpson had failed to keep him up to date on the company's changing attitudes toward the site. When McLoughlin was left with the property after 1842, and when it was clear that land claims south of the Columbia River might be troublesome to sustain, the company gave him no support whatsoever.

The difficulties between Chief Factor McLoughlin and Governor Simp-

---

48. W. Kaye Lamb, "Introduction," HBS, VII, xli. For a different view of company efforts in this region see William H. Goetzmann, *Exploration and Empire: The Explorer and the Scientist in the Winning of the American West* (New York, 1966), pp. 103–4.

49. HBS, X, 99.

50. *Ibid.*, p. 156.

son were worsened by their well-known quarrels. The two men were not particularly friendly to begin with, and they differed on almost every important question confronting them. Simpson disapproved of McLoughlin's generous treatment of settlers, although McLoughlin insisted that generosity in this instance was the better part of wisdom. Simpson favored a maritime approach to the fur trade on the Pacific; McLoughlin's thinking was land-based. The issue that finally estranged them irrevocably was the murder of McLoughlin's son John at the company's fort at Stikine, Alaska. Young McLoughlin had been put in charge of Stikine in 1841, about the time he began drinking excessively. When his treatment of the twenty or more trappers under his command became too harsh, some of the men plotted his murder. He was shot by a Canadian named Urbain Heroux in April 1842. Governor Simpson was required to investigate, but was unable to bring Heroux to justice. The Chief Factor would not forgive this failure, implying that Simpson's investigation had been negligent. McLoughlin's letters became increasingly shrill until at last the London office had to tell him to drop the subject.

Despite McLoughlin's imposing physical presence and his commanding personality he was far from being the undisputed ruler of the company's vast domain in the Oregon country. The Hudson's Bay Company that greeted the first American settlers was not so solid as it seemed. The company was standing pat in Oregon, not standing firm. The Methodist missionaries who came to Oregon in 1834 were emissaries of an institution that also seemed stronger than it actually was. In studying early Oregon, the historian is faced not simply with a clash of institutions and personalities but with a shadow play of dissolutions and changes taking place in British and American ideologies.

The Methodist Episcopal church, after its first century in America, was among the most successful and powerful of evangelical sects. That it was the first missionary group in Oregon was a sign of its efficiency. Yet the haste evinced by the church in sending its missionaries to Oregon is not fully explained by the wish, however genuine, to save heathen souls. There was also real trouble at home. Some people hoped there might be salvation for churches as well as for Indians in a mission to Oregon, that the conversion of Indians in the West might bring peace and unity to quarreling Christians in the East.

CHAPTER 3

Jason Lee, Reform, and the Historical Past

> . . . every new colony of [American] settlers contains
> within itself a nucleus of republican institutions, and
> revives, in a measure, the history of the first settlers. Its
> relation to the Atlantic states is similar to the situation
> of the early colonies with regard to the mother country
> and contains the elements of freedom. Every society
> which is thus formed must weaken the fury of parties by
> diminishing the points of contact.
>   —FRANCIS J. GRUND, *The Americans*

METHODISM has customarily fascinated outsiders, providing a rich yield of generalizations as well as of converts. Historians of the twentieth century have not been slow to see in Methodism clues to the riddles of the American past. The church is said to "have probably influenced the lives of more persons than any other Protestant body in America." [1] It has also been observed that "no non-political organization touched the lives of more people; none reflected the social attitudes of millions of Americans more accurately" than the Methodist Episcopal church. [2] Nineteenth-century churchmen likewise found the followers of Wesley remarkable. Two visiting sectaries, startled by the vehement efficiency of Methodists, exclaimed they "are a hive of bees . . . whatever . . . their failings they have done more both in America and Canada, than any other body of Christians." [3] What all these generalizations clearly proclaim is the inescapable fact of Methodist preeminence among evangelical churches in the period before the Civil War. It is a fact of enormous significance, for religion was the supporting arch of American culture.

1. Colin B. Goodykoontz, *Home Missions on the American Frontier* (Caldwell, Idaho, 1939), p. 161.
2. Donald G. Mathews, *Slavery and Methodism: A Chapter in American Morality, 1780–1845* (Princeton, 1965), p. vii.
3. Andrew Reed and James Matheson, *A Narrative of the Visit to the American Churches by the Deputation from the Congregational Union of England and Wales* (2 vols.; n.p., n.d.), II, 72.

The American Methodists were formally organized in 1784. The growth of the church rapidly outdistanced the hopes of even the most optimistic. Methodist success was due, according to religious historian William Warren Sweet, to the "gospel of free will, free grace and individual responsibility . . . [which] fitted in exactly with the new democracy rising in the West." [4] Unlike the Puritans, for whom God was considered a free agent, awarding salvation as He saw fit, the Methodists and other theological liberals allowed the Deity no such latitude. Instead, men had the option of choosing salvation or declining it. The "logic of Free Grace [which] admitted of no limits to its application" impelled Methodists to seek the conversion of every human being. [5] Since the logic of free grace was relentless and the zeal of Methodists was furious, Americans joined the church in prayerful droves. But the sweep of these generalizations is too great and requires a cautionary digression.

Many Americans, including historians, of whom Frederick Jackson Turner is the best known, have had a great deal to say about possible relationships between democracy and the West. Moreover, few American historians have refrained from assuming or asserting a meaning for such pivotal terms as democracy, equality, and liberty. Indeed, one might say that these words have provided writers of American history with their most important organizational and ideological themes, serving at the same time to justify important categories of analysis—property and class, for example—often said to be inferentially related to these terms and essential to their meaning.

The suggestion, made by Sweet and many others, that Methodism fitted into or paralleled democracy "rising in the West" assumes that the reader knows something of Turner's theories of American development. It assumes too that "democracy" conveys a plausible referent in itself, as well as in association with phrases such as free will and individual responsibility. Sweet's words, although highly abstract, are clear to most readers.

4. William Warren Sweet, *The Rise of Methodism in the West* (New York, 1920), p. 14. Historians of Methodism have generally followed this approach. See, for example, Elizabeth K. Nottingham, *Methodism and the Frontier: Indiana Proving Grounds* (New York, 1966), p. 59.

5. G. G. Findlay and W. W. Holdsworth, *The History of the Wesleyan Methodist Missionary Society* (5 vols.; London, 1921), I, 30. Several good summaries of early Methodism are found in Emory S. Bucke, ed., *The History of American Methodism* (3 vols.; New York, 1964), I. Charles W. Ferguson has written a sprightly popular narrative, *Organizing to Beat the Devil: Methodists and the Making of America* (Garden City, 1971).

The question is whether the clarity is historiographical as well as linguistic. Sweet evidently assents in general to Turner's view that democracy grows or is affected in positive ways through contact with the frontier; Turner claimed that the West, and the process of westering, were responsible for creating American democracy.

Historians are familiar with an enormous body of literature on this subject, almost all of it devoted to testing the theory in one form or another. Surprisingly, however, the term "democracy," basic to Turner's thought, has been accepted with little discussion, its meaning either assumed, or stated in abstract and sentimental language, or else said to be adduced in some vague way in the course of analysis. This lack of attention is hardly limited to literature of the frontier. Definitions and theories of democracy, as of other important and related terms, seem either to exceed the needs of practicing historians or to fall short of them. Irving Kristol has noted what is perhaps one of the most remarkable facts about the writing of American history, namely, that those who write it "appear to have given so very little thought to the various meanings that the idea of democracy might have." Just as true though exceedingly curious is the fact that historians "have little aptitude or interest in . . . problem[s] of political philosophy." [6]

For these reasons, readers of historical texts are more apt to encounter normative faits accomplis instead of explanations. The most obvious, but by no means the simplest, reason is that historians share among themselves, and with scholars in related fields, a certain cluster of values, generally if broadly suggested by the terms *liberalism* and *humanism*. While the level of conscious commitment is more often epistemological than ideological, the practical effects of humanistic historiography are indistinguishable from ideology. Historiography, especially American historiography, is in the mainstream of ideological derivation from the matrix of ideas associated with Anglo-European Enlightenment thought over the past two centuries. Accordingly, research in historical as in other

6. Irving Kristol, *On the Democratic Idea in America* (New York, 1972), p. 49. Better-known historical studies include Merle Curti, *The Making of an American Community* (Stanford, 1959); Stanley Elkins and Erik McKitrick, "A Meaning for Turner's Frontier," *Political Science Quarterly* 69 (1954): 321–53, 565–605; Robert Dykstra, *The Cattle Towns* (New York, 1968). The literature dealing with the frontier and with Turner is enormous. See Ray A. Billington, *The Frontier Heritage* (New York, 1966), as well as his more recent volumes dealing with Turner the man and scholar.

social studies has tended to reflect each new refocusing of Enlightenment visions of man's condition.

The Enlightenment context, or "the temporary triumph, from the Enlightenment to the twentieth century, of the view that ethics . . . proceed unencumbered by the presence of preexperiential data in the psyche," has long been pressed into the fabric of research.[7] Sustained on one hand by a rhetoric fully as seductive as the Enlightenment ideas of progress, reform, change, and rationalism, and on the other by an always increasing mass intelligentsia for whom orthodoxy is vice and change virtue, the Enlightenment context presents the student of the past with an almost impermeable ideological and institutional consensus before research is under way. This consensus, by channeling insight—quite literally censoring it—controls perspective and thereby discourages opportunities for developing historical definitions as differentiated from psychological or sociological definitions. Considered strictly from the standpoint of method, the Enlightenment context requires at the outset an implicit commitment to temporal linearity. This simple idea is a professional commonplace. Like all simple ideas, however, it is difficult to explain and to understand. Provisionally, it may be defined as the approach to the relationship of ideas and events which makes time integral

7. Donald Atwell Zoll, "The Ethical Base of Community," *Modern Age* (1972): 254. Following Leo Strauss's critique of social science, I have attempted to develop these issues by arguing that social science method is the source and model of modern, pluralist democracy. Thus democratic ideology, grounded in Enlightenment ontology which finds a fundamental cleavage between man in nature and man in society (a cleavage that imputes an incorrigible relativism to all human values), received its most lasting formulation in the theories of Max Weber. Weber's classic distinction between judgments of value, which he held to be unverifiable, and judgments of fact which could be verified, continues to inform the social science approach. More important, this distinction has forced a dogmatic and limiting democratization upon students of man and upon the study of ideas. Twentieth-century egalitarianism or the "open society" is the political form of Weber's value-free social science. Identifying democracy, theoretically and historically, with naturalism and ethical relativism, the tasks of the historian have been reduced to the merest sociology wherein the rate and degree of resistance to change or, conversely, opposition to the status quo, provide the basic guides to analysis. An explicit assertion of this exceptionally pervasive view is found in a recent monograph, awarded the Turner prize in 1972, in which the author contends that democracy is "justified, not because anyone could provide or demonstrate certain ethical propositions, but because the idea of an absolute moral demonstration [is] itself a rational impossibility" (Edward A. Purcell, Jr., *The Crisis of Democratic Theory: Scientific Naturalism and the Problem of Value* [Lexington, Ky., 1972], p. 205). Strauss's critique is found in *Natural Right and History* (Chicago, 1953), pp. 35–80 and *passim*, and in *Liberalism Ancient and Modern* (New York, 1968), pp. 203–23.

to both. In other words, historians' "time" is seen not simply as a coordinate of events and ideas, but as a necessary condition for historical meanings of any kind; it is a kind of sociology of historical knowledge.

For most historians this commitment is a tacit one, but that does not mean that it is empty of ideological content. On the contrary, the linear configuration of past ideas and events is irreversibly and insidiously bonded to a series of ideas—change, progress, continuity—which are in turn part of a substrate of professional beliefs about historical methods and about human existence itself. In fact, the context of Enlightenment historiography is incurably teleological.

Broadly speaking, there are at least two reasons for the teleological interpretation. The first is generic in nature. As Robert Nisbet has pointed out, the aim of "students of social change since Aristotle has been to vindicate the principles of continuity and change." And, even though "the normative elements of the idea of progress have been sharply challenged, social scientists have retained the more fundamental conception of the continuity of change." [8] Second, this retention produces and justifies broad agreement upon values, in considerable measure a derivation from method, within the intellectual culture itself. This relationship between method and values has been termed the " 'personal union' of liberalism and value-free social science." [9] The Enlightenment consensus and the methodology imposed by it are clearly not limited to liberal historiography alone, but include Marxism and Marxist variants as well. If the language of development and evolution gives way occasionally to that of catastrophe and strophe, the teleological perspective is clear in both forms. Enlightenment values inform each alike.

The teleological perspective, proceeding, among other things, upon the analogy of cause and effect, imposes a developmental, progressive presumption in the study of human affairs. The concept of direction may be understood and applied in merely structural terms (i.e., trends, tendencies, processes), as it is by most practitioners. For historians who give it a structural interpretation, the teleological perspective is merely an organizational guide, more or less synonymous with chronology, and consequently a mechanical, seemingly objective device. When direction is

8. Robert Nisbet, *Community and Power* (New York, 1962), pp. 86–87. Adrian Kuzminski has clarified some of the matters raised here in "The Paradox of Historical Knowledge," *History and Theory* 12 (1973): 269–89. He calls for a "new ontological context."
9. Strauss, *Liberalism Ancient and Modern,* p. viii.

conceived in overt ideological terms, whether progressivist or revolutionist, teleology and development are made more explicit. However used, the directional focus is obviously basic to an extraordinarily wide spectrum of social studies analysis. And, while humanistic scholarship has raised up whole areas of human activity for study, it is just as true that the huge, untidy Enlightenment conspectus has grown analytically oppressive, if not oppressive in other respects as well.

This oppressiveness takes several forms. Some of these, for example the fallacy of recency, are familiar. Here the present becomes the culmination and focus of the past. This Voltairean view was formalized as the source and the dilemma of historical insight by the Progressive historians half a century ago. Years after the factual misperceptions of Progressive historiography have been corrected, however, historical writing continues to be promiscuously plagued by an array of unintentionally subversive terms such as "prefigure," "anticipate," "progress," and others in which the past is but prelude to the present. Ironically, one of the most frequent justifications for a "new" history or a "new" social science is some unprecedented, hence discontinuous, state of things in the present. Familiar, too, is the format of historical controversy in which people and events are weighed in the scales of Enlightenment values, adjusted to pressures imposed by shifting presents. Such pressures, excused on grounds of methodological inevitability (i.e., that they are mandated by present concerns) and justified on didactic and ideological grounds calling for history to be "usable," urge the historian to know the present and to have visions of the future in order to understand the past.[10] Reasoning of this sort, however widespread, is eccentric and philosophically flaccid. Although the vast implications of these views are beyond the scope of the present discussion, the effects of such approaches bear directly upon my study.

Historians of evangelism in the middle period proceed, as do historians in other areas, as if linear patterns and Enlightenment values reflect enduring contours of reality.[11] Evangelism is said to be concerned with

---

10. For a remarkable exposition of this approach, see Walter LaFeber, "The Impact of Revisionism," in Thomas G. Patterson, ed., *The Origins of the Cold War* (Lexington, Mass., 1970), p. 120. Compare Robert James Maddox, *The New Left and the Origins of the Cold War* (Princeton, 1973).

11. Change thus becomes the only desirable reality, necessarily putting the past at a discount. Perhaps this is the most sensible way to state the "problem" of historicism. See Strauss, *Natural Right,* pp. 1–34.

"democratization," "equalization," and "liberalization." Accordingly students are inclined to ask if the religious were humanistic and benevolent or if, instead, they were advocates of "social control." "Conservative" or "democratic," "backward-looking" or "ahead of their time," are the terms and stakes of controversy.[12] Important here is not the consensus these terms avow, but the narrowing framework created by the larger agreement upon values, a framework all the more constricting for the vague way the consensus is applied. The interdisciplinary emphasis of recent years is directly connected to this problem. Rather than enriching the perspectives of the historian, the interdisciplinary effort, tied to the issues of Enlightenment historiography, has deepened the ideological consensus, further inhibiting the possibilities for new insight and new categories of analysis.

In addition to the fallacy of recency and presentism, the teleological perspective has also enmeshed the problems of writing history in fruitless and inappropriate contexts, the most notorious of which requires history to demonstrate its standing as a science. Historians have suffered no little anxiety in trying to assimilate the ideals of scientists. Had they relinquished the assumption that the present is nothing but the most recent tick of the historical clock, however, much of their anxiety might have been avoided. Challenged to show that history was scientific, practitioners failed to note the queerness of the juxtaposition or to ponder, if only for the sake of logical verisimilitude, the correlative proposition that science was not historical. Unfortunately, historians formulated the problems of objectivity and of presentism in exactly the wrong ways. They reasoned from method to values rather than from values to method. It was not present concerns that impeded historical understanding. Instead it was a reliance upon linearity which made presentism inevitable.

But of all the disabling consequences of the teleological perspective, one is more far-reaching and debilitating than all the rest combined. Teleology imposes upon the historian, whatever his views, the attitude of reformer. The imperatives of teleology are irresistibly linked to the moral superiority of change, and hence to a free-floating antagonism toward the idea that values may be true or false independent of time and place. In other words, the status quo is presumed to be a priori false since no one

---

12. Recent literature is surveyed by Lois W. Banner, "Religious Benevolence as Social Control: A Critique of American Interpretations," *JAH* 60 (1973): 23–41.

value or set of values can be right. Teleologism then expresses the practicing historian's commitment to radical historicism. The historicist approach, especially attractive to historians of democracy for whom ethical relativism is evidence of ontological health and of the growth of democracy, is also an impediment to historical studies, especially to studies of democracies. Thus the presumption that values cannot be known to be true or false except in historical settings, and the view that this proposition constitutes a legitimate basis for studying the past and for defining democracy, shut out the historian who wishes to invoke or establish nonnaturalist, nonrelativist criteria. This in turn amounts to shutting out alternative understandings of the past and of democracy. Historicist and democratist approaches, by assuming that all metaphysical and ethical views are "strictly speaking, untenable . . . as regards their claim to be simply true," reduce historical work to a plausible but relatively unimportant cataloging of ideas and events, limiting its substance and its import to use by demagogues and dilettantes.[13] Also, by relieving us of the need to make judgments of value the historicist approach obscures obvious temporal and conceptual discontinuities. Specifically, historicism has until very recently made it difficult for scholars to realize what Bernard Bailyn has at length made clear, albeit after two generations of scholarly wrangling, namely that "nowhere in eighteenth-century America was there 'democracy'—middle class or otherwise, as we use the term." [14] Despite this vital and long overdue observation it is doubtful if the conceptual apparatus which has so long obscured this obvious fact will soon be dismantled.

A discontinuous, heterodox historiography requires complete disengagement from the Enlightenment context and demands "a new ontological context" altogether.[15] In such a situation ideals may very well be continuous, but in the way that the past, in its broadest connotation, is often said to be distinct from history. In a discontinuous history, differences more than similarities, phases not lines, would predominate. It is one thing to say that the democracy Sweet believed Methodists repre-

---

13. Strauss, *Natural Right*, p. 19.

14. Bernard Bailyn, "Political Experience and Enlightenment Ideas in Eighteenth Century America," *AHR* 67 (1962): 346.

15. Kuzminski, "Paradox of Historical Knowledge," p. 289. A favorable summary of neorelativism may be found in David A. Hollinger, "T. S. Kuhn's Theory of Science and Its Implication for History," *AHR* 78 (1973): 370–93.

sented was a projected vision, more relevant to Sweet than to Methodists. It is another thing altogether, more significant and truer perhaps, to discover that the democracy of Sweet and that of Lee were qualitatively distinct, separated and closed off from each other.

Recent studies of American democracy in the eighteenth and nineteenth centuries which are directly relevant to the present work suggest rather strongly some specific limitations of Enlightenment presumptions and the urgent need for conceptual reordering. Certain residua of data continue to embarrass the categories of Enlightenment historiography in just those areas where research has been undertaken to vindicate Enlightenment presuppositions. Historical literature concerning the franchise is a case in point.

When historians supposed that voting was restricted in pre-Revolutionary America, they concluded that democracy was set loose by the Revolution and by the ideal of "equality." Upon learning the right to vote was extremely broad before the Revolution, historians had to alter their views. Thus mere "franchise democracy" was said to be either predemocratic or not democratic at all. Commenting on Robert Brown's discoveries of widespread enfranchisement in colonial Massachusetts, Michael Zuckerman has observed, correctly it seems, that "concord and concurrence among neighbors" were the objectives of colonial suffrage. A consensual, exclusivist polity, such as that of Dedham or of Haverhill, Massachusetts, Zuckerman adds, "imposed very significant limitations on the democracy of the provincial community, limitations sufficiently severe to suggest . . . the democratic appellation itself may be anachronistic when applied to such a society." [16]

Although the Zuckerman critique reflects an adversarial and pluralist democratic model, something more than a problem of definitions is involved. To say that what eighteenth-century Americans called democracy

---

16. Michael Zuckerman, "The Politics of Consensus: The Social Context of Democracy in Massachusetts," *WMQ*, 3d ser., 25 (1968), reprinted in James Morton Smith, ed., *Politics and Society in American History, 1607–1865* (2 vols.; Englewood Cliffs, 1973), I, 68. Additional evidence and a review of recent literature are found in William F. Willingham, "Deference Democracy and Town Government in Windham, Connecticut, 1755 to 1786," *WMQ*, 3d ser., 30 (1973): 401–22. Also important is John M. Murrin, "Review Essay," *History and Theory* 11 (1972): 226–75, where it is argued that while association of democracy with consensus was the ideal, there were, not surprisingly, lapses in practice. Murrin does not dispute the critical fact that eighteenth-century democracy neither was pluralist nor aspired to be.

is not "democratic" has no real historical meaning. If democracy may be said to possess a historical dimension at all, then comparative assessments over time are clearly not historical matters, but instead logical and ethical ones. Curiously, American historians find little use for the comparative method in studies of race, violence, or power politics. At the same time, however, they are seldom reluctant to invoke the criterion of equality, which is manifestly not historical and just as certainly vague, as a basis for comparison and judgment. The double assumptions that democracy and history are developmental and linear are surely mistaken, whether they are considered separately or together. No real sense, it seems reasonable to believe, will be made of the past—or of democracy—until these questions are thoroughly explored philosophically.

If Zuckerman's view is correct, as it clearly seems to be, it is in reference to it that political, social, and intellectual development must be evaluated. The consistent but baffling confusion, by historians, of vital terms such as "conservative," "liberal," and "democratic" is not a consequence of historical or even of theoretical imprecision. The source of the confusion is directly traceable to the nest of assumptions and values which inevitably make their appearance in analyses such as Zuckerman's. What in fact his and other related works actually explain is that colonial and antebellum democracy was indeed deeply and unashamedly consensual. It was based, ideologically and traditionally, upon the ideal of consent of the governed. This fact, and not the more familiar configurations of heterogeneous, or pluralist, democracy, is what Americans had in mind when they sought, in their various ways, to feel out the implications of equality in the contexts of independence and nationalism.

With Alexis de Tocqueville, American historians have observed the evolution of local autonomies—what Robert Weibe has correctly called "the heart of American democracy"—as these aggregates faced disintegration and reintegration in the first half of the nineteenth century.[17] The well-documented sources of disintegration—the frontier, mobility, ur-

---

17. Robert Weibe, *The Search for Order, 1877–1920* (New York, 1967), p. xii. See also Page Smith, *As a City upon a Hill* (New York, 1966). Historians have long noted these changes. See John Higham, "Hanging Together: Divergent Unities in American History," *JAH* 61 (1974): 5–28. Two recent evocative assertions of the theme are Merle Curti, "Robert Owen in American Thought," in Donald E. Pitzer, ed., *Robert Owen's American Legacy* (Indianapolis: Indiana Historical Society, 1972), p. 68; and Bertram Wyatt-Brown, "Elkins' Anti-Slavery Interpretation Reexamined," *American Quarterly* 25 (May 1973): 175. Also worth noting is the recent reassertion of the provincial-national theme in Ameri-

banization—no less than the ideological resources harnessed for reintegration (particularly the revolutionary psychological adjustments that arose with the age of Jackson),[18] have suggested to students that Americans were alarmed and shaken by the discovery of equality. As William Taylor has put it, speaking perhaps for a wide segment of scholars, "some of the alarm of Americans appears to have sprung from the . . . fact that American institutions were free and that they [Americans] were free to change them for better or for worse." [19] We are to understand that these intimations of cosmic freedom, signifying liberation from all fixities in accordance with the supine truth that there are no truths, were the philosophical bequests of egalitarianism.

Yet, unlike Tocqueville, American historians have consistently de-emphasized and misconstrued the consensualist background, thereby, it seems, leaving out a crucial historical fact. The alarm was probably real enough, but the discovery was not of equality but of increasing disjunction. Post-Revolutionary Americans witnessed the progressive erosion and eventual dissolution of universal structures of spirit and of place, structures traditionally associated with polity and selfhood. Torn, however gradually, from familiar contexts with little more to guide them than the promises and institutions of reason (sometimes called nationalism), Americans were invited to refit their values to a new and radically open-ended cos-

---

can Civil War historiography. See Phillip S. Paluden, "The American Civil War Considered as a Crisis in Law and Order," *AHR* 77 (1972): 1013–34.

18. Lynn Marshall ("The Strange Stillbirth of the Whig Party," *AHR* 72 [1967]: 445–68) indicates that the idea of rotation in office comprehended a view of equality that made men "interchangeable" for all practical political purposes. Marshall's findings suggest certain unexpected resonances in connection with statements such as the following: "Jacksonian democracy bequeathed to America an ideal of fraternal nationalism unmatched even in Rousseau's France or the Italy of Mazzini" (R. Niebuhr and A. Heimert, *A Nation So Conceived* [London, 1963], p. 29).

19. William Taylor, *Cavalier and Yankee* (New York, 1961), p. 99. Bertrand Russell, holding that science has discovered an unfixed, indeed an unhinged universe, calls upon the virtuous man to face incertitudes without aids of any sort. His view may properly be regarded as a perfect expression of the prevailing value consensus among intellectuals. Russell's comments, made more than half a century ago, are now the common property of a mass intelligentsia. See Bertrand Russell, *A Free Man's Worship (Mysticism and Logic)* (New York, 1918), pp. 46 ff. Compare Peter Gay, *The Enlightenment: An Interpretation: The Rise of Modern Paganism* (Vintage ed.; New York, 1968), pp. 418–19. Zoll, "Ethical Base of Community," pp. 246–58. Zoll's brilliant but little-known piece summarizes our "perennial disputes concerning ethics" and provides a basis for challenging nonrelativist departures.

mos. They sought moorings in what was in fact, as we are now beginning to see, an ontological void.

Methodism was part of the search and evangelism was an expression of the "democracy rising in the West." But this democracy did not rest, as we are frequently told, on Locke's view of property. The focus of American democracy was not anarchical, propertied libertarianism or utopian communism even while advocates for both dotted the scene. Reformers who scored the land seeking to exclude, or to include, in their desire for homogeneity, were actuated by a love of harmony, of cooperation, and of consensus. The image of democracy matched the American experience of it for more than two centuries. The image was strifelessness, as much the ideal of democratic theorists like Sidney Camp, John L. O'Sullivan, and George Bancroft, as of Charles Grandison Finney, the leading evangelist of the day. All saw Christian harmony and democracy as two sides of the same coin.

They shared the assumption, fatal and confusing though it proved to be to contemporaries and to students of democracy ever since, that, in the words of two of the more benighted monists of the day, the failure to achieve harmony on a small scale, among a limited number of people, was clear evidence that harmony could therefore be attained on a large scale with many people. "We must combine and associate large masses," exclaimed Albert Brisbane, America's leading booster of Charles Fourier's panaceas, "to develop the harmonies of human nature." [20] Yet America's visionaries had more in common with the nation's most renowned realist, James Madison, than they or later students have supposed. Harmony bound them as it bound Americans generally. The connections were traditionalist as well as aspirational. But the reformers' world differed in one vital respect from that of Madison. Whereas the Virginian believed that harmony might come as a result of equilibrium among diverse forces and

20. Albert Brisbane, *Social Destiny of Man: Or, Association and Reorganization of Industry* (New York, 1840), p. 132. The words are Fourier's; the translation and the book are Brisbane's. George Fitzhugh, the pre-Civil War advocate of slavery, which he called the science of socialism, was especially critical of the communitarian wing of the abolitionist movement. Suggesting that what the abolitionists really wanted was to abolish freedom, Fitzhugh quipped that the communitarians were no less self-deceived. He declared that "each [reformer] has a little Model Utopia or Phalanstery for his new and better world, which having failed on a small experimental scale, . . . is, therefore, the very thing to succeed on a large one" (George Fitzhugh, *Cannibals All*, ed. C. Vann Woodward [Cambridge, 1960], p. 22).

groups, the reformers looked forward to a transcendent equilibrium of intertwined harmonies. Universals, whether spiritual or scientific, would, it was hoped, subdue the residue of resistant particulars. In this respect, Methodist evangelists were transcendental.

For John Wesley, with whose spiritual rebirth at a meeting in London on May 24, 1738, Methodism began, the object of religion was precisely balance. "To balance . . . [not only] sectarian salvation by faith . . . [with] churchly works," but also freedom with security, equality with statism, individualism with the collectivity, and the modern with the traditional, was Wesley's genius. As has recently been observed, "Wesley regarded himself as making real and vital the true message of the Anglican *via media.*" [21] It was this Methodism that Lee hoped to carry to Oregon, the same Methodism Wesley had taken to England's industrial masses. But whereas it had been Wesley's purpose, as Bernard Semmel has shown, to balance Jacobin egalitarian autarky against Laudian passivity, Lee's job was different. His problem, typical of the Jacksonian setting, was to balance and also to transcend homogeneity and diversity. In other words, Lee's object was to maintain Methodist identity for himself and for the church and at the same time to expand the group by including within it all previously resistant diversities—to evangelize, in a word. Religious historians have looked upon this apparent dilemma in socioreligious terms as the problem of sect type (exclusivity) versus church type (inclusivity). Yet this formulation would appear to be only one aspect of much larger problems, involving the conceptual and cultural adjustment that Americans were working through in the antebellum years. Methodism, Wesley had proclaimed, "is essentially a social religion and . . . to turn it into a solitary religion is indeed to destroy it." The paradoxes, social and theoretical, lurking in this proposition did not trouble Wesley, for whom Methodism was explicitly connected with the Church of England. The situation for American Methodism, where the church quickly became independent, and had indeed been virtually so from the start, was more complex and much less secure.

As an Anglican reform movement, Methodism gained its first foothold on American soil in Virginia and North Carolina, where the Church of England had been established. After the formation of the American Methodist Episcopal church at the Christmas Conference on December 24,

21. Bernard Semmel, *The Methodist Revolution* (New York, 1973), p. 188.

1784, Methodists swiftly invaded a hospitable West. Congregational Connecticut and Massachusetts were not so receptive. Thirty-five years later the Methodist Episcopal church was the second-largest Protestant denomination in the country, behind the Baptists. It would soon be the largest. The key to Methodist success and to an understanding of Methodism lies in the recognition that the Methodist church was intrinsically a missionary church.

In the earliest days of Methodism no distinction was made between missionary and preacher, as no distinctions were made among sinners. The logic of free grace admitted of no limitations within the human family. This same logic permitted no limitation on the efforts of the church to reach the human family. In practical fact Methodist doctrine was to make Methodists, and the rule was to preach. The church used the itinerant system, sending its preachers off on circuits and, when they returned, sending them back on revivals. Itinerancy was the perfect system for Methodists and for a frontier, rural society. Likewise, revivalism also seemed to fit the emotional landscape of a mobile people. "The itinerancy," remarked Stephen Olin, a prominent Methodist and the president of Randolph Macon and Wesleyan colleges in the 1830s and 1840s, "is a missionary system. To the efficiency of the missionary principle, inherent in her Constitution, is the Methodist Episcopal Church indebted for her extension and prosperity. . . . What by other Churches are denominated domestic missions, constitute, to a large extent, the regular field of labor of the Methodist ministry in the new states and territories." [22]

The identity of preacher and missionary did not last beyond the second decade of the nineteenth century. The creation of a separate missionary society in 1820, together with a decline in itinerancy and a concomitant increase of stationed (nonitinerant) preachers, reflected the change. With these developments came others, including a desire on the part of the laity and of stationed preachers to exercise more control over local affairs. The conflict between laymen and the episcopacy became a central theme in Methodist affairs.

22. Stephen Olin, *The Life and Letters of Stephen Olin* (2 vols.; New York, 1854), I, 172. In keeping with his Anglicanism, Wesley had carefully differentiated nonordained and ordained ministers. After his death in 1793 even this distinction was eliminated. The identity of missionary and minister was, of course, not merely formal but deeply definitional. Laymen who went on missions were carefully not called missionaries to distinguish them from the ministers who were so called.

Although the widening gap between missionary and preacher and the question of lay representation were problems confronting all Methodists, they were especially serious in America, where vast and extremely rapid demographic and cultural changes were in progress.[23] As receding frontiers were replaced by relatively stable communities, there developed an ever greater need for Methodist ministers to live with the converts won by itinerant preachers. Yet the problems of lay against clerical were more than simply by-products of a successful missionary system or the result of population factors. The changes taking place in the church during the early decades of the nineteenth century reached to the foundations of Methodism. The history of the church to the schism of 1844, if not for a longer period, reflects a frustrated effort to harness incompatible ideals, especially the ideals of world evangelization and of missionary purity.[24] The first was centrifugal, the second centripetal. When internal disparities became too great the harness was stretched, and eventually it snapped.

The schism of 1844 separated the northern from the southern wing of the church. And although slavery was as much the necessary condition for the division between Methodists in 1844 as between the states in 1861, neither the schism, nor the war, is explained by slavery. Both events were embedded in the larger philosophic and cultural matrix, which it is a purpose of this study to explore. Of the era's political philosophy, John William Ward has aptly written that Jacksonians "concluded . . . America had no need for politics." But it is emphatically not "astonishing," as Ward also says, that such a philosophy prevailed.[25] Jacksonian philosophy was fully in keeping with past experience and with all

23. Peter G. Mode, *The Frontier Spirit in American Christianity* (New York, 1923), pp. 130, 134; George Smith, *Polity of Wesleyan Methodism* (London, 1851); George Eayrs, W. J. Townsend, and H. B. Workman, eds., *A New History of Methodism* (2 vols.; London, 1909), II, 119. The scope of these alterations, well known to historians, is not the less difficult to explain and conceive; Rowland B. Berthoff, *An Unsettled People: Social Order and Disorder in American History* (New York, 1971), is a helpful guide.

24. The schism of 1844 divided the Methodist church into northern and southern halves, which did not reunite until 1939. The immediate cause of the break was the decision of a southern bishop to keep slaves he inherited against the wish of a large segment of antislavery northerners. A standard work is John Nelson Norwood, *The Schism in the Methodist Episcopal Church, 1844–1846* (Alfred, N.Y., 1923). New commentaries are always forthcoming. See, for example, Donald G. Mathews, "The Methodist Schism of 1844 and the Popularization of Anti-Slavery Sentiment," *Mid-America* 51 (1969): 3–23.

25. John William Ward, "Jacksonian Democratic Thought: 'A Natural Charter of

visions of the future. Radical egalitarian reformers who sought "patent-office models of the good society" were hardly concerned with marking out the elements of new institutions for the cultural provisioning of unborn generations.[26] Instead, whether free-love communists, secular associationists, evangelicals, or nativists, they all looked for ways to ensure consensus and harmony, and thus to restore the America threatened by diversities, even though they were themselves the products and the creators of diversity, hence of the competitiveness and disharmony they abominated. Reformers longed, with most Americans, for the "return of harmony" which Daniel Webster called for so plaintively after his famous public argument with Senator Hayne.[27] The return to harmony was not conservatism, radicalism, or any ism at all. Nor was it "social control" or "democracy ahead of its time." Harmony was an incantation in the name of what Americans understood to be "republican democracy."

Evangelists, Methodists as well as others, made no effort to hide the fact that outward agreement and harmony among congregants were signs of evangelical success. "The spirit of religion," said Charles Grandison Finney, the famed evangelist noted for disarming simplifications, "is not the spirit of controversy." [28]

Reforming the nation by evangelizing it became the official purpose of the church after 1816. Before that time the church's motto had been "to reform the continent and spread scriptural holiness over these lands." In 1816 the motto was changed. The mission was now "to reform the continent by spreading scriptural holiness over these lands." Here, as elsewhere, Methodists were the offspring, not the authors, of subtleties.[29]

The year 1816 was marked by another significant development in Methodist history. Slavery, expressly condemned by John Wesley, was countenanced by the Methodist Episcopal church. The General Confer-

---

Privilege,' " in Stanley Coben and Lorman Ratner, eds., *The Development of an American Culture* (Englewood Cliffs, 1970), p. 57.

26. Arthur Bestor, Jr., "Patent-Office Models of the Good Society: Some Relationships between Social Reform and Westward Expansion," in *American History: Recent Interpretations,* ed. Abraham S. Eisenstadt (2d ed.; 2 vols.; New York, 1969), I, 412–30.

27. Webster is quoted in Taylor, *Cavalier and Yankee,* p. 114.

28. Charles Grandison Finney, *Lectures on Revivals of Religion,* ed. William G. McLoughlin (Cambridge, 1960), p. 25.

29. Sidney Mead, "The Rise of the Evangelical Conception of the Ministry in America, 1607–1850," in Reinhold Niebuhr and Daniel Williams, eds., *The Ministry in Historical Perspective* (New York, 1956), pp. 207–49.

ence of that year agreed to a compromise law accepting the status quo.[30] But since acceptance of the status quo brought no alteration in the ideological content of church doctrine regarding slavery, the compromise was ideologically unsatisfactory. Methodists adopted gradual emancipation and the colonization of freed slaves as their official position on the slavery issue. Colonization was an exclusionist solution. It proved as unworkable in theory for Methodists as it was unacceptable to most freedmen in practice, for it implied that Negroes or freed slaves were ultimately different and unassimilable. While sending Negroes out of the country was perfectly acceptable to Madisonians, irreconcilability was the death knell of evangelism.

Regenerate men tended to look alike. In this sense Methodists, in the language of sociologist David Riesman, were "other-directed." Missions to the slaves were found to stress the equality of sinners in this world and of the regenerate in the next, while insisting on ineradicable differences among Methodists. The distinction sapped the lifeblood of evangelical ardor even while southern Methodists insisted upon its efficacy and legitimacy.[31] Contrary to modern allegations of a distinctive American racism, the Methodists did not hate Negroes but rather differences, and the differences between slave and free were to them much more defeating than differences of skin color. Methodists spent their "racism" on Catholics, for the most part, and occasionally on Jews. Evangelical Protestantism sought the elimination of differences. The driving power of the missionary ideal was not a passion for social control but for harmony. And as religious leaders talked of harmony, they hoped to "chart . . . the way toward a homogeneous America." [32] The problem of slavery could not be solved by a simple syllogistic deduction from premises of equality and freedom. Instead, it was the fact that slavery was founded on force and conflict which shamed Methodist and American pretensions to equality. The concept of

30. General Conference Journals, I, 139.

31. William Capers to Willbur Fisk, Charleston [S.C.], September 12, 1833, MS C239, Fisk Papers, Wesleyan University, Middletown, Conn. See also Donald G. Mathews, "Methodist Mission to the Slaves," *JAH* 51 (1965): 615–31. Recent efforts to demythologize differences between North and South at this time have gone too far in certain directions and not far enough in others. George Fitzhugh, for example, shared more with the northern abolitionists than either shared with the advocates of popular sovereignty, while the Virginian differed profoundly from both northern groups in other respects.

32. Perry Miller, *Life of the Mind in America from the Revolution to the Civil War* (New York, 1965), p. 48.

equality as both a doctrine of freedom and of consent of the governed involves an obvious, perhaps an incorrigible, dilemma in practice no less than in logic. Methodists were no better able to resolve this dilemma than their contemporaries or their successors. Instead their response was to consume it by reforming themselves and the world.

Reforms, panaceas of all kinds, and do-gooding were at the center of American life, where the mixture of religion and the secular world was often as complete as the separation of church and state was invariable. Communitarians like John Humphrey Noyes, a Methodist, and Bronson Alcott, a transcendentalist, were pledged to an ideal they named equality. Both hunted ways to achieve it without inspiring conflict. Lacking the scientific or romantic assurance of their twentieth-century successors, antebellum reformers most often turned to religion as the first vehicle of reformation. Reformers of every kind, of every political view, saw a way to the promised land along the road either of assimilation or of exclusion of the elements deemed responsible for current evils. All aspirants for virtue hailed equality and the end of strife. Presidents, too, embraced the ethos of nonpartisanship. Before it became mere ritual to say so, Andrew Jackson proclaimed: "If I am elected to fill the presidential chair, it must be by the people, and I will be President of the nation, and not of a party." [33] Willbur Fisk, president of Wesleyan College in Connecticut and "father of the Oregon Mission," hated Jackson with unremitting passion but shared his views of party. "O the spirit of party," he lamented. "What a curse is Jacksonism to our country." [34]

Manifest Destiny, the expansionists' creed, was no less a part of the reform mentality than temperance, evangelism, or, for that matter, nativism. A leading historian of expansionism suggests the Manifest Destiny movement was "perhaps the most important" [35] reform movement of the Jacksonian period. If the more obvious boosters of Manifest Destiny were

33. Andrew Jackson to Andrew J. Donelson, Washington, April 11, 1824, in John Spencer Bassett, ed., *Correspondence of Andrew Jackson,* III (Washington, 1928), 246.

34. Willbur Fisk to [Benjamin F.] Deming, Middletown, Conn., March 15, 1834, folder 2/7/34–25, #340315, Fisk Papers. The rather ineffectual Deming was a representative in Congress from Vermont, a National Republican, and a Whig. See also Leon Litwack, *North of Slavery: The Negro in the Free States, 1790–1860* (Chicago, 1961), p. 117. Fisk was Jason Lee's teacher from 1829 to 1830 at Wilbraham Academy. As the first advocate of the Oregon mission and a formulator of evangelical ideology, he was an important figure.

35. Frederick Merk, *Manifest Destiny and Mission in American History* (New York, 1963), p. 53.

Democrats of the Northeast and the Midwest, the movement, with its promise to "extend the areas of freedom," had many silent partners, just as the slogan had multiple meanings. The movement touched the nation's most sensitive nerve. To Methodists of New York and New England, to whom Andrew Jackson was as much an irritant as the Irish immigrants who voted for him, Manifest Destiny was only too clearly identical with their duty to extend Methodism throughout the world. How awkward was the providential likeness of views between the Methodist mission to save souls everywhere and Manifest Destiny as espoused by the Jacksonian John L. O'Sullivan, professional Irishman and editor of the *Democratic Review*. O'Sullivan believed that growth was "essential" to the nation, that "a federal democracy . . . was better fitted than other forms of government for an almost indefinite increase in territory." [36] He had no criticism of George Sidney Camp's comments concerning immigrants. Camp, arguing against the exclusivist views of native-born Americans, observed that each citizen "ought . . . to rejoice at an event which places the Catholic within his reach, within his means of influence and conversion. . . . The religious Protestant ought to regard with great satisfaction an event which brings Catholics to his own door, to have their belief rectified if it be not orthodox, and thus converts every Protestant neighbor into a Protestant missionary." O'Sullivan saw nothing at all peculiar in this statement, commenting only that Camp was remiss in not having spoken out against the restrictions upon naturalization being urged by Know-Nothings and Whigs. [37]

Whigs who hated Jackson and opposed Manifest Destiny were careful not to reject expansionism directly. Instead they warned of the threat to harmony. They pointed to a fallacy in the Madisonian premise of Manifest Destiny, arguing that an "almost indefinite increase in territory" would open the United States to new conflicts and tensions by requiring absurd annexations of unassimilable colors and cultures. [38] Expansionists countered felicitously, observing that in Mexico "our Yankee young fellows and the pretty senoritas [would] do the rest of annexation" by making

36. Editorial, "Growth of the States," *Democratic Review* (May 1848), quoted *ibid.*, p. 236 n. 10.

37. Review of "Mr. Camp's 'Democracy,' " *United States Magazine and Democratic Review*, n.s. 10 (February 1842): 122–28.

38. Merk, *Manifest Destiny and Mission*, p. 159.

Mexico "Anglo-Saxonized and prepared for the Confederacy." [39] Such annexation by "suffusion," as Congressman Breese of Illinois had the delicacy to call it, would resolve all obstacles to annexing the Mexicans. The Democratic *New York Evening Post* approved such methods and claimed, at a time when national policy dictated a strict cultural separation of Indians and whites, that "Mexicans are Indians" and hence that the best way to proceed would be to "keep our flag flying . . . till the progress of time, and the silent effect of our presence," effected the necessary "suffusion" for assimilation into the confederacy. [40] Significantly, these were the arguments and the methods that Methodists would use in Oregon with the Indians. But while New England Methodists shared methods and forms with Jacksonian expansionists, the two groups differed on more basic matters. They differed in principle. For the Methodists "suffusion," or what Jason Lee later would call "amalgamation," was a substitute for real conversions, the "changes of heart" sought by missionaries. At one stage of the mission's development, amalgamation became a method of lifting the Indians from barbarism to Christianity. In the end, as the missionaries strove at once for group purity and for converts among the Indians, amalgamation became the sign of confusion and failure.

To advocates of Manifest Destiny and to the reform temper prevalent in the nation, the temptations of "an almost indefinite" increment of territory as the means to avoid conflict and provide harmony were hard to resist. Americans of all persuasions and sections were not unaware of what most foreign visitors observed, that "every new colony of settlers contains within itself a nucleus of republican institutions, and revives, in a measure, the history of the first settlers. Its relation to the Atlantic states is similar to the situation of the early colonies with regard to the mother country, and contains the elements of freedom. Every society which is thus formed must weaken the fury of parties by diminishing the points of contact." [41]

---

39. *Philadelphia Ledger*, January 25, 1848, quoted *ibid.*, p. 158.

40. *New York Evening Post*, December 24, 1847, quoted *ibid.*

41. Francis J. Grund, *The Americans* (London, 1837), p. 208. This view was later to be shared by Frederick Jackson Turner. See "The Significance of the Frontier in American History," in *Frontier and Section: Selected Essays of Frederick Jackson Turner*, ed. Ray A. Billington (Englewood Cliffs, 1961), p. 38: "American social development has been continually beginning over again on the frontier." Cf. Earl S. Pomeroy, "Towards a Reorientation of Western History," *MVHR* 41 (1955): 579.

This observation on American life, parts of which would later be used by Frederick Jackson Turner to explain American democracy, was not restricted to Democratic party hucksters. Nor was it always mixed with imperial visions of the kind that sparked the expansionism of midwestern senators such as Thomas Benton and Lewis Cass. It was no ulterior longing for unclaimed territories which provoked Senator Lewis F. Linn of Missouri, for example, to speak of "this farthest west" as a place where "the descendents" of Plymouth's first immigrants would speed with "visions of some *noble futurity* to be realized." Linn's words, prophecy and all, described American reality as contemporaries would have it understood.[42] And Oregonians themselves, curiously extremist, later took up the cause of the Democracy and of Manifest Destiny, at the same time they rejected internal improvements. If territorial expansion could be justified as a way to eliminate conflict, no communication was necessary or desirable between the clusters of people that made up the whole. It seems that the economic and other needs of this fledgling community on the distant periphery of the American continent were no match for the logic of ideals.

Manifest Destiny could hardly be called a new phenomenon in American thought. James Madison's idea that a large republic was necessary for the survival of republicanism had linked democracy and size from the beginning as the conditions for freedom in a nation of aggregates. For men of the Revolutionary generation, conventional liberty within groups and equality between them was the reality to be preserved and the ideal to be perfected. This same freedom, however, was a serious threat, for it held the seeds of tyranny. Factions, parties, interests, and all other "degenerate" forms of group life were spatially conceived by thinkers such as Madison and Jefferson.

The pressures arising in the 1830s and 1840s from the urgency of the Indian problem and the influx of European immigrants were felt in philo-

42. Linn is quoted in Melvin C. Jacobs, *Winning Oregon: A Study of an Expansionist Movement* (Caldwell, Idaho, 1938), p. 35. Even the most belligerent of American expansionist movements, the Mexican war, does not warrant the charge of simple aggressiveness made by Albert Weinberg, among others. See Albert K. Weinberg, *Manifest Destiny: A Study of Nationalist Expansion in American History* (Baltimore, 1935). The most recent effort to see Polk as provoking the Mexican war is Glenn W. Price, *Origins of the War with Mexico: The Polk-Stockton Intrigue* (Austin, 1967). A more balanced view is that of Charles G. Sellers, *James K. Polk, Continentalist, 1843–1846*, III (Princeton, 1966), 213–66. David M. Pletcher, *The Diplomacy of Annexation: Texas, Oregon, and the Mexican War* (Columbia, Mo., 1973), expertly weighs revisionist arguments and presents the best study of the subject available.

sophical as well as in political and demographic terms, because Americans did not readily separate their philosophical visions from politics or politics from demography. When Americans asked who these new men—Indians and immigrants—were, they began a process of redefining themselves. Answers to questions of what constitutes selfhood help determine what men mean by the words "freedom" and "equality." [43] The answers antebellum Americans gave must be pried from layers of political statement and social activities. Historians have always supposed that Indian-white relations must reveal something important about American culture.

Every American president since Jefferson had considered the possibility of removing eastern Indians into the Louisiana Territory, out of contact with whites. Monroe advocated the idea and John Quincy Adams, for lack of an alternative, considered it sensible. It had also been the policy of the federal government from the time of President Washington and Secretary of War Henry Knox to civilize the Indians. This goal was shared by the evangelical churches. After Knox and Washington, who hoped to see Indians learn the meaning of "exclusive property," Secretaries of War John C. Calhoun, defender of slavery, Lewis Cass, Old Northwest advocate of "settler sovereignty," and William H. Crawford, plain Republican of Georgia, all looked to the day when, in Crawford's words, "the Indian should become a member of the family of freemen." [44] Calhoun, Monroe's secretary of war for seven years, urged the Indian agents under his direction to prepare the Indians "for a full participation and enjoyment with . . . [other] citizens of all . . . moral and political rights." [45]

The view from Washington was never very hopeful. The Indian, whether Cherokee farmer of Georgia or dispirited Chinook fisherman of the Pacific Coast, was incorrigibly, frustratingly, Indian. "A tree," said one exasperated government official, "is scarcely more tenacious of the

43. Isaiah Berlin, *Two Concepts of Liberty* (Oxford, Eng., 1958), p. 19.

44. Report of William H. Crawford to Senate, March 13, 1816, *American State Papers: Indian Affairs,* II, 26–28, quoted in Francis P. Prucha, *American Indian Policy in the Formative Years: The Indian Trade and Intercourse Acts, 1790–1834* (Cambridge, 1962), p. 91. See also the same author's "Andrew Jackson's Indian Policy: A Reassessment," *JAH* 56 (1969): 527–39. The more familiar view of Jacksonian Indian policy is Ronald Satz, *American Indian Policy in the Formative Years* (Lincoln, Neb., 1975).

45. John C. Calhoun to the Creek agent, September 29, 1818, quoted in Prucha, *American Indian Policy,* p. 213. The best general study of early national Indian-white relations to appear in recent years is Bernard W. Sheehan, *Seeds of Extinction: Jeffersonian Philanthropy and the American Indian* (Chapel Hill, 1973).

earth than a savage man of his habits."[46] Indians were glad to make use of white culture to adorn their own, but they showed little aptitude or enthusiasm for assimilation with white men.

Whites were amused or mortified by Indians who wore London top hats over hair slickened with animal grease or who added Christian prayers to totem rites. By 1870, after many Indians had been moved from East to West, badgered by a benevolent central government, harassed by frontiersmen, and finally prodded onto reservations, the missionary societies were rewarded with a major role in the implementation of President Grant's new national Indian policy calling for aggressive assimilation of the country's red men.[47] Insistence upon white customs and viewpoints for Indians led some missionaries, Methodist "Father" Wilbur of Oregon among them, to advocate using force to induce the Indians to accept civilization and Christianity, if nothing else would do the job.[48] This postbellum approach differed markedly from earlier methods and ideals.

In 1832 President Jackson carried out the program suggested by his predecessors and recommended to him not only by his own instincts and experiences, but by Georgians greedy for Indian lands. Amid an avalanche of protest from clerics throughout the country, Jackson signed the bill, narrowly passed, removing the Cherokees from Georgia. They were to be sent to "Indian country," an area the size of the existing twenty-four states, running from Lake Superior to the Mississippi, south to the Missouri border, then down the Missouri River to the Red River on the Texas border. Although most of the religious community had fought Jackson on the measure, some looked with favor upon removal because it separated Indians and whites, thus offering the best chance to save the Indian, spiritually and physically. Two years later the same Congress passed a pair of

46. Message of the President to the two Houses of Congress, December 7, 1842. U.S. Congress, House, *Report of the Commissioner on Indian Affairs* [W. H. Crawford], House Doc. 2, 27th Cong., 3d sess., 1842, p. 375.

47. Questions as to the number of Indians in America at various dates have been disastrously confused of late by polemicists. One effort to clarify matters is Don Russell, "How Many Indians Were Killed? White Man versus Red Man: The Facts and the Legend," *American West* 10 (July 1973): 42–47, 61–63. Assessing Indian historiography, and dividing the good from the bad, is Wilcomb Washburn, "The Writing of American Indian History," *PHR* 40 (1971): 261–82.

48. See Alvin M. Josephy, Jr., *The Nez Perce Indians and the Opening of the Northwest* (New Haven, 1965), pp. 485 ff. Wilbur was a personal friend of George Gary, Lee's replacement. For the relationship between Christianity and civilization as Methodist objectives among the Pacific Coast Indians, see chapters 4 and 5.

bills calling for the organization of an Indian department and for a new trade and intercourse act.[49] Livestock grazing as well as trapping were prohibited in the Indian country, though regulated trading was allowed. Whites were to be carefully excluded. In keeping with Jackson's convictions that the Indians held only possessory rights to the lands they occupied and were not to be dealt with as independent nations, the federal government took upon itself the right to interfere in tribal conflicts.

A third bill, providing for territorial government and eventually an Indian state, was tabled, but not before a remarkable debate took place. The discussion revealed how sharply aligned American men and ideals were becoming as what historians sometimes call the democratic experience pressed in upon them. John Quincy Adams, nationalist and continentalist, led the opposition to the bill in the name of states' rights. Although an abolitionist, Adams was joined by slavocrats and negrophobes in this contest against a friend, A. H. Everett, and an enemy, Secretary of War Lewis Cass, a leading advocate of squatter sovereignty.[50] If the lines of conflict revealed incongruities, they also pointed to differences of a more fundamental kind. Men perhaps less plastic and values perhaps less arbitrary than modern social analysts often suggest were heading for fatal collision. Adams, of all contemporaries, owed his forward-looking ideals to a backward-looking set of values. Not only were the external alignments between people dissonant, but so were the internal ones within individuals. Adams's well-known rigidities of character signify no psychopathic puritanism; rather they suggest iron restraints upon warring tendencies. Members of the religious community, however, took no noticeable interest in the plight of John Quincy Adams, although they might well have done so. While politicians wrangled over principles,

49. Prucha, *American Indian Policy*, p. 259. Jurist Henry L. Ellsworth wrote his professor, Yale geologist Benjamin Silliman, from Fort Gibson on the Arkansas River: "Oh! could the contaminating *example* and *conduct* of the *white* be remedied, and the Indians left to enjoy their own country here, supported and defended by the Government—then might they sing for their jubilee had come . . . there is good land enough here for all the Indians, and be assured that it is not philanthropy to urge the natives to remain East of the Mississippi here only can they flourish and be happy." Ellsworth to Silliman [December 5, 1832], Beinecke Library, Western Americana. Ellsworth, son of Chief Justice Oliver Ellsworth, superintended the settlement of Indian tribes south and west of the Arkansas in 1832.

50. *Register of Debates*, pt. IV, vol. 10 (June 25, 1834), pp. 4763, 4768, 4774–75, 4777, 4779. See Annie H. Abel, "Proposals for an Indian State, 1778–1878," *American Historical Association, Annual Report for the Year 1907* 1 (1908): 87–104.

religious societies tried to decide what new methods should be employed now that the Indians were all to be west of the Mississippi.

When they had weighed the prospects for success in the new Indian country against the price of inaction, the evangelists decided to follow the Indian to his western home. Thus began a new phase of western history. The question that most troubled evangelical minds was whether missionaries could civilize the Indians before the whites came and degraded them. This concern was not at all frivolous, however much pre-Darwinian assumptions of racial fixity may jar modern sensibilities. The missionaries were aware that trappers and traders could not be kept out of the Indian country indefinitely, despite the government's best intentions. Anxiety about contamination stemmed from the fear that there would not be time enough—and the religious were very unclear about how much time was actually needed—to provide the Indians with a shield of Christianity as protection against oncoming unchristian white men from civilization. When the missionaries decided to go west with the Indians—a decision more easily made by Methodists than by other leading missionary denominations—they were deciding against the exclusion and separation policy of the government and taking the gamble that they could bring Christianity to the savage before civilized whites brought him liquor and vice.[51] And, as the evangelicals were turning their attention to the West,

---

51. The Methodists did not discuss the difficulties of setting up a mission on the other side of the continent. Even the most thoughtful Methodist publication made no effort to look beyond the church's "satisfaction of having been the means of snatching some of the Indians . . . as brands from the burning" ("Review of the Missionary Society of the MEC," *Methodist Magazine and Quarterly Review* 15 [1833]: 320). Not all missionary societies acted alike, and the differences are meaningful. Whether the Methodist response reflects superior self-confidence or insufficient self-examination is less important than the difference itself. Although Protestants shared general goals, differences over method were often profound, and these led in turn to more fundamental distinctions. The primary place accorded to the mission and the missionary by Methodists, for example, ultimately meant a decisively different evangelism. In contrast, the ABCFM, predominately Congregational and Presbyterian, questioned themselves as follows: "Should white settlers be sent with the Missionaries to provide necessaries for them or should the Missionaries live with the Indians?" The first alternative obviously was too expensive, whereas the second seemed "almost to involve their own return to savage life" (*Twenty-sixth Annual Meeting*, ABCFM [Boston: Crocker and Brewster, 1835], pp. 100–101). The opposite view, that the distinction between civilization and Christianization was procedural only, is found in Sheehan, *Seeds of Extinction*, pp. 125, 127, and Robert F. Berkhofer, Jr., *Salvation and the Savage: An Analysis of Protestant Missions and American Indian Response, 1787–1862* (New York, 1972), pp. 5–6. An interesting if somewhat labored account of the relationship is Gerald

easterners prepared to meet the oncoming immigrant masses who had begun to pour into America from western Europe.

The year of Indian removal (1832) marked the largest increase in European immigration, in both absolute and percentage terms, over previous years. The majority of immigrants were Irish Catholics (44%; 1830 to 1840). For large numbers of American Protestants, no more objectionable class of people could be imagined. In the next several decades a Protestant crusade against Catholics was fiercely waged.[52] By 1854 the Know-Nothing or American party was an important force in national politics, running a former president of the United States, Millard Fillmore, as a candidate for the presidency in 1856. The object of the party was to exclude Catholics and the foreign-born from public office. Methodists were as alarmed as anyone by the influx of these "conspiring" papists in the 1830s. Willbur Fisk, writing in 1834 to Vermont Congressman Benjamin F. Deming, summarized his disapproval and prescribed the remedy.

. . . my feelings are not so much affected by the fact that the Bank of the U.S. is not rechartered or that the disparities have been arbitrarily removed, or that Genl. Jackson assumes kingly authority, or that he presumes to beard the Senate in their own chamber—all these together would be as nothing if the people were true to themselves. My solicitude is that the spirit of party and the love of office can exercise such damnations over the human mind! Over the *American mind!* I almost despair of popular governments. We have committed two awful, irretrievable blunders! The universal suffrage law and the almost unconditional naturalization law. I blush to know that these blunders were committed by the party in politics with which I was bred and reared. The steps however cannot be retraced. All one can now do is to spread religion and education through the land and implore the aid of Divine providence. . . . We who are particularly employed in the cause of religion and literature will endeavor to stamp a better impress upon the minds of the rising generation.[53]

J. Goodwin, "Christianity, Civilization and the Savage: The Anglican Mission to the American Indian," *HMPEC* 42 (1973): 93–110.

52. Alice Felt Tyler, *Freedom's Ferment: Phases of American Social History to 1860* (Minneapolis, 1944); Ray A. Billington, *The Protestant Crusade, 1800–1860* (New York, 1938). For a later period in Oregon, see Priscilla Knuth, "Nativism in Oregon," *Reed College Bulletin* (January 1946).

53. Willbur Fisk to [Benjamin F.] Deming, Middletown, Conn., April 25, 1834, Fisk Papers. The significance of this commentary by Fisk cannot be overstressed. All the issues

As Fisk was writing his letter, Jason Lee, his former student and the man he believed best suited to minister to the Flathead Indians of the Oregon country, was within three days of leaving Independence, Missouri. Lee was about to embark upon the first Protestant mission to the Northwest. Twenty years later, when Lee and Fisk were both gone, the Methodists of the East continued to deplore the Irish Catholic menace in their own region. But their western brethren, while commiserating, had a heavier cross to bear. Writing home in 1854, Kate P. Blaine, wife of a missionary in the newly created Washington Territory, told the same story Fisk had told years before on the opposite coast: "Our legislature . . . have done some thing . . . disgraceful to us as a territory. They have passed a law permitting the half breeds to vote. It will be no difficult matter to get any number of Indians to pass as half breeds. . . . You talk about the stupidity and awkwardness of the Irish. You ought to have to put up with our Indians, and then you would know what these words mean." [54]

In 1833 Fisk saw a "noble futurity" for Methodism and for the world on the western horizon. He yielded his hopes for the Indians to no man, only wishing it were he who was to win glory by bringing the Gospel to them. Lee, who came instead, arrived in response to what the eastern evangelical community believed was a call for the "white man's Book of Heaven." The "Macedonian cry" for help came from a delegation of Indians from the Pacific Coast. They had, so it seemed, come to see their friend William Clark of the Lewis and Clark expedition of 1804–1806, who was now commissioner of Indian affairs in Saint Louis. The evangelical men of the East were eager and willing to believe the Indians had actually gone out in search of *them*.

Jason Lee made the overland trip to Oregon with Nathaniel Jarvis Wyeth, who was on his second journey to Oregon. A buoyant and adventurous entrepreneur from Cambridge, Massachusetts, Wyeth had gone to Oregon two years before, hoping to take advantage of America's right of occupation in the Oregon country. His efforts to break into the fur trade were summarily though honorably quashed by John McLoughlin, who

---

he disregards have, at one time or another, been cited as major determinants of Jacksonian political life.

54. Kate P. Blaine to [her father], Seattle, W. T., May 3, 1854, Beinecke Library, Western Americana.

used the superior resources of the Hudson's Bay Company to undersell and outbid Wyeth. Still hopeful, the courageous Yankee businessman decided to try again. His considerable investment in trading goods sent on to Oregon by sea, Wyeth set out across the continent with Lee in the spring of 1834. His fortitude, however, was not enough to overcome a combination of bad luck and the cleverness of John McLoughlin. After two years of frustration he returned east. Lee stayed longer, but McLoughlin proved as decisive in Lee's affairs as in Wyeth's. The Chief Factor urged Lee to locate his mission south of Fort Vancouver in the Willamette Valley, where a number of retired company employees, mostly French Canadians, had settled. A few Americans formerly with John Jacob Astor's Pacific Fur Company at Astoria, defunct since 1813, had also settled in the Willamette Valley. The old trappers lived with their Indian wives and large half-breed families in isolated simplicity at a place called Champoeg on the east bank of the river, about 18 miles above Willamette Falls. Lee chose his own spot upriver, a dozen miles farther south, at French Prairie. In 1841 he moved south once again, this time to Chemeketa (now Salem), following enlargement of his staff the preceding year. Additional mission personnel were sent to Oregon on three separate occasions, each reinforcement coming by sea. The largest contingent, the so-called great reinforcement, landed in Oregon on June 1, 1840. Chief Factor McLoughlin, along with others in the Willamette Valley, assisted Lee by lending cattle, advancing seed, and selling farm tools.

No sooner had Lee settled than American mountain men began to arrive, starting their farms in Tualatin Plains, west of existing settlements. Among the first of these was Ewing Young, famed Indian fighter, fur trader, and frontiersman, who soon became the wealthiest man in the valley. As the western fur trade slackened in the early 1840s, other American trappers made their way to the Willamette Valley, including Robert "Doc" Newell and Joseph Meek, both of whom became prominent in local politics. A small but important company of men arrived from Peoria, Illinois, in 1839. Tradition has it that they were directly inspired by Jason Lee to emigrate when the missionary stopped in Peoria on his way east in 1838. But the continuing depression of 1837, as well as the eccentricities of the immigrants themselves, probably had something to do with their motives too. Whatever their reasons, they were a peculiar lot. The Peoria party included such figures as Sydney "Blubbermouth"

Smith, Thomas Jefferson Farnham, and Robert Shortess, the man who subsequently wrote a good deal of the provisional government's Organic Law of 1843.

In 1842 Elijah White arrived in Oregon with more than 100 new immigrants.[55] Formerly the mission doctor, White had left the country in the fall of 1840 after a quarrel with Lee. Large-scale migration to Oregon began in late 1843. In the fall of that year about 900 new settlers came to the Willamette Valley, followed by 1,200 more within a single year. The "great immigration," as the influx of 1843 is known, marked the end of Oregon's isolation. Also in 1843, after nearly a decade of effort and an expenditure of more than $100,000, the Oregon mission made drastic cutbacks in personnel and operations.[56] Superintendent Lee was recalled and the Reverend George Gary sent to replace him.[57] Gary, instructed to do what was necessary to restore the mission's "strictly spiritual character," [58] dismantled Lee's large secular enterprises and discharged all but the most essential personnel. Lee had returned to the United States before Gary's arrival.

The mission system Lee built up during his ten years in Oregon was in many respects typical of other aboriginal missions Methodists established elsewhere. It had a central station, a manual labor school for youths, a store, and a hospital. Lee used the mission's physical plant in special, if not always immediately obvious, ways. His approach to the massive and ultimately devastating problem of fashioning Methodists out of Indians was to physically separate the spiritual from the temporal, the Christianizing from the civilizing parts of the missionary work. His methods fol-

55. On White, see Robert J. Loewenberg, "Elijah White vs. Jason Lee: A Tale of Hard Times," *Journal of the West* II (1972): 636–62.

56. January 27, 1843, *Minutes, Oregon Committee, 1842–1853,* Missionary Society of the Methodist Episcopal Church, unpaged (Board of Missions, United Methodist Church, United Presbyterian Church in the USA, Room 1372, 475 Riverside Drive, New York, N.Y.).

57. George Gary (1793–1855) was a New Yorker. A member of the Genesee Conference in 1813, he had entered the New England Conference at the age of fifteen and was the youngest man ever received into a Methodist conference in the United States up to that time. His diary, printed with many serious errors, appears in *OHQ* 24 (1923): 68–105, 152–85, 269–333. His appointment to replace Lee was announced on September 20, 1843, in *Minutes,* Board of Managers of the Methodist Episcopal Church, IV, 286. These volumes, on deposit at the United Methodist Church, the United Presbyterian Church in the USA, Room 1372, 475 Riverside Drive, New York, N.Y., are hereafter referred to as *Minutes, B.M.*

58. Charles H. Carey, ed., "Methodist Annual Reports," *OHQ* 23 (1922): 347.

lowed precisely the conceptual order Methodists perceived as necessary to missionary work. Lee's transition from the conceptual to the physical (the subject matter of the ensuing narrative) proved his undoing and also laid bare certain evangelical contradictions. Under Lee's leadership the mission underwent continuing division and subdivision.

The first headquarters of the Oregon mission was at a place that became known as Mission Bottom, the original settlement 10 miles south of Champoeg. In fact the headquarters of the mission was wherever Lee happened to be. Since Lee traveled much of the time and was at best a mediocre administrator, the mission had no center and only as much focus as Lee's evangelical passion could bring. In 1838 a second station was begun at The Dalles on the Columbia River, about 80 miles east of Fort Vancouver. The mission at The Dalles, far into the wilderness away from the centers of settlement, became the spiritual center of the entire Oregon operation. Although it was four to eight days distant from Mission Bottom, depending on season and weather, Jason Lee made the trip many times.

After the great reinforcement of 1840, stations were opened at Nisqually on the southeastern edge of Puget Sound, at Chemeketa, at Clatsop at the mouth of the Columbia, and at Willamette Falls. After 1840 the mission was like a collection of atoms without a nucleus. Some atoms, such as Willamette Falls, were secular; others, like The Dalles, were spiritual; still others, for example, Chemeketa, mixing secular and spiritual activities, were in the process of becoming one or the other. The three stations at Chemeketa, Willamette Falls, and The Dalles were the only truly functional stations. Those at Nisqually and Clatsop were never fully operable as missions, and Nisqually was abandoned before Lee left Oregon in December 1843.

The mission operated a farm at Mission Bottom under the supervision of Alanson Beers. The mission school, which never had more than forty pupils, was under the direction of the Reverend Gustavus Hines, who came to Oregon in 1840. Cyrus Shepard was the first mission teacher for the Indians. He began instruction in 1834–35 and continued until his death in 1840. In 1841 the school, along with the mission hospital, was moved from Mission Bottom to Chemeketa. The school eventually became the Oregon Institute, a secondary school for civilized children which in turn became Willamette University. The hospital never amounted to anything because only a single doctor was assigned to the mission at any one time, and he was kept busy running from station to station to care for sick missionaries and their wives. The mission store was also relocated in 1841. It was moved, along with the chief accountant or mission steward, from Mission Bottom to Willamette Falls. George Abernethy, head of the provisional government from 1845 to 1849 and a leading merchant, was the mission steward. At full strength in 1840–1842, the Oregon mission boasted six stations, two mills, one store, nine ministers, twelve laymen, and a fluctuating number of hired helpers. They were all working very hard in their own ways. Lieutenant Charles Wilkes, stopping in Oregon in 1841 on an exploring tour of the world for the United States government, was constrained to point out that "no fixed plan of operations has yet been digested." [59] He was not quite right. The Oregon mission was all plans and operations.

About all that is really known of Lee's early life is what he himself recorded in later years.[60] Cornelius J. Brosnan and other historians who have looked into the genealogical background report that the first Lee to land in the New World was John Lee, formerly of Essex County, England. He arrived in 1634 with his pastor, Thomas Hooker. John Cotton, the famous spiritual leader of the Massachusetts Bay Puritans, had been one of Lee's shipmates. When Hooker left Newtown, Massachusetts, for the Connecticut Valley in 1635, Lee went with him. Several generations of Lees continued to inch farther west. In 1800 Daniel Lee, Jason's father, moved north from Vermont over the border into Stanstead, Canada. Here Jason Lee was born on June 28, 1803. After the death of his father in 1806, Jason Lee boarded with an older brother whose son Daniel was also to become a missionary in Oregon.

Jason Lee worked at various trades. He was an experienced woodsman and occasionally directed crews of lumberjacks.[61] In 1826, at age twenty-three, Lee was converted to Methodism. Three years later he enrolled in Wilbraham Academy in Wilbraham, Massachusetts, about 20 miles northwest of Hartford, Connecticut, in the Connecticut River valley. He

59. Charles Wilkes, *Narrative of the United States Exploring Expedition during the Years 1838, 1839, 1840, 1841, 1842* (5 vols.; Philadelphia, 1849), IV, 354.

60. Jason Lee, "Diary," *OHQ* 17 (1916): 116–46, 240–66, 397–430. Also see Lee's testimony before the board in 1844 (Cornelius J. Brosnan, *Jason Lee: Prophet of the New Oregon* [New York, 1932], pp. 246–68). This testimony is an accurate transcription of the original document on deposit at the OHS, Portland, Oregon. Brosnan's transcription, used throughout this study, is hereafter referred to as Brosnan, "Transcript," *Lee.*

61. Lee, "Diary," p. 260.

returned, as it were, to what had been the promised land of the first American Lee who had settled in what is now Hartford, two centuries earlier. The Connecticut Valley town of Wilbraham and the border town of Stanstead, Canada, made up the two sides of Lee's eastern experience, and he cherished memories of both places.[62] How struck Lee must have been when he entered the Willamette Valley for the first time in September 1834 to find an astonishing composite of Stanstead and Wilbraham. The modern traveler seldom fails to note these resemblances and Lee very likely observed them too.

Oregon's forests resemble the fir and oak stands of the Northeast. The fields, meadows, and streams along the Willamette are not very different from those along the Connecticut. And, once again Lee found himself in the midst of a French-Canadian population and in a "border" town. This time, however, there was the vital difference that no border line had yet been drawn.

Lee was chosen superintendent of the "Mission to the Flathead Indians of Oregon" by Willbur Fisk in 1833.[63] Fisk, according to Daniel Lee, had "observed in him [Jason Lee] a tallent of influence and controul and gave him charge of a class of boys in their early teens who needed extra attention being either too fast or too slow, of which trust he made a success." [64] Fisk thought highly of Lee, although he seriously erred in thinking the young man's performance in the classroom would carry over to other areas of leadership. It is noteworthy that Fisk, a man of countless projects and committees, would have made a very poor missionary even though he expressed a sincere wish to accompany the mission himself. Perhaps it was Fisk, oppressed with responsibilities and cares of leadership, who wrote next to Jason Lee's name in the Wesleyan *Merits and Demerits Book* the following laconic observation: "Jason Lee, Gone to Oregon as a missionary." [65]

Lee's missionary career in Oregon cannot be understood apart from its

62. *Ibid.*, p. 26.

63. Mrs. Willbur Fisk to Samuel Luckey, October 1839, Wesleyan University Library, Middletown, Conn., printed in Wade Crawford Barclay, *History of Methodist Missions* (3 vols.; New York, 1949–57), II, 202–3; Willbur Fisk to *Christian Advocate and Journal,* March 22, 1833, p. 118.

64. Daniel Lee, "Copy of a Document Sent to the Chaplain C. C. McCabe, New York, November, 1888," MS 937, OHS.

65. Wesleyan *Merits and Demerits Book* (1833–34), Olin Library, Rare Book Room, Wesleyan University, Middletown, Conn.

contextual underpinnings in American Methodism and American ideology. Nonetheless, Lee's biographers have in the main been too much concerned with defending or criticizing him. For this reason, in part, Lee has been, in Bernard De Voto's words, "a hard man to make out." While Lee may well be of "great importance in American history," he was not himself great, yet he has suffered the treatment accorded great men.[66]

By the end of the nineteenth century Lee, already compared with Caesar, was visualized by at least one admirer as a hero who had "fixed his hand on the skies" in order that Oregon might know Methodism.[67] In 1905 his mortal remains were disinterred in Stanstead and reburied in Oregon.[68] Four years later a Methodist historian, in the language of Sir Walter Scott and with a disdain for accuracy which would have embarrassed Parson Weems, called Lee a "conqueror." The simple missionary was proclaimed "first in point of sanctified leadership . . . of princely mien and kingly birth." The historian believed that nothing "in the history of the world" could equal Lee's role in the settlement of Oregon for a "blending of romance, of patriotism, of sacrifice, of noble deeds, of devotion to God and the welfare of humanity." [69] Brosnan made Lee the "Prophet of Oregon" in 1932, and in the early 1950s Lee was described as the "Father of American Oregon." [70]

Lee's picture, a stylized three-quarter-length portrait, shows him in Napoleonic attitude.[71] The painting, like the historical portrait drawn by

66. Bernard De Voto, *Across the Wide Missouri* (Boston, 1947), p. 179. Lee has been the basis for novels and poems. See Ethel Erford Hewitt, *Into the Unknown: An Historical Novel* (New York, 1957). John Parsons, *Beside the Beautiful Willamette* (Portland, 1924), is an interesting eulogistic narrative. A recent addition to this field is Lewis Judson, *Reflections on the Jason Lee Mission and the Opening of Civilization in the Oregon Country* (Salem, 1971).

67. Harvey K. Hines, *Missionary History of the Pacific Northwest Containing the Wonderful History of Jason Lee* (Portland, Ore., 1899), p. 325.

68. *Memorial Services at the Re-interment of Remains of Jason Lee* (Salem, Friday, June 15, 1906).

69. Albert Atwood, *The Conquerors: Historical Sketches of the American Settlement of the Oregon Country Embracing Facts of the Life and Work of Jason Lee the Pioneer and Founder of American Institutions on the Western Coast of North America* (Cincinnati, 1907), p. 39.

70. William Wallace Youngson, "Why Jason Lee Father of American Oregon Should be One of the Two Historical Figures to be Allotted a Statue in the Statuary Hall in Our National Capital," *Diamond Jubilee of Methodism of the Pacific* (Official Publication, Authorized by Annual Conferences of the Northwest, Seattle, Washington, n.d.).

71. The Lee legend has withstood historians' efforts to deflate it because it is not based on any specific event or series of deeds. The more notorious Whitman legend was debunked in a relatively short time because it rested on a story that was capable of being tested. Dr. Marcus Whitman was physician to the ABCFM mission at Waiilatpu in

his admirers, bears little resemblance to the man. Viewed strictly as an administrator Lee was, as one observer remarked, "unfit for his situation." [72] Although Lee believed enlargement of the mission was essential, each reinforcement tended to impede, not aid, the missionary work. [73] It is true that Lee had some poorly qualified personnel to work with, as George Gary, his replacement, was among the first to admit. [74] Nevertheless the record makes it plain that Lee was to blame for the mission's organizational shortcomings. When the mission consisted of the two Lees, Cyrus Shepard, and two helpers, there seems to have been no trouble. When the first reinforcement arrived on May 28, 1837, the difficulties began, and once begun, they never ended.

In fact, the first reinforcements started their quarrels en route to Oregon. It seems that Alanson Beers, the new blacksmith and farmer, complained to Lee that Dr. Elijah White, leader of the expedition, had mistreated him on shipboard. [75] Beers was a decent, simple soul, but he was an irascible man whose family history was marked by insanity and an exceptional propensity for backbiting. [76] He was, as White said, "a law and testimony man." [77] Lee's response to the blacksmith's charges was to order a trial. When it turned out, as White had predicted, that Beers had exaggerated the episode, Lee became furious with Beers and publicly berated him. But it was only a matter of a few days before Lee's pity for Beers got the better of him and he agreed to reconsider the affair. A second trial was called. This time the procedure took most of a day, but the outcome was the same. To make matters worse, Lee permitted the farce to continue. A committee formed to investigate the entire question condemned Lee's course of action. [78] The "Beers-White Scrape," as White

---

present Washington and was massacred along with his wife and twelve others by a band of Cayuse Indians on November 29, 1847. The Whitman legend has it that his return from Oregon to the United States in 1842 was undertaken with the purpose of saving Oregon from Britain. See Clifford M. Drury, *Marcus Whitman, M.D., Pioneer and Martyr* (Caldwell, Idaho, 1937), and Josephy, *The Nez Perce*, pp. 145–56, 189–93, 214–17.

72. Edmund S. Meany, ed., "Diary of Wilkes in the Northwest," *WHQ* 16 (1925): 301.

73. Margaret Jewett Bailey, *The Grains, or Passages in the Life of Ruth Rover* (2 vols.; Portland, 1854), I, 76.

74. Gary, "Diary," p. 271.

75. Elijah White to Jason Lee, [August, 1840], UPS.

76. Elihu Taylor et al. to Nathan Bangs, Weston, [Conn.], March 18, 1836, UPS.

77. Elijah White to Dr. Nathan Bangs, Sandwich Islands, January 17, 1837, UPS.

78. White to Lee, [August, 1840], UPS.

called it, was followed by another abrasive joust between Lee and White, again provoked by Beers. Lee learned from Beers that indiscretions committed by female missionaries during the voyage had caused White to convene a trial of his own in the Sandwich Islands. Hiram Bingham himself, the masterful leader of the American Board mission in the islands, had attended the proceedings. The verdict was to drop the matter, and everyone promised never to mention it again. Beers, however, could not resist speaking of it after his own troubles with White. Lee unwisely pursued the matter, exacerbating still further his relationship with White. In September, 1837, just as these issues were beginning to cool, the second reinforcement arrived, bringing the Reverend David Leslie and family, the Reverend Henry Kirk White Perkins, and Miss Margaret Smith. Like the first reinforcement, the group had its share of quarrels during the voyage to Oregon and once more Lee reacted ineptly.[79]

This time it was Miss Smith who pressed the superintendent to action. A shrill and even hysterical woman at times, though a keen observer, she called upon the superintendent to discipline Leslie for "crimes of selfishness and falsehood" [80] on the high seas. Lee immediately entered into the squabble. Petitions, meetings, indignant correspondence, and the inevitable committees embittered the winter of 1837–38. The matter dragged on inconclusively until July 1840, by which time Miss Smith was married; in 1839 Leslie had performed the marriage service uniting his female foe with Dr. William Bailey.[81] Under the circumstances, no competent leader would have entertained the complaints of either Beers or Smith. Lee's desire for fairness was real, no less than his Methodist instinct to resolve things by committee. But he willingly fused his ideals with a natural reluctance to make hard decisions.

Lee's famous trip to New York in 1838 is another example of this unfortunate facet of his character. His journey was made for two purposes. His first and formal objective—to gain reinforcements for the mission—is well known. His second purpose, which may actually have had more to do with his timing of the trip, bears upon his relationship with the other missionaries and upon his ability as a leader. A memorial, probably instigated by White, was presented to Lee in December 1837, three months

79. Bailey, The Grains, I, 46–51 and passim.
80. Reportedly Leslie's definition of the charges. David Leland [pseud. Leslie] to J. Lee, [December, 1837], ibid., p. 48.
81. Ibid., p. 91.

before he left.[82] Signed by all the new male arrivals, the memorial advised the superintendent "to return home . . . in the hope that commingling once more in polished society would result advantageously to himself and the mission." [83] In 1840 Dr. White reminded Lee that this memorial "caused you to walk the floor, wring your hands, and cry so much." [84] The superintendent acknowledged the memorial and said that a vote had been taken to burn it, which "being lost a vote to 'return it to those who presented it' was carried and *it was so returned.*" [85] White may well have exaggerated the tone of Lee's initial response to the memorial, but there can be no doubt that by 1837 many of the mission family had begun seriously to question Lee's capacities.

Further evidence of the uncertainty as to Lee's leadership is found in an address from the missionaries in the Willamette Valley to the board in New York City, written just three weeks after Lee departed for the East. The missionaries expressed their fear "that Br. Lee's extream modesty will not allow him to ask of you all which the exigencies of the case demand." [86] They were also apprehensive that Lee would waste the board's time with soulful recountings of his failures as a leader, and their fears were not unfounded. Even though Lee was as eager as anyone that the mission be expanded, correspondence with his nephew Daniel Lee further suggests that he was pushed into the plan of traveling east just as White maintained.

Writing Daniel from Walla Walla in April 1838, Lee appeared deeply preoccupied with soul-searching. Clearly he was trying hard to convince himself that he was doing what he wanted to do. "The more I think about the Missionary work to be done in this country," he wrote his nephew,

82. Elijah White to Jason Lee, July 31, 1840, UPS.

83. The signers included Dr. White, Alanson Beers, W. H. Willson, David Leslie, and H. K. W. Perkins (A. J. Allen, comp., *Ten Years in Oregon: Travels and Adventures of Doctor E. White and Lady* [Ithaca, 1850], p. 92). Clifford M. Drury has recently speculated, admittedly without supporting evidence, that Lee returned to the East to bring a shipload of immigrants to Oregon for the purpose of Americanizing Oregon in keeping with a plan worked out with William A. Slacum and kept secret between them (Clifford M. Drury, *Marcus and Narcissa Whitman and the Opening of Old Oregon* [2 vols.; Glendale, Calif., 1973], I, 285, 300). See my review of Drury's volumes in *JAH* 61 (1974): 482–83.

84. Elijah White to [Jason Lee], Willamette, August 6, 1840, UPS.

85. Jason Lee to Elijah White, Mission House, August 14, 1840 [certified]. A true copy of the original [signed] L. H. Judson, UPS.

86. To the B[oard of] M[anagers], M[issionary] S[ociety] M[ethodist] E[piscopal] C[hurch], from David Leslie et al., Willamette, April 13, 1838, UPS.

"the more I feel encouraged in reference to my anticipated visit to the Union, and the more I am convinced of the necessity of the Measure." [87] Some years later Lee confessed that he had gravely doubted himself and his purposes. Such an admission lends substance to the anxieties that many of those in the Oregon mission had felt about him in 1837. More important, it also suggests that he did have to accept the wisdom of a trip east in 1838 because of a vote of no confidence and a recommendation for a forced vacation. Looking back on these experiences in 1844, after his release from the superintendency, Lee wrote:

> Before I had got across the Mountains on my return my mind was made up that men might be found who would manage that Mission in its future prospects better than myself. And I asked, on my return, if there could not be some way devised for someone to supersede me in that charge. . . . But all would [not] do. You would not hear a word of it, and heavy as the cross was I took it up. I have never yet seen the time when I would not have been glad to relinquish the Superintendancy. [88]

Lee returned to Oregon in June 1840 with fifty-one recruits, and trouble resumed almost at once. Lee and White were quickly at odds again, in a quarrel that was to be their final and most devastating one. It began in late June and ended in September with White's expulsion from the mission. [89] Although the doctor, a transparent opportunist, was in the wrong, Lee let the controversy get out of hand as he had the earlier squabbles. The four-month dispute turned principally upon White's probity in money matters, and secondarily upon his behavior with certain women. It was not the first time the doctor had aroused suspicion because of the way he conducted his business affairs. Before White left his home in Havana, New York, for the Oregon mission, some of his neighbors in nearby Trumansburg had complained to the Missionary Society that the doctor was attempting to run out on his debts. [90] Although White managed to finagle his way out of immediate danger, important members of the soci-

87. Jason Lee to Daniel Lee, Walla Walla, April 25, 1838, OHS, printed in Brosnan, *Lee,* pp. 95–97 (quotation on p. 96).
88. Brosnan, "Transcript," *Lee,* p. 266.
89. See L. M. Lyons, *Francis Norbert Blanchet and the Founding of the Oregon Missions, 1838–1848* (Washington, 1940), pp. 81–84; Loewenberg, "Elijah White vs. Jason Lee," pp. 636–62 *passim.*
90. D. K. McSaller to Nathan Bangs, Trumansburg, [New York], July 6, 1836, UPS: White "has left here . . . without making any arrangements to . . . pay" his debts.

ety, including Nathan Bangs, the corresponding secretary, suspected that White had been a bit too slick. During Lee's absence in 1838–40 White had overdrawn his account at Fort Vancouver. Further, he had drawn upon the mission for what later seemed to Lee to be personal, not mission, expenses. When Lee left for the East in March 1838, he put David Leslie in charge, expressly forbidding all but Leslie to draw supplies at Fort Vancouver on the mission's account. When Lee returned in June 1840, White told him that he had traded on the mission's account at the fort because he was engaged in building the hospital for the mission. Lee was chagrined. He was suspicious as well. Ten days after his return, White insisted that Lee write "settled" across all his accounts,[91] but Lee refused to do so without checking the records, and White flew into a rage. In September White was dismissed from the Oregon mission after a trial by his peers, under the direction of Alvan Waller. Before leaving Oregon, in the same ship that had brought Lee and the great reinforcement just four months earlier, White made a number of charges and threats. He promised to ride Lee on a rail or, failing that, to see him shamed before the board.

The bare facts in the case are not the whole story. Some understanding of White is needed to complete the tale. Elijah White was what might best be called an expectant moralist. He was a man for whom the language and sentiment of righteousness were as needful as the main chance is said to have been to so-called expectant capitalists of the period. The fact is that Lee's return to the Willamette Valley dimmed White's visions. The prospect of the usual routine was deadening to him, and he was ready to look elsewhere. While he certainly did not manufacture the contest with Lee which led to his expulsion, he welcomed the opportunity to display his repertoire of emotions and the benevolent rhetoric that went with them. Once launched, White no doubt found it impossible to suppose that his desire to do good somewhere else had anything to do with his indignation at Lee's refusal to write "settled" across the face of his mission accounts.[92]

91. "Extracts from the Minutes of the Board of Managers of the Missionary Society of the Methodist Episcopal Church," April 21, 1841, UPS; Jason Lee to Nathan Bangs, Willamette, Sept. 15, 1841, UPS.

92. The UPS materials make plain that the White affair was very messy. White would not settle for less than exoneration, once he had returned to New York, and when he could not win that from the board he insisted on being given a job as a fund raiser! Although the board declined, White went ahead and raised funds by giving speeches about the Oregon mission. One confused Methodist from upstate New York wrote Dr. Pitman, newly ap-

White returned to Oregon in 1842, somewhat chastened but still determined to see his enemies at his feet.[93] Meanwhile Jason Lee, saddled with unmistakable dedication to the fulfillment of evangelical purposes, had been driving himself in ways he only half understood himself. Most of his missionaries, on the other hand, darted about fitfully with little direction from Lee and with no comprehension of what he was trying to accomplish. Mrs. Frances Fuller Victor, the talented historian who wrote Volumes XXIX and XXX (dealing with Oregon history) of Hubert Howe Bancroft's multivolume *Works*, can hardly be blamed for calling the spectacle "a curse," comparing the mission's efforts to "a burst peatbog sowing its black mud over the land." [94]

By 1841 the mission's internal affairs were in confusion. Lee added to his troubles by failing to initiate the procedural modifications necessary in a mission far from its home base; instead he relied upon the Missionary So-

---

pointed corresponding secretary, to learn if White had been "restored to his former standing in the M.E. Church and has been authorized to hold Missionary Meetings and take up collections, and also if Revd. Jason Lee has been recalled." The *Christian Advocate and Journal,* he noted, had earlier denied such stories and he thought "all is not right" (Clark A. Smith to C. Pitman, Catherine, [New York], August 13, 1841, UPS).

93. White introduced proceedings against Alvan Waller, who had instigated and directed White's trial in 1840 (Gary, "Diary," pp. 99 ff.). Typically, White failed to win his case and just as typically, having alienated Gary as he had Lee (although Gary said he would not entertain White's "palaver"), White called an open meeting of the settlers to rehear his case against Waller. White took the same course with Lee after his trial and conviction in September 1840.

94. H. H. Bancroft, *History of Oregon,* Vols. XXIX–XXX of *Works* (San Francisco, 1886–88), XXIX, 89. Mrs. Victor's view of the Methodists and of Lee has survived many years of effort by Methodist historians to alter it. Harvey K. Hines, brother to the missionary Gustavus, insisted that it was not a dawning recognition of Oregon's commercial potential which "deflected" Lee's missionary work, as Mrs. Victor claims. Instead, Lee had found "that God had a better and greater design in the planting of the Mission when and where it was planted than [the creation of a] . . . purely . . . Indian mission" (Harvey K. Hines, *Missionary History of the Pacific Northwest* (Portland, 1899), p. 344). W. C. Barclay found it "difficult to conceive how any historian, writing objectively . . . [could miss the] marks of utter sincerity" which Lee displayed in his missionary work (*History of Methodist Missions,* II, 210). Nevertheless, the interpretation of Lee as a colonizer and a businessman prevails alongside the legend of Lee the missionary hero. Examples can be found in almost any text or monograph touching Lee. For Frances Victor's interpretation, see Ray A. Billington, *Westward Expansion: A History of the American Frontier* (4th ed.; New York, 1974), p. 440. John M. Blum et al., *The National Experience* (New York, 1963), p. 264; William H. Goetzmann, *Exploration and Empire* (New York, 1966), p. 167; Arthur Throckmorton, *Oregon Argonauts: Merchant Adventurers on the Western Frontier* (Portland, 1961), pp. 14–30.

ciety in New York to make them. For example, he and the laymen
disagreed as to who could or could not attend the mission's annual meeting. Although Lee insisted that his instructions from the Oregon Committee of the Board of Managers said that only ministers should attend, he
was unable to convince the laymen or adapt the ruling to local circumstances.[95] Predictably, he advised the disgruntled laymen to petition the
board in New York for clarification. The board took no official action although the corresponding secretary, exasperated, suggested to Lee that he
follow common sense in such matters by permitting all those affected to
attend.[96]

A continuing problem for the Board of Managers was Lee's failure to
send a report of missionary accounts and activities. Time and again the
board requested these reports and Lee kept promising to send them.[97] In
fact, he was unable to find time for gathering the necessary data and
incapable of making time. David Leslie, substituting for Lee in 1838–40,
managed to send the board a seven-page account of the mission, including
a "minute & correct . . . view of the . . . Finances," which is precisely
what the board wanted.[98] Lee's habitual delinquency angered board members, some of whom were as doubtful about his sincerity as were many
later historians. Lee was advised in 1843 that the board considered it "one
of the most singular facts connected with the history of the Oregon mission, that although considerably more than a hundred thousand dollars,
have been expended in its support, no account has yet been received from
the Superintendent, of the expenditure of any part of that sum." He was
also informed "that the Board are very much dissatisfied with you on account of [your] apparent neglect. How could they be otherwise?" There
must be, Lee was told, "the strictest adherence to *system.*" [99] By 1843 the
board was well into its second year of discontent with Lee's superin-

95. Jason Lee to Charles Pitman, Mission House, July 27, 1841, UPS.
96. Pitman to Lee, New York, March 18, 1843, UPS. Robert M. Gatke, ed., "A Document of Mission History, 1833–1843," *OHQ* 36 (1935): 83, is in error in stating that the
"Board have taken action on this petition." Compare "Statement of Facts," Board of Missions: "The Board have taken no action on this petition" (unpaged).
97. Charles Pitman to Jason Lee, New York, March 18, 1843, UPS, summarizes the
situation and gives the board's view.
98. Oregon mission to Nathan Bangs, Willamette station, March 5, 1839, UPS. The
board was distressed with Lee, because it was concerned about Missionary Society finances,
even before there was reason to be upset with him.
99. Charles Pitman to Jason Lee, New York, March 18, 1843, UPS.

tendency, and in October he learned, through hearsay, that he was to be called home.[100]

Impulsively, without waiting for official word, Lee sailed for the East in December 1843. Dr. Charles Pitman wrote the new superintendent, George Gary, of Lee's unexpected arrival in New York: "We are not advised as yet," Pitman wrote, "what particular motives induced him to come to this country. . . . My opinion is, that he is under the impressions that he has been very much misrepresented by brethren from the mission, and that justice to himself required his personal presence here. . . . He does not seem at all displeased with what has been done only he would have prefered that you should have gone out in the character of a *special agent*." [101]

The Board of Managers soon learned that Lee's motives were not at all mysterious. It was not his reputation he had returned to protect; the missionary had come to save his mission. Curiously enough, the result of ten years of effort as a missionary was not a church or a new mission, but merely a land claim and a school for the children of civilized white settlers. The school, called the Oregon Institute, was first advocated by David Leslie in 1838. Having arrived in Oregon a confirmed integrationist in 1837, Leslie soon came to realize how enormous were the differences between Methodist and pagan. He insisted upon the need to separate his children—three young daughters—from the Indians. He wrote long, urgent letters to the board in New York in 1837–1839, pleading with them to send a teacher for missionary children and even offering to pay the teacher's passage and her keep in Oregon. Although the board failed to underwrite the idea, the "literary institution" became a major concern of the missionaries, Lee particularly. Ironically, Lee's last "official" connection with the Oregon mission was that of fund raiser for the Oregon Institute in 1842–1844, when the Methodist church was not formally sponsoring it. In time the Oregon Institute became a community effort. Its friends included both Dr. White and Alvan Waller, White's hated enemy.[102]

In 1844 Lee was made the agent of the Oregon Institute. Dr. Pitman

100. Jason Lee to corresponding secretary, Wascopam, October 13, 1843, UPS. This letter is also printed in Brosnan, *Lee,* pp. 206–14.
101. Charles Pitman to George Gary, New York, June 29, 1844, UPS.
102. This story is told in chapter 9.

wrote George Gary a brief "history" of Lee's appointment, suggesting in a wry account the attitude of easterners toward Lee:

Bro. Lee was evidently anxious to retain the relation of Missionary to Oregon. But as he had come home voluntarily, and the Board had heard nothing from you, and as they were not prepared to decide respecting the necessity of his services in Oregon, they of course, could not consistently recommend his return to the Mission, until they heard from you. Meanwhile, the Conference of which Bro. Lee is a member (the [New] England Conference) held its session, and some disposition must be made of him. He was not willing to take an appointment in the regular work, because he believed his ten years location in Oregon, under the peculiar circumstances, had entirely unfitted him for that service. Rather than do that he should ask a location. The brethren did not seem willing that his relation to the Conference should be severed. Nor did *he* desire it only as an alternative. To avoid what seemed to be unpleasant to all parties, a good brother proposed to the Bishop to appoint him agent to the Oregon Institute, having previously learned that such an appointment would meet Bro. Lee's wishes. To this the Bishop replied that he had no authority to appoint an agent to any Institution, not under the patronage of some one or more of the Annual Conferences. To our Yankee brethren, however, this difficulty was nothing. A resolution was submitted and adopted to take the Oregon Institute under the patronage of the New England Conference. That done, the appointment was made, and Bro. Lee was the agent of the *"Oregon Institute."* What the result will be remains to be seen.[103]

Lee became the agent of the Oregon Institute because "some disposition must be made of him," not because anyone in the East except Lee took the institute seriously. The land claim at Willamette Falls, the other part of the Oregon mission that Lee had come east to save, was not considered by the Missionary Society to be any more valuable than the Oregon Institute. Lee thought of the claim as an integral part of his program for Indian salvation; the board regarded it as an embarrassment. Just as Lee was ceremoniously being made agent of the Oregon Institute, George Gary, under orders from the Missionary Society, was selling the mission's land claim at the Falls. When Lee died in Stanstead, Canada, on March 12, 1845, the Oregon mission he created had already been repudiated and destroyed.

103. Charles Pitman to George Gary, New York, January 6, 1845, UPS.

CHAPTER 4

Christianity or Civilization?

> . . . the only effectual way to bring . . . [the Indians]
> to knowledge of the truth is, *first of all*, to carry to them
> the gospel of Jesus Christ and that civilization and do-
> mestic economy will follow a reformation of heart and
> life.
>
> —*Twentieth Annual Report* (1839), Missionary
> Society of the Methodist Episcopal Church

*O*N JULY 17, 1833, Elijah Hedding, the bishop in charge of Methodist missions, announced Jason Lee's appointment as missionary to the Flathead Indians of what is now southwestern
Montana. The announcement was made exactly five months after the
famous Walker letter had first appeared in the *Christian Advocate and Journal.* Published with the letter was a sketch of an Indian in profile, his
pointed or "flattened" head remarkable to behold.[1] President Willbur
Fisk of Wesleyan University at Middletown, Connecticut, was deeply
touched by the sight of the misshapen head and by the Indian's seeming

1. William Walker, a white man married to a Wyandot Indian, had been raised with
the Wyandots in Sandusky, Ohio. His drawing was made from a sketch by General
William Clark, superintendent of Indian affairs in Saint Louis. General Clark of the
famous Lewis and Clark expedition was known to the Indians of that region and, unlike
Walker, had met with the delegation of Nez Percé to Saint Louis. Walker's drawing,
copied from Clark's, is highly stylized. It exaggerated the Indian's flat head.

The Walker letter was sent to Gabriel P. Disosway, a prominent Methodist layman and
merchant and later a member of the Oregon Committee of the Missionary Society. First
published in the *Christian Advocate and Journal* March 1, 1833, p. 105, the letter appeared
a second time in May. The significance of the Indian's flat head as a stimulus to Methodist
activity cannot be overstressed, and indeed it has been too little emphasized. That the Indian's state of civilization, indicated by his distorted head, was as important as his need for
the Gospel is suggested by the fact that only rarely, if ever, did a picture of any kind appear in the *Advocate,* the official newspaper of the church. Founded in 1826, it had a
circulation of 30,000. Cf. Clifford M. Drury, *Henry Harmon Spalding* (Caldwell, Idaho,
1936), pp. 91–92, for a different opinion.

For the Nez Percé delegation to Saint Louis, see Alvin M. Josephy, Jr., *The Nez Perce Indians and the Opening of the Northwest* (New Haven, 1965), pp. 98–101, and Robert Ignatius Burns, *The Jesuits and the Indian Wars of the Northwest* (New Haven, 1966), pp. 17–18.

plea for the "white man's book of heaven." In an emotional letter to the
Advocate, Fisk demanded that a mission to the Flatheads be "established
. . . at once." [2] The Indian's head, as well as his plea for the Bible, was
an irresistible incentive to missionary action.

Science combined with religious benevolence to compel a missionary
response. The intentional distortion of the human skull was uncivilized
and unchristian. Phrenological science, a respected and popular branch of
learning at the time, suggested that the frontal section of the head was the
site of the civilized virtues. The Indian's flattened skull was the sign, and
the product, of barbarism. There was little question in evangelical coun-
cils that the Indian urgently needed civilization and the Gospel. In the
first flush of excitement, however, little thought was given to the difficulties that might be encountered in bringing the combined blessing of civilization and Christianity from East to West. [3]

Fisk's letter to the Board of Managers of the Missionary Society of the
Methodist Episcopal Church, calling for an aboriginal mission to the
Flathead Indians, was read at a regular board meeting on March 20, 1833.
"After some conversation" the board decided to write Bishop Hedding for
his opinion, and in April the Missionary Society put itself on record as
favoring "the establishment of an aboriginal mission among the Flathead
Indians west of the Rocky Mountains." [4] In September the board allo-
cated $1,000 for the new mission and announced that the Reverend
Daniel Lee, a deacon and a member of the New Hampshire Conference,
would accompany his uncle, Jason Lee, to Oregon. [5]

2. *Christian Advocate and Journal,* March 22, 1833, p. 118.

3. The views of phrenologist George Combe were widely known and respected. Jason
Lee sought Combe's professional opinion on the head of William McKay, stepgrandson of
John McLoughlin. "The Round Hand of George B. Roberts, the Cowlitz Farm Journal,
1847–1851," *OHQ* 63 (1962): 234. See O. S. Fowler, *Synopsis of Phrenology* (New York,
1851), p. 1, for a phrenological chart. According to John D. Davies, *Phrenology, Fad and
Science: A 19th Century American Crusade* (New Haven, 1955), phrenological science was
"a humane and optimistic faith" in the view of Middle Period reformers. Davies suggests
(pp. 166–69) that the clergy "as a class" were uneasy about phrenology because they were
hostile to science, although he makes it clear that phrenology "as a plan for man to live in
accordance with the moral law" was readily adaptable to the evangelical program. See
George Combe, *Notes on the United States of America during a Phrenological Visit in
1839–1840* (New York, 1842).

4. *Minutes, B.M.,* II, 174. The Board of Managers of the Missionary Society of the
Methodist Episcopal church, as organized at the General Conference of 1820, consisted of
thirty-two men and seven officers.

5. *Ibid.,* p. 200.

Although the Methodists demonstrated their usual efficiency in mobilizing men and resources for the new mission, Fisk was not satisfied. In October he moved that another $2,000 be granted to the Flathead mission. When that was done he persuaded the board to appoint a standing committee on Oregon with "full powers to correspond &c." [6] Well financed and organized, the Flathead mission had been elevated to a position of first importance before the missionaries left New York. All five members of the Oregon Committee were strong supporters of the Flathead mission and of Jason Lee. Eight years later, when the mission was being severely criticized by the board, none of the original members were left on the committee. Their interests were directed to other missions and other problems.[7] But in 1833 Methodist enthusiasm ran high. The Board of Managers reflected and inspired the excitement of Methodists throughout the country. In keeping with church practice, the Lees spent the fall and winter of 1833–34 seeking funds for their mission.[8]

Trusting largely to providence, neither Lee nor the board expended any serious effort in planning their undertaking. The missionaries were simply to leave for Oregon. They had no clear idea about how or with whom they were to travel. As luck would have it, Nathaniel Wyeth was preparing to make his second expedition to the Oregon country, and in November he agreed to take Lee with him. In December, Cyrus Shepard, a thirty-four-

6. *Ibid.*, p. 206.

7. Original members of the Oregon Committee were Fisk, Nathan Bangs (who was also corresponding secretary of the board until 1842), Gabriel P. Disosway, and Joseph Smith. Francis Hall was secretary of the board and, apparently, a friend of Jason Lee's. See Cornelius J. Brosnan, *Jason Lee: Prophet of the New Oregon* (New York, 1932), p. 270 n. 38. For the Oregon Committee of 1842, see *Twenty-third Annual Report, M.S.M.E.C.,* 1841–1842, p. 104.

8. See *Fifteenth Annual Report, M.S.M.E.C.,* 1834, pp. 43–44, for an account of Lee's fund-raising work. Lee was an excellent fund raiser, and according to Margaret Jewett Bailey, who joined the mission in 1837, fund raising was just what Lee was best suited to do. "His great *forte,*" she said, "was talking." See Margaret Jewett Bailey, *The Grains, or Passages in the Life of Ruth Rover* (2 vols.; Portland, 1854), I, 76. Lee's preaching, according to Alvan Waller, who admired him, was "not of the brilliant, flowery order, yet he [was] a good *sound* preacher." Alvan Waller to Fuller Atchinson, August 19, 1842, in *Christian Advocate and Journal,* November 8, 1843, p. 50.

For Lee's fund-raising itinerary and his movements generally see Brosnan, *Lee.* Brosnan relies on reports of Lee's comings and goings as they were given in the pages of the *Advocate* and of *Zion's Herald.* Lee's arrangements with Wyeth are reported in *Mission Record Book, Methodist Episcopal Church, Willamette Station, Oregon Territory–North America, Commenced 1834,* unpaged, Board of Missions, New York.

year-old schoolteacher from Weston, Massachusetts, was made the third member of the missionary group. Submissive and pietistic, Shepard never caused Lee any trouble. He was an asset to the mission from the beginning. Shepard, the only member of the mission Lee hired personally without seeking outside advice, was exactly the kind of person Lee wanted to have with him.[9]

The two Lees and Shepard left New York in late January 1834, some weeks after Wyeth's brig, the *May Dacre,* had set sail for Oregon from Boston with the missionaries' supplies on board. Although the voyage was seven times the distance of the overland trip, both journeys would take nine months. Communication was obviously going to be a problem. It took more than a year from the time a letter was written on one side of the continent until an answer was received from the other side. But it seems no one was much worried about the correspondence problems that were bound to arise. Lee was not afraid to rely upon divine intercession and, indeed, to give it credit when events took a favorable turn. When his arrival at Fort Vancouver on September 15 was followed the next day by the appearance of the *May Dacre,* Lee was moved to ask: "Is not the hand of Providence in all this?"[10] This fortuitous circumstance, however, was but the illusion, not the promise, of system.

The trip west was uneventful. Two men were added to the mission party in Saint Louis: Philip Leget Edwards, a Kentuckian of twenty-two with brief experience as a schoolteacher, and Courtney M. Walker, a trapper from Pennsylvania who was about thirty. The most significant fact

9. Shepard, who died in 1840 after his leg was amputated by Dr. Elijah White, taught school at Fort Vancouver until February 1835, when he joined Lee at the Willamette and began the first Sabbath school west of the Rocky Mountains in April. His *Journal,* from March 3, 1834, to December 20, 1835, provides important clues to his views and personality. It is in the Beinecke Library. See Jason Lee to Nathan Bangs, Mission House, Willamette, March 15, 1841, UPS. Shepard was "our devoted and indefatigable school teacher" (Z. A. Mudge, *The Missionary Teacher: A Memoir of Cyrus Shepard, Embracing a Brief Sketch of the Early History of the Oregon Mission* [New York, 1848]).

It has often been said that Lee was given authorization to hire the lay personnel for the great reinforcement. (See, for example, W. C. Barclay, *History of Methodist Missions* [3 vols.; New York, 1949–57], II, 227.) The final decision for all personnel for the Oregon mission was, however, the board's. Lee's authority was limited to making recommendations and granting initial interviews to applicants. Lee remarked, for example, that he had objected to the appointment of James Olley, a carpenter from Troy, New York, but was overruled. Jason Lee to corresponding secretary, Willamette Falls, March 30, 1843, UPS. For Lee's account of his trip, see *Zion's Herald,* February 6, 1839, p. 22.

10. Jason Lee, "Diary," *OHQ* 17 (1916): 262.

about Edwards and Walker, though they were not without some importance to the Oregon mission in its early years, is that they were hired by
Daniel, not Jason, Lee. Daniel Lee, thought to be something of an oaf by
the officers of the Hudson's Bay Company,[11] was highly esteemed by his
uncle. At several crucial points in the mission's history, most notably in
1838 when Jason Lee returned to the United States, Daniel's influence was
visible and important.[12]

The five men who arrived at Fort Vancouver in September 1834 were
all unmarried, relatively well educated, and, especially Shepard and the
Lees, devoted to the Indians' salvation. None of the five was a farmer.[13]
This first Methodist missionary contingent fitted exactly Willbur Fisk's
"plan" for the salvation of the Flatheads. Jason and Daniel Lee were "two
suitable men, unencumbered with families, and possessing the spirit of
martyrs [ready to] throw themselves into the nation. Live with them [the
Indians]—learn their language—preach Christ to them and, as the ways
open, introduce schools, agriculture, and the arts of civilized life." [14]
Edwards and Walker would provide secular aid and Shepard would establish schools "as the ways open."

Christianization of the Indians was plainly the first order of missionary
business. After that would come the job of civilizing the Christian Indian
with the help of "the fur traders, and by the reinforcements with which
from time to time we can strengthen the mission." [15] None but evangelists could visualize the difficulties involved in the task, but the implicit
assumption that Christianization would be accomplished with reasonable
dispatch proved to be a fatal one. And yet it was an inevitable assumption.
Not to have made it invited the unwelcome suspicion that Christianization posed something more than merely procedural problems. Methodist
rhetoric tended to become almost eerily abstract, the signal, ironically,
that unsorted emotions, not the results of reasoned analysis, were being

11. Sir Walter Scott "surely must at some time have seen [Daniel] Lee," George Roberts of the Hudson's Bay Company told Frances Victor in 1878. Roberts said that the Reverend Herbert Beaver, Episcopal missionary at Fort Vancouver from 1836 to 1838, "had
many a joke at the Methodists' particularly poor Daniel Lee . . . whom he called that
sapient Dominie Sampson—prodigious." "Letters to Mrs. F. F. Victor 1878–83 [from
George Roberts]," *OHQ* 63 (1962): 196. Compare H. H. Bancroft, *History of Oregon,* Vols.
XXIX–XXX of *Works* (San Francisco, 1886–88), XXIX, 57–58.
12. See chapter 5.
13. Lee, "Diary," p. 262.
14. Willbur Fisk to *Christian Advocate and Journal,* March 22, 1833, p. 118.
15. *Ibid.*

expressed. Jason Lee was no exception. Writing Fisk from Hams Fork, only two months from Saint Louis, he said it would "be easier converting a tribe of Indians at a *Missionary Meeting,* than in the Wilderness." [16] In this assertion the Methodist world view touched the frontier. Was the time between Christianizing the Indians and civilizing them to be so short that civilizing could begin almost immediately and perhaps proceed simultaneously with Christianizing? Or perhaps the distinction between Christianizing and civilizing was unreal. If so, Fisk's vision and the ideas of missionary martyrdom and immersion in the Indian world were only fantasies. In fact, an insoluble dilemma lay at the root of all Methodist professions and practices. The Methodist view of Christianization and civilization did not reflect what Methodism was, but what Methodists believed the church had once been and what it must become again.

The Methodist dilemma, in broad perspective, was a conflict between reality and an ideal. The reality was the Indian, a primitive who was incapable of becoming a Christian in Methodist terms. The ideal, or perhaps it is better called the reality as insisted upon by Methodists, was that Indians must become the sort of Christians Methodists could recognize. This requirement was not idle or speculative. The promise of evangelism was that all men were capable of salvation. However rudimentary, these lines of thought were not the less compelling for their simplicity. Moreover, they were enhanced and deepened by the transparent and familiar differences between civilization and Christianity east of the Mississippi. Of importance, too, was evangelical reliance, among Anglo-Europeans, upon the paroxysmal conversion experience, which invited the Indian to simulate conversion and tempted the missionary to accept it.

The conflict between Christianity and civilization was apparent from the beginning.[17] Paradoxical and often quixotic, the disparity was dis-

16. Jason Lee to Fisk, June 29, 1834, in Brosnan, *Lee,* p. 62.

17. Lee, "Diary," p. 400. Lee agonized over his decision about where to locate his mission. *Ibid.,* pp. 142, 258, 262; Lee to Bangs, July 1, 1834, *Advocate,* September 5, 1834, p. 3; Lee to Fisk, March 15, 1836, in Brosnan, *Lee,* p. 79. On the way west Lee judged possible mission sites by their agricultural potential. Lee, "Diary," pp. 137, 243, 253, 254. After he had decided to settle, his choice of location was influenced by several considerations. McLoughlin advised the Willamette Valley ("Copy of a Document," *TOPA* [Salem, 1880], p. 50). The area south of the Columbia was unlikely to be brought into any dispute between the United States and England as it was universally thought to be American property. Lee was also very likely drawn to the valley because of the way it resembled the Connecticut River valley, where he had attended school. Criticism of Lee's decision to pass the Flatheads by "without saying anything to them . . . and set . . . [himself] on

cernible at all levels of missionary history in the East as well as in the West. Christianity meant personal salvation; civilization designated technology, civility, the "arts and sciences." In the East, where the referents were at best opaque, the distinction between Christianity and civilization was nonetheless self-evident. In Oregon, however, the differences existed unmistakably; but the line between Christian and civilized seemed to preclude meaningful application beyond the civilized themselves, so completely did the Indian's behavior evade analysis. The Indians were neither Christian nor civilized, and the trappers were unchristian and barely civil. The French Canadians, who were Catholics, were beyond the pale altogether in the eyes of evangelical Protestants.

The Methodists who settled Oregon came either from New England or from northern New York, where civilization was not an aspect of salvation but a condition for it.[18] Salvation of sinners was understood to be the work of evangelical ministers. In Oregon, however, civilization was not taken for granted and, while the salvation of souls was undoubtedly minister's work, circumstances called for some redefinition of the ministerial role. While it was perfectly plain to Lee and others that a Christian Indian was still an Indian,[19] no redefinition was forthcoming. Methodists were not content, modern commentators to the contrary, to make Indians into carbon copies of white men. Instead they wanted to make them into

the Multonomah [Willamette]" was first made by the Reverend Samuel Parker (Samuel Parker to editor, *Christian Advocate and Journal,* April 28, 1836, p. 142), who was in Oregon looking for a mission site. For a general discussion of site see W. L. Morton, "The Significance of Site in the Settlement of the American and Canadian Wests," *Agricultural History* 25 (1951): 97–104.

18. The exceptions were the Reverend John P. Richmond from Jacksonville Station, Illinois, and Hamilton ("Cow") Campbell from Springfield, Illinois. The Reverend W. W. Kone from Hillsboro, North Carolina, was the only southerner.

19. Remarks such as this suggested to Mrs. Victor, and to historians convinced of Lee's dedication to Manifest Destiny, that his commitment to missionary work was not sincere. (See, for example, William H. Goetzmann, *Exploration and Empire* [New York, 1966], p. 167; Alvin M. Josephy, Jr., *The Nez Perce Indians and the Opening of the Northwest* [New Haven, 1965], pp. 119–29; Arthur Throckmorton, *Oregon Argonauts: Merchant Adventurers on the Western Frontier* [Portland, 1961], pp. 14–30 *passim.*) The issue is more complex than hypocrisy, however. Lee was as critical of those who thought the Indian was inveterately Indian as historians have sometimes been critical of him, even if he succumbed to the thought himself in times of desperation. He scolded people who insisted that "an Indian will be Indian, do what you will." He demonstrated his view by pointing to the Christian civility of William Brooks, the Indian boy who toured the East with him in 1839. Jason Lee to editor, New York, September 24, 1839, *Christian Advocate and Journal,* October 4, 1839, p. 25; Lee to Daniel Lee, Walla Walla, April 25, 1835, in Brosnan, *Lee,* p. 94.

Christians. At the same time, however, the missionaries found it exceedingly difficult to conceive, or perhaps even to visualize, a Christian who was not also a civilized man. Finally the missionary realized, as sensitive Protestants had always realized, that a distinction between a merely regenerate-seeming man and the true article was absolutely critical.

Throughout Lee's mission the role of gospel preacher was emphatically demanded of Indian missionaries by the ministers and by the Board of Managers. The first objective of the Oregon mission was, and remained, the Christianization of the heathen, to be followed by civilization. The distinction between the two aspects of missionary work was generally understood to be temporal. Lee made it spatial as well by striving to separate secular from spiritual activities. The only exception was that Indian children, when taken from their parents, could be civilized and Christianized at the same time, the presumption being that the "rising generation" were not really or quite yet heathen.[20] For this reason the Reverend H. K. W. Perkins could say that he always felt a "peculiar satisfaction in committing these little ones to their mother earth. I know their spirits are up on high, and forever hence beyond the contamination of heathenism." [21] No amount of mental or terrestrial zoning, however, could alter the fact that the primitive heathens remained and so did the missionary's duty to save them.

After arriving in Oregon, Lee sent out the "Macedonian cry" [22] for single females and married men, without stopping to detail how he had come to be in the Willamette Valley instead of the Rocky Mountains, where the Flatheads were. The board, taking note of Lee's call for farmers,

20. Cyrus Shepard in *Zion's Herald,* July 13, 1836, p. 11. ". . . to benefit the rising generation . . . a location must be made where a large school can be supported by the produce of the soil. . . ." This comment of Shepard's is cited by Barclay, *Early American Methodism,* II, 210, and other historians to counter Mrs. Victor's charge that Lee settled along the Willamette because he was a covert agent of Manifest Destiny. But Shepard, in the *Herald* letter and in his *Journal,* p. 123 (Beinecke), continued on to say that the Willamette location would allow the mission to extend "to other places [Barclay's quotation from the *Herald* ends here] less favorable to cultivation." Shepard was distinguishing two modes of operation to fit the mission's first purpose, which was to Christianize the heathen. His comments appear to supersede, not merely to revise, those of Barclay and Victor.

21. Henry Kirk White Perkins to Charles Pitman, Wascopam, December 4, 1843, *UPS.* This letter is fifteen sheets or sixty pages long; the fifth sheet is missing because Perkins destroyed it.

22. Lee made his first such call before reaching Oregon (Lee to Fisk, June 29, 1834, Brosnan, *Lee,* pp. 59–62). See also Lee to Fisk, Mission House, Willamette River, March 15, 1836 (Brosnan, *Lee,* pp. 78–80).

mechanics, and other workers, did not press him for an explanation.[23] The Missionary Society reported the change of location in the pages of its 1836 annual report with something less than candor, while continuing to underscore the commitment of the mission to Christianization. In October 1835 the decision had been made to change the name of the mission from the Flathead to the Oregon mission [24] on the argument that "the real Flathead Indians were few in number and had no settled habitations." [25] The formal alteration met the needs of rationality and consistency without, of course, affecting Lee's struggle to bring the Gospel to the Indians. The mission's new name was not a factual improvement on the old one, however much it provided philosophical clarification. The "real" Flathead Indians were quite numerous and did have settled habitations, whereas the Chinooks of the Pacific Coast had been reduced by frequent epidemics to a scattered remnant.[26] Thus the actuality was sacrificed to a faith that changes wrought by the missionaries would eventually bring reality into keeping with words. Conscious of having made what might seem to be a retreat, the Missionary Society hastened to point out that the missionaries had "commenced a course of religious instruction . . . reclaiming these wandering savages . . . to the blessings of Christianity and civilized life." [27]

The board's readiness to accommodate Lee and its willingness to em-

---

23. Lee to Fisk, Mission House, Willamette River, February 6, 1835 (Brosnan, Lee, p. 73).

24. Minutes, B.M., III, 9.

25. Seventeenth Annual Report, M.S.M.E.C. (1836), p. 10. "Brother Lee observed [at Bromfield Street Church, Boston] that the . . . Flat Heads have not flat, but round heads, and that the tribe which have flat heads, are the Chenooks." Zion's Herald, February 6, 1839, p. 22.

26. Josephy, The Nez Perce, p. 127. It must be pointed out that Josephy's concern for the Nez Percé and his indignation at white treatment of them leads him to make heatedly inaccurate and distorted statements regarding Lee, the Methodists, and missionary work in general. An excellent map presentation of the course of the intermittent fever is Judith A. Farmer, with Daniel B. Karnes, G. Thomas Babick, Thompson P. Porterfield, and with text by Kenneth L. Holmes, An Historical Atlas of Early Oregon (Portland, 1973), p. 16.

27. Seventeenth Annual Report, M.S.M.E.C. (1836), p. 10. These annual reports served the same purpose as a report to stockholders with the important difference that a deficit in the missionary report was an incentive to invest. Speaking in Boston in 1839 Jason Lee unintentionally contradicted the annual report of 1837, opening to momentary view the incongruities of fact and formula. "We had done but little [up to the spring of 1837] for the spiritual good of the Indians, being under the necessity of laboring much with our hands, as we were far from civilized society, and dependent upon ourselves." Zion's Herald, February 6, 1839, p. 22.

broider the truth represented the first anxious stages of Methodist efforts to deal with the intractable heathenism of the Indian. Lee and the board resolved to permit laymen "to teach the natives . . . agriculture," [28] hoping that the real work of making Christians, and thus the real work of the preachers, would get done beforehand. This type of thinking was characteristic of the Oregon mission experience both in the Willamette Valley and in New York City. Methodist language became increasingly clear in stipulating a separation between spiritual and secular mission functions. Back of it all, however, the Indian remained an Indian and the missionary continued to be checkmated.

Jason Lee's incessant pleas for more temporal workers so he could "attend to spirituals" became a convention among Oregon ministers. Alvan Waller, whose missionary's eye was quick to see a commercial possibility, wrote: "I wish to be so released from temporal cares and responsibilities as to be fully devoted to my ministerial duties." [29] The minister's lament was not reserved for outsiders or for the religious press. Waller made the same complaint to Daniel Lee, who, of course, knew "full well your temporal fetters at your Station, ah when shall they be broken! When? I have longed for such liberty myself constantly." [30] Just a year earlier Daniel, when stationed at The Dalles, had been "at liberty" and unencumbered,

28. *Minutes, B.M.,* III, 10.

29. Alvan Waller to Amos Cooke, Willamette Falls, November 30, 1841, MS 1223, typescript, OHS. Cooke was a member of the ABCFM in Hawaii. Waller's activities are proverbial. His habit of linking secular and spiritual business is instructive. He would make a perfect study, and perhaps an interesting refutation, of the so-called Protestant ethic. Waller noted in his diary while aboard the *Lausanne* that he thought "a steamboat might be stationed in the Straits of Magellan with great advantage to shipping, by towing vessels through the Strait. . . . I doubt not but some enterprising man or company of men (speaking after the manner of men) by stationing a Steam Boat in those Straits would make a fortune. . . . A good Mission Station might also be established on the Southern part of Patagonia. . . . Indeed I feel my heart down out to them with the sanction of the Church I could here stop and cheerfully preach to them Jesus. . . . My soul goes warm as I write on this subject." Diary of Alvan Waller, MS 921W, typescript, OHS. He was fond of possessions and took pleasure in such things as cataloging the books in his library, an exercise he performed in the winter of 1846 for all 426 items he owned. *Waller's Journal,* typewritten copy, pp. 39–46, Beinecke. He was always happy to tell his friends, "I trust I did not come to Oregon to hoard up treasures, but to do good." Waller to Fuller Atchinson, Willamette Falls, May 23, 1843, in *Christian Advocate and Journal,* July 3, 1844, p. 186, or to observe of national affairs: "I am glad that our country has awoke from the dreams of wealth." Waller to Fuller Atchinson, Willamette Falls, August 19, 1842, *Christian Advocate and Journal,* November 8, 1843, p. 50.

30. Daniel Lee to Alvan Waller, Wascopam, July 12, 1841, MS 1210, OHS.

and there were large numbers of Indians within easy reach. Daniel had come to The Dalles in 1838 with Henry Perkins, spending there two of the most outwardly auspicious years in the mission's history. In the fall of 1839 had come the famous "reformation," news of which covered the entire front page of the *Christian Advocate and Journal* on October 14, 1840. Exaggerating numbers as well as facts, Perkins had reported "upward of five hundred native Indians converted to the Christian faith." [31] Clearly these were simulated, not real, conversions (Jason Lee suggested "that many of them knew as little what they were saying as Parrots"),[32] and Daniel Lee understood well enough that there was nothing especially newsworthy in the story. Illustrating one possible response to the missionary dilemma on a personal scale, Daniel abandoned his converted Indians in the spring of 1840 and, with studied aimlessness, drifted down to Fort Vancouver. The great reinforcement was due to arrive. According to Perkins, his missionary partner, Daniel Lee "concluded to take a trip along the river, visiting the Indians as far down as Astoria, indulging the expectation of meeting the reinforcement under his uncle . . . as we were now in weekly expectation of the arrival of the vessel." [33] Francis Blanchet, the Catholic priest at the Willamette, explained Daniel's "trip along the river" with more accuracy. Lee came, Blanchet said, "in order to have the first choice for a wife among the young misses." [34] It was true enough. Although Lee's contemporaries and most chroniclers have sustained the falsehood that Daniel married his fiancée of several years, he in fact married Maria Ware whom he had never seen before. And he married her within eleven days of meeting her.[35]

31. "Journal of H. K. W. Perkins," *Christian Advocate and Journal,* October 14, 1840, p. 33. It was published less than a week after the *Lausanne* had sailed for Oregon to highlight the mission and to reassure its backers. The board, and Jason Lee, lived to regret such excessively zealous public relations.

32. Jason Lee to corresponding secretary, Willamette Falls, March 30, 1843, UPS. Lee's commentary on the reformation is completely in keeping with the facts of life: "I have seen that account in print, and I confess, that, it carries on the very face of it, features which would have made me cautious about giving to[o] great a prominence. Here are hundreds of Indians, locked up in the profound ignorance of perfect heathenism, and in a few hours *all* made genuine Christians. Was this reasonable?"

33. "Journal of H. K. W. Perkins," *Christian Advocate and Journal,* September 13, 1843, p. 11.

34. Clarence Bagley, ed., *Early Catholic Missions in Oregon* (2 vols.; Seattle, 1932), I, 93.

35. Maria T. Ware was from Lowell, Massachusetts. She met Jason Lee in 1839 (Mrs.

In 1844, after Daniel had left Oregon, George Gary, the new superintendent, reported that "from the best account I can get, Rev. Daniel Lee had but little missionary activity or zeal after he was married." [36] But it was not concupiscence that had cooled Daniel's zeal. It was, for him, the hopeless contrariety of the cause he had chosen to support and the imbalance of language and will which paralyzed his efforts and negated his fondest dreams. It is not surprising that Daniel "found it impossible . . . to do [his] work." Nor is it easy to reconstruct how he and others conceived of the job they were expected to do.

To bring some sense to his perplexity, Daniel, alluding to the heroism of the missionary archetype, sought to describe the kind of missionary needed in Oregon. Just two months before retiring from the field, in his first letter to the board since April 1838, Daniel explained why the Oregon mission had not been more successful. Although complete devotion to ministerial work was essential, the preacher's purpose, "the work for which I gave myself and to which I was appointed," had been endlessly frustrated by temporal duties. "The hope of being thus free, which I have

---

Lee incorrectly said 1838), on his fund-raising tour. She was a student at the Newbury Seminary in Newbury, Vermont, where Lucy Thompson, Lee's second wife, was also enrolled. Introduced by a preacher to Jason Lee, she was told to write to the board, which she did. The board responded by accepting her for the mission. Maria [Ware] Lee to Adelia [Judson] Turkington Olley Leslie, Caldwell, Idaho, January 23, 1885, Lewis Judson Papers, Loan Microfilm no. 26, reel 2, Abl. OSL.

Daniel Lee's "intended" was *"Almira Rogers* residing in Stanstead Lower Canada . . . and . . . by all means, she ouaght to accompany any person or persons that the Board should send to our assistance." Daniel Lee to Bishop Waugh, Honolulu, November 20, 1835, UPS. Although Daniel sent "a Draft on the Society in favor of Miss Almira Rogers" to help defray her expenses to Oregon (Daniel Lee to Nathan Bangs, Honolulu, December 20, 1835, UPS), Miss Rogers decided against the trip. On May 18, 1836, the board noted receipt of a letter from Miss "Elvira" Rogers who said she had written Daniel Lee of her decision not to go to Oregon. *Minutes, B.M.,* III, 31. In Jason Lee's letter to Fisk of February 6, 1835 (Brosnan, *Lee,* p. 73), Lee asked that "Daniel's chosen be sent as soon as possible." This letter apparently perpetuated the assumption that Miss Ware was the chosen woman. While the materials at UPS have not been in use among scholars, the reference to Miss Rogers in the board's *Minutes* has been available to, and indeed heavily relied on, by some who have, nonetheless, failed to set the record straight on this point. See Barclay, *Early American Methodism,* II, 239. A correct account is Theressa Gay, *Life and Letters of Mrs. Jason Lee* (Portland, 1936), p. 160. She used the board's *Minutes* and two letters of Daniel Lee then deposited in Philadelphia, now at UPS. As with other marriages (specifically those of Olley, Raymond, and Felix Hathaway, for which see chapter 5), the board and, later on, historians favorable to what they believe are Methodist interests, have been unnecessarily reticent about admitting such things went on.

36. George Gary, "Diary," *OHQ* 24 (1923): 170.

all along sustained, has not yet been realised. . . . I say these things as applying to other brethren as well as to myself." [37]

The "other brethren" agreed that their work was not being done in Oregon. Complaints about temporal duties were universal, and some ministers went even further. John P. Richmond at Nisqually and John H. Frost at Clatsop frankly said that Oregon did not have enough Indians to make preaching worthwhile. Such Indians as they could find were, in their estimation, wretched beyond description.[38] Frost claimed that the damp Oregon winter had conspired with unwonted temporal labors to destroy his ministerial effectiveness; a "disease in [his] throat . . . much aggravated by excessive manual labor" made him unable "to preach for nearly one year," [39] he informed the board. Three days earlier he had told the superintendent, without mentioning the condition of his throat, that it was a fact that his "servises, as a minister of the Gospel, [were] not needed in this country." [40] Jason Lee was quick to correct "Bro. Frost," writing him that it was "as clear as the mid-day sun, that it is *not* a *'fact'* that your labours as a minister of the Gospel are not wanted in this country, [and indeed] one thing, to me, appears *certain,* that, either, the servises of *many more* Gospel Ministers, are needed in this country, or, it is *un*necessary to make known the Gospel plan of salvation to the thousads of Heathen who inhabit this Country." [41]

Dr. John Richmond from Jacksonville Station, Illinois, the best educated and perhaps the most intellectual of the Methodist missionaries in Oregon, also thought the Indians were not worth his time. "Extinction appears to be their inevitable doom," he prophesied airily. "No earthly

37. Daniel Lee to Charles Pitman, Oregon Mission, Dalles Station, May 5, 1843, UPS.

38. The wretchedness of the Indians and their anticipated extinction were commented on by every missionary from Jason Lee in 1834 to Gary in 1844. It was a missionary's response to this observation, not the observation itself, which makes distinctions between missionaries significant. The mere fact that some missionaries stayed while others left is a meaningful distinction although not a conclusive one. While Lee insisted in 1836 that "the Indians are a scattered, periled, and deserted race . . . that unless the God of heaven undertake their cause, they must perish from off the face of the Earth," he was eager that "God grant that a remnant may be saved, as trophies of the Gospel of Christ, and for a seed to serve him." Lee to Fisk, Mission House, Willamette River, March 15, 1836 (Brosnan, *Lee,* p. 80).

39. J. H. Frost to Charles Pitman, Mission House, Clatsop, February 26, 1843, UPS.

40. J. H. Frost to Jason Lee, Clatsop, February 23, 1843, as copied by Jason Lee in Lee to corresponding secretary, March 30, 1843, UPS.

41. *Ibid.*

power can rescue them . . . , they will never be reached by the Voice of Gospel." [42] He found at Nisqually what Lee had encountered at the Willamette seven years earlier. The Indians were few and "so exceedingly scattered and migratory . . . as to render it difficult to operate among them." Richmond recommended, as Lee also had done in part, that the mission "train up their [Indian] children, and educate them in the principles of our holy religion—to learn them to be industrious—and to estimate themselves properly as human beings." [43] But similarities of experience and response did not necessarily lead to the same final results. Richmond was neither so zealous nor so committed as Jason or Daniel Lee. He left the field. For him the dilemma posed by Methodist requirements concerning Christianity and civilization, and therefore the question of his ministerial function, were easily solved. Let the Indians perish. Having said that much, Richmond's next piece of advice was predictable. Educate the children. In effect Richmond evaded the dilemma. For Jason Lee as for others evasion was no solution at all. In the words of H. K. W. Perkins, " 'To save is next to create' and if it be so, to neglect to save is next to destroy, and who of us are willing to take upon us the guilt of destroying the heathen?" [44]

From the perspective of the twentieth century, Perkins's remarks, and the whole cluster of incompatibles at the root of antebellum evangelism, are rich with meaning. The evangelical churches, Methodism among them, did of course find their way out of the dilemma raised by the imperative to Christianize an indifferent world. Instead of continuing to insist upon personal salvation, the evangelicals discovered that world salvation required social reformation, that Christianization was "civilization" in the widest sense. In this view it was not the churches or the Indians, and certainly not the ideal of universal salvation, which was at fault; it was society, its massive but dark array of social, economic, and cultural forces driving men, without their knowing, outside the paths of righteousness. The new evangelists—social gospelers in the early part of the twentieth

42. John P. Richmond to G. P. Disosway, Mission House, Nisqually Station, Puget Sound, Oregon, August 18, 1841, UPS. To the Methodist church which had only a year before reaffirmed its commitment to convert all men, insisting that the Gospel was universally adaptable, this was truly heretical. "Where is Methodism?" Lee sang out to the board. Lee to corresponding secretary, March 15, 1841, UPS.

43. "Journal of the Rev. J. P. Richmond," *Christian Advocate and Journal,* September 8, 1841, p. 13.

44. H. K. W. Perkins to Charles Pitman, Wascopam, December 4, 1843, UPS.

century, ecumenicalists later on—would rely upon the doctrines of John Dewey as strongly as upon the gospels of Paul. The minister would soon find the surroundings of the secular academy more congenial than liturgy. An imperfect society explained the failure of Christianity at the same time that it guaranteed a field of labor and a meaning for cherished ideals. The nineteenth century had not yet ended when a Protestant minister was free to proclaim: "The worst charge that can be made against a Christian is that he attempts to justify the existing order." [45]

For Jason Lee there was no similar salvation. Of halfhearted missionaries, Lee confessed he was unable "to persuade [himself] that there are or ever have been, talents of such superior order, in this country, that work commensurate to the ability could not be found. It may not indeed be such as flesh and blood would choose but it is such as must be done by the followers of our Lord Jesus Christ before the Heathen will be given him for his inheritance." [46] The salvation of the Indian was minister's work, and it could not be avoided because it was difficult or unpromising. Jason Lee never deserted his role as preacher to the Indians. He held fast to the missionary ideal. But his patience was strained; his replacements deserted and he believed the board had failed him. Deeply frustrated, Lee revealed his trials to the corresponding secretary: "If I could get instruction from the Board in these perplexing cases in a few weeks my situation would be *tolerable* but—but—I forbear." [47] Jason Lee may not have fitted the picture of the ideal missionary which others, including his nephew Daniel Lee, were sometimes moved to draw, but he was certainly determined that Gospel ministers would preach to the Indians. The superintendent wished for more time to become the missionary he yearned to be but, like the others, he could never find the opportunity or the means.

When Daniel left Oregon in the summer of 1843, Jason Lee told the board that his nephew was "as well qulified to give . . . correct information on the subject [of Indians] as anyone." [48] Daniel was also prepared to tell the members of the board exactly what kind of Methodist missionary should be sent to Oregon. His description was a larger-than-life portrait of the fabled preachers who brought Methodism out of

45. George D. Herron, quoted in Paul F. Boller, Jr., *American Thought in Transition: The Impact of Evolutionary Nationalism, 1865–1896* (Chicago, 1969), p. 121.
46. Jason Lee to corresponding secretary, Fort Vancouver, April 8, 1842, UPS.
47. Lee to corresponding secretary, March 30, 1843, UPS.
48. Jason Lee to corresponding secretary, Fort George, August 12, 1843, UPS.

Virginia into the hills of Kentucky and beyond in the first years of the nineteenth century. Few men, Daniel began,

are able to do more than one thing well and it is believed that a preacher especially Should be a man of one work and this is more necessary in missions for Several reasons. (1)st From the amounts of direct labor that needs to be done, (2)nd That the missionary's attention may not be divided, nor diverted from his work and (3)rd That his influence may not be injured which must be the case, if he employ himself (no matter from what cause,) in Secular matters—as matter of fact proves. . . . If there was but *one* preacher among us whose whole time was employed in his appropriate work it would be a great relief to my own mind on this subject . . . , there is reason to believe he would do much. In Such a case as much of his journeying would be by water, he must have a canoe *So large* as to be Safe for his provisions, baggage bedding, tents and oillcloth, and So *light* as to be easily carried by portages. His crew of whom one should be able to take from him the whole care of the trip. So that when he arrived at an Indian village, or house, as it might be he would have to lose no time but immediately convene the people for worship and while with them, Spend all his time in giving them instruction, and then proceed to the next place where he might light upon others. He could not give out his appointments, as the Indians are not Stationary, as the high wind might prevent his traveling or the River be frozen a week, or a fortnight, or more.

One of his crew Should be a good interpreter and assist him at every convenient opportunity to acquire the language as when they were detained by Storms, or winds or ice. These detentions would be seasons of rest of reretirement, and no person would need them more. To travel by land he would want .. saddle horse and a pack horse to take his bed, board, and tent, a guide often and an interpreter always that he might travel expiditiously, and Spend as much time in every place as his duty to the whole would allow. . . . if protesant missionaries do not use every christian effort in their power to save the Indians in a case so urgent they will betray their cause! May we be up and doing. . . . In reference to acquiring the language, let me add, it is a work of magnitude. To gain Such a knowledge of a written one as to be able to preach therein would take, I Suppose three years. I am told that the A.B.C.F.M. allow that to their missionaries for this purpose. It will take double that time probably to conquor an unwritten language and to write a few books and translate some of the most easy portions of Scripture in it. But to Succeed in this well, a man Should be at the very foundation a thorough linguist. He Should be well acquainted with Hebrew, Greek, and Latin, and the grammatical construction of the French,

Spanish and German languages . . . , with the knowledge of the English only, he must frequently meet with difficulties which will consume much of his time to remove, or in unavailing attempts to do So.[49]

Few men, and fewer Methodist ministers, could have met these requirements or withstood the strain of such unusual labor. But Daniel Lee believed he knew of one man who certainly could have done the job—the great John Wesley himself. Wesley was a man of God who thought the work of a minister was to preach. There was, he said, "no gospel without salvation from sin."[50] Methodists could not possibly mistake Wesley's emphasis; saving souls was the single objective of the Gospel preacher. In the early days of American Methodism, when the preacher was identified with the missionary, it was the missionary, the evangelizing circuit rider, who set Methodism apart from all other sects. The itinerant preacher won the church its fame and its membership. The primitive, early American missionary was the glory of the church. A volunteer for breaking new ground, he depended entirely on benevolence for the support that encouraged and justified his incessant preaching, his tireless traveling, and his hardships. With the creation of the Missionary Society in 1820 came clear and symbolic evidence that the day of the preacher-missionary was over.[51] But the Methodists did not abandon the ideal of the missionary martyr. The historic office of the indigent, long-suffering Methodist minister was transferred, informally of course, to the missionary in distant lands and to the revivalist.

The Missionary Society was established to provide for the health of the church at home just as much as to rescue heathens abroad. But should the missionary fail to save the souls of men, however alien or uncivilized, the

49. Lee to Pitman, May 5, 1843, UPS. Also see Robert J. Loewenberg, " '. . . : Not By Feeble Means': Daniel Lee's Plan for Oregon," *OHQ* 74 (1973): 71–79.
50. John Wesley, *The Letters of Rev. John Wesley* (8 vols.; London, 1931), VI, 327.
51. The formation of the Missionary Society of the Methodist Episcopal Church was intimately connected with the struggle between Methodist laymen and the clergy for control of the church, the former espousing local control, the latter opposing it. This struggle has been unnecessarily confused by some students who, employing a rigid semantic fundamentalism, suppose as a matter of course that older groups on top are "conservative" and emergent ones on the bottom are "democratic." See, for example, Peter G. Mode, *The Frontier Spirit in American Christianity* (New York, 1923), pp. 128 ff.; William W. Sweet, *Methodism in American History* (Nashville, 1954), p. 211. A recent study, using definitions one might easily question, has nevertheless urged scholars to avoid this typology on empirical grounds, to say nothing of definitional ones. James Q. Wilson, *Political Organizations* (New York, 1975).

consequences for evangelism could be devastating. The prospect that foreign missionaries, sent to bring souls to salvation, should not preach was a mockery of the entire evangelical effort. If preachers at home were no longer missionaries and missionaries abroad did not save souls, the Methodist church had indeed faltered. Methodists were perfectly aware of what was at stake in their missionary undertakings. They recognized that their goal of world evangelization, while the duty of Christians, was essential to Methodism itself: "If we abandon any part of the field, the effect will be no less disastrous at home than abroad. A disease at the vitals often appears first at the extremities. . . . The connection of the cause of Christ abroad and at home is intimate, and is well expressed by a remark of a member of the Massachusetts Legislature, who said, 'This piety is a peculiar thing. The more we export of it, the more we have at home.' " [52]

The board, supported by the church membership, and the missionary ministers in Oregon were in agreement with Fisk. All shared the same image of Methodist preachers: martyrs as of old, ready, as Fisk said, to "throw themselves into the nation" for Christ's sake. But the real facts of life at home were pushing Methodists in the other direction, toward a located ministry, each minister the focus of a church-centered community where the preacher was not only a man of God but a model Christian. Lee justified his call for white females, for mechanics, farmers, and married men, as well as his own two marriages and the marriages of others as examples to the heathen. An exemplary Christian was, of course, an exemplary American, and an exemplary American was at the very least a civilized man. But the missionaries did not set out to civilize the Indians or to recreate eastern life in the West. While the modern reader, familiar with a later, harsher image of the evangelist, finds it difficult to grasp, Methodists were interested above all in the spiritual life of the Indian and only secondarily in civilizing him. Unfortunately for Methodist plans, however, western missionaries were forced to contend with Methodist experiences in the East. Methodist wishes and professions notwithstanding, the Oregon mission tended from the very beginning to reconstitute eastern life. The Methodist minister in Oregon played a role quite different from the one he wanted to play.

Pressed from the past to live up to hallowed remembrances of ministerial purity, Methodists were also forced to witness the practice of their

---

52. *Twenty-fourth Annual Report, M.S.M.E.C.* (1843), p. 7.

ideals by their most hated competitors in the present. Who but the Jesuit was unencumbered and unfettered, free to preach, a scholar and a martyr ready to lose himself in the midst of heathenism to save perishing souls? Celibate, transnational, with a tradition of scholarship older than Methodism itself, the Jesuits struck the Indians as "people removed from the human concerns of family, country, and acquisition." [53] Such was Daniel Lee's perfect missionary as he had recalled him from historical accounts and as he imagined him. Perversely the beholding eye would not report to the conceiving brain the image it sought, but returned instead the image reversed. Professing, and believing, the promise of universal salvation, insisting upon the eternity of the next world and the impermanence of this one, the Methodist missionary appeared nonetheless a man very much of the world. That at least is the way the Indians saw him. It is also the way many outsiders saw him, and it is the way he knew he must appear to observers. Whereas the Methodist claimed, along with the Jesuit, to speak on behalf of God, stressing the rewards of happiness in an unseen world after death, it was clearly the Jesuit whose unworldly ways symbolized the religious life. The Indian found the simpler, universal vocabulary of ritual gesture far more convincing than the Methodist's "religion of the heart." [54] Methodists, like Jesuits, looked to Paul the Apostle as the missionary prototype and believed that "whoso loveth father or mother more than me is not worthy of me, and whoso loveth wife or children more than me is not worthy of me, and whosoever taketh not up his cross and followest after me is not worthy of me." But it was the Jesuits, without families and, as Protestants never failed to point out, with

53. Robert I. Burns, *The Jesuits and the Indian Wars of the Northwest* (New Haven, 1966), p. 49.

54. As mentioned earlier, the problem of distinguishing sinners from the regenerate was not original with the American Methodists or even with their Puritan forebears who brought parts of the Reformation to the new world in the seventeenth century. Christian efforts to separate sinners and saints parallel the advent of Christianity and represent a species of the deeper, more abiding human problems of knowing and acting, meaning and purpose. Some theorists maintain that primitive, true Christianity is based on faith alone, making life and distinctions among individuals meaningless and thereby reserving all meaning to the afterworld. See Karl Löwith, *Meaning in History: The Theological Implications of the Philosophy of History* (Chicago, 1949). This view of Christianity ("antinomian" or "existentialist"), irresistible to secular romantics in all ages, presents grave dangers to the evangelical sects because their theology pushes them in an antinomian direction to begin with. Methodist episcopacy met and largely controlled this danger.

ambiguous national allegiances, who were free to follow these austere injunctions.

When it came to teaching Indians the arts and civilized virtues, the Jesuits had no problem deciding whether civilization or Christianity came first because religion overtly encompassed both. The creedal expressions of Catholic worship such as chants, relics, and other kinds of ritual were easily distinguished from the specifics of conventional Christian morality. Methodists disparaged the Catholic reliance on ritualism as Protestants had always done. But the Indians knew nothing of the Reformation, and they no doubt found the preacher an indifferent religious sensation. Also, the spasm of the conversion experience, however emotional, was after all a civilized aberration. Its context was civility. Although Lee welcomed the conversion ecstasy of an Indian sinner, he knew it was, at the very best, a most unreliable sign of regeneration.

The Jesuits approached the Indian with a willingness to accommodate him. They were trained, says historian Robert Ignatius Burns, to make "cultural transmigrations" into the worlds of those whom they wished to change. To make these transmigrations the Jesuits followed a program of excluding all nonnatives from their model communities ("reductions") among the aborigines.[55] The reduction called for the missionary to immerse himself in the world of the native. The Jesuit's comparative independence from family, society, and convention made such a course possible. The reduction provided a way for the missionary to draw himself into the Indian world as the first step toward changing it. The Methodist, whose goals for himself as preacher and missionary implied a similar approach, was unprepared for cultural transmigrations. Inescapably he brought his culture with him. Instead of excluding nonnative elements from contact with the heathen, Methodists were more likely to exclude

55. Burns, *Jesuits*, p. 38, the " 'incarnational attitude.' " On reductions, see *ibid.*, pp. 48–55 and *passim;* also, H. C. Spicer, *Cycles of Conquest* (Tucson, 1962), pp. 290, 292, 344–45. While a study such as that by Robert F. Berkhofer, Jr., provides interesting contributions and many new materials to the student, his view that Protestant missionaries sought to make Indians into carbon copies of whites because the "missionary held the basic values of his culture in common with other Americans" is an example of the conceptual obscurantism of social science in its pure form. In addition to being a tautology, Berkhofer's statement is radically antiempirical and obscure in its claim, however commonplace, to comprehend a "common" culture. (*Salvation and the Savage: An Analysis of Protestant Missions and American Indian Response, 1787–1862* [New York, 1972], p. 9.)

Indians from what became a transplanted white society. Believing they could inspire Christianity among the Indians, Methodists made homes and mills their first structures in Oregon. The Jesuits, preparing to create model civilized communities of Indians, built churches before anything else. The Jesuits, an international society, purposely suppressed their varied cultural backgrounds in order to subvert that of the Indians. Methodists, more culture-bound than Jesuits, unintentionally suppressed Indian culture as they tried to adapt to the Indians they hoped to convert.

The further Methodists fell from their expectations, the more vigorously they pursued them. The deeper ministers became involved in secular life as a result of calling for laymen to relieve them from temporal cares, the more laymen were called. The tension between practice and profession, between the realities achieved and the reality promised, forced Methodists to make adjustments in the missionary program and in the ways they described and perceived it. Jason Lee managed the conflict in several ways. Instinctively he contrived to separate physically the work of civilization from Christianizing. This division was the real meaning, and the original justification, for choosing the Willamette location instead of an area more heavily populated with Indians.

Separation complicated the distribution of responsibilities and programs. Surely the most important part of the Methodist program was the extraordinary attempt to create a microcosm of the original relationship between the Oregon mission and the Missionary Society. The mission at The Dalles, begun in March 1838, was to become the new wilderness station where Fisk's original plan for Christianizing the Indians would go into effect without the hindrances of civilization or the trappings of eastern culture and language. Like the mission itself in its relation to the East, the mission at The Dalles would revive the piety of Oregon at the same time that it paved the way for the basic work of Christianizing. Jason Lee and Cyrus Shepard had thought in these terms from the beginning. Lee's thinking followed clearly the paths initially marked out by Fisk for the Oregon mission. The superintendent proposed to send "two suitable men unencumbered . . . and possessing the spirit of martyrs" to The Dalles, where they would learn the Indians' language and generally proceed as Fisk had expected the Lees to do.[56]

56. Elvira Perkins to Mrs. May [sister], Willamette River, March 26, 1838, in Grace C. Albee, comp., "A Portion of the Autobiography of Rev. Henry Kirk White Perkins with the Addition of Letters Found among His Papers" (typescript, n.d.), WSHS, p. 65.

Plans for the new station began to jell in early 1837, and the designated missionaries anticipated departing the Willamette in the fall of 1837. The rainy season, however, forced them to wait until spring of the following year.[57] On March 14, 1838, Daniel Lee and Henry Perkins set out to begin a "purely Indian" mission by proceeding "up the Columbia beyond the Cascade Mountains . . . [until they] should find enough Indians and a location suitable. . . . [Here they were to] pitch tents, and await further instructions from Jason Lee." [58] Thus, with the same haphazard travel plan that had launched Lee four years earlier, the mission at The Dalles was begun. From the start The Dalles was the special, truly Indian mission among all the Oregon stations. Henry Perkins, recalling his feelings upon leaving Fort Vancouver for the wilderness the first time, outlined what would soon become prescriptive for other missionaries: "I could hardly restrain my tears," he said. "I felt I was going for the first time beyond the pale of civilization, with but one with whom I could converse in English. I do not know that the prospect of earthly gain would have inclined me to proceed, but calling to remembrance the perishing Indians, I at once took courage, and in a little while began to feel quite cheerful." Having arrived at his new station he was a changed man, or at least he wrote as if he believed he was. "I feel much happier here than at the Willamette," proclaimed the missionary to his wife of five months. "The Indians are far, far superior in intelligence to the Calapooyas. . . . It was a great satisfaction to me to kneel down in the midst of forty Indians for the first time and commend their souls to God. . . . I just begin to feel I am a missionary." [59]

Other missionaries would make the same discoveries and describe their experiences in ways remarkable for similarity of expression and emphasis.

Lee conceived the plan as one calling for single men and he chose Perkins accordingly. By the time the mission was ready to begin, however, Perkins was married. This of course is just what had happened in Lee's case. The permutations of Methodist logic in Oregon suggest that the next step would be to find a place for marriage itself in the missionary scheme to capture the Indians' souls and this is in fact what occurred. See chapter 5, *passim*.

57. *Ibid.*

58. *Ibid.,* p. 68, Henry Perkins to Elvira Perkins, Willamette River, March 26, 1838. For a biographical sketch of Perkins and a discussion of the role of the mission at The Dalles see my "The Missionary Idea in Oregon: Illustration from the Life and Times of Methodist Henry Perkins," in Thomas Vaughan, ed., *The Western Shore: Oregon Country Essays Honoring the American Revolution* (Portland, 1975), pp. 151–80.

59. Albee, "Perkins's Autobiography," p. 76.

George Gary, for example, arriving at The Dalles for his first visit, immediately sensed a different atmosphere from the one prevailing in the Willamette Valley. "Never," he was sure, "did I feel so much like being a missionary." [60] It comes as no surprise to learn that it was at The Dalles that Methodist missionaries made their only serious attempt to learn Indian languages. Understandably, it was the last station to be disbanded when the Oregon mission was closed down.

In practice, physical division of the civilizing and Christianizing functions often meant separating children from adult Indians. The practice had obvious advantages at stations such as those in the Willamette Valley, where the Indians were demoralized and culturally adrift. Subdividing Indians by age allowed the missionary to satisfy the demands of logic even while actually failing to Christianize. The bulk of his time could safely be given to civilizing the children, a legitimate evangelical undertaking, while the failure of the adult Indians to respond to preaching was readily taken as the sign of their nearly total degeneracy and dehumanized condition, further underscoring the necessity to save and segregate the children. In time there were other distinctions as well. In the end the impetus to convert, to include, and encircle the heathen became a narrowing, even exacting, process of exclusion and division. The missionary dilemma was finally stabilized by the unspoken rule that made the Willamette mission the center for teaching and civilizing, and the mission at The Dalles the Christianizing agency.[61] All these physical adjustments were matched and reinforced by corresponding revisions made at home in the East.

The Missionary Society agreed with Jason Lee in 1839 that the mission should be enlarged by adding more laymen so as to "establish . . . the institution of Christianity . . . before the natives become yet more defiled by the proximity and intermingling of unprincipled white men [who will be arriving] at no distant period." [62] Methodists assured the world they were not planning to colonize Oregon. "The main object of this mission

60. Gary, "Diary" p. 170. Alvan Waller was stationed at The Dalles in 1844 and struggled with Gary and the board to continue operating the station; but it was finally sold to the missionaries of the ABCFM. Alvan Waller, "Diary," Wascopam, April 27, 1847, UPS, unpaged.
61. In the Lee–Fisk plan of 1839 for revising the Oregon mission (Brosnan, Lee, p. 115), the Willamette mission was the only station assigned a teacher. The other stations had a farmer and a missionary. The farmer was to allow the missionary to devote his full attention to spiritual work.
62. Twentieth Annual Report, M.S.M.E.C. [1839], p. 12.

. . . ," the board said, "is to convert the natives to the knowledge of the truth as it is in Jesus." Two years later, when the mission was fast becoming a secular colony, the board despaired of the superintendent's poor administration.[63] Lee, while regretting his lack of expertise in administrative affairs, could not understand how the Board of Managers failed to see that he was doing all in his power to save the Indians.

In its annual reports the board soothed the fears of the faithful by extolling the good work being done in Oregon. The reports emphasized the activities of the Willamette station because the majority of mission personnel was located there. Since Willamette was the civilizing, not the Christianizing, mission, there was no need to talk of conversions. Predictably the reports concentrated on the missionary work among the "rising generation." The annual report for 1841 [64] is typical. After a reassuring if vague statement that the Gospel was foremost in the mission's approach to the Indians of Oregon, it went on to say:

> In addition to the labors of the missionaries in preaching the gospel, they have organized schools, in which they and their wives are employed, with the male and female teachers, in instructing the children of these poor natives, not only in letters, but in the arts of civilized life. The boys are employed in agricultural labors upon the farms, which at every station are cultivated for raising the necessaries of life; while the girls are instructed in sewing, knitting, and household work of all kinds . . . the farmers, who have been sent out for the purpose, superintend the pattern farms at the principal settlements, and teach the Indians how to cultivate the soil. The wives of all these working men, by their example and influence, with the Indian women, are training them for civilized life to which the gospel is destined to introduce them . . . we may look, with the divine blessing, for a nation to be raised up in the Oregon territory from the wretchedness of barbarism to the blessedness of a civilized and Christian people.[65]

63. The first official record of concern was registered on September 24, 1841. *Minutes, B.M.,* IV, 50. Barclay (*Early American Methodism,* II, 318) states incorrectly that the board's "earliest" sign of concern came in October.

64. The annual report bears only a slight resemblance to events in Oregon, but a strong and curious resemblance to Jedediah Morse's famous report of 1822 to the secretary of war for Indian affairs. See Jedediah Morse, *Report to the Secretary of War of the U.S. on Indian Affairs, Comprising Narrative of Tour Performed in Summer of 1820 under commission from President of United States for use of Government, actual state of Indian Tribes in our Country* (Washington: Davis and Force; New Haven: Howe and Spalding; printed by S. Converse, 1822).

65. *Twenty-second Annual Report, M.S.M.E.C.* [1841], p. 13.

On the Methodist home front, no one demonstrated more clearly than Willbur Fisk, the father of the Oregon mission, how completely reality and the ideal were susceptible of rationalization and compartmentalization. So completely did Fisk fuse the goals of civilization and Christianity that he was able to accept as wholly reasonable the Methodists' demand that salvation precede the introduction of arts and the civilized virtues, while at the same time supporting a program for doing exactly the opposite. It is possible that Fisk was simply too busy to notice that he was endorsing opposing doctrines simultaneously, but it is most unlikely. Willbur Fisk was a methodical man and an intelligent one, and, what is more, the Oregon mission was of overriding importance to him.

Fisk's ability to reconcile opposing views and policies is well illustrated by a letter he wrote in the fall of 1838 to the editor of the *Oregonian and Indian's Advocate,* the short-lived organ of the equally short-lived Oregon Provisional Emigration Society, whose purpose was to settle Oregon with "persons of good moral character . . . who are believers in the Christian religion, and no others." [66] The editor of the periodical was the Reverend F. P. Tracy of Cambridge, Massachusetts, who had advocated sending "not less than two hundred men, with their families," [67] to Oregon. Tracy believed that the Indian character and mode of life were such that "no lasting reform can be effected among them by mere spiritual instruction." Missionary efforts had been misguided, he thought: "The Indians were not taught to be farmers and mechanics at the same time they were taught to be Christians," as they should have been. "Some were induced to become Christian, but they were Christian *Indians.* Their souls might be saved thus . . . but the race could not in this way be preserved." Tracy's views about priorities suffered no ambiguities: "It is useless," his editorial continued, "to attempt, among Indians, to push on Christianity before civilization." [68]

Although the plan of the Emigration Society, vigorously supported by Tracy's editorial, to send men and their families to Oregon to help civilize the Indians directly contravened the Methodist position that Christianiza-

66. "Constitution of Oregon Provisional Emigration Society," House Report no. 101, 25th Cong., 3d sess., Vol. I (Jan. 4, 1839), App. M, p. 27.
67. Letter of Mr. F. P. Tracy, Lynn [Mass.], January 6, 1839, *ibid.,* pp. 25–27. Compare HBS, VI, E. E. Rich, ed., *The Letters of John McLoughlin from Fort Vancouver to the Governor and Committee,* 2d ser. (Toronto, 1943), pp. 14–15 n. 3.
68. Editorial *Oregonian and Indian's Advocate,* November, 1838, pp. 54–55.

tion must come first, Fisk was able to write a letter of commendation to the *Oregonian's* editor in November 1838, in which he declared that the emigration plan was "doubtless feasible." [69] How could Fisk have reconciled views that clashed so openly with his own views, as well as with those of Jason Lee? Lee, it will be remembered, begged for helpers so that at least "a remnant" could be preserved from the diminishing tribes "as trophies to serve Him."

Fisk's reasoning was tailored to fit the shape of Lee's thought and the adaptations Lee had already made to accommodate Fisk's original plan. Their thinking came together like two parts of a puzzle. Fisk readily slipped into considering the problems of the Oregon mission in the comfortable realm of "system," as if the work Lee was doing in the wilderness was all preliminary, merely a technical adjustment transitional to the commencement of full-scale Christianization. The response of Lee himself, when he first began to recognize the dimensions of his task on the trail to Oregon, had taken the same form. No ideological or theoretical transposition, permitting the support of two opposed programs, had taken place in Lee's mind or in Fisk's. Instead Fisk was simply relying on system to put everything right, just as Lee was doing. Gratifying alike to Fisk's benevolent instincts and his peace of mind, the system called for sending more men and women to support the mission.

The Missionary Society of the Methodist Episcopal Church was intent upon its plan of making Christians of the Indians before teaching them civilized ways. Officially reconfirmed in Lee's presence and with his assent, the plan was made the guiding philosophy of the great reinforcement bound for Oregon in 1839. In May of that year, the Missionary Society at its annual meeting resolved, after hearing Lee's address "on the state and prospects of the Oregon Mission, [that] as all attempts to save the heathen by teaching them letters and the arts of civilized life *first* have failed, therefore, in the opinion of this meeting, the only effectual way to bring them to the knowledge of the truth, is, *first of all,* to carry to them the gospel of Jesus Christ and that civilization and domestic economy will follow a reformation of heart and life." [70]

Methodist commitment to Christianity as the first duty did not end with the closing of the Oregon mission. Surveying the wreckage after the

69. Willbur Fisk to editor, November 10, 1838, in *Oregonian and Indian's Advocate,* November, 1838, p. 78.
70. *Twentieth Annual Report, M.S.M.E.C.* [1839], pp. 3–4.

schism of 1844 had divided the church into northern and southern halves, the Missionary Society acknowledged that a "mixed dispensation everywhere prevails." [71] Yet the society wanted it to be understood that schism had not altered in the smallest degree the course of evangelism. Methodists were glad to turn their attention in 1845 to the work of the Reverend John Seys, missionary to Sierre Leone in West Africa. Seys, a truly ideal missionary, was successful, sacrificial, even Christlike. He lost a son in his African mission but counted his work "too high, and holy, and godlike to be marred by any personal complainings." [72] He urged the society to furnish him with "fifty good zealous missionaries, with their hearts yearning for the establishment of Christ's kingdom." Sierra Leone was a British-run enclave for former Negro slaves from around the world, hardly to be compared with Oregon as a mission field. But Methodists were understandably sensitive about comparisons that implied that evangelical efforts were at the mercy of circumstances. Seys maintained that his mission had completely vindicated the hope that Christianity might come "first of all" in the missionary program. The northern remnant of the Methodist Episcopal church called on "the Spirit of the God of missions" and pressed all men to rededicate themselves to the ideal of "the Niger expedition, and others . . . that conversion to the truths of the gospel must precede civilization." [73]

The distinction between Christianization and civilization was as emphatic in 1845 as it had been in 1833 when the Oregon mission was conceived and in 1839 when the mission was reinforced. Although it was easier to make the distinction in New York or to find it in the Methodist tradition than in the midst of heathens, a truly good missionary insisted on making it wherever he was. He did not yield to reality without a struggle. The marks of the missionary dilemma are evident not only in Fisk and in the early physical division between civilizing and Christianizing missions, but in all aspects of mission life.

The dilemma permeated the daily affairs of Oregon missionaries. Lee tried desperately to separate the secular activities of the mission from the vital spiritual ones so that the business of Christianizing the Indians could get under way. He succeeded only in postponing the time when Methodists would act as if Christianization was not really separate from civiliza-

71. *Twenty-sixth Annual Report, M.S.M.E.C.* [1845], p. 10.
72. *Ibid.*, p. 5.
73. *Ibid.*, p. 4.

tion. But postponement itself was a success, even though Lee was not rewarded for it. Like the advocates of Manifest Destiny, who promised that the annexation of Mexico would be accomplished by "our Yankee young fellows and the pretty senoritas," [74] the Methodists discovered that amalgamation was a promising conversion technique. Lee had come upon this solution by accident. Amalgamation was a by-product of one of the more important methods for dealing with the missionary dilemma in Oregon—the method of marriage.

74. Frederick Merk, *Manifest Destiny and Mission in American History* (New York, 1963), p. 125. The term "amalgamation" was widely used in this period, denoting among other things the practice of rewarding the spoils of office without regard to party. President Monroe and J. Q. Adams were open amalgamationists.

CHAPTER 5

The Dilemma Resolved

. . . native Elisha's shall go forth declaring to their
Red Brethren "in all things ye are too superstitious,"
and "this same Jesus which is preached unto you is the
very christ." Could *you* see, what *I* have seen . . . you
would not think me wandering in the regions of poetic
fancy.
—JASON LEE to Charles Pitman, March 30, 1843

ALL THE resources and the institutions of eastern Methodism
were brought to bear on the problem of converting Indians into
Methodists. The study of missionary methods in Oregon as
elsewhere is difficult. Until the remarkable collections of Methodistica
were acquired by the Collins Memorial Library, University of Puget
Sound, and by the Washington State Historical Society, both in Tacoma,
historians of the missionary period had to rely on scattered and sparse evidence. These materials provide a fairly complete picture of Lee's mission
and therefore increase our knowledge of the early history of Oregon.

Some idea of the richness of these collections is suggested in the notes
to this and subsequent chapters. While these documents resolve old questions and raise new ones, they also reveal that Lee was a thoroughly dedicated missionary, loyal to church and doctrine. His greatest challenge was
an internal struggle between his earnest wish to satisfy the Methodist
ideal by Christianizing the Indians and his tendency to civilize them. The
struggle was not his alone, but that of evangelical religion as practiced by
mid-century Methodists. Out of Lee's missionary dilemma came unusual
and deeply significant variations of standard missionary measures, not
reasoned enough to be called programs, but not entirely haphazard either.

The reality that Methodists had to face in Oregon was that Indians did
not readily become Methodists. Methodists, famous as practical, systematic men, strove to overcome that obstacle. Painful contradictions

developed until mission affairs, inwardly as well as outwardly, became hopelessly tangled. Attempts by Jason Lee and the Missionary Society to coordinate Methodist practices with Methodist professions were as unsuccessful as they were constant. For example, when the society protested publicly in the *Christian Advocate and Journal* that the great reinforcement of 1839 had "nothing to do with planting a colony in Oregon," people questioned Methodist sincerity. When the Oregon mission came to resemble a colony, the Mission Board of Managers and other Methodists seemed to be genuinely surprised by its "secular" character. The worldly-wise never did believe the *Advocate*'s assertion that the "successful prosecution of [the] mission . . . [required] . . . farmers and mechanics, to build houses and to cultivate the land, that those who go as missionaries may devote themselves entirely to their spiritual work." Either the missionaries were trying to fool other people or they were fooling themselves. Neither supposition was true. The missionaries' primary object was just what they claimed it to be: "the salvation of the souls of the people in that region." [1]

Methodists, no less aware than others that noble purposes may disguise less noble intentions, also knew that men are sometimes willing to deceive themselves. Before he reached Oregon, Jason Lee knew full well that sincerely good work for the Indians must be distinguished from pretended good work. Coming upon a letter from the secretary of an emigrating society called the Western Colonization Society while in Saint Louis, Lee wrote a criticism of the society's plans which is remarkably like the criticism that would later be made of him. "The ostensible object of the society," he pointed out,

> is the good of the Indians. But is their enterprise likely to effect their object? I think not. Their first object is to get a title to land, and hence circumscribe the boundary of the Indian. When they arrive they must, in the very nature of things, turn their attention to providing for themselves, and I am satisfied that such a colony will find enough to do for a long time, without looking after the welfare of the Indian. And it would have a tendency to collect the abandoned and disaffected traders and trappers; and, like every other colony that has been planted among the Indians would ultimately scatter and cause to become extinct the very tribes which they designated to save. [2]

1. *Christian Advocate and Journal,* April 5, 1839, p. 130.
2. Jason Lee to corresponding secretary, July 1, 1834, *Christian Advocate and Journal,* September 26, 1834, p. 18.

These comments on the Western Colonization Society are no different from Frances Victor's on Lee.[3] By 1840, when Lee's own colony began to fulfill his predictions for the settlement of the Western Colonization Society, he would insist upon the importance of distinguishing between true evangelists and mere colonizationists. Lee believed there was an unbridgeable gap between a secular colonization society and its colony on the one hand, and a missionary and his mission on the other. A mission settlement would be guided by religious objectives and be dedicated to the Indians' spiritual welfare. In his mind there was simply no common ground for comparing a mission with the kind of operation the Western Colonization Society had in view. When Lee was asked by the Board of Managers in 1844 to explain hostile reports about the mission, to defend it against charges of speculation and secularity, he responded as any board member might have. Where, he asked them, "are Christians not slandered?" [4]

Actually the colonization issue has been misconstrued. Lee did not oppose colonization, as his criticism of the Western Colonization Society makes plain. "Everything else apart," Lee concluded, "I think the difficulty of establishing a colony at present is almost unsuperable." [5] Nor did the Missionary Society oppose colonization. Dr. Nathan Bangs, the corresponding secretary of the board in 1837 and perhaps the single most powerful man in the church, did not think a colony would be in conflict with Methodism. He wrote H. K. W. Perkins—a man whose ability to keep secrets was not remarkable—that "if the mission prospers, a colony will rise up, so we hope a foundation will be raised thus early for its future prosperity." [6] The Missionary Society, caught in 1844 between its own

3. H. H. Bancroft, *History of Oregon*, Vols. XXIX–XXX of *Works* (San Francisco, 1886–88), XXIX, 311, 313, 425.

4. Cornelius J. Brosnan, *Jason Lee: Prophet of the New Oregon* (New York, 1932), "Transcript," p. 252. Also Lee to corresponding secretary, March 30, 1843, UPS. Lee found the board's criticism hard to bear. "Have not I forsaken all, and labored incessantly for ten long years in the service of the Board, with no other object in view but to build up the kingdom of Christ in this dark land?" Lee asked of the board members. He demanded that they take his word and not the words of others. Jason Lee to corresponding secretary, Wascopam, October 13, 1843, UPS.

5. Jason Lee to corresponding secretary, July 1, 1834, *Christian Advocate and Journal*, September 26, 1834, p. 18.

6. Nathan Bangs to H. K. W. Perkins, January 16, 1837, Perkins Collection, WSHS. When the great reinforcement left New York in October 1839, it was Bangs who insisted that the Missionary Society had "nothing to do with planting a colony in Oregon." *Christian Advocate and Journal*, April 5, 1839, p. 130. Bangs's comments should dispel the idea

dashed hopes for Oregon and Methodists clamoring for success in a very
costly mission, made Lee's alleged colonization or "secularization" a
scapegoat for much larger issues. Chroniclers, pro and con, have continued the error.

A colony did, of course, develop in Oregon. It attracted trappers and
others, and Indians did die before they could be saved. The missions in
the wilderness failed to Christianize the Indians. After spending a few active but aimless years watching Indians and being watched by them,
many of the Methodist clergy went home or drifted to the main headquarters on the Willamette. The retreat cannot be blamed on the fact that
Lee was an exponent, open or covert, of Manifest Destiny. It happened
because Methodists felt they had, above all, to make "praying Christians"
of the Indians by "preaching to them Christ and the resurrection." [7] But
if praying Christians could have been made from the Indian groups of the
Pacific Northwest, family men from New England were not the ones to do
it.

The new missions were fatally encumbered from the start. Every minister except Alvan Waller and Jason Lee deserted his post, and in most instances a man's family obligations provided the readiest and most realistic
excuse.[8] True, many of the ministers chosen for Oregon were poorly

---

that Lee was working behind the society's back to colonize Oregon, indicating as well that
Methodists such as Bangs and Lee really did have a special approach to their work, the
approach that secular historians tend to deny and religious historians insist only believers
can appreciate. It might also be pointed out that Bangs's thoughts on colonization predate
by two years a supposed "dawning conception" in Lee's mind that he should forget about
the Indians and concentrate on white immigrants. See Harvey K. Hines, *Missionary History
of the Pacific Northwest* (Portland, 1899), p. 344.

7. Both phrases were standard usage among evangelists. See "Journal of Rev. Jason Lee
of August 18 to September 4, 1840," *Christian Advocate and Journal,* August 25, 1841, p.
5.

8. Daniel Lee stayed the ten years required by the board but left Oregon with John H.
Frost in August 1843. In March 1844 Daniel Lee told the board he "left his mission field
in Consequence of the severe indisposition of his wife." On Daniel Lee's decision to leave
Oregon see H. K. W. Perkins to Charles Pitman, Wascopam, July 29, 1843, UPS. His
departure from Oregon is recorded in many places. See, for example, "Journal of John H.
Frost, 1840–43," ed. Nellie B. Pipes, *OHQ* 35 (1934): 50–73, 139–67, 235–62, 348–75;
the quotation is on p. 374. Daniel Lee's testimony is in *Minutes, B.M.,* III, 333. Frost had
many complaints. Appearing before the board with Daniel Lee in 1844 he mentioned the
troubles with his throat and observed that Oregon was much too hard on females. Daniel
Lee agreed with him. *Ibid.* In a letter to Jason Lee dated at Clatsop, February 17, 1841, as
copied by Jason Lee in his letter to the corresponding secretary, March 15, 1841, UPS,

chosen, but even the most capable missionaries—Jason Lee, for example—were unable to convert the Indians.

When the new missionaries with their wives and families arrived in Oregon, little time was lost before they began to call for schools, for more lay helpers, and for stronger emphasis on the "rising generation" of Indians. In doing so they were simply repeating Lee's own earlier responses. Other ministers could return home and blame their failure on the Indians, said to be either degraded beyond saving or simply dying out, but Lee, having brought the banner of Methodism to Oregon, could not easily relinquish it. For him, desertion would be capitulation; it would be an ad-

Frost told Lee he was going to "return to the U. States with my family . . . [because] Mrs. Frost's health fails very fast."

Gustavus Hines left the Oregon mission for New York on September 6, 1845. Gustavus Hines, *Wild Life in Oregon* (New York, 1881), p. 264. Lee believed Hines's "wife . . . never wished to go into the country." Brosnan, "Transcript," *Lee*, p. 259. Hines's letter of March 15, 1834, in Robert Moulton Gatke, ed., "A Document of Mission History, 1833–43," *OHQ* 36 (1935): 71–95, 163–81, is highly critical of Lee. Jason Lee told the board that he understood "Bro. Hines' mind was made up to come home *before* he wrote, and *that* is the key to this communication from Bro. Hines." Brosnan, "Transcript," *Lee*, p. 259. Lee had written earlier from Oregon that "perhaps no poor woman was ever more literally *dragged* into the Missionary field than Mrs. Hines and I doubt not, she will succeed in *draging* him out." Lee to corresponding secretary, Fort George, August 12, 1843, UPS.

William Kone, just twenty in 1840, had married his wife in late August of that year. See minutes of the Estimating Committee of the Board of Managers, M.S.M.E.C., in *Minutes, B.M.*, III, unpaged. (These minutes, at the back of the volume of board minutes, are written upside down in relation to them.) Kone's wife's parents were unable to persuade the bishop in charge of missions, Beverly Waugh (Waugh replaced Bishop Elijah Hedding in the summer of 1839), and Nathan Bangs to release the Kones from their commitment to go to Oregon. "They [Mrs. Kone's parents] fear that the marriage was too much hurried for suitable deliberation and they desire a release of Bro. Kone . . . , neither Bro. Kone nor his wife are very desirous on the subject" of becoming missionaries. Beverly Waugh to Nathan Bangs, Baltimore, September 2, 1839, UPS. Lee disliked Kone, the mission's only southerner. "Mrs. Kone determined to return from Rio Jeniura [de Janeiro] before she had been but a few weeks at sea and he resolved while on the passage to the S[andwich] I[slands] to return from that place; and further, that he was several times *whining* and *sniveling* . . . about going home, while here [Willamette] before he went to Clatsop." Lee to corresponding secretary, Mission House, March 15, 1841, UPS.

The Reverend David Leslie lost his wife and then two of his five daughters in January 1843. Even before coming to Oregon he experienced the loss of a child, his only son, in 1836. Leslie to Bangs, October 10, 1836, UPS. Stationed at the Willamette, Leslie had relatively little to do with Indians. His wife's health and, after her death in 1841, the welfare of his daughters occupied his time. He was acting superintendent from 1838 to 1840 when Lee was in the United States. Leslie, charged with deserting his post to look after his personal affairs, defends himself in Leslie to Pitman, Willamette, January 1, 1845, UPS.

mission of evangelical miscalculation and failure, not simply of personal defeat.[9] Correctly sensing himself a part of important changes taking place within the church, he was unwilling to brand the Indians "a doomed race" and be done with them.[10]

The Board of Managers of the Missionary Society, particularly the new corresponding secretary, Charles Pitman, who replaced Bangs in 1842, shared Lee's annoyance with deserters. The board was entirely out of patience with the "semi-infidels" who returned to the United States. Criticizing Gary, and by implication all others who deserted the field on grounds that "the Indians are so deeply degraded . . . that their regeneration is utterly hopeless," [11] Pitman sounded like Lee, who never, even in the mission's darkest days, spoke the language of unrelieved despair. In March 1843, although "some dark clouds have seemed to hang over the prosperity of this Mission for two or three years past," Lee assured the board he "never . . . despaired of the *ultimate success* of *Oregon Mission,* and . . . never shall." [12] Only days after learning that his nephew Daniel was going home, when he felt that "final success *among the Indians,* seemed enshrouded in such a cloud of *impenetrable* darkness," [13] Lee continued to insist that "Oregon is still of infinite importance, as a field for Missionary operations among the Indians. All that is wanting is a proper system of operation and the right sort of duly qualified Missionaries." [14]

Members of the board could not have agreed more, and while they blamed Lee for the lack of "system" in Oregon, their views concerning missionaries were perfectly in accord with his. "No Missionary Soy.," wrote Charles Pitman to George Gary, "has ever been more unfortunate than we have been in the selection of many of our Missionaries." [15] Other missionary societies had similar problems, as Lee and the board members both knew. But no church other than the Methodist claimed to be a missionary church or insisted it was "Christianity in earnest." [16]

9. See Brosnan, "Transcript," *Lee,* p. 248; and *Minutes, B.M.,* IV, 212.

10. Jason Lee to Daniel Lee, Willamette Falls, August 1, 1843, Willamette University, Salem, Oregon.

11. Charles Pitman to George Roberts, New York, November 12, 1847, UPS.

12. Jason Lee to corresponding secretary, Willamette Falls, March 30, 1843, UPS.

13. Jason Lee to Daniel Lee, Willamette Falls, August 1, 1843, Willamette University.

14. Lee to corresponding secretary, Willamette Falls, March 30, 1843, UPS.

15. Charles Pitman to George Gary, New York, September 24, 1845, UPS.

16. Like "Methodism a continuous revival," this was a familiar Methodist phrase of the period.

Jason Lee discovered "a proper system" when he realized that the institution of Christian marriage might be used as a device for converting Indians. Marriage had served, and confounded, Methodism before. In the earliest days of American and British Methodism, the preacher was expected to be celibate, to accept penury, and to travel incessantly. None of these requirements was enjoined by written law, but each was part of the Methodists' definition of themselves. Bishop Francis Asbury, head of the American Methodist church from its formal beginning in 1784 until his death in 1816, opposed any changes in the preacher's mode of living. But his fidelity to ministerial purity had its disadvantages. A dwindling supply of Methodist clergymen was perhaps the most serious result of Asbury's orthodoxy. Pious and promising young men, deeming themselves fully capable of preaching God's word as married men, joined other sects. In fact, married men who wanted to serve as Methodist preachers were turned away by the church. In defending his stand on married clergy, Bishop Asbury disclosed a view of the Methodist missionary-preacher as a special man, even an ascetic. It would, he said, be "neither just or generous" for a Methodist minister to marry because his "voluntary absence [would] subvert the whole order and economy of the marriage state." [17] But of course the state of marriage was fundamental to the coherence of Methodism which was, as John Wesley said, a social religion. Like itineracy itself, the ideal of celibacy yielded to necessity, as the need for stationed preachers outpaced the need for itinerants. For still another reason the issue of marriage was especially problematical for Methodists. Missionaries were also preachers, and preachers were preeminently married men.

Marriage was as much a part of Methodism and the clerical life as celibacy was a part of the missionary tradition. The strain resulting from efforts to make marriage, as well as celibacy, functional parts of a preacher's creed was never more painfully demonstrated for Methodists than in the life of John Wesley himself. Wesley was adamant that celibacy be observed by Methodist preachers, but he was equally convinced of the need to keep Methodism a social religion, resistant alike to sectarianism and asceticism. The social aspect of Methodist worship which Wesley had in mind was not limited to the spiritual sphere, but included the full spec-

17. Francis Asbury, *Journal of Rev. Francis Asbury, Bishop of the Methodist Episcopal Church* (3 vols.; New York, 1821), III, 143, quoted in Wade Crawford Barclay, *History of Methodist Missions* (3 vols.; New York, 1949–57), II, 358.

trum of religious life. A Methodist preacher should be, as Wesley was, an exemplary man and a family man as well as a tireless preacher. These goals, theoretically compatible, nevertheless seemed to require the use of methods that were incompatible: marriage on the one hand and celibacy on the other. What seemed perfectly sensible in theory became awkwardly and embarrassingly contradictory in practice. John Wesley, a tireless preacher, was also a married man.

Jason Lee's situation in Oregon was exactly the reverse of Wesley's. His principal difficulty was converting the Indians. He saw the exemplary function of Christian marriage as a means of saving Indians and of composing the peculiar contrarieties of the missionary dilemma. Marriage might be just the way to liberate the missionary from his enslavement to temporal duties. It could also relieve him from the compulsion to follow the heathen into their wilderness homes in order to convert them. Marriage was a halfway measure between tacitly requiring civilization from the Indian on the one hand and demanding full-time evangelizing from the missionary on the other. Marriage seemed a way of coaxing the Indian out of his barbaric fastness and into a social context that made sense to the missionaries. The marriage of the missionary would, it was hoped, set off a chain reaction that would ultimately reach into the heathen universe and prod the Indian to climb out of it into the world of the missionary.[18]

Conversion by example, an obvious insight, seemed eminently plausible in its simplicity. The missionary's marriage would inspire emulation among the white-Indian couples living in the valley. These couples, with familial and other links to the Indians, would in turn influence the heathen. When all had been set in motion and the Indian was unknowingly on his way up to civilization, the work of Christianization could begin. The missionary was not to be idle during the process of exemplification. He was to climb down toward the Indian who was on his way up to meet him. The hope was to create a context that would embrace both worlds. The great reinforcement would help to accomplish the purpose. The missionary was to be, as it were, on a continuous revival, reaching out to the

18. The missionary's tendency to civilize was complemented by an equally strong attraction for agricultural settings and a resistance to mountainous and forested ones. Lee, for example, considered the Umpqua country south of Salem inappropriate for a mission. "Civilization itself," he said, "would run wild in such a place." Jason Lee to corresponding secretary, Mission House, Willamette Falls, March 15, 1841, in *Christian Advocate and Journal,* August 25, 1841, p. 5.

Indians who were now, thanks to marriage, linked at last to the touch-stones of meaning upon which Christian men and their families relied.

While the missionary's wife and family industriously carried on the continuing business of exemplary piety, the missionary was to be abroad upon a martyred and unfettered itineration, just as he would have been in Kentucky or Tennessee thirty years earlier. At last the missionary would be employed in the spiritual labors he had come to Oregon to perform, and the Indians would be receiving the benefits of Christianization before any overt attempt had been made to civilize them. Marriage was to be the bridge between two mutually incomprehensible worlds. When Jason Lee and his nephew arrived in Oregon, they called for married men to come and join them. Thus began a policy that led to Jason Lee's return to the United States for reinforcements in 1838. By 1837 he had already begun to seek clarification of his ideas by putting them in practice. Typically, he made an effort to set them down on paper at the same time.

Later on, when peculiar and unsatisfactory results—not conversions—followed upon Lee's uses of marriage as a missionary technique, he did not ask why it should be so. Wesley himself had not given any real study to the incompatibility of his own views and acts on the issues of marriage and celibacy. Lee, like Wesley, looked upon marriage and celibacy as missionary methods, mere systems serving the church's objective of world evangelization. But the fact that such methods led to contradictions does not appear to have suggested that evangelization, theoretically intelligible, might similarly involve practical contradictions with equally grave implications for theory. Methodist devotion to system helped, perhaps intentionally, to shield first principles from too careful inspection. Lee was most secure, just as Wesley apparently was, when he could give order and system to life's complexities by writing things down. Unlike Wesley, who wrote endlessly, Lee was slow to take pen in hand. But when he finally did so, self-explanation occupied his attention.

In August 1837, after almost three full years in Oregon, Jason Lee turned to his diary to explain his dealings with the heathen and "record . . . the dealings of God with" him.[19] Lee had not written anything in his diary since 1834. In the first months after his arrival in Oregon, long hours of physical labor had left no time to think about the saving of souls. He had been content to observe, at the end of the fifth month, how "God

19. Jason Lee, "Diary," *OHQ* 17 (1916): 402.

is able to speak to the heart," even if the Indians could not yet make any sense of Lee or his preaching.[20] Later on, he admitted having "no evidence that we have been instrumental in the conversion of one soul, since crossing the Mountains. . . . [T]he faithful herald of the cross . . . [could] not *but* feel straitened, if . . . he is not permitted to see the accomplishment of this most desirable object." [21]

Lee had no cause to question his purpose or his dedication. "I know full well," he wrote, "the main object I have kept in view has been the glory of God in the salvation of souls." To the extent that temporal affairs kept him from his proper work, he feared there was only "a little in reference to my *own* conduct . . . I should be willing to exhibit to others, for their *imitation.*" [22] Although the details of his activities suggested an immersion in temporalities, he felt he could "safely say concerning my own conduct, that the more prominent features, or rather the general outlines of the picture, have been such as be, would be, in the main, approved of by even the judicious." [23] Lee was questioning the content of his activities, not the spirit in which he had acted or the object he had pursued. It was a system, not an ideal, which Lee was looking for: "the *filling up,* the FILLING UP" of the outlined picture, "there is the difficulty." [24]

Lee's imagery is significant. "Filling in" matched his habits of mind; outlining was uncongenial to him. Lee's was a literalizing mind. He dealt with problems by defining them orally or by putting them down on paper.[25] Having put his failure to make Indians into Christians into literary form, Lee was ready to close his diary for another year. He resumed his calls for additional helpers so that he would have more time to preach. The reinforcements came, but instead of giving him time to preach, they

20. *Ibid.*

21. Jason Lee to Willbur Fisk, Mission House, Willamette River, March 15, 1836, in Brosnan, *Lee,* p. 78.

22. Lee, "Diary," pp. 402–3.

23. *Ibid.,* p. 403.

24. *Ibid.*

25. Lee's most crucial failures—to Christianize the Indians and to send a report to the Mission board—were occasions for the assertion that he hated to write. The point has multiple significance. First, Lee was literal-minded to begin with, and second, the stress of his situation exacerbated this tendency. Third, Lee's habit, and his response to his dilemma, fitted neatly with Methodism. Methodism, not a dialectician's religion particularly, produced and attracted men such as Lee who were, in all respects, Methodism in action. Examples of Lee's "aversion to writing," are Lee, "Diary," p. 402, and "Extract from Diary of Jason Lee," UPS.

added to his secular burdens. He called for more help.[26] The significant fact is that neither Lee nor the Missionary Society ever thought about changing the "more prominent features or . . . the general outlines" of the projected evangelization of the Indians of Oregon, even as the mission grew daily to look more like Lee's evaluation of the Western Colonization Society.

No man felt the stress of the Methodist dilemma more than Jason Lee, and few demonstrate its paralyzing effects so clearly. Although he was by all accounts a persuasive speaker, his oratorical effectiveness was the result of a good voice, a prepossessing manner, and unmistakable sincerity. Most important, his speaking ability did not reflect an ability to lead, but was instead a substitute for leadership. Lee's stature among his contemporaries stemmed from the fact that he was considered a pioneer, not from the fact that he was a missionary. For this reason Frances Victor could, in the end, grant "honor to . . . Jason Lee," [27] even though she believed he duped the Missionary Society. But Lee wanted the missionary honor that comes with "The glory of God . . . in the salvation of souls." It is most unlikely that Lee, who spoke and believed the evangelical idiom of his day, was "self-deceived" any more than most men or that, in the words of Bernard De Voto, history had passed him by.[28]

Jason Lee had a logical mind; given a premise or an idea, he tended to make semantic deductions rather than draw inferences and analogies. His tendency was to reduce abstractions to objects of sense and, conversely, to translate the data of experience into abstractions susceptible of semantic manipulation. His habit was reinforced by the large organizational and even larger conceptual demands of his job. Lee had a committeeman's intellect. Ordering and naming came naturally to him. When he transposed the product of his thinking onto the real world the processes of his reasoning stood out plainly.

Lee's mental processes were clearly revealed in the divisions he made between the civilization of children and the Christianization of adult Indians and in the geographical separations that maintained the divisions. His organizational efforts to supply the new missions set up in 1840 also re-

26. For example, Margaret Jewett Bailey, *The Grains, or Passages in the Life of Ruth Rover* (2 vols.; Portland, 1854), I, 76. Also Lee to corresponding secretary, Mission House, March 15, 1841, UPS.

27. Bancroft, *History*, XXIX, 221.

28. Bernard De Voto, *Across the Wide Missouri* (Boston, 1947), pp. 179-80.

flected these divisions.[29] Mrs. Margaret Jewett Bailey knew Lee at close range. Although she was herself erratic and emotionally unstable, her literary portrait of Lee is perhaps the most astute ever drawn by a contemporary. "The Rev. Jason Lee," wrote Mrs. Bailey of her former supervisor, who had not always, in her judgment, dealt fairly with her,

> was a *good* man, and possessed the true missionary spirit. He was devotedly pious, ardent and dauntless, but deficient in judgment; easily influenced by those whom he considered his superiors, but obstinate and unyielding to his inferiors. His great *forte* was in talking. He could keep the whole body of the people around him, listening to his conversation and waiting for his nod, but he could not set them to work or decide on any work for himself which gave him satisfaction . . . , his mind was ever vacillating and fluctuating. . . . [His] tardiness of operation, arose, too, perhaps in consequence of his entertaining so great a conscientiousness on the subject of *time* . . . Mr. Lee declared that he did not consider "the time in which he wrote his letters home to be his own," therefore *time* was unimproved because belonging to no one.[30]

Lee was not temperamentally disposed to be indecisive. He knew well enough how to boss a crew of woodsmen or how to tutor youngsters in a classroom.[31] But he was nevertheless the soul of vacillation when it came to running the mission because he was pulled in two directions at once and could not legitimately abandon either. The mission came to a "dead stand," not because Lee was equivocating between alternatives, but because he was balancing alternatives and a "dead stand" in mission affairs was a testimonial to his "success." The balancing of the Willamette mission against the mission at The Dalles, of Indian children against Indian

29. Jason Lee made efforts to divide his time between the mission at The Dalles and missions in the Willamette Valley. The trip on the Columbia took about a week each way and Lee made the journey many times. H. B. Brewer, the farmer at The Dalles, said Lee "visited us time and again." H. B. Brewer to [his mother], The Dalles, September 26, 1844, Brewer Collection, WSHS.

30. Bailey, *The Grains*, I, 76–77. It is only fair to point out that while Mrs. Margaret Jewett Bailey's acuity as a character analyst was in some respects considerable, her probity as a polemicist was another matter. She was quite willing to piece together one sentence from the December issue of the *Oregonian and Indian's Advocate* with another from the same periodical of twelve months later without mentioning what she was doing or even providing ellipses. *Ibid.*, p. 106.

31. Lee's youthful experiences as a woodsman are recorded in Brosnan, "Transcript," *Lee,* p. 260.

adults, of the contradictory demands made on the mission steward,[32] reflected Lee's efforts to appease opposed sides of his dilemma. He could not commit himself to a theoretical justification of the program of civilization to which his colonizing efforts naturally led, and he could not abandon the goal of Christianization which those same efforts compromised and ultimately precluded.

The mechanical, self-induced stasis of the Oregon mission was a small-scale version of what the church was experiencing nationwide in an effort to bring all its affairs into harmonious equilibrium. There are fascinating similarities between Lee's response to the missionary dilemma in Oregon and the efforts of eastern churchmen to deal with the slavery issue. Methodist compromises on slavery were directed, simply and practically enough, to harmonizing discordant Methodists. Conflict caused the parliamentary wheels of the church to spin rather than turn, as if movement itself would soothe differences. As in Oregon, there were efforts to find mechanical solutions that did not touch the dilemma at hand, but instead allowed irreconcilable elements some form of common ground. In the conflict between slavery and abolition, Methodist churchmen, North and South, embraced the "wistful" solution of colonization,[33] which was "the very essence of inaction because it lacked even the power of moral suasion." [34] But inaction, the semblance of harmony, was the essence of Methodist resolve, signifying the utmost in institutional exertion. In Oregon, where the problem was not simply to hold off two warring factions but somehow to align a predilection with an ideal, the use of marriage would seem to have been an even more wistful solution than colonization. The similarity between the mission's use of marriage and the church's use of colonization extended beyond the structural level to an identity of personnel. The advocates of colonization for freedmen were often involved with the Oregon mission. Willbur Fisk, for example, a central figure in founding the Oregon mission, was also the "most respected and outstanding colonizationist in the Methodist Episcopal Church." [35]

32. See below this chapter.

33. Donald G. Mathews, *Slavery and Methodism: A Chapter in American Morality, 1780–1845* (Princeton, 1965), p. 110.

34. *Ibid.* The American Colonization Society, formed in 1820, undertook to return freed slaves to Liberia in Africa.

35. *Ibid.,* p. 106.

Marriage and colonization of the freed slave were not really "wistful" solutions. They were no solutions at all, but rather institutional adjustments to insoluble dilemmas. In the Oregon wilderness, the marriage policy amounted to inaction because it never really touched the Indians. More important, it did not make missionaries of Methodist ministers. Theoretically, however, marriage as a means for converting the Indians was irresistible. If unencumbered missionaries were the customary ideal, married ministers were the conventional value. Of all civilized institutions marriage was the most obviously religious. The prospect of married life came as naturally to Jason Lee as it had to his ministerial forebears of four or five decades before. But whereas the earlier itinerants had crowded the margins of their diaries with covertly worded distress at enforced celibacy, Jason Lee, arriving in the Willamette Valley in 1834, "commenced building a house." [36] Once it was built he "made the best shift [he] could without female assistance . . . feeling more sensibl[y] than it is possible for a man to feel, in the enjoyment of civil society, that it is not good for a man to be alone." [37]

For Lee's missionary predecessors the problem had not been how to use marriage but how to evade its attractions. Lee's problem was objectively dissimilar but equally frustrating. He hoped to make marriage attractive to potential converts without actually evading his duty to Christianize Indians. Lee's impulse was to use the traders and their Indian wives in two roles. First, these couples would be examples to surrounding Indians; for this reason Lee ardently believed "their influence must be corrected." Second, settlers with Indian wives had prestige among the Indians and Lee hoped to exploit it for missionary ends by winning the confidence of the settlers and then using it to reach the Indians. Speaking in Boston in 1839, Lee explained his approach:

> We have . . . done something in Oregon. We have thrown a moral influence around that settlement of white people, in which the mission is located. . . . These men have long been there, but they are not calculated to exert a moral influence upon the Indians; and to allow the community to grow up in this manner, would be to paralyze missionary efforts. We

36. Speech of Jason Lee in the Bromfield Street Church, Boston, published in *Zion's Herald,* February 6, 1839, p. 22.
37. Lee, "Diary," p. 408.

thought it necessary that one of our first objects should be, to prevent the bad influence of the white men.[38]

The proposed conversion of the heathen by direct contact with them and indirectly by means of settlers did not resolve the dilemma. Although Lee's objective was to link the Indian and the civilized worlds, both functionally and spiritually, what he actually accomplished was their physical separation. The mechanical and yet eminently Methodist quality of Lee's thought is suggested by comparing it with Fisk's. Reasoning out his solution to the problems Lee faced in Oregon, Fisk was able to perceive the missionary dilemma with as much clarity as Lee, who lived at the center of it. Fisk knew, better than most, how to balance contrarieties and explained how they might sensibly be welded into harmony. In a letter to the *Oregonian and Indian's Advocate* he recommended "a suitable settlement" which "would greatly aid the mission . . . and the mission already established may greatly sub-serve the establishment and ultimate propriety of the settlement." The mission and the proposed settlement were to be separate but interdependent. Fisk's syntax, like Lee's logic, was not wholly a substitute for solving problems, but neither was it prescriptive. Rather, both were indicative of an excessive reliance upon the effectual agency of words and systematic formulas. Fisk joins the ideals and the realities of missionary work together by commas as if ideal flowed into reality in practice. His balanced commentary extended from missionary theorizing to getting "a grist mill entire, with a double set of gears," to Oregon, imputing a harmony to his presentation which was obviously lacking in the mission itself.

The settlement, as Fisk described it, would give its "support to the missionaries—a civilized society to which the missionary could occasionally resort." And then, on the other hand, "should a proper settlement once be established in Oregon its influence would be most salutary." [39] Significantly, distinctions are carefully drawn between the

38. Jason Lee, speech, in *Zion's Herald*, February 6, 1839, p. 22. See also Bailey, *The Grains*, I, 77.

39. Willbur Fisk to the Reverend F. P. Tracy, *Oregonian and Indian's Advocate*, December, 1838, p. 78. The balanced approach was traditional and scientific, just as the response to the flat-headed Indian had been in 1833.

The importance of equilibrist thinking (affecting style, as here, and value) to egalitarian theory and political science has gone without adequate analysis. See Cynthia Russett, *Equi-*

exemplary, didactic roles of Christians in a heathen land and the missionary's proper work of converting the heathen. In outlining tactical maneuvers for reaching and converting the Indians, Fisk's thinking presented any number of practical difficulties, difficulties that would soon cause the mission to founder. Yet Lee was in full agreement with his former teacher.

On his return to the United States in the spring of 1838, Lee had time to think about marriage in general and his own especially. Stopping on July 30, 1838, in present-day Nebraska, he spent "part of the day . . . noting a few reminiscences of self and days gone by . . . the perusal of which may be gratifying at some future day if life should be spared." In this entry, the longest in his diary, Lee recalled his adolescence and the "glowing interest," shared with "most others," in wooing "a beautiful, wise and lovely daughter of Eve." He remembered admitting "the full force of the assertions of holy writ, that 'it is not good for man to be alone' and was fully satisfied that the man who was destitute of a helpmate . . . was wanting what was better calculated to smooth the ragged path of life, lessen its ills and increase its pleasure than anything else of an earthly nature, that this world . . . can possibly afford and for which, man with all his diligence and assiduity can never find a substitute." When he reached the age of twenty-three, Lee decided it was time to look "about for her who was to be the solace of future years," but his search was interrupted by an unlooked-for, yet emotionally related, event, his conversion. For the next seven years religious duties did not permit him to entertain the "fair prospect of maintaining a wife comfortably." Finally, his decision to "cross the R. Mountains, to labour among the Indians of Oregon," [40] ruled out marriage for the time being. Lee insists, and his honesty is not in doubt, that duty had directed him not to marry for the first thirty-three years of his life, at which point duty, with equal imperiousness, required him to marry. It was this sense of duty, aided somewhat by Providence, which led him to marry Miss Anna Maria Pittman on July 16, 1837.

Miss Pittman, a decent and very plain woman, arrived in Oregon in the early part of 1837 when she was several months into her thirty-fourth year.[41] Lee "had seen her before in N.Y. City" but had not been "favoura-

---

librium in American Social Thought (New Haven, 1966), and Floyd Matson, *The Broken Image* (New York, 1964). Compare Leo Strauss, *Liberalism Ancient and Modern* (New York, 1968), p. 222.

40. Lee, "Diary," pp. 405–8.
41. Theressa Gay, *Life and Letters of Mrs. Jason Lee* (Portland, 1936), pp. 1–10.

bly impressed with her personal appearance." [42] As her portrait, painted in New York at her own expense, [43] makes clear, Miss Pittman was hardly a beautiful daughter of Eve. And, despite her penchant for acrostics and dolorous rhymes, she was not so talented as Lee had once hoped his wife would be. Although Miss Pittman did not suit his fancy, for which, he said, "there is no accounting," the finger of Providence had again intervened in his life as it had during the first days of the mission. Lee concluded that, "perhaps, he who looketh not upon the outward appearance but upon the heart, has chosen her as far better calculated to increase the joys and lessen the sorrows of life, than any that my *fancy* would have prompted me to choose." [44]

Everything about Lee's marriage, the ceremony included, was mission business of the highest order. Mission plans to hold the first public communion in Oregon on July 16 had already been made before Lee's decision to wed. The day was eagerly and widely awaited, and when it arrived at last there were "some," according to Daniel Lee, "who awakened and appeared tremblingly alive to the great interests of their souls. . . . [W]e anticipated great and good things. . . . Brother [Cyrus] Shepard had determined to be married . . . believing it would have a beneficial influence upon those who were living with native women, without the ceremony of marriage." Telling no one except Daniel, his nephew, "who was to do the business," Jason Lee and Anna Maria decided they would marry on the same day. At eleven in the morning on July 16 the "whole Mission Family . . . and between 20 and 30 children, Indians and half breeds, repaired to a beautiful grove of firs 40 rods in front of the Mission House where were assembled nearly every white man in the settlement with their native wives and children . . . besides a goodly number of Indians." [45]

The communion setting, like those of the classroom and the podium, provided the right kind of circumstances for Lee's distinctive talents. Dramatically putting the audience in a "devotional frame"—"Bro. J. Lee . . . gave out the Hymn, 'When all thy mercies O my God' " [46]—he

42. Lee, "Diary," p. 409.

43. Anna Maria Pittman to [her brother], Williamsburgh, [New York], March 15, 1836, Rosenbach Foundation Collection, Rosenbach Museum, Philadelphia.

44. Lee, "Diary," p. 409.

45. Daniel Lee to editors, *Christian Advocate and Journal,* Mission House, Willamette, December 11, 1837, UPS. Daniel's account bears a close resemblance to his uncle's rendering of the marriage. The superintendent's account was written after Daniel Lee's.

46. *Ibid.*

then rose to address the assembly "upon the subject of the holy institution of marriage and . . . the importance of that duty." Then, perhaps smiling as the moment of surprise was near, he said, "I intend to give you unequivocal proof that I am willing, in this respect, at least, to practice what I have so often recommended to you." With these words, he "stepped forward," [47] plucking "Miss P." from the assemblage. Silently he led her to the altar. If "Miss P.," rescued at last from spinsterhood, resented her part in Lee's "sacrifice," she did not record the fact. But of course Lee wanted to marry and their "affections for each other" [48] increased so that their brief marriage was a happy one.[49] Most important, Lee had done his duty, which was not simply to marry but to see that others did too. The exemplary function of marriage and of married missionaries was explicit in Lee's premarital lecture and in the union itself.

Because the half-breeds were the missionaries' entrée into the Indian world, they too had their place in Lee's compartmental scheme. Lee, thinking as it were in layers, saw a didactic role for the half-breeds and an even larger one for half-breed children. They were "the future hope of the country, they *will,* they *must* have the influence, unless a colony be introduced from the civilized world," [50] in which event white children would assume the role of half-breed youngsters. And for the Methodist preacher, children again held the promise of the future.

Lee's thinking here, which had to wait upon fully ten years of failure before maturing, marks the high point of his intellectual creativity. At the same time it fits into the larger puzzle of evangelical thought—typified in the change from a gospel of personal salvation to the social gospel—which engaged Methodists and others at mid-century. Inverting completely the terms of the original missionary ideal that had brought him to Oregon, Lee dreamed of the day when Christianized Indian boys would begin to tutor their red brethren: "Native Elisha's," he said, "shall go forth declaring to their Red Brethren 'in all things ye are too superstitious.' . . . Could *you* see, what *I* have seen, could you hear, what I have heard; I am sure, you would not think me wandering in the regions of poetic fancy." These native Elishas would proclaim "the Gospel of our 'com-

47. Lee, "Diary," pp. 410–11.
48. *Ibid.,* p. 413.
49. *Ibid.;* Gay, *Life and Letters of Mrs. Jason Lee,* pp. 169–80.
50. Lee to corresponding secretary, Mission House, October 8, 1835, *Christian Advocate and Journal,* July 1, 1836, p. 182.

mon' salvation" by learning "the english." [51] The impracticality of the plan and its obvious contradiction with the continued Methodist emphasis on learning the native tongues did not trouble Lee's poetic fancy. Furthermore, the Indian missionaries were to follow Fisk's plan for Lee in all respects. They would learn the New Englanders' language and then go out to "range these [their] native hills and delightful plains . . . the *heaven appointed* means of elevating . . . [their] degraded countrymen to the rank of *civilized* and *christianized* men." [52]

The outward logical and psychological aspects of Lee's thinking are uncomplicated. While the actual conversion of the heathen had barely moved ahead in the ten years from 1833 to 1843, when Lee announced that the idea of using red missionaries was "in embryo," the progress of the Methodist ideal had kept pace with events. To be sure, the native Elishas were inevitable under Lee's system. They followed in logical order behind Daniel Lee and Henry Perkins, who went off alone to The Dalles in 1838, preceded of course by the two Lees who had earlier gone to the Flatheads in 1833. Fisk's original plan, which was as much a hope as a plan, had not changed, although Lee's "poetic fancy" and his ten years of failure had turned it inside out. But as Lee trekked eastward in the spring of 1838, this visionary and desperate plan had not yet occurred to him. He was occupied with the more obvious, and outwardly more reasonable, problem of finding white adult missionaries for Oregon.

It was no easy matter to find qualified candidates for missionary work in the best of times.[53] The late 1830s were a particularly uneasy period of national history. Economic depression and jarring social changes, while often providing more potential volunteers than normally, did not necessarily mean that a larger number of qualified applicants would be available. Perhaps the reverse was nearer the truth. There may well have been relatively more unqualified than qualified applicants in hard times, even though in absolute terms more people were available. Certainly Lee faced this difficulty in 1839. It was easier to raise funds than to find qualified

51. Lee to corresponding secretary, Willamette Falls, March 30, 1843, UPS.

52. *Ibid.* Perkins at The Dalles was laboring night and day to learn Walla Walla. The Dalles was the only station where an effort was made to learn the native language. At the Willamette missions only English was taught.

53. The total amount spent for the Oregon mission from April 1839 to April 1840 was $42,499.77. *Twenty-First Annual Report, M.S.M.E.C.* [1840], p. 36.

volunteers. Methodists, it seemed, could raise money from the heathen themselves. They were masterful at the task. Jason Lee led the largest and most successful campaign, up to that time, for a single mission.[54] In nine months he marched from Baltimore to Maine and back again, accompanied by an exemplary Indian boy from Oregon named William Brooks. But Lee knew before his fund-raising tour began what his real problem would be: "I am persuaded," he wrote in November 1838, that "money can be forth coming, but it will be more difficult to procure proper persons."[55]

Methodists had high standards in choosing missionaries. Pious and industrious men were wanted above all. The Missionary Society also hoped to employ only those who were professionally competent, as well as solvent. The society proposed that all recruits promise to stay in Oregon for ten years.[56] Further, all volunteers should be married to wives who had had some teaching experience. No foreign mission, and no domestic one either, could attract such paragons, especially in the numbers that Methodists hoped to find. Moreover, no one, it seems reasonable to assume, really believed these standards would be met. Publication of personnel specifications in the *Advocate* during the early stages of recruitment advertised, in effect, that Methodist values were intact. The paper also suggested that Methodists countenanced neither the land-grabbing schemes nor the fly-by-night organizations espousing various do-gooding enterprises which were prevalent at the time. No doubt some gentle self-delusion was involved too, as when the *Advocate* announced that no applications would be accepted until a "reserve list" of missionary candidates had been interviewed.[57] When the society felt that enough time had been spent getting its several messages across to Methodists and to anybody else who might be interested, the long and tedious work of scraping together a group of missionaries began.

It was clear that most Methodists were prepared to give money to the mission cause but few were willing to become missionaries. Judging from the men and women who were chosen to go to Oregon and, equally important, from the letters of those rejected by the Missionary Society, there is

54. A fairly complete account of Lee's campaign is Brosnan, *Lee,* pp. 104–41.
55. Jason Lee to Cyrus Shepard, New York, November 21, 1838, WSHS.
56. *Christian Advocate and Journal,* April 5, 1839, p. 130.
57. *Ibid.,* December 21, 1838, p. 70.

not much doubt that few were adequately prepared for the life they proposed to undertake. Applications were received from people plainly not of the missionary type. For example, a retired sailor deemed himself adequately trained for missionary work on the strength of having "given chase to pirates." The inferences to be drawn from the sailor's comments regarding the labors of Methodist missionaries are only slightly less flattering than his view of Indians. At all events, he had no references except the witness of the "Island of Candia" to testify to his exploits.[58]

Another application came from a man who "whoul like Some assistance as . . . perhaps fifty Dollars Sent"[59] before leaving. From Meadville, Pennsylvania, a group of more than twenty men and women, all related to one another, offered themselves for Oregon. They evinced an effusive interest in Oregon but only minimal curiosity about Indians. The Meadville family was looking for a subsidized trip to Oregon. Even so, the board, which was in no position to dismiss anyone out of hand, gave consideration to their applications until deterred by the candid remarks of the local preacher, who wrote: "Religious motives are probably united with others in inducing them to offer themselves to the missionary society. . . . [T]hey might be wanting in the missionary Spirit—mingle with it too much of the Spirit of the world."[60] Most of the many others who applied were misfits, and almost all of them were clearly unreliable.[61] Clarke Cummings offered to go as a hatter or a farmer. Although Cummings's letter does not reveal him to be a particularly desirable candidate, the letter was "shown to J. Lee."[62] A stonemason from Oswego, New York, wanted to go. Directed to reapply as a farmer, he did so but was evidently turned down, perhaps because his wife was ill.[63] A likely prospect from West Stewartstown, New Hampshire, a town within 50 miles

58. W. C. Choate to Jason Lee, Washington, D.C., December 31, 1838, UPS. Choate was also unmarried.

59. Elias Crawford to [Jason Lee?], Cohoes, [New York], June 4, 1839, UPS.

60. H. J. Clark to Nathan Bangs, Meadville, [Pennsylvania], February 23, 1839, UPS. Also James Doughty to Nathan Bangs, Meadville, Pennsylvania, January 24, 1839, UPS. Like Lynn, Massachusetts, Meadville had its own Oregon emigration society.

61. The society was also repeatedly embarrassed by its employees, some of whom accepted appointments and then failed to report. Others, such as Elijah White and Adelia Judson, used the society when it suited their purposes. Still others simply failed to exert themselves once in the field.

62. Clarke Cummings to Nathan Bangs, Mount Mims, [New York], July 8, 1839, UPS. Also Clark[e] Cummings to Nathan Bangs, Mount Mims, July 22, 1839, UPS.

63. Letter to Nathan Bangs, Oswego, [New York], March 22, 1839, UPS.

of Lee's old home in Stanstead, Canada, was not hired.[64] Some applicants who were accepted backed out after their appointments had already been announced in the *Advocate*.

The great reinforcement was manned, as were earlier reinforcements, by individuals often hired solely on the basis of correspondence and the written recommendations of elders and ministers. In a pious and closely bound society such as Methodists wished to be, these procedures might have been sufficient. Instead, the society was obliged to take people whose only real qualification was their availability. Elijah White, it will be recalled, who led the first reinforcement of 1836, was in debt.[65] Alanson Beers who went to Oregon with White was regarded by his neighbors as a cranky and irritable individual who should not be trusted with a responsible post in the Oregon mission. There was apparently a thread of insanity running through the Beers family.[66] Lewis H. Judson was married to a sick woman and his children were uncontrollable. Desperately needing able bodies, the society took a chance on such people.[67]

The story of James Olley, a member of the great reinforcement, was the strangest as well as the most pertinent. Olley, as a carpenter, was a first-rate candidate for the Oregon mission, for carpenters were badly needed and extremely difficult to find. Olley was unmarried and, at forty-nine, he was the oldest man hired. But when the time came to sail for Oregon in

64. Lorenzo D. Blodgett to Nathan Bangs, West Stewartstown, New Hampshire, April 9, 1839, UPS.

65. D. K. McSaller to [Nathan Bangs?], Trumansburg, [New York], July 6, 1836, UPS. White had written the board for a loan of $1,000 and an advance on his salary. Elijah White to Nathan Bangs, July 2, 1836, UPS. His request was granted on the day McSaller's letter was written. See *Minutes, B.M.*, III, 37.

66. Elihu Taylor (and six others "all Members of the Society to which he belong[s] and Members of the Missionary Society of the Methodist E. Church") to Nathan Bangs, Weston, [New York], March 18, 1836, UPS. "Beers . . . [is] altogether an improper person and one that would be a reproach on the Missionary cause. . . . [W]e do not consider him the right kind of Smith his business has been that of making edge tools. He is also of a verry irritable disposition and of a visionary mind the Family to which he belongs some of them have been and still are mentally deranged and he is considered to be laboring under the same complant." Elijah White wrote that Beers "though a law and testimony man— and not quite so pleasant in his manners as some," was improving. Elijah White to Nathan Bangs, Sandwich Islands, January 17, 1837, UPS. Beers turned out to be an honest, simple soul, if a bit unusual.

67. L. H. Judson to Adelia Leslie, Astoria, Oregon Territory, February 4, 1858, Loan Microfilm no. 26, A3c4; L. H. Judson to Adelia Leslie, Vancouver, June 5, 1859, OSL. Of course some of these men and women made fine citizens even if they did not become the sort of missionaries with whom Lee could be satisfied.

November 1839, James Olley was a married man. To understand his story, the plans for enlarging the mission must be looked into.

At least three plans were suggested for the reinforcement of the Oregon mission. They all gave preeminence to woodworkers—carpenters, millwrights, and coopers.[68] The so-called Lee-Fisk plan, conceived and written down at the home of Willbur Fisk on January 16, 1839, stipulated four kinds of professional men, including six ministers, five physicians, a secular agent, and a teacher. To these thirteen men were added four farmers, a blacksmith, and seven carpenters or woodworking "mechanics," making twenty-five men in all. Since Lee had asked the board for twenty-six men upon first arriving in New York from Oregon and before his session with Fisk, a fair inference would be that this plan was largely of Lee's own devising.[69]

The board's plan, agreed upon on December 5, 1838, and announced the following month in the *Advocate,* called for seventeen men. Like the Lee-Fisk proposals drawn up a month later, it also specified more carpenters than any other category including ministers, who came second in both plans. The third plan was Daniel Lee's written April 30, 1838, just ten days after Jason Lee had left the mission at The Dalles, where he had stopped briefly on his journey to the United States. Daniel's plan stipulated that fifty men should go to Oregon, twice the number sought by Jason Lee. Again, Daniel's plan asked for more woodworkers than any other occupational group. Daniel Lee's plan was exceptional in requesting as many teachers as woodworkers; he wanted ten of each. Jason Lee recommended only one teacher. The board, hoping to find farmers whose wives were teachers, called for no teachers. Four teachers, all single women, were actually sent to Oregon.

Except for teachers (the board wanted married women and had to settle

68. The Lee–Fisk plan "Sketched by Jason Lee and Dr. Fisk at Middletown on the Afternoon of January 16, 1839," Brosnan, *Lee,* pp. 115–16; the board's "Plan," in *Christian Advocate and Journal,* December 21, 1838, p. 70; and Daniel Lee's plan in Daniel Lee to corresponding secretary, April 30, 1838, Wascopam, UPS. Fisk probably saw Daniel's letter which gives considerable space to a trading plan (one requiring the society to buy a ship and trade in Canton), which Fisk also mentions, although the older man thought "it would be out of the ordinary course of the Missionary Society to purchase or charter a ship for regular passages and permanent service, yet it would be perfectly in accordance with the object and interests of the proposed settlements." Willbur Fisk to F. P. Tracy, in *Oregonian and Indian's Advocate,* November 10, 1838, p. 78.

69. Lee to Shepard, New York, November 21, 1838, WSHS.

for single ones) and physicians (Jason and Daniel wanted five and six respectively, the board only one), all three plans were in close agreement. The board was able to meet all its personnel requirements except in the categories of farmers and woodworkers. Although conclusive evidence of applications in these categories is not easily at hand, what is available suggests that at least six of eight farmers who applied were turned down. Of carpenters applying to join the mission, only Joseph Wheeler of Rochester, New York, who "suffered much opposition . . . in the early part of his experience" [70] from his wife, was turned away along with Smith Beers of Yates County, New York.[71] Smith Beers had applied for the steward's post, but, unlike Judson, who also applied for the job, he did not say that he would serve as a carpenter if he should prove unqualified for the job of secular agent.

By the first week in April the Missionary Society had engaged three carpenters: Hamilton Campbell of Springfield, Illinois, Lewis H. Judson of South New Berlin, New York, and Orlando Beers of Cheshire, Connecticut. When Orlando Beers changed his mind about going because of "the failure of a man of verry extensive businness with whom [he] had some connexion [involving him] in debt and trouble," [72] the board wrote James Olley offering him the job. The aging bachelor lost no time in accepting the chance to join the missionary expedition.[73] Lee, however, was displeased with the appointment because he thought Olley was too old.[74] But the board, not Lee, did the hiring. Olley, however, was not married. He was the only unmarried man preparing to sail for Oregon with thirteen missionary couples on October 10.

Many missionary marriages among evangelical denominations were made in haste and sanctioned by duty, but Olley's was more hasty than most and clearly more expedient than dutiful.[75] The story of Olley's

70. M. Tooker to Nathan Bangs, Pittsford, [New York], April 22, 1839, UPS.

71. Elijah Hebard and three others to Nathan Bangs, Pennsylvania, May 11, 1839, UPS.

72. W. W. Brewer to [Nathan Bangs?], Cheshire, [Connecticut], April 15, 1839, UPS.

73. James Olley to Nathan Bangs, Troy, [New York], April 17, 1839, UPS. He mentions that the board's letter "dated April" was "received."

74. Jason Lee to Charles Pitman, Willamette Falls, March 30, 1843, UPS.

75. Typical of this period, brevity was studied in most of the Methodist marriages in Oregon. Jason Lee married his first wife five weeks after she arrived in Oregon, his second within four months of meeting her. Cyrus Shepard married Susan Downing, his fiancée,

eleventh-hour nuptials is a humorous one. The more important features of this marriage, however, concern the Board of Managers of the Missionary Society. The board knew there was a new Mrs. Olley, and indeed paid her passage to Oregon, yet failed to acknowledge her existence to the society's membership, a failure that accounts in some degree for the fact that the number of Methodists who went to Oregon in the great reinforcement has always been unclear.[76]

The tale of numerical misadventures touching the *Lausanne* passenger list began in December 1838 when the society, announcing its plan to send thirty-two adults to reinforce the Oregon mission, advertised thirty-four positions in the *Advocate*.[77] Nine months later, on September 28, 1839, when the Oregon Committee met in New York, a resolution was passed to "hold a public meeting before the sailing of the missionary family [for Oregon]." [78] The Methodists hoped for a large audience for this

five weeks after she arrived in Oregon. Perkins married Elvira Johnson on November 21, 1837, two months after she reached Oregon. W. H. Willson married Chloe A. Clark within two months of her arrival, although he had been an ardent suitor of the then Miss Jewett, who did not like him because he lacked the "strength of intellect and sedateness of mind which I should wish to find in a man with whom I was destined to be engaged in missionary labors." Bailey, *The Grains*, I, 84. (Miss Jewett made two marriages, both disastrous.) When she learned of Willson's marriage she observed sardonically that "Miss [Clark] . . . consented . . . giving as a reason for the change of sentiment [she too had not yielded immediately to Willson's attentions] towards him, that she thought it her 'duty.' " *Ibid.*, p. 119.

Almira Phelps married Joseph Holman, an Englishman who was not a member of the mission family. This marriage took place nine months after the couple met despite Lee's efforts to prevent it. Once she was married to an outsider, the mission could no longer require her services.

Susan Downing married Joseph Whitcomb several months after the death of her first husband, Cyrus Shepard. Mrs. Olley wed David Leslie, her third marriage and his second, within a year of Mr. Olley's death by drowning.

76. The question of how many Methodists sailed in the *Lausanne* was confused by Frances Fuller Victor. Without giving a specific number she lists all the individuals who she believed actually sailed. The list was apparently generated by her research. When she came to Olley she simply added "wife and children" as a guess. Had she known of his marriage she would certainly have mentioned it as but another example of what she saw as Methodist worldliness and hypocrisy. She also states that Mr. and Mrs. Campbell brought their "children," though the Campbells had just one child. See Bancroft, *History*, XXIX, 177; and Hamilton Campbell to Nathan Bangs, Springfield, Illinois, November 4, 1838, UPS. Also Robert J. Loewenberg, "The *Lausanne* Mystery Solved: A Note," *OHQ* 74 (1975): 359–67.

77. *Christian Advocate and Journal*, December 21, 1838, p. 70.

78. "Meeting of the Com: on Saturday evening Sep: 28, 1839," *Minutes*, Oregon Committee, UPS, unpaged.

publicity function. To prepare for the crowd, and to attract it, twenty-five hundred copies of a program, called the "Order of Exercises," were printed. The program listed the names and occupations of the fifty-one men and women going to Oregon, including Thomas Adams, the Indian boy, and the Lees. The turnout at the public meeting on October 3 handsomely rewarded Methodist efforts. The committee delightedly announced that the gathering was "among the largest, and most interesting . . . assemblies . . . ever called together in this city," that 2,000 "bills of the order of Exercises on the occasion were distributed," [79] and that "both male and female [speakers] . . . addressed the audience." [80] At least 2,000 people listened to thirty-two white adults and watched them as they sat "on a platform sufficiently large to accommodate the Mission party and the Mission Board." [81] The meeting had been a success. The Oregon mission and its members were big news.

As the Methodists were savoring these auspicious beginnings, an unwelcome visitor threatened to disrupt both their plans and their peace. Just two days after the public meeting on October 3, the Board of Managers learned that "bro: L. H. Judson's sister had arrived in the city, wishing to embark with his family for the mission." [82] No one could have anticipated a favorable response, and the Oregon Committee resolved that "it [was] inexpedient for her to go, as the whole arrangements are now completed for the necessary and comfortable accommodation of the mission party; nor could an additional individual be taken on board with propriety." [83] Seriously underestimating the ingenuity of Adelia Judson, the committee directed Dr. Bangs to inform Judson of its resolution, no doubt confident that nothing more would be heard about the matter.[84] Although Dr. Bangs must have carried out the committee's instructions, three days later Judson's sister had become a bona fide passenger. She had

79. "Meeting of the Com: on Saturday evening Oct. 5, 1839," *Minutes,* Oregon Committee.

80. *Ibid.* John M. Canse, ed., "The Diary of Henry Bridgeman Brewer," *OHQ* 29 (1928): 191. Although many authors refer to this flyer as if it were part of Brewer's diary, it does not in fact appear with the original in possession of OSL.

81. "Meeting of the Com: on Saturday evening Sep: 28, 1839," *Minutes,* Oregon Committee, UPS.

82. "Meeting of the Com: on Saturday evening Oct 5, 1839," *Minutes,* Oregon Committee.

83. *Ibid.*

84. *Ibid.*

married James Olley. Twenty-four hours after the wedding the newlyweds boarded the *Lausanne* for Oregon. Months later, as the ship neared the equator, one of the new missionaries noted in his diary that "Sister Olley . . . met in band" with some other women and "felt her burden removed." [85] The exact nature of her burden can only be guessed.

When the Missionary Society published its annual report in 1840, Mrs. Olley's existence was obliquely acknowledged. She was counted with the others in the "company of fifty persons . . . includ[ing] six missionaries their wives and children, a physician, wife and child, a missionary steward, wife and two children, two farmers, wives and children, a cabinet maker, two carpenters, and a blacksmith their wives and children, and five single female teachers." [86] This literary sleight of hand corrected the "Order of Exercises," raising the total number of adults from thirty-two to thirty-three. One child underwent figurative demise. No mention was made of the Indian boy Thomas Adams, leaving the reader free to assume that he was the fifty-first person.

The Missionary Society did not want married missionaries badly enough to engage in this kind of trickery, but they were forced to allow it for Adelia Judson Turkington Olley. Even so, the married missionary was highly valued.[87] Married men were free "from that overwhelming longing

85. Brewer, "Diary," p. 306.

86. *Twenty-First Annual Report, M.S.M.E.C.* (1840), p. 11.

87. Bishop Beverly Waugh to Nathan Bangs, Baltimore, January 17, 1840, UPS. This letter is a key document in several respects. Bishop Waugh had replaced Bishop Hedding as bishop in charge of foreign missions. Waugh wanted experienced men for Texas in 1840 and recognized he would have to send married men with families. Married men without families were a rare find, particularly when the exemplary role of the nonministerial members of the mission was considered important as in Oregon. The only large families hired for Oregon in 1839 were those of Judson (three children) and Richmond (four children). Judson was a carpenter and Richmond was well qualified on paper. He was a minister as well as a doctor, and his wife had had previous missionary experience with an earlier husband. Important too is the way Waugh, along with others, was drawn to the Texas mission and to the domestic missions for the German immigrants both of which were, not surprisingly, far more successful in the creation of Methodists than Lee's mission to the Indians of Oregon. Although it is true that the society's financial debt was in fact part of the reason for disbanding the Oregon mission, funds were available for other more promising missions in Texas and in the immigrant ghettos. Waugh was cool on the Oregon mission before the board learned to be displeased with Lee. As early as September 1839 Waugh told Bangs that "we are sending a larger reinforcement to that field [Oregon] than our means and other calls justify." Bishop Waugh to Nathan Bangs, Baltimore, September 2, 1839, UPS.

which must at times sicken [the missionary's] heart." [88] They were explicitly required for the Oregon mission, and small families rather than large ones were preferred.

The society overcame its objection to the fait accompli of the Olley marriage just as it had earlier overlooked Olley's advanced age and his bachelorhood. The reasons are obvious. The society was desperate. It had to have carpenters and it had to have married men. Better an older carpenter than none, and a married carpenter was better still. Mrs. Olley's resort to marriage testifies as much to Methodist views of marriage as to hers, and Olley's marriage was not the only one made in more than ordinary haste.

William W. Raymond, a strapping young man from Ballston Spa, New York, had a most unromantic view of marriage. Indeed, he was openly coarse. The society's acceptance of him and of his marriage is further evidence of how short was the supply of qualified personnel. For Raymond, too, the Methodists compromised their already ambiguous standards where marriage was concerned. Raymond wrote to the board in the winter of 1838–39. In January 1839 the corresponding secretary asked him for references, reminding him that married men were wanted for the Oregon mission. Raymond's answer was direct: "Let not this [marriage] be an obstacle in my way. . . . [T]here are female missionaries here and if you advise probably one might go especially if you consider it advisable. . . . [P]lease give some advice respecting the manner I go whether single or not." [89] Evidently Bangs advised Raymond to marry, and Miss Almira David of Amsterdam, New York, became the new Mrs. Raymond.[90] In the main, Raymond proved to be an unsatisfactory lay missionary. Capable of hard work, he seldom worked to capacity. Nothing in his recommendations or in his correspondence had suggested that he possessed much of the "missionary spirit." In Oregon he took advantage of his position as the keeper of the boarding school at the Oregon Institute to get the "Institute claim recorded in his own name" in 1844. "It is a

88. The phrase is Fisk's. Fisk to F. P. Tracy, *Oregonian and Indian's Advocate,* November 10, 1838, p. 78.

89. W. W. Raymond to Nathan Bangs, Ballston Spa, [New York], February 4, 1839, UPS.

90. Mrs. Almira David Raymond's letters are deposited at the University of Oregon, Eugene.

reproach to the mission," said Superintendent Gary, "to have had such a man connected with it." [91]

In 1839 Jason Lee himself remarried in the United States. Having learned on his way east that his first wife and his infant son had died, Lee was advised by Dr. Nathan Bangs and Willbur Fisk to take a second wife.[92] Although the decision displeased many people, including the mother of his first wife,[93] Lee was not reluctant to marry a second time. He found nothing contradictory in writing, in the winter of 1838–39, that he loved his first wife "more than all other earthly objects" [94] and that he would marry Lucy Thompson in the spring. Lee's behavior simply revealed his devotion, and that of the society, to the cause of securing married missionaries for Oregon.

Methodists were just as eager to promote marriages in Oregon as in the East. The Oregon missionaries missed no opportunity to use persuasion or their authority with the Indians under mission care when a marriage could be arranged. At the annual meeting of the Oregon mission on May 16, 1842, the ministers reported themselves "in favor of marrying our mission children when they arrived at sufficient age &c." [95] For example, Mary Sargeant of the Molalla tribe, who had been at the Willamette mission for two years, was married to Felix Hathaway, an American settler who had extensive dealings with the Methodist mission. The marriage lasted for five years until Hathaway learned that "Mary was constrained to give her consent . . . to marriage through fear of those persons having controll over her at that time . . . although your petitioner [Hathaway] was utterly ignorant of such constraint at the time." [96] Mary had repeatedly deserted Hathaway, and he looked to the provisional government for release from the bonds of his Methodist marriage.

The Methodists had to listen to even graver accusations against their policies. The Reverend John Smith Griffin, an independent missionary to

91. George Gary, "Diary," *OHQ* 24 (1923): 300.

92. Jason Lee to Mrs. George W. Pittman [mother of Lee's first wife], on the *Lausanne*, November 27, 1839, in Gay, *Life and Letters of Mrs. Jason Lee*, p. 188.

93. *Ibid.*, p. 187.

94. Lee to Cyrus Shepard, New York, November 21, 1838, WSHS.

95. "Annual Meeting [of the Oregon mission]." Extracts from the diary of Alvan Waller (typewritten copy), p. 6, OHS.

96. Petition of Felix Hathaway to Legislative Committee [Oregon Provisional Government], June 28, 1845. *Papers of the Oregon Provisional and Territorial Governments*, Microfilm #54, reel I, doc., frame 690, OHS.

the Oregon Indians from Litchfield, Connecticut, accused the Methodist mission of "taking sides in favor of adultery," [97] an extremely serious charge. A fiery Congregationalist, Griffin excoriated the Methodists for being "very quiet on the subject of adultery." He deplored their willingness to baptize the children of common-law marriages and to become "preachers to all such families and as many others as could be obtained." [98] He imagined that the missionaries' decision to build these people "a house of worship" was intended to curtail his influence, although Griffin's presence had not the slightest effect on Methodist operations.

Obviously the mission did not "take sides in favor of adultery," but neither was the eastern church in favor of slavery. The resemblance between Lee's use of marriage and the church's use of colonization was real enough. John Griffin was quick to see a connection. "The subject of adultery in Tualatin county," he said, "Was in '42 in the same position as slavery in the states between '35 & '38, admitted to be wrong abstractly, but practically not to be rebuked." [99] Methodists, seeking in their dilemmas to erect bridges from what were essentially barriers, were open to such criticism. Endurance seemed the only defense; the great reinforcement was perseverance above all. All the reinforcements came to Oregon to maintain the ministers with a secular base from which the work of evangelization could go forward. And even though Lee's first experience with secular helpers was not encouraging, he remained unshakable in the belief, not appreciably different from secular democrats who favored expansionism, that "Satan [would] not relinquish his empire . . . [to] a few men and a few dollars." [100]

After the majority of the great reinforcement had been selected, the society advertised in the *Advocate* on April 26, 1839, for a mission steward "to take charge of the temporal interests of the mission." [101] George Abernethy was well qualified for the job. He received the best of recommendations from his fellow workers and from his preacher. Respected at

97. J. S. Griffin, "Notes on an article in the *Christian Advocate and Journal* for October 14, 1846." Griffin Papers, Pacific University, Forest Grove, Oregon. These materials are uncataloged.

98. J. S. Griffin, "History of Tualatin Plain" (January 1, 1843), Western Americana, Beinecke.

99. Griffin, "Notes," Pacific University.

100. Jason Lee, speech reported in *Zion's Herald*, February 7, 1839, p. 22.

101. *Christian Advocate and Journal*, April 26, 1839, p. 17.

work and as a leader in his home church, Abernethy was a model Methodist layman.[102] His postmissionary career as a businessman and as sole governor of the provisional government from 1845 until 1849 establishes his reputation for competence and talent beyond question. Nevertheless, George Abernethy was no match for the job of mission steward.

By dividing missionary efforts into spiritual and temporal activities, Lee really created two separate missions. The mission steward had not one but two jobs, each with its own special duties. In order to perform his work properly he would have needed to be in two places at once, because the spiritual and temporal affairs of the mission were physically separated.[103] Writing from the Willamette mission, Abernethy pleaded with the society in New York to tell him which of the two jobs he was supposed to perform. "All I want," he said,

> is either to be under the control and direction of the Board or to be entirely under the direction and control of the Superintendent, but not in a certain sense under both, unless both correspond in their requirements. . . . [His problem was that] the Brethren on the ground when Br. Lee left for the U.S. from what I can learn wished a person to be engaged as a steward for the Oregon mission, that is to furnish supplies to the different families the same as a steward of a Circuit, provide them with Beef, Pork, flour, Butter . . . and that this should be his business.[104]

Abernethy had taken the job with the understanding that the steward would "take charge of the temporal interests of the mission, keep the accounts &c," and perform the duties of bookkeeper and accountant. In order to do the job he was hired to do, the one the society had clearly advertised, he had to be "on the Columbia River where I can receive the goods at once, and charge them to the different individuals as they leave the main depot [the depot to be established at the Columbia] but if my place is to furnish the families of course I must be where most of the families are." [105] Abernethy was soon relocated between the Columbia and the Willamette mission; that is, he was stationed at the Falls with Waller

---

102. Opinions vary concerning the ability and character of Abernethy. Recommendations were received from Marvin Richardson and Samuel Halsted, who testified to his piety, and from George Krasse, Isaac Anderson, James R. Rikey, all of whom were coworkers. UPS.

103. George Abernethy to Charles Pitman, Willamette, November 11, 1841, UPS.

104. *Ibid.*

105. *Ibid.*

who, predictably, divided his time between secular and ministerial duties.

The Oregon Committee of the Missionary Society, unsympathetic to Abernethy's dilemma and furious about Lee's ambivalence, told Abernethy to do both jobs, denying that they were incompatible.[106] It did concede, however, that the "principal Mission station" should perhaps be moved to a more "eligible" situation, that is, to a location where the majority of the mission family lived and where a store could conveniently be operated.[107] This was exactly what Lee did not want to do. If the store was built on the premises of the "principal mission," then the distinction between Christianizing and civilizing missions would be lost. When construction of the mission store was begun at Willamette Falls north of Mission Bottom, the "principal mission" was immediately and irrationally moved farther south. By 1840 the division betwen civilizing and Christianizing missions was a physical fact of mission life. Abernethy's instructions mocked his circumstances. It was geographically impossible to carry out the wishes of the board.[108]

The civilizing mission on the Willamette was, as Abernethy suggested, more like a circuit in the East than a western missionary outpost. The duties of the ministers bore out the comparison: Jason Lee was endlessly engaged in administrative affairs; Alvan Waller's first job in Oregon was to direct the building of a church at Chemeketa; Gustavus Hines was in charge of the Manual Labor School; and David Leslie, the oldest minister in Oregon, was an administrative jack-of-all-trades when he was not handling problems and projects of his own. More than twice the number of people lived at the Willamette mission than in all other stations combined. It needed a steward to attend to its people as on circuit. On the other hand, those who lived at the outlying stations, where more than half of the ministers were stationed, needed a centrally located mission store where they could get their supplies with a minimum of difficulty. Yet, as perverse as it must have seemed at the time, the outlying stations were

106. Meeting of January 16, 1843, *Minutes, Oregon Committee, 1842–1853,* Board of Missions, New York, unpaged.

107. *Ibid.*

108. Abernethy's instructions were to keep "a regular and exact account of all the goods, merchandise, clothing, farming and mechanical utensils, the produce of the farm and the mechanical shops, the stock of the farm, at a fair valuation, together with the work of the Houses, barns, mills, and shops or whatever else may belong to the Mission." George Abernethy to Nathan Bangs, Willamette, November 11, 1841, UPS.

organized in circuit fashion and should have received the attention of a steward as on a circuit, attention that was being demanded by those stationed on the Willamette where a centrally located store could have operated to advantage. From New York the affairs of the mission looked bleak when they did not seem altogether ridiculous. The society was persuaded that its interests in Oregon had "been very injudiciously managed." Moreover, the Oregon Committee was afraid "that there is a want of competency in the Superintendent, and of efficiency in many of the missionaries." [109]

Lee's problems as a missionary did not end when he sealed his occasional letters to the board, nor were easterners rewarded with a revival of piety at home when missionaries such as Lee went into the field. Methodism was a social religion, as John Wesley had said, and evangelists were inescapably active men. Lee's role in local secular affairs, an extension of spiritual purposes, was ideologically indistinguishable from his role as emissary of the church. Indeed, his secular or political activities in the Willamette Valley should be seen as only contextually distinct from his evangelical ones. The relationship between the secular and the spiritual, between civilization and Christianity, was the essence of evangelism. The conversion of the world was an intimate part of the reformation of the world. Evangelism was in this sense a political program. Yet the primary object of the program was the elimination of politics. Lee could only regret his failure to bring the evangelical ideal to fruition so "that like the faithful beast man might answer the end for which he was created." [110] The objective of world conversion was the reward of grace in life and the assurance of heaven after death. The sign of grace in this life was agreement. The passage most often quoted by Methodists promised that "If two of you agree on earth about anything they ask, it will be done for them by my Father in heaven. For where two or three are gathered in my

109. Meeting of January 16, 1843, *Minutes, Oregon Committee.* This sentence is in parenthesis marked with an asterisk to show that the committee did not adopt it as part of a series of resolutions to be sent to Lee. The resolution (numbered 2) directing Lee to relocate the mission was laid on the table. Both gestures indicate prudence, though the resolution and the negative comment on Lee are suggestive of the committee's feelings.

110. Lee, "Diary," p. 249. Wesley's view that Methodism was to be a "social" religion has tempted modern humanist Methodists to derive a social reform gospel from Wesley, though it is plain he was no activist. For example, see Richard M. Cameron, *Methodism and Society in Historical Perspective* (Nashville, 1961). Actually, Lee was carrying out Wesley's view quite explicitly in Oregon as he strove to bring about a social order that was religious and hence harmonious.

name, there am I in the midst of them." [111] Where two or more were not gathered, but were simply together, however, conflicts arose and politics became necessary. Lee's outward involvement in local politics, an important part of his story and of the early history of Oregon too, is in certain significant ways a religious history. It is not, as Frances Fuller Victor believed, the history of a missionary gone to seed. Unfortunately, the generally credited accounts of early political life in Oregon need considerable revision before some of the wider implications touching Methodism can be discussed.

111. Matt. 18:19–20.

CHAPTER 6

Early Political History in Oregon

. . . the majority . . . [was] disposed to declare . . .
an Independent State.
—JOHN McLOUGHLIN to the governor and committee,
November 20, 1844

*W*HEN the Oregon settlers created a provisional government in 1843, their action was seemingly an expression of popular sovereignty and self-government. Jason Lee is usually credited with having played a major role. Yet much is still obscure about Oregon's first government. For many years historians have presented the political meetings of 1841–1843 as a continuous series of events leading inevitably to the government that was voted into existence at Champoeg on May 2, 1843. In fact there was no continuity. The friends of government in one year were often the foes of government in another. The government envisioned in 1841 was not the government created in 1843. In this chapter I reexamine those political meetings in an effort to reach an understanding of Lee's purposes in Oregon.

Seven important political meetings took place in Oregon in the period 1841–1843. The first three were held in 1841, two of them at Mission Bottom on February 17 and 18 and the third at French Prairie on June 1. The last four meetings took place in 1843. Two of them, at the Oregon Institute on February 2 and at the home of Joseph Gervais just north of Mission Bottom on March 6, are known as the "wolf meetings." The third 1843 meeting, held in mid-March, was probably the one that gave birth to the settlers' government. The seventh and final meeting was the Champoeg conclave on May 2, 1843.

As the leader of the Methodist mission, Jason Lee could not have avoided playing a part in local affairs. It has never been quite clear, however, exactly what role he played in bringing the provisional government into being. Frances Victor believed that Lee and the mission conspired to form a "Missionary Republic." In her view the provisional government was the creation of the "missionary party . . . [which] won the day . . . by encouraging the settlers to believe that it was their own government." [1] Others who have looked upon Lee as a farseeing exponent of Manifest Destiny have credited him with an active role in the political events of 1843. Actually there is no evidence of a Methodist conspiracy, and there are few indications that Lee engaged in political activity in 1843. Cornelius J. Brosnan, finding nothing to connect Lee with the formation of the provisional government, concluded that Lee's "political acumen made him realize that a local provisional government was not the direction where lay Oregon's true interest." [2] Lee's "political acumen" and "Oregon's true interest" are pertinent factors, but his feelings toward the provisional government were not affected by either. Instead, it was his recognition—which he of all men did not mistake—that his mission's true interest in 1843 did not lie in a provisional government.

Lee's personality and his views of governing and authority make much of what has been said about his political activity irrelevant. The cycle of letters from Lee to the Missionary Society seem clearly to vindicate the claims of Methodist historians that Lee's first concern was the salvation of Indians. Lee, along with other Methodists, wanted to see the "rise, spread, and glory of Methodism" in Oregon and throughout the world. He differed from others only in his tenacious, almost literal, allegiance to the evangelical ideal. At times his dedication was almost fanatical. His desire to see a "missionary republic" in Oregon is as indisputable as it is unexceptional. His wish for Oregon was the western half of Fisk's hope for Connecticut; it was the wish of all Methodists for the world.

Jason Lee's goal was not ambiguous, but the roads he and others took to reach it were circuitous, even tortuous. Because the evangelical enterprise called for the conversion of every man and woman in the world, it depended on the assumption that everyone could be converted. [3] Even

1. H. H. Bancroft, *History of Oregon,* Vols. XXIX–XXX of *Works* (San Francisco, 1886–88), XXIX, 305.
2. Cornelius J. Brosnan, *Jason Lee: Prophet of the New Oregon* (New York, 1932), p. 218.
3. Charles I. Foster, *An Errand of Mercy: The Evangelical Front, 1790–1837* (New York, 1960), pp. 26, 129. Also on this topic see the following: Clifford S. Griffin, *Their Brothers' Keepers: Moral Stewardship in the United States, 1800–1865* (New Brunswick, 1960); Wil-

though failure was the common lot of missionaries in Oregon, outright failure could not be accepted without impugning the ideal of world salvation. Lee learned very quickly that the shortest distance between heathenism and Christianity was not a straight line; the Indians simply did not respond. In order to reach the Indian and bring him to Christianity Lee turned to various methods, including marriage and the separation of adults and children. All his devices were essentially political because they plunged him and the mission into the social and economic life of the Oregon settlements. Lee's own involvement was at once literal and symbolic. In the mission's secular affairs Lee expressed the political implications of evangelical Protestantism, which in turn reflected aspects of American political thinking. Whereas any assessment of Lee and the mission calls for some understanding of Methodism, Lee's role in the politics of forming a provisional government clearly requires an account of the larger community. What was the provisional government, who wanted it, and how did it come about?

The vote of May 2, 1843, favoring what the minutes of the meeting call "organization," marks the beginning of the provisional government. It is also said to mark the culmination of earlier "steps." Although settlers evinced a continuing concern for some form of government from the mid-1830s to 1843, there was by no means a consensus about the kind of government they wanted. Before the provisional government came into being, there were numerous meetings, petitions, and other political events, but the connections among them are by no means obvious and certainly not teleological.[4] Even though historians agree that the death of

liam A. Clebsch, *From Sacred to Profane America: The Role of Religion in American History* (New York, 1968); Sidney E. Mead, "The 'Nation with the Soul of a Church,' " *Church History* 36 (1967): 262–83.

4. Sources for the political history of early Oregon include original manuscripts of minutes of important meetings. An invaluable published collection is David C. Duniway and Neil R. Riggs, eds., "The Oregon Archives, 1841–1843," *OHQ* 60 (1959): 211–80. Also J. Neilson Barry, ed., "Documents: Primary Sources to Early Government [in Oregon]," *WHQ* 35 (1934): 139–47; J. Neilson Barry, "First Local Government, 1841 Index to Primary Sources," *OHQ* 41 (1940): 195–202. The three most important accounts by contemporaries published with documents are Gustavus Hines, *A Voyage Round the World: With a History of Orgeon Mission* (Buffalo, 1850); William H. Gray, *A History of Oregon, 1792–1849* (Portland, 1870); Charles Saxton, *The Oregonian, or History of the Oregon Territory* (Washington, D.C., and Oregon City, 1846). Letters, diaries, and other documents by contemporaries, published and unpublished, include items by William Gray, Robert Newell, George LeBreton, Josiah Parrish, and F. X. Matthieu (see bibliography). A renowned battle between Gray and Newell in 1867 is an entertaining addition to the docu-

Ewing Young in mid-February of 1841 made some form of government desirable, there is no reason for thinking that the provisional government of 1843 was the end product of events that began in 1841. Actually Young's death marked an alteration of a government already in place as much as it signaled the start of a new one. When Ewing Young died intestate, the problems of settling his estate led to meetings of a government created when Lee was in the East in 1839. The result was the establishment of a probate "court" with a "supreme judge with probate powers" to preside over the court. The probate judge administered the estate of Ewing Young and the estates of others until the provisional government began to function on July 5, 1843. The connection between the "probational" government created in 1841 and the provisional government erected in 1843 is not a straightforward one.[5]

Shortly after Young's death two meetings took place. The first one, held on February 17 and chaired by Jason Lee, was sparsely attended. At the second meeting, on the eighteenth, David Leslie, who had been chosen justice of the peace in 1839, replaced Lee as chairman. Presumably Leslie would have taken charge of the first meeting too had not his wife

mentary background and an important part of the evidence for this chapter. Testimony from witnesses of the Hudson's Bay Company is significant of course, as much for its occasional falsehoods as for the information it contains.

5. Accounts that maintain the provisional government followed a series of steps toward final completion in May are Charles H. Carey, *A General History of Oregon Prior to 1861* (2 vols.; Portland, 1935), II, 318–32; Marie Merriman Bradley, "Political Beginnings in Oregon: The Period of the Provisional Government," *OHQ* 9 (1908): 42–72; Robert Carleton Clark, "How British and American Subjects United in a Common Government for Oregon Territory in 1844," *OHQ* 16 (1915): 313–29; Peter H. D'Arcy, "Historical Review: Champoeg, the Plymouth Rock of the Northwest," *OHQ* 29 (1928): 217–24; James Rood Robertson, "The Genesis of Political Authority and of a Commonwealth Government in Oregon," *OHQ* 1 (1900): 3–59; Harvey W. Scott, "The Formation and Administration of the Provisional Government of Oregon," *OHQ* 2 (1901): 95–118; Leslie M. Scott, "Modern Fallacies of Champoeg," *OHQ* 32 (1931): 213–16; Russell Thomas, "Truth and Fiction of the Champoeg Meeting," *OHQ* 30 (1929): 218–37; George H. Himes, "Organization of Oregon Provisional Government," Oregon, Secretary of State, *Oregon Blue Book, 1915–1916;* Frederick V. Holman, "A Brief History of the Oregon Provisional Government and What Caused Its Formation," *OHQ* 22 (1921): 89–139; Mirth T. Kaplan, "Courts, Counselors and Cases: The Judiciary of Oregon's Provisional Government," *OHQ* 62 (1961): 117–63; John A. Hussey, *Champoeg: Place of Transition* (Portland, 1967), pp. 161–63; Dorothy O. Johansen and Charles M. Gates, *Empire of the Columbia: A History of the Pacific Northwest* (2d ed.; New York, 1967), pp. 178–89. These last two accounts, Hussey's particularly, are sophisticated integrations of previous scholarship, but both continue to stress a cumulative and continuous series of links between the meetings.

died on the fifteenth. The meeting on February 18 called a third meeting for the first Tuesday in June.[6] The June meeting appointed a committee to ask John McLoughlin and Lieutenant Charles Wilkes of the United States Exploring Squadron, then visiting Oregon, for their opinions on forming some kind of government for Oregon. Both men opposed the idea.[7]

In early 1843 two meetings were held in the upper settlements above the Falls, on February 2 and March 6. These two gatherings are remembered as the "wolf meetings" because they were called for the purpose of forming an organization to deal with the dangerous predator. Wolves were a menace to Willamette settlers, French Canadians and Americans alike. At the second wolf meeting on March 6, there appears to have been some comment on the propriety of forming a government,[8] as shown by an entry in the minutes. Two further entries reveal the formation of a committee to discuss the question of government. Neither the committee nor the minutes, however, can be accepted at face value. An analysis of both will be necessary as the discussion proceeds. In March of 1843 meetings were also going on at the Falls, and at these meetings government was the chief question. It was at one of these meetings in mid-March that the May 2 meeting at Champoeg was planned.[9] Once "organization" was agreed to on May 2, 1843, a series of legislative meetings followed. A legislative committee of nine drafted a code of laws which was called the

6. Duniway and Riggs, "Archives," p. 217. This collection uses Gustavus Hines, *Life on the Plains of the Pacific* (Buffalo: G. H. Derby & Co., 1852), as "Version B," using as "Version A" La Fayette Grover's *Oregon Archives* (Salem, 1853). Hines's book was reprinted under various titles, e.g., *A Voyage Round the World: With a History of Oregon Mission* (Buffalo: G. H. Derby and Co., 1850); *Life on the Plains of the Pacific* (Buffalo: G. H. Derby and Co., 1850). Concerning Leslie's wife see Jason Lee to David Leslie, Mission House, February 15, 1841, Barker Collection (unsorted), OHS.

7. Charles Wilkes, *Narrative of the United States Exploring Expedition during the Years 1838, 1839, 1840, 1841, 1842* (5 vols.; Philadelphia, 1849), II, 352–53; Edmund S. Meany, ed., "Diary of Wilkes in the Northwest," *WHQ* 16 (1925): 48–49. See Carey, *General History*, II, 323, who points out that Wilkes ignored the civil aspects of the proposed government in favor of the merely criminal ones which Carey says were less important. Herein lies at least a part of the confusion concerning these affairs since it was a specific crime—the theft of Methodist goods in January 1841—which brought the "government question" into the open. See Duniway and Riggs, "Archives," p. 219.

8. Duniway and Riggs, "Archives," p. 223.

9. This meeting has traditionally been referred to as the March 17 meeting. Hussey, *Champoeg*, p. 152, incorrectly ties the mid-March meeting and the wolf meeting of March 6, 1843, by suggesting that the so-called Committee of Twelve dominated both. This incorrect interpretation is basic to Gray's view of how the government was formed.

"Organic Laws." [10] This committee met in the granary of the old Methodist mission from May 16 to May 19 and again on June 27.[11]

Political concern was affirmed not only by the settlers' meetings but also by three petitions sent to Congress in the years antedating the provisional government. They are the petition of March 16, 1838, the Farnham petition of 1839, and the Shortess petition of March 25, 1843. The 1838 petition, though prepared by Philip Leget Edwards, is plainly the work of Jason Lee. This petition (discussed in chap. 7) asked for the extension of American jurisdiction south of the Columbia River. It spoke favorably of Oregon and the Hudson's Bay Company alike and was signed by most of the residents in the valley.

The Farnham petition of 1839 is anomalous in several respects. Thomas Jefferson Farnham led the group of men from Peoria, Illinois, who came to Oregon in the fall of 1839 with the grand design of making the area part of the United States. The "Peoria party" set out for the Far West like medieval crusaders, complete with a banner, the handiwork of Farnham's lady, which bore the motto "Oregon or the Grave." The petition grew in part out of what Farnham called the "unpardonable negligence" of the United States in protecting Americans from the Hudson's Bay Company and from England.[12]

The petition was formulated when Lee was in the East. Frances Victor

10. Robert Shortess wrote most of the Organic Laws and the term "organic" emerges without explanation from the minutes of the Legislative Committee meetings of May and June 1843. Robert Shortess to Elwood Evans, Astoria, September 1, 1867, MS 174, Evans Papers, Beinecke Library. Duniway and Riggs, "Archives," p. 245. The document adopted on July 5, 1843, was called the Organic Laws for the same reason that the legislative and executive powers of the government were vested in committees, that is, "to avoid as far as possible even the appearance of an independent and permanent government." Jesse Applegate, *Views of Oregon History,* microfilm, reel I, part 2, frame 39, Bancroft Library. Peter Burnett, an illustrious immigrant of 1843, capitalized on this fact to justify his treating the Organic Laws as if they were statutes and not a constitution. See Peter H. Burnett, "Recollections and Opinions of an Old Pioneer," *OHQ* 5 (1906): 186.

11. Duniway and Riggs, "Archives," pp. 240–51. According to Barry, the second session of the Legislative Committee was held at the Falls. See "First Local Government in Oregon," *OHQ* 41 (1940): 200. Since the provisional government was, among other things, part of a conflict between town sites (see chapter 8), this conclusion can not be ruled out. Hussey reports that David Duniway believes the second session was held in the mission hospital. See Hussey, *Champoeg,* p. 354 n. 25.

12. Bancroft, *History,* XXIX, 231. Thomas Jefferson Farnham, *Travels in the Great Western Prairies, the Anahuac and Rocky Mountains, and the Oregon Territory,* in Reuben Gold Thwaites, ed., *Early Western Travels, 1748–1846* (32 vols.; Cleveland, 1904–7), XXIX, 25.

claims that it was drawn up by the well-known British settler, Dr. William J. Bailey. If so, there is reason to believe that his role was no more important than Edwards's had been in devising the 1838 petition.[13] The document, though insulting to the French Canadians on its face, was signed by many of them because they were told that it asked for nothing more than had been set forth in the 1838 petition.[14] Nevertheless, the Farnham petition was aggressively anti–Hudson's Bay Company and anti-British. Actually, David Leslie and Elijah White, both of the Methodist mission, seem to have been responsible for the petition and for the way the signatures were gathered. White, at any event, did not deny the accusations of the Catholic priest, Francis Norbert Blanchet, who claimed that White and Leslie had tricked the French Canadians.[15]

One of the most important features of the 1839 petition is that it purports to speak for "residents of the Oregon Territory, and citizens of the United States, or persons desirous of becoming such." [16] In contrast with the other two petitions, which are carefully limited to "settlers South of the Columbia River," the Farnham document is insensitive to local feelings. In style and tone it resembles memorials typical of the Oregon fever which, just beginning to arrive in Washington, called for the federal government to assume authority in Oregon. The Farnham petition, explicitly hostile to the company, upon which settlers depended in many ways, calls for American jurisdiction to be extended "north of the Columbia river." [17]

The Farnham petition reflected the political views of the Peoria party. The missionaries were responsible for the anti–French Canadian or, as they thought of it, the antipapist contribution to the petition. Father Blanchet, arriving at the Willamette in November 1838 in response to a request by the French Canadians, represented a serious threat to Methodist hopes. Catholics not only were enemies, but they seemed to enjoy greater success among the Indians than did Protestants. Methodists in Oregon, like evangelists in the East, could be relied upon to favor almost

13. Bancroft, *History*, XXIX, 213 n. 10.
14. F. N. Blanchet to Elijah White, February 1, 1840, PAA, printed in L. M. Lyons, *Francis Norbert Blanchet and the Founding of the Oregon Missions (1838–1848)* (Washington, D.C., 1940), pp. 79–80.
15. *Ibid.*
16. U.S. Congress, Senate, *Petition of a Number of Citizens of the Oregon Territory*, S. Doc. 514, 26th Cong., 1st sess., 1840, p. 1.
17. *Ibid.*

any scheme that promised to get rid of Catholics. Before leaving Oregon for the East in 1838, Lee had remarked, more hopefully than truthfully, that "he sufficed to serve the habitants of the Willamette."[18] With the advent of Blanchet in the Willamette Valley, a kind of holy way began.

The third petition sent from the Willamette to Washington before the provisional government was established was the Shortess petition of March 25, 1843. Robert Shortess, like Farnham a member of the Peoria party, joined with George Abernethy of the Methodist-run Island Milling Company and others hostile to the Hudson's Bay Company to press the United States for the extension of American jurisdiction south of the Columbia River.

These meetings and petitions form the bulk of the traditional evidence for the early political history of Oregon. On the simplest level, the documents point to the conclusion that formation of the provisional government in 1843 was mainly a local affair. To think of it as a national contest, as is frequently done, does not accord with the evidence.[19]

18. F. N. Blanchet to James Douglas, February 10, 1840, PAA, printed in Lyons, *Blanchet,* p. 77. Lee certainly believed he was "priest" enough for the French Canadians. His interest in keeping them as his parishioners was part of his hope to reach the Indians by example and contiguity. The French Canadians were in close contact with Indians because of their marriages with Indian women. Lee told the board in 1844 that "Previous to the Priests going there, I was [McLoughlin's] intimate friend. . . . Such was my influence with the Canadian part of the settlement, that they would have been pleased to give me their church and have no Priest come." Brosnan, "Transcript," *Lee,* p. 253. This was an exaggeration, the French Canadians having sent at least two petitions for priests to the bishop of Juliopolis in 1834 and 1836.

19. American tourists were particularly afflicted with the international bias. They found national rivalries at every turn when simpler and more relevant local explanations of events were at hand. William Slacum of the United States Navy was directed in 1837 by the State Department to find "the sentiments entertained by all in respect to the United States, and to the two European powers having possession in that region." Slacum followed his instructions with an advocate's vigor. His distortions of fact and local sentiments were so remarkable that McLoughlin found it necessary to publicly refute him and Jason Lee felt compelled to swear to the Chief Factor's veracity. John Forsyth to W. A. Slacum, Washington, November 11, 1835, in "Document: Slacum's Report on Oregon, 1836–1837," *OHQ* 13 (1912): 180. Lee to McLoughlin, Vancouver, October 27, 1840, HBS, VI, 31 n. 2 (E. E. Rich, ed., *The Letters of John McLoughlin from Fort Vancouver to the Governor and Committee,* 2d ser. [Toronto, 1943]).

While settlers such as William McCarty and William Johnson are often referred to in the literature as American and British, respectively, it is at least as important to remember that they were Catholics and were friendly with the French Canadians. When the Catholics in the Willamette Valley petitioned the bishop of Juliopolis for priests in 1836, McCarty and Johnson, both of whom voted for the provisional government on May 2, signed the pe-

International rivalry was as inevitable in Oregon as the need for legal convention was inescapable, but extranational allegiances, dependencies, and enmities replaced and refined national ones. Settler interest in local government was erratic, owing to the multiplicity of groups of settlers in the Willamette Valley. They demonstrated a concern for law and order when external circumstances seemed to warrant it. From the earliest days of settlement there had been law of one form or another and frequent attempts to bring order into the wilderness.

The first governmental agency in the Oregon country was a criminal court set up to try Thomas Jefferson Hubbard for killing a man on Sauvies Island in 1835. The verdict was justifiable homicide, and Hubbard soon drifted to Champoeg.[20] In 1839 a more formal, substantial government body was brought into being when David Leslie of the Methodist mission was "unanimously chosen" justice of the peace.[21] The theft of Methodist goods in early 1841 by a Catholic connected with the Hudson's Bay Company brought political questions to a head at a time when sharp hostility was embittering relations between the Catholic and Methodist missions.[22] Further, this culmination of two years of sectarian warfare coincided with the death of Ewing Young in February, when Lee and Blanchet were looking for ways to prevent each other from wielding influence south of the Columbia.[23]

tition. Of the sixteen French Canadians who signed the petition for priests, four voted for the government and the other fourteen divided about equally between those voting against the provisional government and those not voting. See "Petition to the Bishop of Juliopolis," March 22, 1836, typewritten copy, Bancroft Library. It should also be pointed out that a request for priests preceded the arrival of Methodists in Oregon by several months, and that it was apparently at McLoughlin's suggestion that the first petition was made. See Lyons, *Blanchet*, p. 1.

20. Carey, *General History*, I, 317; Bancroft, *History*, XXIX, 76, 95; H. H. Bancroft, *History of the Northwest Coast, 1800–1846* (San Francisco, 1884), p. 596 n. 14.

21. Jason Lee to F. N. Blanchet, January 7, 1841, PAA, printed in Lyons, *Blanchet*, p. 88.

22. See Lyons, *Blanchet*, pp. 85 ff.

23. Jason Lee to corresponding secretary, Fort Vancouver, September 23, 1841, UPS. Brosnan made some effort to play down Lee's anti-Catholicism, which was as virulent as any evangelist's. Compare Jason Lee to Mr. and Mrs. Gustavus Hines, Mexico, April 24, 1844, Rosenbach Museum, Philadelphia, and the same letter printed in Brosnan, *Lee*, pp. 239–41. At page 240 Brosnan leaves out the following paragraph without ellipses: "The catholic is the *only* religion [in Mexico]! The Priests are notoriously corrupt. Most of them keep one or *more* women, whom they call their Nieces and by them have large families. The religion appears to be *all all* form! I can discover nothing that looks like *devotion* from the least to the greatest."

In 1841 three distinct social entities—the two missions, Catholic and Methodist, and the Hudson's Bay Company—existed in Oregon, a territory that all agreed would sooner or later become American. Of the three, only the company exercised anything resembling police functions. Lee suggested that everyone acknowledge the "powers that be," namely, the little "government" begun in 1839. He told Blanchet he had made a check of the inhabitants and found that "all with one accord declare, that certain individuals have been duly elected and qualified . . . [to] take cognizance of the misdemeanors of the citizens of this community . . . until Great Britain, the United States, or some other nation, establish some superior civil jurisdiction over this country." [24] In response, Blanchet said he would "await the establishment of good government"; until then the French Canadians would govern themselves "under the protection of the Hudson's Bay Company, much better than you could do it for us." [25]

This exchange shows the bitterness of the antagonism between Methodist and Catholic. Lee objected to what he correctly believed was an unfair advantage given Catholics by McLoughlin's special sympathy for them. Interestingly, while Lee erroneously supposed company policy reflected McLoughlin's pro-Catholic bias, the company supported Catholics in the valley out of an equally mistaken suspicion of Lee's territorial ambitions. The affair of the Methodist goods stolen in 1841 proved to be more than the de facto government could handle. McLoughlin, aware of the need for some kind of governing authority south of Fort Vancouver, asked London for instructions. [26] The area was a legal vacuum. Before Ewing Young died the two missions had fought to a standstill, Lee trying to weaken the Catholic-company connection and Blanchet resisting Lee. With the necessity of disposing of Young's estate Lee gained the upper hand, but only momentarily. Methodist attempts to strengthen the government of 1839 soon fell flat because Blanchet would not cooperate. He instinctively feared that the lessening of company authority south of the Columbia would work to his disadvantage. Lee, on the other hand, hoped for the es-

24. Jason Lee to F. N. Blanchet, Mission House, Willamette, January 11, 1841. MS B. III, 2–26, f9–f11, PAA (copied in unidentified hand).
25. F. N. Blanchet to Jason Lee, January 18, 1841, PAA, printed in Lyons, *Blanchet*, pp. 91–92; citation on p. 92.
26. John McLoughlin to governor, deputy governor, and committee, Fort Vancouver, October 31, 1842, HBS, VI, 76.

tablishment of a jurisdiction separate from the Hudson's Bay Company. He favored government and Blanchet opposed it on sectarian grounds, although the two men agreed that some kind of civil and criminal code was desirable. Lee used the incidents of 1841—the criminal case in January and the civil case in February—to try to break the Catholic-company liaison. It was to be the last time he looked upon the idea of local government as a solution to the mission's problems.

The meeting of February 17, 1841, called after the death of Ewing Young, was directly concerned with the issue of a separate settlers' government south of the Columbia. Only the problem of jurisdictional limits was resolved at the meeting.[27] Contrary to what is so often claimed, however, the meeting was not the first step in the establishment of the provisional government. It was, rather, part of Lee's quarrel with Blanchet, especially the recent disputes over the thievery case. The minutes of this February 17 meeting, the only one Lee was to chair, bear the stamp of his personal concerns and visions. At issue were precisely those legal problems Lee and Blanchet had been unable to solve. Lee sought to establish a uniform jurisdiction applying to all noncompany people wherever they might reside and to all areas south of the Columbia. As Blanchet had made clear the month before, he, and not any makeshift government, would discipline Catholic felons. Such views, the very essence of the Jesuitical approach, as Lee saw it, were clearly unfavorable to Methodist plans.

Lee did not intend to exclude the French Canadians south of the Columbia; rather, his contemplated jurisdiction was meant to include them. Lee put his case to Blanchet in terms that leave no doubt about the broader outlines of his thinking. He insisted in February, as he had in January, that a community already existed and that Blanchet's failure to submit to the already established authority created two separate communities.[28] The conclusion is inescapable that Lee was completely dedicated to the idea of local government in 1841. His sectarian purposes are just as clear. What is more, Blanchet's purposes were precisely the same as Lee's. The Catholic resisted Lee's attempt to make what the Methodist called "one community," for he was not unaware that such a plan would establish two jurisdictions, one on each side of Columbia.

Historical accounts of the formation of the provisional government and

27. Duniway and Riggs, "Archives," p. 217.
28. Jason Lee to F. N. Blanchet, January 11, 1841, PAA.

of the 1841 meetings require two comments. First, as already indicated, the problems of Lee and Blanchet in January 1841 were also their problems in February after Ewing Young died. The meetings of February 17 and 18 must be seen against a background of the preceding month's events. Second, Young's death, from Lee's point of view, rather than creating a need for government, provided an excuse and a provocation for making clearer the distinction between Hudson's Bay Company jurisdiction (hence Catholic influence) and settler jurisdiction. Even so, it should be stressed, Lee's preference for local government in early 1841 was rooted, not in any predilection for government as such, but in his desire to cut the Catholic-company connection.[29] More important than Lee's apprehensiveness concerning Blanchet, however, was a deeper anxiety about the very nature of company power in the Willamette Valley. Lee objected to the combination, in the company, of legal authority and what he called "moral authority," or the company's power to ensure stability because of its economic power.

Lee's objections were based on several considerations, some theoretical, others personal. His most important theoretical objection was that the company's economic and moral powers were not being used to benefit Methodists. Lee's personal objection to the company's position was financial and perfectly straightforward. The mission, and the missionaries, were both in debt to the company store at Fort Vancouver. This most unsatisfactory arrangement ultimately landed Lee in the impossible position of fighting the company even while the mission, in debt to the company, was approaching bankruptcy. Lee's efforts to free himself and the mission from the company's moral and economic authority in the Willamette Valley provide the key to company-mission affairs from 1841 to 1843. The superintendent's objective in 1841 was to keep the Hudson's Bay Company out of the politics of the settlements, not to see a government created simply for its own sake.

The settlers' meeting on February 18, 1841, with Justice of the Peace David Leslie in the chair, chose a committee to formalize the de facto government of 1839. A code of laws was proposed,[30] but the committee

---

29. It was for this same reason that Blanchet opposed Lee in January 1841, and not because he opposed "government."

30. The committee of nine men included four French Canadians, two of whom later voted for the provisional government (Etienne Lucier and David Donpierre), one who voted against it (Charlevon), and one, Father Blanchet, the chairman of the committee,

selected to draft the code never convened. When the settlers met again on
June 1 the committee reported no progress.[31] The Island Milling Company, formed in the fall of 1841, was an undisguised mission operation.
To operate successfully it needed the water power of Willamette Falls.
Thus the mission came into direct conflict with McLoughlin, who himself
claimed the mill site. The ensuing dispute over the Falls claim was in reality a contest for moral authority and economic power between the mission
and the Hudson's Bay Company. After 1841 there were no more Methodist-inspired meetings.

The next meetings for which records exist are the wolf meetings of
1843, in which William Gray, a testy if colorful person, was evidently the
leading spirit. Less clear are the direction and the quality of his leadership. Gray was an original member of the missionary contingent sent to
Oregon in 1836 by the American Board of Commissioners for Foreign
Missions of Boston, the organization responsible for sending the famous
Dr. Marcus Whitman to the Cayuse Indians in present-day Washington.
After four years of bickering with his fellow missionaries, Gray decided to
quit his evangelical labors. In 1842 he went to the Willamette where
Jason Lee employed him as director of the as yet unbuilt Oregon Institute,
a school in Chemeketa for white children. In his book, *A History of Oregon,
1792–1849* (1870), Gray takes full credit for organizing the wolf meetings.

The minutes for the two gatherings, held on February 2 and March 6
and marked with more than the usual number of scratchings and erasures,
present a maze of possible interpretations to the historian. According to

who did not vote. Jason Lee, Gustavus Hines, and J. L. Parrish were the Methodists on the
committee. The other two members were William Johnson, who had signed the Catholic
petition for priests in 1836, and Robert Moore who came to Oregon with the Peoria party
in 1839. These important differences are submerged by Frances Victor's now conventional
perspective. See, for example, Kent Richards, who says the committee consisted of "five
Methodists and four French Canadians." "The Methodists and the Formation of the
Oregon Provisional Government," *PNQ* 2 (1970): 90. Hines did not attend the May 2,
1843, meeting and Parrish may not have. Both "independents," Moore and Johnson,
voted for the government. Johnson was one of several settlers who told Lieutenant Wilkes,
leader of the American Exploring Squadron reconnoitering in the Pacific in 1841, that
"there was no necessity for lawyers or magistrates" in Oregon at all. Wilkes, *Exploring
Tour,* II, 349.

31. The meeting was called for the first Tuesday in June, when it took place. Hines, *A
Voyage,* p. 419. The eleventh could not have been the first Tuesday and Blanchet verifies
the June 1 date. Duniway and Riggs, "Archives," pp. 218–19; report of F. N. Blanchet to
Quebec, June 1–October 12, 1841, PAA, printed in Lyons, *Blanchet,* p. 95.

Robert Newell, one of the more reliable witnesses, his own name and that of "the Frenchman" were falsely entered in the minutes. "I did not attend one of these meetings," said Newell many years later, "nor give consent to use my name" [32] for the Committee of Twelve assigned to look into the possibility of forming a government. The "Frenchman" would almost certainly have been Etienne Lucier, because only two Frenchmen were named to the committee and the other one was Joseph Gervais, at whose house the meeting took place.

The first wolf meeting was held at the Oregon Institute, where Gray was then living. According to the minutes, which cover less than half a page, it was a "public Meeting of a number of citizens of the Colony . . . called to . . . take into consideration the propriety of adopting some measures for the protection of our herds against the beasts of prey in the country." The mission doctor, Ira L. Babcock, who had been designated supreme judge with probate powers in February 1841, served as chairman. On the motion of Alanson Beers, mission farmer at the Willamette station, the participants agreed that a "general meeting" take place on "the first monday in March next . . . at the house of Mr. Joseph Gervais." [33] When Gray came to write his own bombastic history of Oregon's early days, he called the first wolf meeting the "point of conception and birth of the *oldest State on the Pacific,* for as justice to our effort and a proper understanding of our rights should have admitted us as a State instead of subjecting us to a Territorial *annoyance,* under such *demagogues* as were sent among us up to the time we became a state." [34]

Although Gray proudly and promiscuously clouded his presentation of documents with his hatred for Catholics and the Hudson's Bay Company, creating a history that runs crazily from Homeric pretensions ("LeBreton with his ready pen") to farcical displays of spleen ("Dr. White, the notorious blockhead"), his work is exceedingly valuable. It is also a foil for the angry barbs of the ex-trapper Robert Newell, who despised Gray as "the smallest specimen of our race . . . speaking professionally." [35]

Gray's *History* tells of a patriotic conspiracy under his leadership to win

32. Extracts from Robert Newell's copy of *Oregon Archives* with his marginal notes. MS 1197, p. 11, Bancroft Library.

33. Duniway and Riggs, "Archives," pp. 221–22.

34. Gray, *History,* pp. 263–64.

35. Robert Newell to editor, *Oregon Herald,* January 10, 1867, Box 1 of 2, Evans Papers, Beinecke.

Oregon from a counterconspiracy of Jesuits and British monopolists. Gray's lieutenants in this imaginary "filibuster" were George LeBreton of Boston, Massachusetts, who was shot and killed by Indians in 1844, and James O'Neil, an American who came to Oregon with Wyeth and Lee in 1834. Newell, though granting that a few other men were sympathetic to Gray's undertaking, denied that Gray's objective in the winter of 1842–43 was patriotic; indeed, it was quite the reverse. Gray's literary efforts were an attempt to cover up his real plans to "secede from the Union." [36] In 1867 Newell wrote lawyer and chronicler Elwood Evans in Idaho Territory that Robert Shortess, David Hill, and James O'Neil were part of a conspiracy in 1842–43, as Gray said, but claimed that it was a conspiracy against the Union: "Who was those men . . . who agitated organisation by a System of bounties for the purpose of extermination of wild Animals . . . why . . . the most of them were the verry men who went first for an independent Government and for that verry thing I dislike those men's professions to this day." Note that Newell does not say that LeBreton was in league with Gray. Newell also described the would-be hunters as incompetent men who "could not kill a wolf nor had they any Animals to protect save Oneille. we knew those men were not hunters [and] never kept a gun, but office was their object." [37]

Newell would seem to have had more integrity as a witness than Gray, but he had his flaws. He drank too much, especially toward the end of his life. Yet whatever his defects, he was plainly a man of character. Gray, on the other hand, was excessively quarrelsome and faultfinding. He disliked almost everyone and was disliked in return. He was capable of a meanness of spirit which was unlike any quality that Newell manifested. Yet Newell could be caustic. In 1867, an embittered, tired man, he lost his job as Indian agent to J. L. Parrish, a Methodist missionary, thanks to the connivance of Oregon's first territorial delegate, Samuel Thurston. Thurston, also a mission man, was, in Jesse Applegate's measured view, one of the "most desperate cases" of demagoguery he had ever known. [38] In 1861,

36. Robert Newell to editor, *Oregon Herald,* March 8, 1867, Box 1, Evans Papers.
37. Robert Newell to Elwood Evans, Lewiston, I[daho] T[erritory], August 8, 1867, Box 1, Evans Papers.
38. Jesse Applegate to Elwood Evans, Yoncalla, [Oregon], October 13, 1867, Box 1, Evans Papers. Thurston was the "most unscrupulous and mendacious" demagogue, Applegate told Evans, but, notwithstanding, Evans wrote of him with high praise as a man of "decided ability . . . untiring industry and earnestness of purpose. . . . Let the remembrance of intellectual greatness and successful labor so conspicuous . . . efface the recol-

just five years before Newell's newspaper feud with Gray, the Willamette had flooded and Newell had lost his home and belongings in Champoeg. One of his half-breed children had been hanged as a horse thief and it was rumored that the old mountaineer, never an abstainer, was drinking heavily.[39] In May 1867, three months before Newell began his correspondence ·with Evans, his second wife died.

During the provisional and territorial periods Newell was affiliated with the Democratic party, originally the antimission, later the anti–Know-Nothing, party in Oregon.[40] Even more important is the timing of

lections of any error in the short but brilliant career of a youthful, impulsive, perhaps too impatient, seeker for political fame." Elwood Evans, *History of the Pacific Northwest* (2 vols.; Portland, 1889), I, 323. Gray was a historian in the same vein and an interested participant in addition.

39. James Nesmith, "Address" to 12th Annual Reunion, TOPA (Salem, Oregon, 1885), p. 31. Mrs. Margaret Bailey, who came to Oregon with the first Methodist reinforcement in 1837 as Miss Jewett, thought little of Newell. She said his drinking habits led her husband astray. Margaret Jewett Bailey, *The Grains, or Passages in the Life of Ruth Rover* (2 vols.; Portland, 1854), I, 149. On Newell see George Guy Delamarter, "The Career of Robert Newell" (M.A. thesis, University of Oregon, 1924), pp. 63–65. Also Dorothy O. Johansen, ed., *Robert Newell's Memoranda* (Portland, 1959).

40. It is too often forgotten that the term "Mission Party" postdates Lee. It is properly assigned to prominent laymen such as Abernethy, Judson, and Willson, or to Methodists who came to Oregon during the superintendencies of George Gary and William Roberts. Gustavus Hines and Alvan Waller belonged to the Mission Party, but they did not become active in it until the late 1840s. Waller was at the mission at The Dalles from 1844 to 1846 and Hines was in the East from 1844 to 1848. Further, not only does the Mission Party come after Lee, but the term really means "Methodist Party," since the mission was effectively defunct at the end of Lee's tenure.

Newell's assertion that Gray, Shortess, Hill, and O'Neil were "camp-followers" of the Mission Party is equally misleading. See Newell to Evans, August 8, 1867, Evans Papers. All three had some connection with the mission at one time or another as did many people, yet only Gray was employed by the mission. Moreover, Alanson Beers was a member of the mission and a stockholder in the Island Milling Company, but nevertheless he was on Newell's "side" in May 1843. In addition, Newell thought well of Babcock. See extracts from Robert Newell's copy of *Oregon Archives*, p. 10, Bancroft Library. And, one of the mountain man's children boarded with H. B. Brewer, farmer at the mission station at The Dalles. Thus Newell was himself not completely hostile to the mission or to Methodist missionaries. Brewer and Beers both signed the Shortess petition of 1843, a document Newell abominated.

All in all, Newell's account of political events in 1843, while perhaps the single most reliable source, is suffused with the political feelings of the 1860s. The missionaries certainly did not support Gray and they opposed independence. Newell's "camp-followers" idea and the designation "Mission Party" are both the result of his foreshortened historical perspective. In addition to the several genuine reasons Newell had to dislike Methodists in the 1860s, his state of mind was also affected by the recent elevation of Gray to the ranks of

his quarrel with Gray. By calling Gray "Secush [secessionist] No. 1" at a time when the Civil War had only just ended, Newell was openly exploiting the issues of the day in order to disparage Gray with, as Newell himself said, "as much contempt as possible." [41] In 1843 the prospect that Oregon, or even the entire Northwest and Texas, might become an independent republic was not a subversive view. Independence was openly discussed in Oregon, and "secessionist" is an inappropriate word to describe those who favored it. It is not without significance, however, that Gray denied he approved of independence, if, as Newell says, he actually had favored it in 1843, or even in 1846, when McLoughlin reported to his superiors that a sizable number of Americans in Oregon supported independence. In the fall of 1844 McLoughlin believed "the majority . . . [was] disposed to declare . . . an Independent State." [42] Finally, if Newell made more of Gray's disloyalty than he had a right to, his assertion that Gray favored independence in 1843 is very probably true. Gray's *History* is a mixture of lies and truths.

Whatever else the wolf meetings might have been, they were not the "point of conception" for Oregon's political history, as Gray so grandly proclaimed. They were, however, the point of departure for Gray's conception of the history of Oregon. His *History* was written just after the Civil War and when the United States Congress was debating how much money to pay the Hudson's Bay Company as reimbursement for properties forfeited south of the 49° parallel in the Anglo-American boundary settlement of 1846. Robert Newell argued that Gray's purpose in writing his history was to support congressional opponents of the Hudson's Bay Company and also to make sure that posterity never discovered his "secessionist" leanings in the 1840s. [43] Indeed, his work might well be regarded as an attempt to prove that his apparently proindependence activity in 1843 was, in reality, a patriotic conspiracy to save Oregon from British-Jesuit malefactors. William Gray wrote for a receptive, sympathetic audience in 1870. Oregonians were outdoing one another in professing love

---

federal officialdom, a fact that could not have softened Newell's dislike of "the second John Brown." See Newell to *Oregon Herald,* January 10, 1867, Evans Papers.

41. Robert Newell to Elwood Evans, I.T., May 7, 1867, Evans Papers.

42. John McLoughlin to the governor and committee, November 20, 1844, HBS, VII, 32 (E. E. Rich, ed., *The Letters of John McLoughlin from Fort Vancouver to the Governor and Committee,* 3d ser. [Toronto, 1944]).

43. Newell to *Oregon Herald,* January 10, 1867, Evans Papers. See William Gray to editor, *Pacific Tribune,* September 15, 1865, MS 229, Beinecke Library.

for the Union and hatred of secession. Jesuits and Catholics were widely despised and feared, and the view that Oregon had been "won" from England was becoming popular.[44]

Like Frances Victor, Gray claims that a conspiracy of some kind brought the provisional government into existence. In his view the settlers conspired to win toleration from the Methodists, who opposed a government. In Victor's account it is the Methodists who conspired to create the government, which the settlers only think is their own. In both histories the provisional government is said to be a settlers' government, and in both there is in fact no evidence of a conspiracy. The creation of the provisional government, while by no means a simple event, was not the product of conspiracies. The conspiracies were concocted by the historians; in fact, Gray's *History* is itself somewhat conspiratorial. The key to Gray's conspiracy lies in the wolf meeting of March 6, 1843. The minutes reveal that a committee was to be "appointed to take into cunsderation the propriety of taking measure for the civil and military protection [of] this colony." [45] This resolution is the foundation for Gray's conspiracy theory. He argues that it signified the success of the progovernment forces whose purpose all along had been to bring a government into being, not to deal with wolves. Deception was necessary, Gray says, because almost everyone opposed the idea of forming a government, the French Canadians most of all. Gray, and those who have followed his account, see the wolf meetings as part of a larger national and ethnic conflict.

The proceedings of the March 6 assembly were ordered presented "to the Recorder of this Colony," [46] George LeBreton, who had been chosen to that office in February 1841. Obviously the wolf meetings were considered a legitimate function of a government in existence prior to the advent of a decision to destroy predators. Furthermore, the members of a committee chosen at the first wolf meeting, who submitted ten resolutions for discussion on March 6, were by implication members of a preexistent government entity. Although these factors do not necessarily preclude a conspiratorial use of the second wolf meeting, they make clear that the meeting itself was part of a specified series with specific objectives. To consider

44. Gray's anti-Catholicism was especially fervent. Writing Evans in 1880, he referred to the *Catholic Sentinel,* a religious paper, as the "Smut Machine." William Gray to Elwood Evans, Olney, [Oregon], June 8, 1880, Evans Papers.
45. Duniway and Riggs, "Archives," p. 223.
46. *Ibid.,* pp. 223, 227.

the idea of a government at either of these meetings would seem either redundant (since a government of sorts already existed) or revolutionary. It could also be that what was offered for consideration at the second wolf meeting was not government, but some special sort of government. As the sequel will show, that is precisely what happened.[47]

In both the report and the minutes, the two items that supply Gray with documentary evidence for the importance of the meeting of March 6, numbers are inserted, crossed out, or superimposed on others. The changes strongly suggest that the accounts were tampered with. The tenth resolution, for example, became the eighth, but since the minutes show that both the tenth and the original eighth resolutions were adopted, there is no possible way of deciding what really was intended. To complicate matters further, each paragraph of the minutes is numbered after the entry showing that the ninth resolution was adopted. The paragraph numbering begins with 10 and goes up to 21.[48] One cannot be sure whether the numbers refer to resolutions, to articles, or simply to statements. Finally, these numbers—10 to 21—were changed at some point to 11 to 22, the new digits written in over the older ones. The numbering of paragraphs, both times, and the renumbering of the resolutions were almost certainly done in an effort to simulate continuity. Significantly, the pattern of alterings ties in with the entry at the end of the meeting calling for a committee to discuss the government question. Hidden within the tenth resolution is one of the keys to the wolf meeting of March 6 and at length to the real story of the provisional government.

The sequence of events following the numbering of the paragraphs in the minutes turns upon the number 10. The first nine resolutions of the report were discussed and voted on in sequence; the tenth resolution was not voted on until the meeting was almost over. The first numbered paragraph in the minutes was given the number 10 because the entry preceding it referred to the adoption of the ninth resolution. Presumably

47. That is, the committee of Gray, Beers, W. H. Willson, Joseph Bernabe, and Etienne Lucier. This report is not in the handwriting of any of these men, and all the names of the committeemen appended at the end of the report have been erased.

48. The excellent and otherwise literal transcription of these documents by Duniway and Riggs does not show this alteration. Compare Duniway and Riggs, "Archives," pp. 223–24, and Document 421, Archives of the State Library, Salem, Oregon. Newell said that Gray tampered with official documents, although he specifies only the documents of the legislative committee in May and June 1843. Newell to *Oregon Herald,* March 8, 1867, Evans Papers.

whoever did the numbering wanted to give the paragraph he numbered 10 as much significance as the preceding entry, though it was only a seconded motion. Then, when he finished numbering paragraphs 10 to 21, he discovered that following his number 13 was the entry, "Resolved that the 10th resolut be accepted." He thereupon renumbered the paragraphs from 11 to 22.[49] The effort to make it seem each paragraph in the minutes, after the adoption of the ninth resolution of the report, was of sufficient importance to receive a number was connected with the other oddity in these minutes, the resolution calling for a committee to consider the propriety of civil and military protection. The relationship of this twentieth "resolution" [50] to the rest of the minutes is ambiguous.

The minutes show that a good deal of business was transacted between adoption of the ninth and adoption of the tenth resolution of the report, because the latter was merely a resolution to adjourn and turn the minutes over to the "Recorder of this Colony." [51] Before it was adopted five motions, all concerning the problem of wolves, were made and seconded. Then, after the resolution to adjourn was passed, eight more entries, all termed "resolutions," were made in the minutes, but they are much less important than earlier resolutions. They simply tie up the loose ends of resolutions agreed to earlier in the meeting. In fact, the meeting began to break up after adoption of the tenth resolution, though the eight additional "resolutions" are duly entered in the minutes. Then follows an entry clarifying details of the arrangements made for controlling the depredations of wolves (the nineteenth "resolution").[52] The final "resolution," the twentieth, concerns "government."

Everyone who attended the wolf meetings knew that other meetings were going on at the Falls where political issues were being considered. They also realized that the focus of discussion was not government per se, but whether Oregon would remain loyal to the United States or become an independent republic. No American doubted that the Willamette Valley was American territory awaiting the technicality of actual posses-

49. Duniway and Riggs, "Archives," pp. 223–24. That is, the tenth resolution of the report. The entry noting the adoption of the tenth resolution is not a numbered paragraph, which supports the view that the numerator began his numbering from the adoption of the ninth resolution.

50. Whether or not this entry, number 20, is to be considered a formal, technical resolution is not clear in the minutes.

51. Duniway and Riggs, "Archives," pp. 223, 227.

52. *Ibid.*

sion by the United States government. Certainly there was no expectation that the lands south of the Columbia were to be turned over to England. Also of importance in light of the historical literature on the "Oregon question," no settler expressed any interest in taking "All Oregon" either for the United States or for an independent government. The idea that the wolf meeting of March 6 was the "point of conception" of the provisional government is not an inference from the available evidence, but rather an intuition or an impression drawn from the aura of the Oregon question and the legend of international rivalry in the area.

The genesis of the twentieth resolution of March 6, 1843, was not subterfuge or a hidden plan. What probably happened was that when the meeting was breaking up, someone asked: "Shall we discuss here the political matters that are being discussed at the Falls?" The numbering of resolutions at least warrants such a development, and the very starkness of the twentieth resolution gives an impression that it had attracted scant interest. The membership of the Committee of Twelve, chosen either before or after the meeting adjourned, suggests that a local discussion group, not a planning body, was in prospect. All the appointees were Champoeg residents except for Dr. Elijah White, who lived at the Falls; as United States Indian subagent, he was the only federal official in the area.[53] The members of this group, subsequently made famous by Gray as the "Committee of Twelve," were, according to Gray, the prime movers in bringing government to Oregon. But the idea seems not to have caught on. The would-be statesman was waved down.

This reconstruction of events is fictional, but the chronology suggests that it may be correct. A vitally important point is that the Committee of Twelve was not directed to meet again, though settlers' meetings in Oregon, without fail, gave committees such authority. A deleted phrase—"move that the Committee"—would suggest that an attempt to put the committee to work was scotched.[54] Gray makes his way around this difficulty by linking the May 2 meeting to the March 6 meeting. His linkage has remained unbroken for more than a century, but it is something less than firm. Gray claims that when the minutes of the May 2 meeting refer to a previous committee and a report from it, that committee was none other than the Committee of Twelve in its capacity of leader-

53. White had some property at Champoeg but he did not live on it.
54. Duniway and Riggs, "Archives," p. 226.

ship at the mid-March meeting. The extant minutes of the May 2 meeting do assuredly declare that the meeting was called "in accordance with the call of the committee, chosen at a former meeting," [55] but there is no evidence that such a call was issued by the wolf meeting of March 6 or by the Committee of Twelve at any other time. Robert Newell insisted that "no report . . . of a former Committee on wolves" was presented on May 2,[56] but the minutes of that meeting do refer to a "report" delivered by "The Committee." This report, in keeping with conspiracy theories and Gray's story,[57] has never been found. Nevertheless, it is possible at last to refute Gray and begin revising his picture of the forming of Oregon's provisional government. Robert Newell had placed one of his sons at the Methodist mission at The Dalles. Writing to the mission farmer, Henry B. Brewer, from Fort Vancouver on March 18, 1843, the mountain man gave his account of local affairs.[58] He described a meeting that is obviously the mid-March meeting, the one that generated the "report" referred to in the May 2 minutes. Newell wrote that "the citizens of this colony had a public meeting a short time since at the Falls and discussed the wants of the people and a majority is in favor of forming a code of laws and resolved that a governor, three magistrates, three constables, one sheriff, one colonel with subaltern officers be elected and on the 2nd Tuesday of May next a meeting will be held to nominate and make laws and enforce the same." [59] It was at the same mid-March meeting that a majority voted to make the settlements an independent republic. This move was checked by a resolution presented by George Abernethy, secular agent of the Oregon mission, which called for postponement of independence for four years,

55. *Ibid.*, p. 236; Gray, *History,* pp. 268–69.

56. Newell to Evans, August 8, 1867, Evans Papers.

57. Gray, *History,* p. 279. Compare Hussey, *Champoeg,* p. 152.

58. Robert Newell to H. B. Brewer, Vancouver, March 18, 1843, Brewer Collection, WSHS.

59. *Ibid.* The meeting was held on May 2, the first Tuesday in May. Since this letter was written from Fort Vancouver, it is reasonable to suppose that McLoughlin got his information from Newell. McLoughlin wrote Governor Simpson on the 20th that the March meeting at the Falls had taken place on the 17th and the proposed meeting was to take place on May 12. John McLoughlin to Simpson, Vancouver, March 20, 1843, in Robert C. Clark, *History of the Willamette Valley* (3 vols.; Chicago, 1927), I, 793–94. My guess is that Newell somehow fused Tuesday and Tuesday the second, to come up with the second Tuesday in May. How McLoughlin came upon his dates is unclear although he may simply have forgotten what Newell told him. The recurrence of the number two in all these variations might suggest a connected series of communication miscues.

during which time the United States would be given the opportunity to take the settlers under its wing.[60]

The Abernethy resolution and Newell's letter to Brewer clarify much that has formerly been obscure. The question of whether or not to include a governor in the proposed government was raised, not in March as Gray said, but at the meeting on May 2. This again is a fundamental distinction and it completely reorients the traditional picture. One of the first things done at Champoeg on May 2 was to decide that "we should have no Governor." [61] Gray, on the other hand, insisted that the matter of a governor had been raised at the mid-March meeting, when "blockhead" White said he would be governor or else.[62] White may have made such a pronouncement, but the Newell letter states clearly that a governor's office was agreed to in mid-March and that elections would be held in May. Reliance upon Newell instead of Gray, personalities aside, is required by the logic of surrounding evidence and by the logic of events as well. Gray is not telling the truth.

Gray recounts how the Committee of Twelve met at the Falls "by *mutual* understanding . . . about the middle of March, 1843." [63] We know through Newell, however, that he and "the Frenchman" referred to in the minutes of the March 6 meeting, along with two other nominated committeemen, Dr. White and Ira Babcock, took no part in any of this committee's conferences, if indeed there ever were any. If, as Gray also maintains, these four men were assigned to the Committee of Twelve for reasons of "prudence," what exactly could have been the "mutual understanding" among the twelve members of the committee since the prudence Gray refers to is that these four committee members did not know what he and his conspiring cohorts were up to? [64] Gray so thickened his plot that he confused and contradicted himself. The affairs of the Falls "were known," he says, "to the getters-up of the 'Wolf Organization.' . . . In fact LeBreton had participated in the discussions at the Wallamett Falls, and reported them to those of us in the valley." [65] LeBreton,

60. George Abernethy to W. H. Gray, Portland, March 11, 1866, printed in Gray, *History*, p. 269.

61. Newell to Evans, August 8, 1867, Evans Papers.

62. Gray, *History*, p. 269. "The main question at issue before the committee at the Falls meeting was the office of governor."

63. *Ibid.*, p. 268. Italics added.

64. *Ibid.*, p. 267. It is Gray who asserts that Babcock and White were not present.

65. *Ibid.*, p. 261.

the recorder elected in February 1841, probably did attend meetings at the Falls as well as the wolf meetings, but there was no need for any spying on his part. Gray knew this, of course, since he also attended meetings in both places and avers, eight pages after recording LeBreton's undercover activities, that the entire Committee of Twelve attended the mid-March meeting at the Falls![66] Gray's conspiracy is imaginary. Meshing the wolf meetings, the Falls meetings, and the May 2 meeting in a specious continuity, let alone merging them into a patriotic conspiracy to save Oregon, has distorted the real lines of cleavage and action in the spring of 1843. The major issue, the divisive one, concerned the kind of government that ought to be established. The government idea became a matter of debate because of the independence advocates who sought to promote their cause early in 1843. There was no ground swell of popular interest in government, and, as the following chapters explain, the Methodist missionaries certainly did not initiate the proposal in 1843.

That the central political question was the allegiance of a prospective government is also clear from the issues that occupied voters on May 2 at Champoeg. By that time the issue was plainly not if a government was to be formed—that had been decided in March—but what direction it would take. The terms of conflict, set in mid-March, were independence versus nonindependence. These terms, defining practical political possibilities, focused upon the relative strength of the new government. Not surprisingly, the major questions of May 2 were whether the new government should have a governor and the powers to tax. The proindependence faction favored such proposals; others opposed them.[67] Although the independence forces had managed to bring the government idea to life in 1843, the settlers made sure the regime that was actually created was low key. They outlawed taxes and insisted that there be no governor. In place of a chief executive a three-man executive committee was agreed on. The reason for having a committee instead of a governor, Gray claims, was to placate the antigovernment forces, but all other contemporary observers, including Robert Shortess, the sage Jesse Applegate, and Robert Newell, recognized that the real purpose was to avoid the appearance of having set up an independent government.[68] Gray noted, however, that Ira Babcock

---

66. *Ibid.*, p. 269.

67. Newell to Evans, August 8, 1867, Evans Papers. "At the first mass meeting in Oregon the People voted that we should have no Governor nor pay a tax. . . ."

68. For Newell see *ibid.* Gray (*History*, p. 349) admits Shortess favored the executive

opposed the executive committee because it looked "too much like a per-manent and independent government"! [69]

The executive committee was created not just because a patriot such as Robert Newell wanted to dispel the suspicion of independence in the new government. Many opposed independence for more practical consider-ations, reflecting differing views about government among settlers and special-interest groups. There were, as Robert Newell sagaciously de-tected, two contesting wings at Champoeg on May 2,[70] and it was compromise that finally gave birth to the executive committee. An argu-ment between Gustavus Hines and Newell reveals the nature of the com-promise. On July 5, 1843, the day the Organic Laws were to be approved by the settlers, Hines delivered himself of a lengthy diatribe against the executive committee, calling it a hydra-headed monster. Newell begged Hines to change the subject lest "all . . . fall to the ground before he got through speaking." [71] Newell's plea was based on the understanding that the executive committee was the bond that had brought the two wings together on May 2.[72]

David Hill, a member of the executive committee, favored the Gray, or strong-government, wing. Alanson Beers of the mission farm in the Wil-lamette Valley had Newell's vote for the small-government forces. Joseph Gale, the third member of the committee, represented the farmers, in-cluding Robert Shortess, chief author of the Organic Laws, who opposed taxation, though their interests and their anglophobia aligned them with Gray's wing. In 1844 Gale, still fighting the battles of 1843, told tax collector Joseph Meek that he would pay no taxes.[73]

The wolf meetings did not lead to the May 2 meeting. The mid-March

---

committee, and Applegate, writing of Shortess and the Organic Laws, states that the pur-pose of the committee was to avoid the appearance of independence, implying that Shortess favored the executive committee for that reason. See Applegate, *Views of Oregon History,* p. 39.

69. Gray, *History,* p. 349.

70. Newell to Evans, August 8, 1867, Evans Papers.

71. *Ibid.* Hines is a complex figure in many respects. He wrote the letter to the Mis-sionary Board in 1843 condemning Lee's administration at the same time that he be-friended Lee by caring for his daughter. In 1845 he wrote the board once more, this time condemning Abernethy. There is good reason to suspect that he was a tyro in his political opinions. His support for Dr. White and his criticism of Lee and Abernethy, both of whom disliked White, suggest that perhaps he had some hopes for office.

72. Robert Newell to editor, *Oregon Herald,* October 25, 1866, Box 1, Evans Papers.

73. Leslie M. Scott, ed., "Oregon Tax Roll, 1844," *OHQ* 31 (1930): 16.

meeting at the Falls, which did summon the May meeting, turned upon the abstract question of the new government's allegiance. In practical terms this question was reflected in the major dispute at Champoeg on May 2 concerning the degree of power the government should have. The wolf meetings were exactly what they purported to be—meetings to deal with wolves. In fairness to Gray it should be pointed out that Newell overdid his criticism of the meeting's leaders. All of them, he said, "save Oneille," had no livestock to protect and no experience with firearms even if such were needed. But Gray and Shortess both had stock to protect,[74] and Hill, though not listed in White's census of 1842, also had some, according to a local census of 1844.[75] Although Gray may indeed have been "a Pink," as Newell claimed, the mountain man was not above a little friendly dissembling of his own. His views of government were not alone motivated by his opposition to independence.

Newell said that he and the mountain men of Tualatin Plains first saw the wisdom of an organization for keeping law and order in 1842, when the house of Mr. Littlejohn, an independent missionary, was broken into by an Indian,[76] who took "all the contents including his [Littlejohn's] and his wife's clothing bedding &c." [77] Newell, William Dougherty, Caleb Wilkins, John Smith Griffin, and Joseph Meek apprehended the culprit and brought him to justice. The story is no doubt true, but Newell's comment that it led him and others to consider an organization merely for an "understanding as to how was best to act in" similar cases omits more than it conveys.[78] Just as the theft of Methodist goods in 1841 had stirred mission efforts to control Catholic influence, as well as to protect Methodists, so the Littlejohn affair prodded Newell into finding ways to turn government to profitable effect. Newell was not so much interested in moral influence as were Methodist missionaries. When he started thinking about government, his mind turned from mere protection against criminals to the incorporation of towns, the sale of government ferry contracts, and other matters of interest to an enterprising man of the world.

74. Elijah White, "Census Report," *Annual Report of Elijah White,* Letters Received by the Office of Indian Affairs, 1824–1881, Oregon Superintendency, 1842–1880, NAM, 234, roll 607, frames 112–19. Gray had twelve horses and forty-four cows; Shortess had eleven horses and twenty-seven cows.

75. Scott, "Oregon Tax Roll, 1844," p. 17.

76. Newell to Evans, August 8, 1867, Evans Papers.

77. *Ibid.*

78. *Ibid.*

Newell had been living at the Falls for about a year when the mid-March meeting agreed to form a government. Quietly arranging to exchange some property with a new and energetic immigrant named Walter Pomeroy, Newell made up his mind to return to Champoeg.[79] Like John McLoughlin, Newell subscribed to the theory that, though the Falls was growing daily in importance and population, Champoeg would eventually become the leading settlement south of the Columbia River.[80] As Newell prepared to return to Champoeg, McLoughlin discovered that his own favorable opinion of this location had revived. The Chief Factor began to plan business projects for Champoeg, mixing, as always, his own personal affairs with those of the company.[81] While McLoughlin and Newell were contemplating new investments in the spring of 1843, the Methodists in Oregon found the world growing increasingly inhospitable to their interests.

At the mid-March meeting the Methodists were confronted with Lansford W. Hastings's proposal that the Oregon country become an independent republic. Hastings, a freewheeling frontiersman, had been in Oregon for less than a year and had drawn little attention from the mission. But the independence movement was widely supported, and the Hastings resolution favoring independence had been accepted by a majority in mid-March. Although it was successfully countered by George Abernethy's resolution postponing independence for four years, the missionaries were made painfully aware how close Oregon had come to being cut off from the United States. In Lee's view, an independent Oregon was an intolerable idea. Furthermore, Hastings was John McLoughlin's lawyer and was therefore trying to beat the mission out of its Falls claim. Lee, who was in debt to his chief antagonist, John McLoughlin, learned, at the same time Hastings advocated independence, that the board in New York was not going to send him the money he needed to get out of debt. The Falls had become the mission's lifeblood, as Lee saw it; it was an integral part of the mission's moral influence. The importance of the mill site at the Falls was part of a situation that transformed the missionary dilemma. Unfriendly critics of Methodism might be inclined to prefer the word "evade" to "transform," but in fact there was no evasion. The transformation was

79. Hussey, *Champoeg*, pp. 107–8.
80. John McLoughlin to Governor Simpson, Fort Vancouver, March 3, 1845, printed in Hussey, *Champoeg*, p. 198.
81. See chapter 8.

part of a deeper and less accessible gray area of the evangelical enterprise, where the religious and the profane ran together. If the political elements implicit in the goal of world conversion were buried deep in Methodism, the politics of personal conversion lay just beneath the surface of the experiences every Methodist knew.

Lee had discovered in his own life and in observing the lives of others that conversion was primarily a matter of consent. In describing his own conversion, Lee employed the familiar language of American political discourse: he had been "ushered into the liberty of the Children of God. I was now, by my own consent, the property of another, and his glory and not my own was the object of my pursuit." [82] Indians, however, did not willingly give consent to regeneration. Nor did they withhold consent, as many missionaries pointed out. They simply did not seem to care. To convert Indians Lee relied entirely on the belief that God's miraculous power could save sinners. But he also hoped—the hope was surreptitious and almost wayward—that he might induce salvation by preparing the heathen for the work of God's miracles through tinkering slightly with the environment. God's grace alone, assisted by the preacher's exhortation and concern, was ultimately the only acceptable means of salvation. But the fact that Indians were not really changed by their occasional conversion experiences was disconcerting.

Although failure did not shake Lee's faith in God and in His power to save, it did shake his faith in his own powers as a preacher. Lee's failure pushed him to adopt "other methods" to save the Indians, even while seeking to preserve the central ideas and the old, purely religious methods. The Falls claim controversy, for example, was a contest for power and authority; in a word, it was a political endeavor. But because evangelism was dedicated to eliminating politics, Lee chose not to regard his secular missionary efforts as political. The Missionary Society in New York took a different view; insisting that Lee had contravened the meaning of religious life, it dismissed him because of his secular activities. Lee had certainly not betrayed evangelical principles; on the contrary, he had followed them closely. More than exhortation was needed to achieve the conversion of the world; power and authority were also required. Lee was discharged before he could accomplish very much, and in truth he was too simple a soul to make much headway in a difficult situation. He directly pursued the evan-

82. Jason Lee, "Diary," *OHQ* 17 (1916): 408.

gelical ideal and his secular concerns expose some of the ideal's deepest contradictions. Lee's life in Oregon also helps to clarify, to some extent, how the egalitarian ethos underwent a series of transformations.

Lee was forced to grapple openly with political, secular matters. Easterners could dismiss him for dirtying his hands, just as they could dismiss political meanings of evangelism along with partyism and partisanship. Methodists strove with other Americans to find and maintain the ways of righteousness. They were usually more successful than others with the same objective because they were more committed to the task. For them, it was a holy as well as an ethical imperative. To some observers antipartyism was a pose assumed by jealous clerics who found themselves unable to compete with politicians for the allegiance of American voters; [83] to others it was a self-deluding hypocrisy directed ultimately toward disguised hopes of social control for the sake of a special interest or class.[84] Although sectarian jealousy of politicians and a wish to control things may have been factors in the evangelical movement, they are probably not peculiarly Methodist traits, and their assessment is better fitted perhaps to sociological or anthropological analysis than to historical probing. The historical element in Lee's experience was the drive, not to ensure social control or to compete with politicians for a constituency, but to achieve equality for America's sake and for Christ's sake.

83. For example, Bertram Wyatt-Brown, "Prelude to Abolitionism: Sabbatarian Politics and the Rise of the Second Party System,"*JAH* 57 (1971): 316–41.

84. John L. Thomas, "Romantic Reform in America, 1815–1865," *American Quarterly* 17 (1965): 656–81. This dispute among historians is summarized in Lois W. Banner, "Religious Benevolence as Social Control: A Critique of American Interpretations,"*JAH* 60 (1973): 23–41.

CHAPTER 7

Moral Influence and Economic Monopoly

> I hope no time will be lost in making arrangements
> with some house in London, that we may, at least, be
> able to pay the Com. a year from next March. . . . We
> cannot *depend* on Vancouver.
> —JASON LEE to corresponding secretary,
> September 23, 1841

*J*ASON LEE first became aware of the problems of power, authority, and control in the early months of 1837. For him as for other Methodists the disapprobation of party and of politics was much more than a ritual; it was an integral part of the evangelical world view. The secular ventures of the mission were joined to the business of making Christians, and the whole was imbued with aspirations to harmony. If conflict and the corruption of politicians were indications of man's fallen state, so economic power, if it lessened competition and decreased the influence of politicians, could be turned to religious ends.

While honesty compelled Lee to inform Willbur Fisk and others in the East that two years of Methodism on heathen soil had brought not even one Indian to God, he could also say, just as truthfully, that "we have not spent our strength entirely for naught." Lee, referring to the Temperance Society he had organized in February 1836, informed his eastern brethren, eagerly awaiting news of converted heathen, that if the "temperance reformation succeed," that outcome was enough, for the moment, to make "crossing the Rocky Mountains" worthwhile.[1] In less than a year's time, however, even this modest reformation was threatened. Temperance reform was a fundamental part of Lee's struggle with the missionary dilemma. Achieving it in Oregon, he believed, would save the mission. When he discovered that temperance was endangered by a plan to build a

1. Lee to Fisk, March 15, 1836, Cornelius J. Brosnan, *Jason Lee: Prophet of the New Oregon* (New York, 1932), pp. 78–80; quotation on p. 79.

distillery at the base of the Chehalem Mountains, he organized a community response. Therein lay the real beginnings of government in Oregon. The episode indicates the changing tone and direction of Lee's Oregon career and suggests as well the effects of mission affairs on life in the settlements.

Rumors that Lawrence Carmichael and Ewing Young were planning to build a distillery across the river from the mission and slightly to the north were circulating in the valley during the fall and early winter of 1836. By January 1837 Lee had won support for a petition asking the two men to give up their enterprise. The petition was backed by all segments of the community including the Hudson's Bay Company. Young and Carmichael, chastened and no doubt surprised by the strength of the opposition, agreed to halt their project "for the present." [2] Purser William Slacum of the United States Navy, who offered to take Young and others to California to buy cattle, was undoubtedly a factor in the decision to abandon the idea of liquor manufacture. But the real reason for the success of the petition was that most settlers were dependent upon the supply and market functions of the Hudson's Bay Company. Thus it was not the legendary intercession of Slacum with McLoughlin on Young's behalf which convinced Young to quit the distillery business. To be sure, the company did refuse to sell supplies to Young for a short period (for reasons to be discussed later), but McLoughlin had been ready to lift the ban in late 1835 before Slacum appeared on the scene. Rather, what discouraged Young was the silent intercession of the company in all settler affairs, for the company, as the source of supply, was also the source of what Lee called "moral influence."

With the tension caused by the distillery project relieved, all elements in the Oregon country joined together to form the Willamette Cattle Company. Tranquillity returned to the settlements as Slacum's brig *Loriot* sailed for California with the new company's eleven-man cattle-buying group on board. The expedition was under the command of Ewing

2. Ewing Young and Lawrence Carmichael to the Oregon Temperance Society, Willamette, January 13, 1837, C. H. Carey, "The Mission Record Book of the Methodist Episcopal Church, Willamette Station, Oregon Territory, North America, Commenced 1834," *OHQ* 23 (1922): 251. The original document is at the Board of Missions, New York, and differs at several points, some of them significant, from the edited version used here. The transcription of the other documents in the distillery affair are accurate. See also "Slacum's Report on Oregon, 1836–7," *OHQ* 13 (1912): 211–13.

Young.[3] For Lee the looming catastrophe of liquor production was averted, at least "for the present." In little more than a year Lee left for the United States with another petition, this one addressed to the federal government. It was drawn by Lee and copied by Philip L. Edwards, who had since returned from California with the cattle company's representatives and more than 600 head of cattle.

Once in the East, Lee found himself among statesmen and government officials. Of these the most interesting and important was Caleb Cushing, a political maverick whose career touched upon all the controversial questions of the day. As a member of a mercantile family from Newburyport, Massachusetts, he was interested in the Northwest because he had long been concerned with the China trade.[4] In 1839 he was a member of Congress and had been assigned to the House Foreign Affairs Committee. Cushing asked Jason Lee to draft a formal letter for use in a forthcoming report on the Oregon country. Lee's dealings with Cushing were tied to his experiences with Young.

Ewing Young arrived in the Willamette Valley in October 1834 with a motley band of companions. Hall Jackson Kelley, an Oregon booster from Cambridge, Massachusetts, was a member of the group. Winslow Anderson, a free Negro whose death-dealing blow to the Indian Cockstock in 1844 focused attention on the need for law and order, was another. The group had left California with horses and mules and numbered in its ranks some men "with a character not of the best," known to be horse thieves.[5] In fact, Governor José Figueroa of California sent a letter to the Chief Fac-

3. The most important fact about this trip was that it gave employment to a number of individuals. The cattle, 830 head purchased and 200 lost on the trip back from California, were not of lasting importance. See "Copy of a Document Found among the Private Papers of the late Dr. John McLoughlin," *TOPA* (Salem, 1881), pp. 51–52; HBS, IV, 216 (E. E. Rich, ed., *The Letters of John McLoughlin from Fort Vancouver to the Governor and Committee*, 1st ser. [Toronto, 1941]). H. H. Bancroft, *History of Oregon*, Vols. XXIX–XXX of *Works* (San Francisco, 1886–88), XXIX, 138–50. Mission Record Book, p. 26, Board of Missions, New York.

4. Cushing wrote on the back of his notes taken during his talk with Lee: "No cotton has ever been planted whether it would grow or not." Caleb Cushing, "Notes with Rev. Jason Lee," container 220, Cushing Papers, OHS. For a summary of his view of the possible connection between Oregon and China see Richard E. Welch, Jr., "Caleb Cushing's Chinese Mission and the Treaty of Wanghia: A Review," *OHQ* 57 (1958): 328–57.

5. Bancroft, *History*, XXIX, 90. On Kelley see Fred W. Powell, *Hall Jackson Kelley on Oregon* (Princeton, 1932); F. G. Young, ed., "The Correspondence and Journals of Captain Nathaniel Wyeth, 1831–6," *Sources of the History of Oregon* (Eugene, 1899), p. 12; HBS, IV, 127.

tor of the Hudson's Bay Company condemning the entire group as thieves. McLoughlin could not risk trading with Young and his party for fear of receiving stolen goods until Governor Figueroa's charges were clarified.

McLoughlin told Lee and the French Canadians about Figueroa's letter, but softened the accusation by adding that "Mr. Young had been met by our people in their trapping excursions and . . .[they] always found him . . . an honest upright man." Young chafed at the restriction imposed upon him by McLoughlin, though others in his party were willing to accept it. Having left California with high hopes for Oregon, Young was eager to make a beginning once he had landed there. The Chief Factor's willingness to "let [the immigrants] have what they demanded" as a gift until the question of thievery could be laid to rest meant that trade and the development of capital and resources would have to be postponed. Young tried to avoid delay by evading McLoughlin's proscription. Late in 1835 or early in 1836 one of the company's trappers, an American, came to McLoughlin with a large quantity of furs. As the Chief Factor recorded it, the trapper

> expressed . . . doubts of its all being his. When he told me some of it was Mr. Young's who wished him to get certain articles which he wanted, I gave the articles but would not take the Furs, and desired him to take them with my compliments to Mr. Young and to tell him privately, that I sent him the articles he demanded which I requested him to accept as while these accusations remained against him, I could not take any Furs or anything else from him. The bearer of my message instead of what I told him exclaimed before all the People "Mr. McLoughlin won't take your Furs, and sends them back to you, but sends you the things you requested." Which Young considered as an insult.[6]

Although Young was cleared of the charge of horse stealing by 1836 at the latest, he had no dealings with the company until he returned from California in 1837 at the head of the Willamette Cattle Company.

The incident McLoughlin recounted took place when "Mr. [Nathaniel] Wyeth was trading" at Fort William on Sauvies Island, located at the junction of the Willamette and Columbia rivers northwest of the company's fort. Young "might have had his supplies" from Wyeth,

6. HBS, VII, 277 (E. E. Rich, ed., *The Letters of John McLoughlin from Fort Vancouver to the Governor and Committee,* 3d ser. [Toronto, 1944]).

McLoughlin pointed out, implying that Young and Wyeth did not trade.[7] Young, however, was in close touch with Courtney M. Walker, Wyeth's agent at Fort William, headquarters of Wyeth's erstwhile Columbia River Fishing and Trading Company. This enterprise, lacking all the essential ingredients for success except Wyeth's own gumption, had closed down in the spring of 1836. McLoughlin took the precaution of buying off Wyeth's agent Walker, who had been equipped with traps by the American as a ruse, McLoughlin believed, "to go about and acquire a knowledge of the Country Which would be of Great use to Wyeth if he comes back to oppose us again." [8] Paying Walker a higher salary than his duties merited, McLoughlin sent him off to Nisqually and Young was left high and dry with no one to barter with for supplies except the company, with which he was now welcome, but unwilling, to trade.

Events proved that McLoughlin should have used the money he paid out for Walker's salary to buy the American trader's leftover equipment, for it was Young's acquisition of a pickling caldron, almost certainly obtained from Wyeth, which won him the necessary measure of independence. With this slim margin of real capital, Young proposed to set himself up as a supplier, and therefore as a market, in opposition to the company. The supply he planned to offer was liquor, distilled in his caldron. Young's enterprise dovetailed conveniently with his occupational preferences, his prejudices, and his desire to be independent of the company. Young was different from most other settlers in the valley, French as well as American, in that he raised practically no wheat. Consequently he did not need the company as a market for his labor. Furthermore, wheat was the decisive factor in the spirited contest between the forces of temperance and the Young-Carmichael partnership. In fact, wheat was fundamental to all aspects of life in the settlements. As wheat is basic to

7. *Ibid.,* p. 278.

8. HBS, IV, 171. Young's most recent biographer, Kenneth Holmes, says that wheat was the most important crop in Oregon, as it was, and that it was as important to Young as to others. As evidence for this assertion he cites White's census of 1842 to the effect that Young had "150 acres of wheat." This is either a mistake or a misprint. White's census credits Young with 150 bushels (not acres) of wheat, a poor man's portion in 1842. Moreover, White's census does not say that Young had 75 acres of wheat under cultivation, as Holmes implies, but that he had 75 acres of land "under improvement." The outstanding fact about Young in White's census is that he had 400 horses and 600 head of cattle. No other individual had anything like these numbers of livestock. See Kenneth L. Holmes, *Ewing Young, Master Trapper* (Portland, 1967), p. 140. "Census Report," *Annual Report of Elijah White,* NAM, 234, frame 114.

an understanding of the distillery project, so the demise of the distillery project is essential to an understanding of the political developments of 1842–43.

By November 1836 McLoughlin was ready to justify his policies in the Willamette in light of their relationship to wheat production and trade. It was his plan that retired company employees be permitted to remain in the Oregon country. At first Simpson and the London committee thought little of this idea, but by 1836 the resettlement of retired company personnel in the Willamette Valley had become a standard practice. Yet the company's policy, reflecting political factors in England, was erratic.[9] One of McLoughlin's arguments in favor of allowing discharged company people to settle in the valley was his belief that they would remain loyal to and dependent upon the company in an agricultural area that was bound to become American territory. This plan committed him, just as much as it compelled the retired employees, to trade in wheat.

Ironically, the company, or rather the Chief Factor, soon became more dependent upon the wheat growers than the Willamette farmers were dependent upon the market and supply functions of the company. When McLoughlin advised the London office on November 16, 1836, that the company "might Make [grain] a Branch of our Business—confer a Benefit on these men and Raise a population which would join us in opposition to that which is likely to come," [10] he ensured his own involvement along with that of the company in the economic and political life of an area England would never enter and where the company could not remain. Protection of company property from American "predators" forced McLoughlin to take wheat grown in the Willamette and to sell supplies for fear, as he believed, of being attacked. Here was an example of a modification of

9. Frederick Merk, *Fur Trade and Empire: George Simpson's Journal* (rev. ed.; Cambridge, 1968), p. 201. Following the suggestions of the governor and committee, James Douglas urged the Willamette settlers to move to Cowlitz, but they were unwilling to go. Douglas to governor and committee, Fort Vancouver, October 18, 1838, HBS, IV, 240. In March 1842 Simpson continued the committee's policy of discouraging retired company employees from settling south of the Columbia. Simpson to McLoughlin, Honolulu, March 1, 1842, HBS, VI, 271 (E. E. Rich, ed., *The Letters of John McLoughlin from Fort Vancouver to the Governor and Committee*, 2d ser. [Toronto, 1943]). But in September of 1843 the governor and committee reversed their position and advised McLoughlin to encourage employees to settle in the Willamette Valley. Governor and committee to John McLoughlin, London, September 27, 1843. *Ibid.*, p. 313.

10. McLoughlin to governor and committee, Fort Vancouver, November 16, 1836, HBS, IV, 174.

policies forced upon the company by the uncertainty of the boundary. The usual procedure was simply to take wheat from the settlers and sell them supplies in order to ward off competitors.[11]

McLoughlin's early plan to use the company's retired employees to settle the fertile Willamette Valley was based on recognition that the area would be settled quickly. Buying the settlers' wheat was also a logical step and made a virtue of necessity. In time, however, the Chief Factor became prisoner to his own power. In 1839, after the Hudson's Bay Company agreed to ship wheat to the Russian American Fur Company in Archangel, interdependence between company and wheat grower on the Willamette became stronger.[12] Wanting to use the Columbia department to advantage, the company established the agricultural program involving sale of wheat to the Russians. This plan conflicted with the initial hope of the London directors to keep company people out of the Willamette Valley. The demands of the wheat contract in 1839, together with political factors in England, brought a change in policy concerning French-Canadian settlers in the Willamette Valley. Retired employees were now encouraged to remain.

In any event, the company's policy of discouraging settlement south of the Columbia had never been successful. The Frenchmen already there did not leave or sell out to the oncoming Americans, as the company originally had hoped they would. The additional wheat anticipated from the company's Puget Sound Agricultural Company, also begun in 1839,

11. The fears of McLoughlin, Douglas, and Simpson of American acts of violence were perfectly genuine, but while occasional fanatics made threats to attack the company, the Americans were never the dangerous renegades company officials often assumed. The company's directors in London were more responsible for the trepidation of their officials than the Americans. After the arrival of Elijah White in Oregon in the fall of 1842, the governor and committee included the area south of the Columbia as a part of the "disputed territory," thereby altering their views about settling that vicinity with supposedly pro-British retired company employees. They believed, incorrectly, that "the meetings . . . and petitions got up at the Walamet" were hostile to British interests by design. Frances Victor later shared this view, and she relied heavily on Hudson's Bay Company authorities. See governor and committee to John McLoughlin, London, September 27, 1843, HBS, VI, 313.

12. HBS, X, 85–86 (E. E. Rich, ed., *Simpson's 1828 Journey to the Columbia: Part of Dispatch from George Simpson, Esqr., Governor of Rupert's Land, to the Governor and Committee of the Hudson's Bay Company, London, March 1, 1829, Continued and Completed March 24 and June 5, 1829* [Toronto, 1947]). John S. Galbraith, *The Hudson's Bay Company as an Imperial Factor, 1821–1869* (Berkeley and Los Angeles, 1957), p. 195. HBS, VI, xi–xii, 196, 209, 230, 299, 400.

could not compensate for the loss that would have been entailed if the company did not take Willamette wheat.[13] But there was never any thought of refusing to take the settlers' wheat, because McLoughlin, and company men generally, believed that such a course of action would bring violent reprisals from the farmers. Wheat bound McLoughlin and the settlers together. Oddly and, where McLoughlin was concerned, typically, the company itself was more flexible. Predictably, McLoughlin's personal interests became immersed in those of the company, so that his links south of Fort Vancouver grew stronger as the company's power there grew weaker. And naturally the wheat nexus became more complex as the settlements grew. The situation spelled trouble for McLoughlin.

Growing complexity was reflected in changes in the relationships of wheat grower, shipper, supplier, and miller. Towns began to emerge with competing interests. Of these the first and most important were Willamette Falls and Champoeg. Growth and change had been implicit in 1837 when the economic power of the company compelled Ewing Young to forgo his distillery project. Young knew perfectly well that the majority of his companions of 1834 were no more teetotalers than were the French Canadians, around whose homesites researchers continue to dig up the evidence of heavy liquor consumption.[14] But he had not fully analyzed the consequences of his desire for independence on others, whatever they might think of alcohol. He soon learned. There was also a lesson for Jason Lee in the distillery experience. It was simply that his powers were very limited and the mission was gravely imperiled as a result.

Lee's response to the rumor about the distillery was immediate and im-

---

13. On the Puget Sound Agricultural Company see E. E. Rich, *Hudson's Bay Company* (3 vols.; New York, 1961), III, 686–87; Galbraith, *Imperial Factor*, pp. 193–96. As of 1843 the largest percentage of company wheat for sale and for use came from the Willamette settlers. The crop at Vancouver was 3,000 bushels; at Puget Sound it was 5,000. "We expect from Settlers" 10,000. McLoughlin to governor and committee, November 15, 1843, HBS, VI, 125.

14. See Harriet D. Munnick, "The Transition Decades on French Prairie, 1830–1850," *Marion County History* 4 (1958): 41. "Whatever their motive in signing the petition against the distillery of their friend, Ewing Young, it could not have been a love of temperance *per se,* because the quantity of liquor bottles they left is prodigious." F. N. Blanchet forbade his parishioners from having anything to do with the Temperance Society after his arrival. His reasons were both religious ("there is more virtue in the practice of it") and political. Blanchet to Elijah White, February 1, 1840, PAA, in L. M. Lyons, *Francis Norbert Blanchet and the Founding of the Oregon Missions, 1838–1848* (Washington, 1940), pp. 79–80; quotation on p. 79.

pulsive and, as it turned out, decisive. He called a meeting of the Temperance Society, enlisting in its ranks such unlikely opponents of the "desolating scourge" as John Howard, whose notoriety as a drinking man was a byword. Seven Frenchmen joined Lee's society. Eight more inhabitants, five of them French Canadians, supported the petition to Young and Carmichael of January 2, 1837, but did not become members of the society. The petitioners asked that the still be disbanded "forever." [15] But Lee could hardly have fooled himself into believing that it was his petition that stopped Young. He knew it would take more than preaching to keep liquor out of the Willamette Valley; he had to meet the threat with legal instruments, for no one had to tell him that appeals to divine laws would not move the likes of Ewing Young. Lee, believing that the solution was to be sought in legal or administrative terms, not political ones,[16] looked to the federal government for help.

The fundamental emphasis in Lee's petition against the distillery is that American law strictly regulated the sale of liquor to Indians and provided severe sanctions for lawbreakers. Lee listed four reasons for discontinuing the manufacture of ardent spirits "to be sold in this vicinity" in order of importance to him, and in what must be supposed was the reverse order of effectiveness on Young. First, the "vending of spiritous liquors . . . [would] paralyse our efforts for the promotion of temperance." Second, the prosperity of the settlement would be "materially affected by . . . [a distillery] both as respects . . . temporal and spiritual welfare." Third, the Indian "will be made far more" wretched than he is already. Finally, almost as an afterthought, the petitioners suggested that the distillers could hardly be "ignorant that the laws of the United States prohibit American citizens from selling ardent spirits to Indians under the penalty of a heavy fine." [17]

Two years later Lee was in the United States. Writing from the home of Willbur Fisk on January 17, 1839, to Congressman Caleb Cushing, Lee noted that it would be "especially desirable that the introduction of ardent spirits into the country . . . be prevented. These, as all know, are ruinous to the white man and the Indian." The best way to deal with mercenary and evil-minded persons trading in ardent spirits would be to require the "establishment of wholesome laws to regulate our infant but rising

15. Carey, "Mission Record Book," p. 249.
16. For a further discussion of Lee's social and political views see chapter 8.
17. Carey, "Mission Record Book," p. 249.

settlements." Only Congress, Lee was certain, could provide such laws. Oregon needed "two things at the hand of Government for . . . protection and prosperity . . . [first] a guarantee from Government that the possession of the land we take up, and the improvements we make upon it, will be secured to us . . . should the Indian title ever be extinguished." He claimed he was sure that the "pioneers in this arduous work will be liberally dealt with," though of course he was most unsure. The second item required from the United States was "the authority and protection of the Government and laws of the United States to regulate the intercourse of the settlers with each other, to protect them against the peculations and aggressions of the Indians, and to protect the Indians against the aggressions of the white settlers." Both objects could be secured without "much of a military force . . . [because] the settlers would sustain, [the authority of] a suitable person . . . sent out as a civil magistrate and governor of the territory." [18] As proof of his contention Lee offered the Memorial of March 1838 which he had brought from the Willamette; it was signed by thirty-six settlers, fifteen short of the total male population.[19] In petitioning Ewing Young in 1837 Lee had said that legal restraints already existing in the United States were adequate to prevent Young from entering the liquor business. In discussions with federal lawmakers in 1839, Lee made every effort to impress them with the "commercial advantages" of the Oregon country. Explicit in Lee's petition to Young and in his eastern discussions was the assumption that economic power had definite religious and moral dimensions.

The petition of March 16, 1838, is the clearest and most complete statement Lee ever made of his political philosophy. A basic clue to his behavior in later years, it is also vital to an understanding of his first four years in Oregon and to the Cushing letter of 1839. After pointing out Oregon's "happy position for trade with China, India, and the western

18. Jason Lee to Caleb Cushing, Middletown, January 17, 1839, U.S. Congress, House, Report no. 101, 25th Cong., 3d sess., 1839, Appendix H, pp. 3–4. Compare Lee's approach to that of F. P. Tracy of the Oregon Emigration Society who found that Joel Poinsett, secretary of war, was not eager to make any promises about the United States government's future disposition of lands in the Northwest. *Oregonian and Indian's Advocate* 5 (1839): 3.

19. U.S. Congress, Senate, *Petition to the Honorable the Senate and House of Representatives of the United States of America, March 16, 1838,* S. Doc. 154, 25th Cong., 3d sess., 1838, pp. 1–3. The only study of this document is C. J. Brosnan, "The Signers of the Oregon Memorial of 1838," *WHQ* 24 (1933): 174–80; see also C. J. Pike, "Petitions of Oregon Settlers, 1838–48," *OHQ* 34 (1933): 216–35.

coasts of America," which by then was common knowledge in the United States, he went on to say that "the growing importance . . . of the islands of the Pacific, . . . not so generally known and appreciated," should encourage the government to "take formal and speedy possession" of the Oregon country "south of the Columbia River." The possibilities for trade, which Lee was already exploring, would become "new channels of supply," which in turn would erode the economic power of the Hudson's Bay Company, heretofore the source of "moral influence . . . [and] . . . the pledge of our safety." Continuing, Lee observed that although "our social intercourse has thus far been prosecuted with reference to feelings of honor, to the feeling of dependence on the Hudson's Bay Company, and to their moral influence . . . we cannot hope that [this influence] will continue." Like McLoughlin, Lee recognized that the company's position as sole market for the settlements was the source of its power. In addition, the "agricultural and other resources of the country cannot fail to induce emigration and commerce." [20]

He believed, as did almost everyone else, that the fertile Willamette Valley would soon attract settlers in large numbers. The petition of 1838 was one of the steps he was taking to prepare for this eventuality. McLoughlin also expected the valley to become the chief area of settlement in the near future. His objective was to ensure the company's safety and economic power by stifling the new channels of supply which Lee said must come with accelerated growth. Even while McLoughlin justified the importance of Fort Vancouver by pointing to profits from the sale of wheat and supplies, his primary responsibility was to protect the company from hostile settlers. In time Lee would be in McLoughlin's position. As Methodists began to fill the new channels of supply, the mission assumed the burdens of moral influence and the liabilities of supplier. [21] When that happened Lee found he was deserted by the home office, just as McLoughlin would be, while menacingly surrounded by unfriendly groups in Oregon.

In 1838, however, Lee's first matter of business was to ask where the replacement for the moral influence of the company was to come from when "our settlement begins to draw its supplies through other channels." Although "legal restraint" and "moral influence" were certainly not mutu-

20. Petition, March 16, 1838, S. Doc. 154.
21. George Gary, "Diary," *OHQ* 24 (1923): 176: ". . . the mission has [in 1844] the curse or rather their superintendent's Bro. Lee, for monopoly and speculation."

ally exclusive in Lee's mind, they were nevertheless distinct. In fact, it seems the two were related inversely. In the absence of the company's economic power, and therefore its moral influence, legal restraint was needed to handle "so mixed a population." [22] Such a population was bound to come to Oregon unless a code of laws discouraged would-be settlers. Lee's reasoning is circular but his meaning is clear. A code of laws and American jurisdiction were essential to ensure a law-abiding population. The implication is that American law and good citizens would replace the company's moral influence, or, put another way, a competitive economy ("new channels of supply") and a lawful community would replace, with their own moral influence, the company and its noncompetitive monopoly. On the other hand, if no laws were provided, good people would not come to Oregon, but the inevitable increase in population, tantamount to new channels of supply or competition, would require some form of restraint. The logical source of this restraint would be another monopoly.

Lee's reasoning did not rest upon a commitment to competition (new channels of supply) or monopoly (the company's moral influence), either in principle or in logic. Instead, his interest in economic matters was a reflection of his political objective. McLoughlin's thinking was just the opposite. The difference, important in a number of respects, explains much of their "misunderstandings" in 1842–43 when both were seeking control of the Falls. With the latitude men customarily grant themselves when dealing with means, not ends, Lee seemed to play fast and loose with the morality of the marketplace to achieve the higher morality of the missionary goals he hoped to fulfill. [23] By 1843, when the question of legal restraint was enlarged by Lansford Hastings to include independence, Lee wished more avidly than ever for American jurisdiction and a code of laws. He was just barely willing to tolerate some kind of interim government. [24] And in 1843, although he was more dependent on the company

---

22. Petition, March 16, 1838, S. Doc. 154.

23. A nonsectarian but sympathetic historian, Charles H. Carey, "Lee, Waller and McLoughlin," *OHQ* 32 (1931): 193–200, struggles to exonerate Lee while actually convicting him of unethical behavior.

24. William H. Gray, *A History of Oregon, 1792–1849* (Portland, 1870), pp. 268, 347, and *passim*, emphasizes Lee's position to give credibility to his conspiracy theory of the creation of the provisional government. Thus while it was the company and the Jesuits who wanted to "steal" Oregon, it was Lee and the mission who had to be coaxed into nonopposition. The fact that the Methodists were actually cool to the provisional govern-

than in 1838, it was no longer the pledge of his safety, but his most dangerous enemy.

In the East, in 1838, Lee was ready to say what people such as the Reverend F. P. Tracy of the Oregon Emigration Society wanted to hear, if it would help to bring a pious and industrious population to Oregon. Lee was equally pragmatic in appealing to Caleb Cushing for a code of laws and a governor. A law-abiding population, however created, would tend to attract good people and to repel a bad or a "mixed population." Nor did the missionary attempt to disguise his economic plans for Oregon. His 1838 petition made it quite plain that the most significant point about the well-known "fertile valleys of the Willamette and Umpqua . . . , varied with prairies and woodlands," was that all were conveniently "intersected by lateral streams, presenting facilities" for sawmills and gristmills to prepare the produce of the fertile valleys and the woodlands for use and trade.[25] Accordingly Lee saw to it that the *Lausanne* hauled milling machinery, paid for by the society, to Oregon in 1839. The project was strongly endorsed by Fisk, the eminent president of Wesleyan College, who thought the mission should build as many mills as it possibly could.[26] Lee summarized his views and the views of most Methodists when he wrote Cushing that, whereas the "exclusive object of the mission [was] the benefit of the Indian tribes west of the Rocky mountains, . . . it is [just as] necessary to cultivate the soil, erect dwelling houses, and school houses, build mills and in fact, introduce all the necessaryies and helps of a civilized colony." [27]

Just three months before leaving for the United States with the 1838 petition in hand, Jason Lee wrote the Missionary Society that

Capt. Joseph Thing who crossed the Mountains with us is to leave . . . for Boston. He talks of coming here to establish himself in Mercantile business. I think he is a very proper person for that business here, for he promises to bring no spiritous liquors. He thinks of bringing a loaded Vessel from Boston here, and then procure his supplies through a firm at Oahoo, S.I. . . . I

---

ment while sectarian interests at the time of Gray's writing were fiercely against the company accounts for much of the work's plausibility.

25. Petition, March 16, 1838, S. Doc. 154.
26. Willbur Fisk to F. P. Tracy, November 10, 1838, *Oregonian and Indian's Advocate* 2 (1838): 78.
27. Lee to Cushing, January 17, 1839.

think you would do well to make arrangements with him to have our supplies sent by the same conveyance.[28]

Such a development, along the same lines as the Willamette Cattle Company but far more extensive, was precisely the kind of "new channels of supply" Lee referred to in his petition of 1838.

McLoughlin, meanwhile, did his best to keep the mission dependent on the company store at Fort Vancouver. He asked the governor and committee to permit him to supply the missionaries "at the present or even a Lower Rate of Advance or give them freight, as if you refuse them they will get their supplies from Wahou." [29] McLoughlin was correct in his conviction that failure to give the mission special rates would drive in the entering wedge for troublesome competition. Arrangements with the Sandwich Islands were exactly what the Methodists had in mind. "If navigation opens suitably," wrote Alvan Waller in 1841, "much grain or flour may be exported from here to the Islands in a few years." [30]

The governor and committee of the Hudson's Bay Company did not support McLoughlin. There was "no objection to [the missionaries] being supplied from our stores, with such absolute necessaries . . . as they may require," the committee wrote McLoughlin, "if they be in a condition to pay for the same [and if] these Missionaries confine themselves strictly to the avowed objects of their residence in the country." By 1839 the Methodists had worn out even this slim welcome. In December of that year the company protested a mission draft for £1,000 drawn in its favor by Lee on the firm of Sands, Hodgson, Turner, and Company of London. The draft was eventually paid, but the Hudson's Bay Company was much annoyed by the inconvenience and by the imposition of having to supply American missionaries who were suspected of designs against company interests.[31] Indeed, English churchmen were bothersome enough to the company without the additional burden of Americans, and Methodist Americans at that. But the Missionary Society in New York left Lee stranded just as the governor and committee of the Hudson's Bay Company undercut McLoughlin's efforts to keep the mission in check.

28. Jason Lee to [corresponding secretary], Mission House, December 8, 1837, UPS.
29. John McLoughlin to governor and committee, Fort Vancouver, November 16, 1836, HBS, IV, 174.
30. Alvan F. Waller to Amos Cooke, Willamette Falls, November 30, 1841, MS 1223 (typewritten copy), OHS.
31. Governor and committee to John McLoughlin, December 31, 1839, HBS, VI, 18–19 n. 2.

During his stay in the East, Lee told the Board of Managers of the Missionary Society that the company was no longer honoring drafts on the society's New York office; it would accept payment only through London bankers. Unfortunately for Lee, the society made light of this development, for it believed that the great reinforcement sent out in 1839 would relieve the mission of dependence on the company altogether.[32] This assumption proved fatal in several ways. First, the board's anticipation of economic independence undermined its confidence in the superintendent, who insisted that he had never promised that the mission would become self-supporting.[33] Second, the board's unwillingness to authorize Lee to pay for his supplies with drafts on London, and the irregularity and inadequacy of supplies from the society in New York, made Lee dependent upon the goodwill of McLoughlin. McLoughlin had goodwill in large supply, but by making use of it, Lee found he was digging the mission ever more deeply into debt and dependence, just as the "moral influence" of the company was buckling in the face of competition from Methodist enterprise. The board preferred to pay the company in New York because it was cheaper to handle one's own bills than to pay an agent for the service. When Lee asked for money, therefore, the board directed him to draw on the society, not on the London outfit. Lee followed instructions even though he "anticipated . . . a refusal [by McLoughlin] to accept such a draft." [34]

Lee, though complying with the society's instructions, complained bitterly: "We are cut off from paying anything to the Company," he wrote in September 1841, "until we receive from you *authority* and direction on whom to draw in *London.*" [35] Lee's position was uncomfortable. Even worse than the accumulation of debt on the books at Fort Vancouver was the interest charge of 5 percent, which linked the mission to the company more closely than even the debt of gratitude incurred by McLoughlin's willingness to supply the mission without demanding immediate payment. Scarcely a single letter of Lee's written to the board after 1841 is free of complaints that the mission was being deserted: "Since the first

32. *Minutes, B.M.,* IV, 121.

33. Jason Lee to corresponding secretary, Wascopam, October 13, 1843, UPS. As early as June 1841 Lee told the board: "One thing is evident that it will take no small sum to support the number we have in this field." Jason Lee to corresponding secretary, Clatsop, June 18, 1841, UPS.

34. Jason Lee to corresponding secretary, Fort Vancouver, September 23, 1841, UPS.

35. *Ibid.*

draft drawn after I left for the States. *The Oregon Mission* was in debt, till the last drawn, and I did hope, that we should never be obliged to go in debt again at Vancouver; but I see no way to avoid it." [36] Lee's situation worsened when the ship *Peacock* of Charles Wilkes's United States Exploring Squadron was wrecked in the Columbia in 1841 and all the supplies put on board by the society in New York were lost. Lee, calling upon an ebbing reservoir of patience, said bravely: "We shall look for goods from N.Y. next summer" (i.e., in 1842). [37]

Lee was approaching the time when his inability to pay the company and the society's reluctance to help him pay would converge with other factors impinging on mission life, the two most important being the contest over the Falls site and the movement toward independence. In 1841 the Oregon missionaries made a new effort to survive and to achieve their goals in circumstances that had become decidedly unfavorable. The year had barely begun when Ewing Young's death made necessary the establishment of legal machinery to administer his estate. Lee was also under personal attack from Dr. Elijah White, who was diligently seeking ways to discredit him in the eyes of the Missionary Society and the New England Conference to which the superintendent belonged. In 1842 Lee would learn that White had succeeded. [38] During the latter part of 1841 the Oregon Institute, later to become Willamette University, was being launched in what is now Salem. While the mission was providing for the education of white children in Salem, the Island Milling Company was being formed at Willamette Falls. [39]

36. *Ibid.*

37. *Ibid.*

38. Charles Pitman to Jason Lee, New York, February 28, 1842, UPS. Jason Lee to corresponding secretary, Vancouver, October 18, 1842, UPS. "Dr. White has arrived. Learning from him, that nothing had been done to effect a withdrawal of the 'Bill of Objections' pending against me in the New England Conference, I took immediate measure to secure a passage to England, hoping to be able to reach the States before the next session of the New E. Con.

"Dr. White in the meantime, learning my intention expressed to me his ardent desires that a reconciliation might be effected between us *here* and that he should then make such representations, as would doubtless prevent any further prossecution of the subject before the N.E. Con." In sum, White won the official exoneration he craved and, having in fact been in the wrong to begin with, he rested satisfied.

39. The Island Milling Company was begun in the late fall of 1841. See Waller to Cooke, November 30, 1841, OHS; HBS, VII, 220, 207, 211, 213, 218. The Oregon Institute held its first official meeting in January 1842. Gustavus Hines, *A Voyage Round the World* (Buffalo, 1850), pp. 139–52. Lee advised the board in June 1841 that "We shall

These enterprises were rooted in Lee's two-sided approach to the missionary dilemma. They both presupposed the extension of American jurisdiction as the ultimate guarantor of all lands claimed in Oregon. The Island Milling Company and the Oregon Institute were formed as companies on the assumption that United States jurisdiction would mean incorporation. But in the uncertain legal atmosphere of "probational" government in 1841, both entities were companies in name only. The mission believed it was necessary in its ownership of the institute, as with the claim at the Falls, to disguise for legal purposes either the Methodist or the corporate ownership by Methodists of any property in Oregon. The missionaries knew of course that only individuals could preempt public lands. The purpose of the disguise was to validate future claims, not, as has often been said, to fool local Oregonians or the Missionary Society in New York.[40]

Developments in 1841 give every indication that Lee was beginning to fear that he was being deserted in the midst of his enemies. On September 18 he wrote, "We cannot *depend* on Vancouver at all," though just three years before he had said the company was the "pledge of our safety." Lee's report continued:

soon have a good deal of property, in buildings &c in this country." Lee urged the appointment of a board of trustees to hold the property "and not intrust all the funds here in the hands of *one* man." The board did not act on Lee's proposal, providing a further incentive, along with the legal uncertainty of property in the Oregon country, to divide ownership of Methodist properties among mission members. When the Linn Bill of January 3, 1843, granting 640 acres to every inhabitant or cultivator, showed signs of passing the Congress, Pitman, Ames, and Waugh went to Washington. On their copy of the Linn Bill the land grant provision (sec. 1, ll. 12–23) is amended in longhand (unidentified, although it is not the writing of either Pitman or Waugh) with a proviso to prevent any sale, alienation, or contract of granted lands before a patent was issued. This provision, evidently intended to prevent Methodist lands from being taken by individual Methodists, was not incorporated in the final bill. The Linn Bill, passing the Senate on February 28, failed in the House and never became a law. Nevertheless the board's caution was justified. On February 3, 1846, William Raymond claimed the Oregon Institute! Lee to corresponding secretary, Clatsop, June 18, 1841, UPS. The board's copy of the Linn Bill is endorsed "Oregon Documents received principally in 1843" in the handwriting of Charles Pitman. Bill, S. 22, 27th Cong., 3d sess., January 3, 1843. Ordered to be printed as amended in Committee of the Whole, UPS. Arrangements for Ames, Waugh, and Pitman to meet in Washington recorded on February 3, 1843, *Minutes,* Oregon Committee (unpaged). On Raymond see Gary, "Diary," p. 300. Lee had been required to declare that all lands claimed by him in Oregon would become the possession of the society. "Copy of the Declaration of the Rev. Jason Lee . . . ," in *A Statement of Facts,* Board of Missions, New York, pp. 4–5.

40. See, for example, Read Bain, "Educational Plans and Efforts by Methodists in Oregon to 1860," *OHQ* 21 (1922): 79.

Dr. M. Laughlin, took a freak that we have done something by way of trade that did not suit their interest and consequently, refused to let me have a pair of Blankets; alledging as the reason, that Blankits were scarce. But when I learned the real cause, I conversed with him on the subject, and he was convinced that he has been misinformed. This however, shows how little dependence is to be put upon the Com. for our supplies.[41]

Lee underscored the danger of depending on McLoughlin in terms that Methodists everywhere would instantly credit, even when they might refuse to hear him out on other matters. McLoughlin was a Catholic, and aided Catholics in preference to Methodists. Actually McLoughlin did not become a practicing Catholic until November 1842.[42] Lee's comments reflected his recent troubles with Father Blanchet and McLoughlin, but by far the most significant feature of his letter is an unintended prophecy. In retrospect it provides the most believable explanation of Lee's behavior in March 1843, when Lansford Hastings proposed that Oregon become an independent republic.

In order to be relieved of his debt to the company, Lee pleaded with the society to send authorization to draw on London. He was convinced that the mission's future was mortgaged so long as he remained dependent on the Hudson's Bay Company. Calculating his indebtedness, his plans for expansion, and, not least of all, the mail schedule between coasts, Lee decided that if "no time [is] lost in making arrangement with some house in London, . . . we may, at least, be able to pay the Com[pany] a year from next March" (i.e., March 1843).[43] From 1841 on Lee became even more anxious about mail deliveries than he had been before. Mail entered Oregon in several ways, all more or less irregular. Some of it came by ship, some with overland travelers, merchants, or government officials. The most efficient route, requiring about six to ten months for the round trip, was the Hudson's Bay Company's overland express, which Lee repeatedly advised the Missionary Society to use.[44] The corresponding sec-

41. Lee to corresponding secretary, Fort Vancouver, September 23, 1841, UPS.
42. F. N. Blanchet also anticipated McLoughlin's reconversion to the faith of his parents. He reported to the bishop of Quebec on March 8, 1843, that McLoughlin had been "Catholic in heart and acts for a long time before becoming a Catholic in fact." Carl Landerholm, trans., *Notices and Voyages of the Famed Quebec Mission to the Pacific Northwest* (Portland, 1956), p. 170.
43. Lee to corresponding secretary, Fort Vancouver, September 23, 1841, UPS.
44. For example, Jason Lee to corresponding secretary, The Dalles, April 23, 1842, UPS.

retary announced the receipt of Lee's letter at a board meeting on May 16, 1842. He entered an abstract of it in the minutes along with sundry "letters from Oregon." Visible even in his brief entry is the secretary's annoyance over Lee's "complaining of the act of the Board in withdrawing the permission to draw on England for the amount the Superintendent needs to carry on the operation of the Mission." [45] The other letters from Oregon were also called "complaints." The board had in fact washed its hands of Jason Lee. The meeting had been called especially to reaffirm plans to send an agent to Oregon. [46]

In April 1842 Lee wrote again. The situation, from his point of view, was more desperate than ever: "Unless the Board send us some goods, or letters of credit on London the Mission will be Bankrupt next year, and then we shall be forced to do, what we have been accused of doing in a paper published at Oahoo, *Viz,* all turn Farmers." [47] Lee complained of the board's failure to send its mail via the express as he advised. His frustration with the board's inattention to regularity in correspondence was at least as great as the board's distress with the superintendent's failure to send a financial report. The irritability on both sides was undisguised, justifying a comment in 1844 by Charles Pitman, who looked to the "establishment of a monthly mail" between New York and Oregon to provide relief "from half the difficulties under which we have hitherto labored." [48] The board's decision in May 1842 to alter the Oregon mission and bring it into line with eastern expectations was preceded by Jason Lee's decision in April to look for no changes from the board regarding Oregon. The express had brought not "one line from the states. . . . But a truce to this subject," he said, "if *all* I have written produces no effect I shall submit in silent dispair." [49] As always, Lee submitted and despaired, but he did not relent in his determination to see that the mission planted Methodism in the soil of Oregon, though he still had no sure converts among the Indians. Indeed, there were only a few among the whites.

The year 1843 opened with no promise of improvement. Lee told the board he had nothing of particular interest to report, but the corresponding secretary pressed him often for signs of good work as aids to "our

45. *Minutes, B.M.,* IV, 121.
46. *Ibid.*
47. Lee to corresponding secretary, The Dalles, April 23, 1842, UPS.
48. Charles Pitman to George Gary, New York, June 29, 1844, UPS.
49. Lee to corresponding secretary, Vancouver, April 8, 1842, UPS.

begging operations." [50] Lee, with little to offer, could not resist suggesting, rather testily, there was "no want of uninteresting matter . . . to extend my correspondence to any desirable length." [51] Two exceptionally long letters by Lee in March show that he was deeply depressed. Significantly, the missionary chose a trip to The Dalles as his nostrum. On January 23 he hurried through his morning chores and, after arranging for the care of his one-year-old daughter, took off for a visit with Daniel Lee and brothers Perkins and Brewer at The Dalles. [52] As usual on such trips, Lee stopped at the Falls to confer with Alvan Waller and the mission steward and storekeeper, George Abernethy. On his return trip he spent the latter half of March there attending the settlers' political meetings. [53] Lee's stops at the Falls at this time were especially important because the land controversy with McLoughlin was reaching its climax.

In addition to the particular point at issue, this famous dispute involved questions of wheat, trade, supply, and milling, as well as political and philosophical matters. The controversy, formalized by the petition of March 25, 1843, the so-called Shortess petition, was basically a "fight between two milling companies," as Henry Perkins aptly put it. [54] The contestants were the Methodists who owned and ran the Island Milling Company and the Hudson's Bay Company with its mills and stores, including a competing mill at the Falls. Waller and McLoughlin were the agents of their respective superiors, Lee and Simpson. Lee, for his part, was legally bound to hold all mission lands in the name of the Methodist church. McLoughlin had no legal arrangement with the company concerning the

50. Charles Pitman to Jason Lee, New York, February 28, 1842, UPS.

51. Lee to corresponding secretary, Willamette Falls, March 30, 1843, UPS.

52. Jason Lee to corresponding secretary, Willamette Falls, March 27, 1843, UPS.

53. Lee wrote two letters from the Falls in March 1843, one on the twenty-seventh and the other on the thirtieth. His letter of the twenty-seventh is in the form of a journal. In dating this journal (which appears to have been written after his trip) Lee slips from February to March. Writing about February in the month of March apparently explains this error.

54. Gray, *History,* p. 297. Gray quotes Perkins from memory and the language may well be incorrect. But the sentiment is accurate. Perkins made a great deal of his opposition to Jason Lee's handling of the Falls controversy in 1844, although his criticism was closely allied with his overriding desire to get away from Indians and from Oregon. He was a friend of White's. The two men were emotionally and intellectually compatible. For all of Perkins's protestation against Jason Lee in 1843–44, once he was in the East he became a warm partisan of the former superintendent. H. K. W. Perkins to Daniel Lee [n.p.], November 11, 1845, WSHS.

Falls site; he had only Simpson's instructions of 1828 to take the site for the company.[55]

Writing to the Chief Factor in November 1842, Lee more than hinted at the agent's role Waller was playing at the Falls. "[If] your claim failed," said Lee, speaking of McLoughlin's claim of 1828 made at Simpson's direction, "and the Mission did not put in a claim he [Waller] considered that he had a better right than any other man and should secure a title to the land if he could." [56] The claim controversy began in earnest in November 1842, when McLoughlin invited Stephen Meek, a settler, to pick a building lot for himself at the Falls. Waller refused to honor McLoughlin's right to grant a lot to Meek.[57] Basic to the controversy was Lee's assumption that the Falls would ultimately become American territory, and tied to that assumption was the belief that American laws would one day be extended. As in all legal questions in Oregon, most notably in the distillery affair, Lee had recourse to the laws of the United States as he understood or had knowledge of them.

When the immigrants led by Elijah White and Lansford Hastings arrived in November 1842 they brought news of a land bill then pending in the Senate. While it has often been pointed out that Oregon immigrants came west because they expected passage of Senator Lewis Linn's preemption bill granting 640 acres of land to each man, it should also be noted that laws already on the statute books gave immigrants certain rights as to landownership.[58] At least as important as the pending Linn bill was a law passed on September 4, 1841, the so-called Distribution-Preemption Law, which revised land policy fundamentally in favor of the preemp-

55. On Lee's obligations to the society see, *A Statement of Facts,* pp. 4–5. A succinct account of McLoughlin's difficulties with the governor and committee and his problems with the Methodists in this affair is W. Kaye Lamb, "Introduction," HBS, VII, ix–xiv, xl–li. See also HBS, VI, 187–89, and Brosnan, *Lee,* pp. 291–315.

56. Jason Lee to John McLoughlin, Willamette, November 28, 1842, HBS, VII, 201.

57. John McLoughlin to Jason Lee, Fort Vancouver, November 18, 1842, *ibid.*

58. Immigration to Oregon did not begin until after 1841. It had little to do with Jason Lee and a great deal to do with the Distribution-Preemption Act of 1841. The cluster of folktales surrounding the settlement of Oregon must contend with the sobering fact that the vast majority of immigrants to Oregon in 1842, as well as during the years 1843–45, were neither desperadoes nor political ideologues. The idea that they would have ventured 2,000 miles for the sake of winning Oregon or that they would have risked the sale of a farm in Missouri or Illinois on the chance, however good, that Linn's bill would pass, is most implausible.

tor.[59] The 1841 law was a moral if not a legislative triumph for the views of Senator Thomas Hart Benton of Missouri, the strongest Oregon booster in the land.[60] The new legislation accomplished two things. It altered the emphasis of federal land policy from revenue to settlement, and, by making cultivation and residence legal prior to purchase, it conceded the principle of preemption. Oregon, of course, was not a part of the public lands of the United States, but everyone knew that in time it would become American territory.[61] The settlers of 1842 relied upon this fact just as Lee had done in the distillery dispute; indeed, unlike the missionary who contested McLoughlin's claim, they had the best of two worlds: McLoughlin's largesse and their own government's promise that the lands they took up would be secured to them. Once they had settled in Oregon, all they found lacking was some form of police authority, and they made haste to supply this need within less than a year after their arrival.

What Lee was doing in his encounter with McLoughlin at the Falls was putting the claim of cultivation and residency against the more speculative claim of McLoughlin's which was based upon priority but flawed by absenteeism. He was not jumping McLoughlin's claim, rather he was

59. Roy M. Robbins, "Preemption: A Frontier Triumph," *MVHR* 18 (1931): 331–49; Roy M. Robbins, *Our Landed Heritage* (Princeton, 1942), pp. 85–89, 427–29. "The preemption provisions of the Act of 1841 . . . recognized that settlement prior to purchase was no longer per se a trespass." *Ibid.*, p. 89. Of course this law had as much to do with Clay-Tyler warfare and the more central matter of the tariff as with either preemption or distribution directly.

60. There are several fine studies of Benton, but the best way to study him is through his autobiography, *Thirty Years' View* (2 vols.; New York, 1854–56).

61. The mistaken view that American-British rivalry in Oregon itself was more important than the question of dependence on or independence of the United States government is an adjunct to the wider misconception that Oregon pioneers directed their efforts to winning Oregon. A comment of Anna Maria Pittman, Jason Lee's first wife, upon her arrival in Oregon is typical. Stepping ashore in Oregon after her voyage from the East she remarked how good it was "once more . . . [to] trod on the shores of America." Anna Maria Pittman to [her sisters and brothers], May 11, 1847. Theressa Gay, *Life and Letters of Mrs. Jason Lee* (Portland, 1936), p. 151. Also K. B. Judson, ed., "Documentary: Letter, Doctor John McLoughlin to Sir George Simpson, March 20, 1844," *OHQ* 17 (1916): 234. ". . . the immigrants [of 1843] have placed themselves all on the South Side of the Columbia River . . . and give out that they believe the Columbia River will be the boundary and they think it is settled by this time." This fact, together with the prevalence of a sentiment for independence, makes it clear that a large number of Americans, Lee and the missionaries included, had no idea there was an "Oregon Question." Oregon was not quite so much an issue in the East either at this time. See Edwin A. Miles, " 'Fifty-four Forty or Fight'—An American Political Legend," *MVHR* 42 (1956): 291–309.

putting in a claim, through Waller, so that if the McLoughlin claim failed the mission "should secure title to the land." This was his position, and Waller's, in the last months of 1842. Lee clarified his stand to Elijah White in 1843, recounting a conversation with McLoughlin, the same conversation that McLoughlin recorded, from his own point of view, in a letter of 1844.

In his letter to White, Lee gave the mission's side of the controversy as of April 1843. McLoughlin's sale of deeds to settlers, about which the Chief Factor spoke so often, was, Lee believed, a ridiculous undertaking for anyone in the circumstances. McLoughlin "mentioned to me," Lee told White,

> that he had put up a notice, requiring all who wished to take lots, to take deeds, of his agent [Lansford Hastings, an American] within a specified time. I made enquiries as to the *kind* of deeds he gave, and told him very pleasantly, that I thought it assuming rather high grounds for a private individual to give deeds to land in this neutral Territory to which the Indian title had not been extinguished. In short to do what no Government could do. . . . I could not conceive that his Deeds could be of the least use to any one.[62]

Waller was more contentious and aggressive than Lee, but unlike Lee he was willing to talk about the lands at the Falls as if the Indian title had been extinguished and the lands had been made part of the public domain. Waller wrote the superintendent for advice early in May, asking how to proceed with mission plans for building a church at the Falls. Lee thought it was understood that the conflicting claims should be determined by "Government" when the time came. He insisted that Waller disregard McLoughlin's deeds because they were not "of the least use to any one." Waller, somewhat more businesslike than his superior, was still not sure of his position and asked Lee once again, on June 23, 1843, what he should do. The answer was decisive: "Let the Church build a Chapel upon the ground, and it shall have it,—without money and without Deed."[63] The superintendent, frustrated at every turn, was fed up with McLoughlin's pretensions. He came "to the conclusion" in April that he

---

62. Jason Lee to Elijah White, [n.p.], April 25, 1843, as transcribed in Elijah White to John M. Porter, Secretary of War, [n.p.], March 20, 1844, *Annual Report of Elijah White*, NAM, 234, frame 163. Also Alvan F. Waller's Diary, 1842–1845, OHS, p. 1.

63. Jason Lee to Alvan Waller, Willamette, June 29, 1843, Rosenbach Foundation. That is, without McLoughlin's leave.

should not pay Dr. McLaughlin Ten Dollars for a quit claim deed to every few feet square, we needed at the Falls for our Missionary purposes, as I considered his Deeds good for nothing and especially as we were the first permanent residents at the Falls. I resolved to set up no opposition claim to anyone to land in that place, but simply occupy it till government made some disposition of it unless we were driven away by force, of which indeed, I had no apprehension.[64]

Lee was clearly resting his claim upon preemption, an approach that news of the land law of 1841 could only have strengthened. "We were the first permanent residents at the Falls," he told White. As with Young in 1837 so in 1843 Lee leaves no room for doubt about his strategy. It was both simple and logical. He acted on both occasions as if the laws of the United States were going to be applicable to Oregon. On his second and final trip to the East in 1843, Lee carried yet another petition to the Supreme Court. It referred to Waller's claim of 640 acres, which fitted exactly the terms of the Linn bill while ignoring the law of the provisional government excluding claimants from holding acreage on town sites.[65] All these facts, including the mission's demand that it receive special treatment from the provisional government in May 1843, strongly suggest that the mission did not trust the settlers' government of July 5, 1843.[66]

Lee stopped at the Falls on his way to The Dalles on January 25, 1843, and talked with "Bro. Waller about the interests of the Miss. &c until a very late hour." After spending two weeks at the mission at The Dalles, Lee returned to the Willamette. These were Lee's darkest days since the winter of 1836–37. Arriving at Chemeketa he was greeted by an empty house, his second wife having some time since followed the first to the

64. Lee to White, April 25, 1843, NAM, 234, frame 164. It is clear that "government" refers to the United States government.

65. Since the Organic Laws of the provisional government made a special exception of missions, allowing them to hold such claims, it is reasonable to infer from Lee's effort to have Waller's claim recognized as an individual claim by the U.S. Supreme Court that the missionaries had very little confidence in the authority of the provisional government. Many of the important official documents in this controversy have been published and are readily available. See HBS, VII, 195–219, and Brosnan, *Lee*, pp. 291–318.

66. Henry B. Brewer wrote his brother and sister "concerning my [land] claim. I think I have a good one. It is not thought best to leave it until I can get it secured to me from government." H. B. Brewer to [his brother and sister], Oregon City, October 6, 1847, MS 979.5/B75, OSL. Filmed by the Oregon State Library for the author, September 1970. WSHS possesses a typescript of Brewer's letter.

grave. His child Lucy Anna, in whom he took such great joy, was visiting at the mission hospital in the care of Gustavus Hines, later to become her stepfather.[67] In addition to his loneliness, Lee was physically unwell, entering the first stages of an illness that claimed his life two years later. The mail from the East had brought a letter from the board, but Lee searched in vain for authorization to pay for goods bought at Fort Vancouver by drafts on a London bank, as McLoughlin had demanded.

The board's letter was dated April 7, 1842, more than a month before Lee's letter had arrived in New York.[68] But it was now March 1843 and, as Lee had predicted eighteen months earlier, the mission was bankrupt. In fact, it was worse than bankrupt because in April 1842 the superintendent, having anticipated authorization and unwilling to continue his dependence on the company, had paid McLoughlin, including 5 percent interest, by drawing on Sands, Hodgson, Turner, and Company of London for £400.[69] Lee answered the board's letter on March 30, 1843. He needed no prophet's talents this time to predict what kind of a reception his unauthorized payment to the company would receive: "Judging from the tenor of your letter [of April 7, 1842], and especially from one recd from Bro. Lane [treasurer of the Missionary Society] I fear you will be embarrassed by the drafts we drew . . . but I am persuaded, nothing better could have been done."[70] This news, combined with a very meager record of conversions, did more than embarrass the board's members; it enraged them.

---

67. Lee to corresponding secretary, Willamette Falls, March 27, 1843, UPS. Hines's behavior toward Lee appears to have been a mixture of genuine affection and jealousy. He was friendly to Elijah White and wrote a glowing letter to the commissioner of Indian affairs commending the work of the Indian subagent. Hines to J. M. Porter, secretary of war, Willamette, April 3, 1843. Gray, *History*, pp. 216–17 (an accurate copy). Hines wrote a letter to the board in 1843 condemning Lee's administration and in 1845 he wrote the board once more, this time in criticism of George Abernethy. See Hines to corresponding secretary, Willamette River, March 15, 1843, UPS; Gustavus Hines to [Board of Managers], Willamette Falls, March 21, 1845, UPS. The only area of the mission that escaped Hines's criticism was the Manual Labor School, for which he was responsible. Hines may have been one of those individuals whom Lee considered, in Mrs. Bailey's words, to be "his superior." Lee delegated *"all* the business of the" Manual Labor School to Hines. Jason Lee to Gustavus Hines, Willamette, November 18, 1841, Beinecke. Margaret Jewett Bailey, *The Grains, or Passages in the Life of Ruth Rover* (2 vols.; Portland, 1854), I, 76.

68. *Minutes, B.M.,* IV, 121.

69. Lee to corresponding secretary, March 30, 1843, UPS.

70. *Ibid.* Lane's letter has not been located.

Given Lee's circumstances in March 1843, little imagination is necessary to guess what his response to a movement for independence must have been.[71] Bankrupt and deserted by the society at home, dependent on the company at the same time he was contending with it over the Falls claim, Lee had paid the mission's debt without authorization, only to discover that authorization would not be forthcoming. The claim at the Falls, based upon the prospect of ultimate protection under American law, was in grave jeopardy because of the mission's debt to the company and the movement for independence. Any government that was not transparently linked to the United States would be unwelcome to Lee, and all but the weakest of local governments would obviously have to be resisted. The Shortess petition, praying for laws to protect the weak against the strong and calling for the elimination of the British monopoly and a boundary at the Columbia River, was the mission's response to all the provocations of March 1843. Lee saw that it was his duty "to immediately petition the Government of the United States to secure to the Missionary Soc. the right of possession . . . [to lands that the] Mission had obtained by possession [that is, by preemption] in Oregon." [72] For Jason Lee, Oregon had suddenly become an "expatriated country." [73]

71. See Gray, *History,* pp. 268–69. He points out that Lee and Abernethy were "disposed to ridicule the proposed organization as foolish and unnecessary." John Hussey, *Champoeg: Place of Transition* (Portland, 1967), p. 147, following Gray, remarks that the behavior of Lee and Abernethy was sparked by "some unspecified reason." Since they did not favor the government idea, the remarks of Lee and Abernethy are perfectly reasonable.

72. Brosnan, "Transcript," *Lee,* p. 249.

73. Lee to corresponding secretary, Willamette Falls, March 30, 1843, UPS.

CHAPTER 8

The Shortess Petition and the Champoeg Meeting

The history of the matter is this; The Settlers became
convinced that the H.B. Co. wished to monopolize the
commerce. This injured the settlers and the Mission.
They believed they could build a Mill at the Falls that
would bring in other vessels beside the H.B. Co's.
—Testimony of Jason Lee
before the Missionary Society, 1844

*I*N DISCUSSING the provisional government established in the
Oregon country on May 2, 1843, it is important to distinguish between the forming of the government and its actual
operation. The government which history remembers, a makeshift effort
made necessary by the many immigrants who came to Oregon in 1844
and 1845, is something quite different from the government begun in
1843. The latter enterprise was not really a government at all, but
rather a nongovernment.[1]

As already suggested, the creation of the provisional government has
traditionally, and mistakenly, been seen as a series of steps leading to the
vote for organization on May 2, 1843. My purpose in this chapter is to
explore and refine the implications of the two preceding chapters. It is
suggested in chapter 6 that Jason Lee's view of politics, together with the
problems confronting the Oregon mission in 1843, could not possibly
have led him to favor any but the strongest American government. By
focusing on the relationship of the May 2 meeting and the Shortess petition of March 25 in this chapter, I am seeking to clarify the differences between Lee's views and those of others. Once again it becomes necessary to
revise a long-held view, the view that the Shortess petition and the May 2
meeting were complementary events.[2] Instead, each was a self-contained

1. A summary of the provisional government's activities from 1845 to 1849 is Dorothy
Johansen and Charles M. Gates, *Empire of the Columbia* (2d ed.; New York, 1967), pp.
211–27.
2. This view has been expressed by most historians over the years. For example, see
J. W. Bashford, *The Oregon Missions: The Story of How the Line Was Run between Canada and
the United States* (New York, 1918), pp. 240–48; John A. Hussey, *Champoeg: Place of Tran-*

event, and in several important respects they were antagonistic. Those attending the mid-March meeting at the Falls had consented to a government of sorts, not because anyone especially wanted the government that finally came into being, but because certain powerful groups—of which the mission was one—did not want an independent government.

The meeting at Champoeg on May 2, 1843, has long been the thematic linchpin of Oregon's early political history. On that day, it is said, old Joe Meek, the mountain man, challenged the gathering of about 100 men to join him in urging the organization of a government. When more than half of those present heeded the call, the organization to be known as the provisional government was launched. Based on only a few reminiscences, the Meek story is more legend than history, more folktale than fact. As time went on, the May meeting gained importance as much because it was thought to mark the start of an American community as because it was considered the end of a chain of creative events. Actual participants may not have been aware that they were making history, but posterity, discovering meanings for the past in later events, reinvested the earlier event with a significance it never had. Fame and homage have taken their toll on this celebrated gathering, as they have just as surely distorted the reputations of Jason Lee and John McLoughlin. Like the two men, whose memory has been honored by statues, the May 2 meeting also has its monument, an obelisk in Champoeg State Park.[3]

Most of Oregon's Methodists did not attend the May 2 meeting, and a majority of the settlers who did attend favored a small, simple organization. Many were indifferent to the advent of full-fledged government. The missionaries were much more concerned with a camp meeting scheduled for July 14 than they were with the inauguration of a government; the ministers, almost to a man, were visibly disinterested in political affairs. Jason Lee commented sarcastically in June 1843 to Alvan Waller that he found very "little said about the *Fourth*—and *I* have not *begun* to prepare, *'an Oration forty minutes long,'* yet." [4] The Presbyterian John Smith Griffin

---

sition (Portland, 1967), p. 144. Mirth Tufts Kaplan, "Courts, Counselors and Cases: The Judiciary of Oregon's Provisional Government," *OHQ* 62 (1961): 125.

3. For a picture of this monument on the occasion of its unveiling on May 2, 1901, see Hussey, *Champoeg,* p. 248.

4. Jason Lee to Alvan Waller, Willamette, June 29, 1843, Rosenbach Foundation, Philadelphia.

of Tualatin Plains echoed Lee's sentiments. He thought the "great swellings" of those who advocated "big government," such as Gray, Shortess,
and LeBreton, overstepped the bounds of necessity and sense.[5] Waller
made only offhand reference to Willamette politics, calling the organization that resulted from the May meeting a "sort of government." [6] David Leslie spent the early days of July in amorous pursuit of
Sister Olley, a widow of seven months and the lady who had captured the
affections of James Olley in New York City four years before. Although
Leslie wrote to his future wife about local affairs, he said nothing, even on
July 3, about the new government.[7] Henry Perkins, who toured the
Willamette Valley with his wife Elvira in the spring and early summer of
1843, took no notice at all of the doings at Champoeg. In his journal he
mentioned only missionary events, secular as well as spiritual. He wrote
enthusiastically of the coming camp meeting and the claim controversy at
the Falls.[8]

Although the men who wanted a big government on May 2 did not win
the day, the formation of the provisional government has been recounted
in their terms. The Newell wing was not made up of activists.[9] Its
members were mostly back-benchers whose main interest in getting
power was to keep others from getting it.[10] Activist George LeBreton is
typical of the big-government wing. His account of the provisional government has suggested to Dorothy O. Johansen, who recently uncovered
LeBreton's letter of 1844 to Caleb Cushing, that the supposed contest of
ethnic and national rivalries was genuine.[11]

LeBreton saw the provisional government as a victory for Americans

5. John Smith Griffin, "Record of a resolution which I attempted to substitute instead
of the great Swellings brought forward by the committee of twelve at Champoeg." Archives, Pacific University, Forest Grove, Oregon. (This document is dated simply "May,
1843.")

6. Alvan Waller to Amos Cooke, Willamette Falls, Oregon, August 2, 1843, MS
1223 (typewritten copy), OHS.

7. David Leslie to Adelia Judson, July 3, 1843, OHS.

8. H. K. W. Perkins to Charles Pitman, Wascopam, July 29, 1843, UPS.

9. On the classification of the May 2 assembly into wings see Newell to Evans, August
8, 1867, Evans Papers. Newell's typology is used here.

10. On this Tory approach to power see, for example, Roland Van Zandt, *The Metaphysical Foundations of American History* (The Hague, 1956), p. 176.

11. Johansen and Gates, *Empire of the Columbia,* p. 189. A copy of this letter is in OHS;
the original is in the Cushing Papers, Library of Congress.

over French Canadians who, he said, were under the company's thumb. He warned Cushing about the danger of a move toward independence, favored, he said, by the Hudson's Bay Company and the Chief Factor. Unlike Gray, LeBreton believed that the primary objective of the government was to protect settlers from Indians. Newell and his friends in Tualatin Plains gave the same reason for their interest in an organization of some kind.[12] But LeBreton's account blurs the existence of the two wings that Newell describes. LeBreton emphasized the ethnic dimension, insisting that French-Canadian reluctance to support the kind of government he wanted was the same as opposing any organization. More important, LeBreton gave the mission all the blame for taking a less ambitious course than he would have pursued on May 2. His argument is not wrong so much as it is incomplete and therefore misleading. It was Newell and his wing who favored a cautious approach at Champoeg. The mission did not really favor local government at all. LeBreton told Cushing that Hines and Lee were knowledgeable about the country but that the congressman would have to make "allowance for any prejudices which they may have with regard to the length to which the organisation &c has been carried." [13]

Protection from the Indians was perhaps the most widely shared reason for considering an organization in the years 1839–1841. LeBreton was himself killed by Indians at the Falls in 1844. But just as there were no steps toward a provisional government in the years 1841–1843, so the Indian question did not lead inevitably to the establishment of a government in 1843.[14] Nor was the basis of the provisional government the desire of older immigrants to protect their land claims against new immigrants, another theme that permeates the literature dealing with the provisional government.[15]

12. Newell to Evans, August 8, 1867, Evans Papers.

13. George LeBreton to Caleb Cushing, Willamette Settlement, December 1, 1843 (photostat), OHS. This sentence does not appear in the excerpt printed in Johansen and Gates, *Empire of the Columbia,* p. 189.

14. When LeBreton was killed on March 4, 1844, in the "Cockstock Affair," it was George Abernethy who wrote the Missionary Society to advise the United States that "an experienced and effective Indian Agent" should be sent. George Abernethy to corresponding secretary, Willamette Falls, March 29, 1844, UPS. Incidentally this letter sets to rest the speculation that there were two Indian skirmishes at Oregon City in March 1844. See Maurice O. Georges, "A Suggested Revision of the Role of a Pioneer Political Scientist [William Gilpin]," *Reed College Bulletin* (April 1947), p. 72.

15. See, for example, H. H. Bancroft, *History of Oregon,* Vols. XXIX–XXX of *Works*

It is now clear that the issue that provoked the formation of a provisional government in spring of 1843 was independence. Lansford W. Hastings, the man who urged independence for Oregon in the early months of 1843, explained in 1844 that his idea had been responsible for the decision to organize. This decision had come, not on May 2 but in "the winter," that is, in mid-March. Hastings claimed that the discussion of independence "resulted in a determination to organize a government subject to the control of the United States, and in the spring following [in May], in accordance with that determination, an organization took place." [16]

It was Newell's view that the men who favored independence in the winter and early spring of 1843, or those who purposely or unwittingly gave support to independence by urging a strong local government, were the same men who years later loudly blamed the Hudson's Bay Company and other foreign influences for fostering the movement for independence. If John McLoughlin ever favored independence, as he was accused of doing by numerous contemporaries, there is no supporting evidence. Indeed, he seems to have believed that the idea was especially favored by the most hostile American element. He was right, but not completely. Certainly the Methodists were anticompany, but they were just as surely against local government and they opposed an independent government. Furthermore, McLoughlin could hardly have welcomed the prospect of keeping company with a crowd of monopoly-hating independent Americans just south of Fort Vancouver. [17]

It is a mistake to think that the French Canadians opposed government per se and to suppose that the contestants at Champoeg on May 2, 1843, can be divided into progovernment Americans and antigovernment French Canadians. Many of the French Canadians who lived at French Prairie favored the kind of organization Newell said he and the mountain

---

(San Francisco, 1886–88), XXIX, 313. Also Kaplan, "Courts, Counselors and Cases," p. 121.

16. [Lansford Hastings] letter in the *Saint Louis New Era*, March 25, 1844, *OHQ* 2 (1901): 202. If the question of government was still an open one in the spring of 1843, Hastings would have made some effort to influence the gathering on May 2 in favor of his favorite scheme of independence. Instead he did not attend the meeting. It should be added that the easterner could not possibly confuse an Oregon May with "winter." See the same author's *The Emigrant's Guide to Oregon and California*, ed. Charles H. Carey (Princeton, 1932), p. 61.

17. Governor Simpson certainly did not favor the idea of "self-government" in Oregon. See Hussey, *Champoeg*, p. 147.

men wanted, an "understanding as to how [it] was best to act" [18] if there was trouble with the Indians. The problems of criminal jurisdiction, which first gave rise to a concern for government among the mountain men, had as its corollary the larger issue of Indian-white relations; this problem had been crucial since the late 1830s, when organization was deemed advisable by all groups living in the Willamette Valley.[19] Only rarely, as in 1839–1841, did religious differences become the center of conflict, even though religion colored all issues, including political issues, throughout the period. By 1841 the Methodists had deserted Champoeg, an area of Catholic preeminence, for points north and south, even moving their landing for supplies eastward and downriver from Champoeg to a place called the Butte.

Jesse Applegate tried to make all these things clear to Elwood Evans in 1867. "If you persist," he wrote,

> in believing the Canadians were opposed to a provisional government (which is not true) their opposition *did not* arise from any opposition to the Government of the U.S. or partiality for British rule. . . . Father Blanchett has frequently said to me . . . that he was in favor of government so far as it was necessary to preserve peace and order but wished not to go so far as to jeopardize his flock with the British Government until the boundary was settled and they were freed from their obligations to the British Crown.[20]

The French Canadians were opposed, both in 1843 and in 1844, to a strong government "not suited to our purposes." [21] Indeed, Blanchet's views on government in 1843 were the same ones he expressed in 1839. The priest outlined his thinking to his colleague, Father Modest Demers,

18. Newell to Evans, August 8, 1867, Evans Papers.

19. L. M. Lyons, *Francis Norbert Blanchet and the Founding of the Oregon Missions, 1838–1848* (Washington, 1940), pp. 74–82, 85–93.

20. Jesse Applegate to Elwood Evans, Yoncalla [Oregon], October 13, 1867, Evans Papers.

21. P. J. Frein, trans., "Address," *OHQ* 13 (1914): 341. The "Address" of the French Canadians to the Americans is dated March 4, 1843, although the correct date apparently should be 1844. See J. N. Barry ("The Champoeg Meeting of March 4, 1844," *OHQ* 38 (1937): 425–32. While internal evidence suggests to Barry that the "Address" was presented in 1844, the views expressed in it were those of the French Canadians, and others, after 1839. See n. 21 above and Newell to Evans, August 19, 1867, also above. Also see Newell to Evans, August 8, 1867: ". . . the French protest [i.e., the "Address"] . . . was intended to be submitted as a code of laws for the time being but it was not presented." The question is not whether a French petition or remonstrance was presented, or by whom, in 1843, but whether the "Address" is the specific one presented.

explaining his activities at the settlers' meeting of February 18, 1841: "I suggested that the election of the officers for the different posts be delayed until the first Tuesday in June, with the exception that the nomination of a committee to draw up a constitution and the selection of a supreme judge, a sheriff and constables might be carried through." [22] Blanchet's view of government closely resembles the organization actually endorsed on May 2, 1843, the chief point of similarity being the priest's omission of the governor's office. On May 2 a majority vote accepting organization was possible only when an agreement was reached that the new government would have no chief executive. The French-Canadian opposition on May 2, like Blanchet's opposition to the proposals of February 18, 1841, was specifically directed to the office of governor. When the objection was removed, as it was at Champoeg on May 2, the French-Canadian opposition to organization disappeared.

The issue of independence, raised in mid-March, brought the government question to a head. The meeting on May 2 concerned more practical matters. Both meetings suggest that the provisional government was not an American, anti-British movement. Although the attendance figures are not accurate, the standard estimate that more than 100 men voted at Champoeg on May 2 is almost surely too high. One historian has implied that perhaps as many as twenty-four men, long reputed to be on the "American side," may not have attended the meeting at all.[23] Even more important than numbers is the fact, pointed out earlier, that the Americans at Champoeg did not speak with one voice. Frances Victor's story that the provisional government was a Methodist conspiracy is not borne out by the evidence.

There was, however, a Methodist conspiracy of sorts in the Willamette Valley in March 1843. Its purpose was to defeat independence and to make sure that American jurisdiction was extended to Oregon. The Shortess petition to the United States Congress on March 25, 1843, reflected this effort. The petition was symbolic, among other things, of the mission's evolution brought about by Lee's attempts to resolve the missionary dilemma.

22. Blanchet to Jerome [Modest] Demers, February 11, 1841, PAA, in Lyons, *Blanchet*, p. 93.

23. J. N. Barry to Mr. Armstrong, June 18, 1959, Archives, OSL (Highway Division, Highway Building, Salem, Oregon). I am grateful to Elisabeth Walton, park historian, for making available to me a copy of the attachments to the cover letter to Mr. Armstrong.

In ten years the mission had undergone curious changes in its pursuit of missionary goals. In 1843, at the Falls, the mission found itself repeating some of the Hudson's Bay Company's earlier experiences, and by the autumn of 1843 missionaries heard settlers speak spitefully of the monopoly on the south side of the Columbia.[24] Governor Pelly had urged the British government to consider drawing a boundary simply for the sake of rationalizing trade; the mission suggested the same thing in 1843 in the Shortess petition. The mission's years in Oregon were closing on the historic antagonism of missionary and fur trader, but there were some ironic twists. Lee and McLoughlin were both dismissed, each for not being either fur trader or missionary enough, even though it was in truth the tenacity of both men in clinging to the programs of their respective home offices which brought about their discharges. Lee could not have been more persevering in pursuit of the goals set for him by the Missionary Society, nor could McLoughlin have served the company with more fervent loyalty.

McLoughlin had no reason to fear that the company would desert him in his fight to keep the Falls claim. It was George Simpson's idea in 1828 to take up the Falls site as a means of controlling the economic life of the Willamette Valley, thereby ensuring that Americans did not begin to drift northward. The Shortess petition, calling on the United States to protect Americans south of the Columbia, proved the success of Simpson's strategy of 1828. Of course, Simpson's plan had undergone subtle changes in emphasis over the past fifteen years. Yet so involved was McLoughlin in the life of the Willamette Valley, and so strong was the antagonism be-

24. George Gary, "Diary," *OHQ* 24 (1923): 177. Concerning the Shortess petition itself Frances Victor was probably right in thinking that Abernethy took advantage of Shortess. Bancroft, *History,* XXIX, 207. But the issue went deeper than Abernethy's unwillingness to sign the petition for fear of being refused supplies at Fort Vancouver. Abernethy took advantage of Shortess's temperament and his ideological antipathy toward the Hudson's Bay Company to enlist what became a swing group in joining the Island Milling Company in its efforts to get American protection from the Hudson's Bay Company. Shortess may well have been the first to conceive the idea of complaining to the United States about the company. He told Elwood Evans in 1867 that he "drew up a Summary of the subjects I intended to embrace . . . [and] it was decided to request Abernethy to write it out in proper form which he did. . . . I had it copied by A. E. Wilson and in his hand it was circulated." Shortess to Elwood Evans, Astoria, September 1867, MS 174, Evans Papers. (Note that David C. Duniway and Neil R. Riggs, eds., "Archives," *OHQ* 60 1959: 232, state erroneously that Waller was the author.) The "subjects" embraced in the petition are really only one: alleged usurpations by McLoughlin and the Hudson's Bay Company.

tween him and Simpson, that he failed to realize how tenuous his relations with the governor and committee had become. McLoughlin continued to immerse himself, and his money, in projects on the south side of the Columbia, serving the company's interest and his own, without taking into account the growing disparity between his concerns and those of the company.

By 1844 McLoughlin had bound himself to the settlers by overextending company credit, although his original purpose had been to keep them from coming north for land. The same motive lay behind his decision to locate a new store at the Falls. He congratulated himself on its success, telling the governor and committee that some Oregon residents "are Desirous that the Columbia be the Boundary because it will afford them a Double market and if the policy I pursued while in charge of the Hudson Bay Co. Business of selling at an advance of 100 p. cent and at this place [the Falls or Oregon City] of selling at the same price as the American traders, say 33⅓ in Vancouver is followed—the Desire will increase." [25] But it all came to nothing. The American and British negotiators in 1846 took as little notice of Oregon settlers as the company took of McLoughlin.[26] Just as Lee made sure he got the land claim at the Falls, so McLoughlin managed to hold back the tide of American settlers. Perversely, the mission's claim was sold by George Gary while the Hudson's Bay Company, discharging McLoughlin in 1845, left him holding the claim in his own name and offered him absolutely no legal assistance.[27] McLoughlin lost the claim and a good bit of money as well. The curtain on this classic conflict was brought down when McLoughlin, agent of a vast monopoly, was released for alleged philanthropy beyond the call of duty and Lee, the standard-bearer of the religious life, was dismissed for demonstrating too much concern for business matters. The events of

25. John McLoughlin to J. H. Pelly, Oregon City, July 12, 1846, HBS, VII, 162 (E. E. Rich, ed., *The Letters of John McLoughlin from Fort Vancouver to the Governor and Committee,* 3d ser. [Toronto, 1944]). The Shortess petition makes the remarkable assertion that the petitioners acknowledged the "right" of the United States to extend its jurisdiction over them, "the settlers south of the Columbia River." No one, not even George Simpson, ever doubted the United States had at least that right. The comment further demonstrates that the petition reflected local not national issues, and specifically the issue of independence. See Duniway and Riggs, "Archives," p. 228.

26. McLoughlin's view that his acts were influential at Whitehall suggests how little he understood the Oregon dispute. HBS, VII, xli. Also see chapter 2 above.

27. An excellent brief account of McLoughlin's relations with the governor and committee in London is W. Kaye Lamb, "Introduction," HBS, VII, xl–lx.

March 1843 brought the drama of Lee's ten-year search for moral authority to a pathetically ironic close.

The Shortess petition was a transparent bid for American protection by
the Island Milling Company, situated at the Falls on land claimed both by
the mission and by the Hudson's Bay Company. The petition neatly ties
McLoughlin's supposedly illegal land claim at the Falls to his power as the
only supplier in the Willamette and generalizes his usurpations to include
his "claims in other places south of the Columbia River . . . [for ex-
ample] at Tualatin Plains and Klakamus Plains [where] he had huts
erected to prevent others from building and such is the power of Doct
McLoughlin, that many persons are actually afraid to make their situation
known, thinking if he hears of it, he will stop their supplies." The petition recommended that the surest way of breaking McLoughlin's power
was to protect "American settlers south of the Columbia . . . with laws
to protect the weak against the mighty," or in other words to exclude the
company from operating in American territory. But the petitioners attacked McLoughlin from two sides. Not only was McLoughlin's land
claim illegal because he was the agent of a foreign monopoly but, agent or
no, he could not justly claim lands he did not live on. As the Shortess petition pointed out, "During the years 1841 and 1842 several families
settled at the Falls, when Doct McLoughlin who still resides at Fort Vancouver, comes on the group and says, the land is his, and any person
building without his permission is held, as a trespasser." [28] By March
1843 Lee's hopes for the mission's economic independence from the company and for Methodist influence were hanging on the land claim. [29] Of
utmost significance is the fact that the provisional government could win
toleration from the mission only by exempting it from the land laws everyone else was required to observe. The special proviso in the Organic
Laws, making an exception of the mission's claim at the Falls, identifies

28. Petition to the United States Senate, March 25, 1843, Territorial Papers of the
U.S. Senate. Duniway and Riggs, "Archives," pp. 228–33. Quotation is on p. 231.
29. Lansford Hastings, the man who moved that the settlements become independent
at the mid-March meeting, was also McLoughlin's lawyer and confidant. The man who
later offered to become McLoughlin's lawyer in the Falls controversy was John Ricord.
Frances Victor has noted that Ricord asked for a larger retainer from McLoughlin than he
asked from the Methodists. There is a very good reason for his request which Mrs. Victor
does not mention. It is that McLoughlin did not have a very good case. It follows from this
fact that Hastings's partiality for independence and his lawyer's solicitude for McLoughlin
may not have been unrelated. See Bancroft, *History*, XXIX, 212–13.

the mission's relation to the local government as that of a pressure group seeking favors, not as a majority granting them.

Lee had decided in November 1842, when McLoughlin sent Stephen Meek, a settler, to pick out a lot for himself at the Falls, that he would base his dealings with the Chief Factor on current American land law. News of American laws had come to Oregon the month before with the arrival of the overland emigration led by Elijah White and Lansford Hastings. The most important news the emigrants brought concerned the Distribution-Preemption Law of September 8, 1841.[30] In what has become the standard analysis of the Falls controversy, Charles H. Carey comments that Lee "knew that there was no law, as yet, that made it necessary for a land claimant to reside upon his claim, or to be a citizen of the United States." [31] Although Carey refers to the 1841 law, he seems to have overlooked provisions that make it quite clear that a claimant did have to reside on his claim and did have to be a citizen of the United States. The law also made specific provision for deciding between two claimants to the same piece of land. Thus, "when two or more persons have settled on the same . . . land, the right of preemption shall be in him or her who made the first settlement." [32] This law put Lee and the mission in the clear because McLoughlin had never settled the Falls claim. The Shortess petition argued the mission's case with an eye to the provisions of the Distribution-Preemption Law. Lee's future dealings with McLoughlin indicate, as does his correspondence with others concerning the claim, that he assumed American land laws would ultimately operate in Oregon, that is, that American jurisdiction would eventually extend to Oregon south of the Columbia.[33] As in 1837, when he had invoked the Intercourse Acts prohibiting the sale of liquor to Indians, Lee was once again relying on the imminent Americanization of Oregon.

The Shortess petition, not a simple document, was intended to serve mission interests. Because the Methodists were not all-powerful, in order to achieve their own objectives they had to make the petition satisfy others besides themselves. The sixty-five men who signed the Shortess petition

30. See chapter 7.
31. Charles H. Carey "Lee, Waller and McLoughlin," *OHQ* 33 (1932): 206.
32. *Statues at Large,* V, sec. 11, 456 (1841).
33. For Lee's handling of the distillery affair see chapter 7, p. 170. The outstanding study of the Intercourse Acts and of American Indian policy to 1834 is Francis P. Prucha, *American Indian Policy in the Formative Years* (Cambridge, 1962), *passim* and pp. 261–69.

were not all sympathetic to Methodism or even to the interests of the Island Milling Company. The common bond among them was antipathy toward the Hudson's Bay Company and, specifically, the desire to break the company's hold on the wheat market. An evaluation of the relationship between the petition and the provisional government must take into account the differences among those who signed the petition. These differences must in turn be superimposed on the limited but pertinent data available for the groups that participated in the voting on May 2, 1843.

The relationship between the Shortess petition of March 25, 1843, and the vote on May 2 is complex. Three different groups participated in either or both of these events: (1) forty-three men who signed the Shortess petition only; (2) twenty-one men who signed the petition and voted on May 2 (the "swing" group or, as Newell called it, the "big-government wing"); (3) approximately twenty-eight men who voted on May 2 only (Newell's "wing").[34] The two important elements separating these three groups were geography and wheat production. The geographical factor, later to become crucial in territorial politics (1849–59), was significant from the beginning.[35]

The Willamette River, flowing north into the Columbia, was the main transportation link between settlements. Above the Falls the most convenient entrepôt was Champoeg. Wheat from Clatsop and Tualatin Plains west of Champoeg could be routed overland to Fort Vancouver via the old Hudson's Bay Company trail or else sent down to Champoeg for shipment north to the Falls. Communication and transport between the Falls and the western farming areas of Clatsop and Tualatin were impractical because of the dense forests and precipitous cliffs on the eastern side of the Willamette River at the Falls. The voting pattern on May 2 and the signing of the Shortess petition on March 25 reflected the geography.[36]

The most obvious difference between the May 2 meeting and the Shortess petition is that they happened in different places, a highly significant point. The Shortess petition represented the interests and the people

---

34. Dealing in signatures and numbers for these two events is of course an act of faith. All things considered, however, it is perhaps no less hazardous than reliance upon more accurate but more abstract data, such as census reports or voting returns.

35. An excellent study of territorial politics in Oregon is James E. Hendrickson, *Joe Lane of Oregon: Machine Politics and the Sectional Crisis, 1849–1861* (New Haven, 1967).

36. See maps in Hussey, *Champoeg*, p. 42, and HBS, VII, opposite p. 128.

at the Falls; the provisional government was a Champoeg affair. For this reason, contemporaries who knew less than either Newell or Gray were convinced of the causal importance of ethnic and international factors. Champoeg was predominately a French-Canadian settlement, and the behavior of such men as Gray, who was at least as hostile to papists as he was to monopolists, strengthened the notion that mighty events were in progress. But the early history of Oregon has long been obscured by the tendency to see events in light of what developed from them. In due course the provisional government became as much the property of the Falls as of Champoeg. The local and separate character of the two events reveals the difference in the populations of the two communities. The Falls was an American community, but French Canadians as well as Americans resided in the farming regions that spread around the Falls in the shape of a horseshoe, from French Prairie in the southeast to the plains of Clatsop and Tualatin on the west and southwest.

Champoeg was the only settlement in the Oregon country south of the Columbia with a French-Canadian majority. The attendance at the May 2 meeting was a consequence of this population factor rather than of a supposed predilection of Canadians for or against government. Because the meeting was held at Champoeg, French Canadians could more easily be present. No more than 37 percent of all the Americans and others in the Willamette Valley attended the meeting—about fifty men at the most, out of a possible 135 or 175. The fifty or so French Canadians who years later were said to have been at Champoeg (although the total attendance, to repeat, was almost certainly less than this) made up about 50 or 60 percent of the 85 Canadian males in the Willamette settlement.[37] Eight French Canadians almost surely voted for the organization: Bernier, Billeque, Donpierre, Gervais, Ladaroute, Lucier, Matthieu, and Compo.

37. Here as everywhere else numbers are more impressionistic than otherwise. The number 135 is taken from White's census. The higher figure is a guess at the maximum possible number of American males in 1842–43, based on a rough count of names in addition to those that show up in White's census. The exact number of French Canadians in the Willamette Valley in 1843 is not known. There were eighty-five, according to White's census, but this figure is certainly smaller than the actual number. According to Father Modest Demers, there were "about a hundred Canadian families . . . at Wallamette" as of February 13, 1844. Carl Landerholm, trans., *Notices and Voyages of the Famed Quebec Mission* (Portland, 1956), p. 185. J. Neilson Barry compiled a list of "practically all the French Canadians [males] who were living or had lived in the Willamette valley by 1844." It includes 121 names. J. Neilson Barry, *The French Canadian Pioneers of the Willamette Valley* (Portland, 1933), p. 5.

Newell, who is the authority for the attendance of Bernier and Billeque, said there were "others." [38] Five of the eight are mentioned in the minutes of the May 2 meeting and their affirmative votes are therefore as certain as records can show. [39]

The American attendance at Champoeg, while small relative to the entire American population, was quite sizable when considered in terms of a district, specifically of the Champoeg-Tualatin-Clatsop or horseshoe district. From this point of view, American attendance at Champoeg may have been as high as 75 percent. The disparity between American attendance and local American participation on May 2 strongly suggests that the issues at Champoeg in the spring of 1843 were local issues in every sense.

The Americans, 60 percent or more, who stayed away from the May 2 meeting were mostly residents of settlements to the north and south of the horseshoe, such as Salem, Lee's spiritual enclave, and the Falls, the mission's temporal bastion providing "moral influence" in the "mixed community free of all legal restraint." [40] Most Salem residents were Methodists and they had their own mills. In keeping with Lee's policy of spatial division and separation of the spiritual from the temporal, his own house was in Salem, at the most remote part of the settlement. [41] The two wings who attended the May 2 meeting were chiefly dwellers in the horseshoe area, whereas the 60 percent of those who signed the petition without attending the May 2 meeting were residents of the Falls.

By far the most interesting and in some ways the most important group comprised the twenty-one men who signed the Shortess petition and also voted on May 2. [42] This swing group, or big-government wing, had economic as well as ideological differences with the larger Newell wing,

38. Newell to editor, *Oregon Herald,* October 25, 1866, Evans Papers. In a letter to Evans, Newell said he "saw five or six of them [French Canadians] last winter [1866–67] some of them have past away." Newell to Evans, August 8, 1867.

39. The eighth name is that of Xavier Ladaroute. The authority for this name is J. L. Parrish, who may not have been at the May 2 meeting himself. J. L. Parrish, *Anecdotes,* Bancroft Library, Berkeley, California, p. 100. In 1866 Newell included Ladaroute. Newell to editor, *Oregon Herald,* October 25, 1866, Evans Papers.

40. U.S. Congress, Senate, *Petition to the Honorable the Senate and House of Representatives of the United States of America,* March 16, 1838, S. Doc. 154, 25th Cong., 3d sess., 1838, pp. 1–3.

41. George T. Allan, "A Gallop through the Willamette in November 1841," *TOPA* (1882), p. 59. Also published in *Oregon Native Son* 1 (1899): 153–55.

42. Gustavus Hines and David Leslie were not present on May 2.

whose members attended only the May 2 meeting. The swing group included the largest American wheat growers in the Oregon country, most of whom lived in the plains of Tualatin and Clatsop. Their chief reasons for interest in the provisional government were their hatred for the Hudson's Bay Company and their jealousy of its control over the export market. In this stand they were in complete agreement with the merchants at the Falls. The farmers and their neighbors in Tualatin and Clatsop who voted for the provisional government without signing the Shortess petition were interested in developing the Champoeg settlement.

The farmers in the swing group differed from other farmers in their willingness to risk elimination of the company as the area's primary market because they believed they would gain more if American traders were brought into Oregon to replace the company.[43] The Methodist-run Island Milling Company at the Falls was a step in this direction, although swing-group support of this company was less an endorsement of Methodist merchants than it was a protest against the Hudson's Bay Company. Strong government was, for this group, an alternative to the extension of American jurisdiction. For the Newell wing and for the Methodists there was no alternative to American jurisdiction. The differences in productivity in wheat growing among the three major groups are an instructive index to their other differences. The signers of the Shortess petition who did not vote on May 2 were city folk who grew practically no wheat. The members of Newell's wing, who voted on May 2 but did not sign the petition, produced wheat at a mean of 300 bushels per year. The swing-group farmers, who participated in both the petition and the May 2 meeting, were the planter aristocracy of the valley. Each of them raised about 450 bushels in 1842.

Thus the group comprising the largest number of people (the petition signers) produced the smallest amount of wheat, as might be expected of a mill town such as the Falls. The total annual wheat production of this group (614 bushels) was substantially less than the production of any one of three single producers in the swing group. Furthermore, no single pro-

43. These farmers were the forerunners of a group of Tualatin wheat growers who tried to establish an import-export cooperative in 1846–47 to circumvent the high-priced suppliers of Oregon City, the company and the American merchants. The farmers realized "that their real problem was the inadequate export market for their wheat which, in turn, prevented an inflow of supplies." Arthur Throckmorton, *Oregon Argonauts: Merchant Adventurers on the Western Frontier* (Portland, 1961), pp. 60–61.

ducer of wheat in the Newell group produced more than 400 bushels. This group had a fairly even distribution of middle-range producers, whereas the swing group included the largest producers in all three groups.

The swing group and the Newell group were differentiated in several other important respects. The latter, made up largely of French Canadians and Americans, was a farmers' group, though some nonfarmers from Champoeg were also included. Among them was Dr. William J. Bailey, Margaret Jewett's first husband and a friend of the French Canadians. Bailey, Solomon Smith, and Joseph Cannon were all old-timers who at one time or another had been employed by the Hudson's Bay Company. The Newell group included only two entrepreneurs, Robert Moore and Robert Newell, while the swing group, as might be anticipated, had the lion's share of this class.[44]

Robert Moore, arriving in Oregon in 1839 with the Peoria party, claimed the land directly opposite Willamette Falls. His dream was to make the west side of the Willamette River the equal of the eastern or Methodist side and he spent his life in the attempt.[45] Robert Newell was the most important figure in this group, "the proprietor," as a recent observer has aptly said, "of Champoeg's ambitions."[46] Generally speaking, the men of the Newell group were the ideological descendants of Ewing Young and lived, as he did, in the plains of Champoeg-Tualatin. As farmers they depended on others to mill their wheat and supply them with the necessities of life. They stood to gain by competition between mills and suppliers.

The swing group included not only the largest wheat producers in the country but also most of the budding merchant population of the Falls, or what would soon become Oregon City. Two agents of a New England mercantile firm, George LeBreton and A. E. Wilson, who opened a store together in 1843, belonged to this group, as did J. L. Morison who became one of the first major property owners in the city. J. R. Robb was deeply involved in Falls business projects. Morison, Robb, and Medorum Crawford, immigrants in 1842, were all initially employed by William Gray who may well have influenced their thinking. Two other recent immigrants in the swing group, J. C. Bridges and Reuben Lewis, both held

44. On Newell's entrepreneurship see below, this chapter.
45. Howard Corning, *Willamette Landings* (Portland, 1944), pp. 37–57.
46. Hussey, *Champoeg,* p. 235.

posts in the provisional government and they too may have come under Gray's influence. Significantly, these five men were among the youngest men in their group.[47] They were also the only new arrivals in the group, having come with the White-Hastings party in 1842.

Seventeen new immigrants signed the Shortess petition without voting on May 2. And although Frances Victor called the Shortess petition "a puerile . . . recital of injuries [to which] the signers affixed their names without caring to know the tenor of the document . . . , half of them [having been no] more than six months in the country," the fact remains that only 40 percent of the new arrivals took any action at all in 1843 and those who did were overwhelmingly in the group that signed the petition only.[48] The value of these men to confessed conspirators such as Gray or reputed conspirators like Lee was not exploited on May 2, for the simple reason that there were no conspiracies. Men who had just arrived and were living at the Falls patently had little interest in the affairs of Champoeg.

The special nature of the swing group has been ignored not only because the factors of geography and wheat production have gone unnoted, but because historians have often assumed, just as they have assumed that the provisional government was Methodist-oriented, that the men who participated in both events were sympathetic to the Methodists or were even special friends of Jason Lee.[49] The reverse is true. The men in the swing group had had serious difficulties with the mission before 1843, the best evidence being a petition of 1840 condemning Jason Lee; it was circulated among the settlers in the Willamette Valley by Elijah White.[50] Eight of the ten men in the swing group who were in the country in 1840

47. Crawford was twenty-four in 1843, Lewis twenty-nine, Morison twenty-four, and Robb twenty-seven; Bridges' age was unknown. No other member of group 2 was in his twenties and the average age of the group was about forty.

48. *Bancroft*, XXIX, 209 n. 33.

49. Frances Victor said that Shortess was a "convert of the Mission," although his conversion did not affect what Jesse Applegate called his "savage independence." Bancroft, *History*, XXIX, 207; Jesse Applegate, *Views of Oregon History*, microfilm, reel 1, no. 2, Frame 40, Bancroft Library. Shortess is an important figure inasmuch as he wrote the Organic Laws, but knowledge of him and of his motives is scanty. While he was, as Mrs. Victor comments, "the extreme of American fanaticism" and an avid supporter of all moves to bring some form of government to Oregon, he opposed paying taxes to the provisional government. As an Indian agent in Clatsop County he demanded fair treatment for the Indians and a government to take care of matters of probate. Bancroft, *History*, XXIX, 207. Robert Shortess to Joseph Lane, Astoria, April 21, 1850, MS 762, Shortess Papers, 1843–54, OHS.

50. Petition: To whom it may concern [n.p.; n.d.], UPS.

signed the 1840 petition. They and others, "more than half Canadians," according to Jason Lee, who had gathered at or near "the Roman Catholic Church . . . on Monday 2 O'Clock PM" [51] on September 14, 1840, are the same men who have so often been suspected of harboring Methodist or mission sympathies. Besides Charles Compo, Joseph Gale, William Mc-Carty, and John Edmunds Pickernell, this group also included Robert Shortess, T. J. Hubbard, James O'Neil, and Webley Hauxhurst, who were "converted" to Methodism and evidently friendly to the mission at one time or another.[52] The two men who refrained from signing White's petition, John Howard and William Johnson, had no special attachment to the mission. Howard was a drinking man and Johnson, an Englishman, was remarkable for his bovine ways. He may have failed to sign the petition simply because he was asleep.[53]

Seven of the twenty-four signers of White's petition were members of the Newell group.[54] One of them, Etienne Lucier, was usually thought to be a great friend of Lee's. Ewing Young also signed the petition, although Young told Lee that he regretted having done so.[55] The only men who signed White's petition from those who only signed the Shortess petition were James Bates and John Turner. The latter was exceptional because his wheat production of 300 bushels was almost half that of the entire group. Bates's behavior on both occasions may simply have been the result of his penury. He was working for the mission in both 1840 and 1843, although he alone of the twenty-four who signed the White petition was penniless in both years. He may have been indebted to White who was a creditor of some dimension in the settlements.[56]

51. Lee to corresponding secretary, Mission House, September 15, 1840, UPS; Petition: To whom it may concern, UPS.

52. James O'Neil and T. J. Hubbard were both much affected by a Methodist love feast in December 1838. O'Neil was in fact converted, as was Shortess. See H. K. W. Perkins to Daniel Lee, Mission House, January 4, 1839, folder M-Z, Deady Papers, OHS. Hauxhurst was the first white convert in Oregon. See Hussey, *Champoeg*, pp. 75–76. O'Neil lived on what was originally Leslie's homesite, about one mile from the Willamette near Mission Bottom. In 1841 Leslie was living with O'Neil. Charles Wilkes, *Narrative of the United States Exploring Expedition during the Years 1838, 1839, 1840, 1841, 1842* (5 vols.; Philadelphia, 1849), IV, 356.

53. *Ibid.*, IV, 347, 349.

54. The seven were Joseph Holman, Peter Bilake [Bellique], George W. Ebbert, Caleb Wilkins, W. J. Bailey, William Canning, and Etienne Lucier.

55. Jason Lee to corresponding secretary, Mission House, March 15, 1841, UPS.

56. By means of an ingenious form of "protection" White managed to keep many settlers in his debt. See [W. W. Raymond] to the board of the Missionary Society of the

A final group of men whose activities in March and May require explanation comprised the mission personnel who participated in the meeting on May 2. There were only five: Dr. Ira Babcock, W. H. Willson, L. H. Judson, Alanson Beers, and Josiah L. Parrish.[57] Babcock, supreme judge of probate, could not easily have avoided putting in an appearance at the May meeting, and he is the only one of the five who did not sign the Shortess petition.[58] Although Babcock was a member of the Island Milling Company, he was obviously not part of the company's "inner circle," as shown by a letter he wrote McLoughlin in late 1841. He assured the Chief Factor that he would "withdraw from the company" if it was true that McLoughlin really did have a claim at the Falls and that the Island Milling Company was challenging that claim.[59] This kind of behavior led George Gary to praise Babcock as the only layman in the mission family with "the courtesies of a gentleman." [60] The doctor's willingness to withdraw from the company was perhaps just as genuine as his ignorance of the operations of a company in which he was a director.

W. H. Willson was an eccentric who cherished a consuming passion for cats and was addicted "for many years [to] the habitual use of tobacco . . . even immoderately." [61] He was also a quack who judged himself competent to practice medicine, though his only training had been acquired "since he engaged as Carpenter for Oregon Mission," a pretension

---

Methodist Episcopal Church, Willamette, September 2, 1840, UPS. Raymond was White's amanuensis during the exchange of letters between White and Lee in 1840. The fact that White may have used this leverage to get some of the names on his petition of 1840 against Lee does not necessarily destroy the importance of the petition. Indeed, it strengthens the petition by underlining the implausibility of Lee's hold on the men who signed it.

57. David Leslie did not sign the Shortess petition. Although he is usually considered to have voted on May 2, actually he did not. Leslie went to Hawaii in 1841 and returned on the brig *Fama,* which did not reach Oregon until after May 2. Although Frances Victor does not say that Leslie was a member of this ship's company, a letter from Waller to Amos Cooke indicates that Leslie did in fact return to Oregon on the *Fama.* See Bancroft, *History,* XXIX, 422; Alvan Waller to Amos Cooke, Willamette Falls, August 2, 1843 (typewritten copy), OHS.

58. Duniway and Riggs, "Archives," p. 236.

59. McLoughlin to governor and committee, December 4, 1843, HBS, VI, 188 (E. E. Rich, ed., *The Letters of John McLoughlin from Fort Vancouver to the Governor and Committee,* 2d ser. [Toronto, 1943]).

60. Gary, "Diary," p. 271.

61. J. H. Brown, "Sketches of Salem from 1851–1869," *Marion County History* 3 (1957): 21.

that Lee believed would bring "some of us . . . to an untimely grave." [62]
But most important here, Willson was not a member of the mission in
1843. Lee told the board that Willson had "reported himself incapaci-
tated by a local infirmity . . . and ask[ed] some lighter employment" as
early as March 1841. It was the opinion "of those best acquainted with
him he [was] not fit for a school teacher, and what we shall do with him I
know not." [63] By October 1842 Willson asked to be discharged from the
mission. Lee, thinking it "best for all concerned that he be released,"
decided to give Willson "a written discharge and take receipt of him in
full of *all* demands upon the Missionary Board." [64]

L. H. Judson, elected justice of the peace in 1841, was an emotional
man with pronounced views on the subjects of laymen's rights, slavery (he
was an abolitionist, along with Brewer and Raymond), and temperance.[65]
Writing Brewer in 1846 of an event six years earlier which still rankled,
Judson insisted that "we all had as *good* a right as any other members of
the Mission . . . [to] a seat and a voice in the yearly meeting." [66] Judson
believed there was a need to reform the church in the matter of its "over-
grown Episcopal powers and prerogatives," even though he thought "the
history of . . . church reform" promised "little or no hope . . . of success." [67] His emphatic support for laymen's rights led him to be more
sympathetic than other members of the mission (or more than the facts
warranted) to Elijah White when White was tried and dismissed from the
mission in September 1840.[68] At that time White told the superintendent that Judson was willing to consent to Lee's "continuance in office
for at least a little longer time." [69] Judson's signature on the Shortess petition would seem to have been an expression of duty, and his participation in the May 2 meeting, an expression of independence. In November Judson resigned from the mission "to spend . . . time in business
. . . and not to receive any support from Oregon Mission for the ensuing

62. Lee to corresponding secretary, Willamette Falls, March 30, 1843, UPS.
63. Lee to corresponding secretary, Mission House, March 15, 1841, UPS.
64. Lee to corresponding secretary, Vancouver, October 18, 1842, UPS.
65. L. H. Judson to H. B. Brewer, October 20, 1841, Brewer Collection, WSHS.
66. *Ibid.* Judson refers to the question of laymen's rights in Oregon about which there
was some difficulty owing largely to Lee's administrative ineptitude. See chapter 3.
67. [L. H. Judson] to H. B. Brewer, Chemeketa, March 16, 1845, Brewer Collection,
WSHS.
68. L. H. Judson to Elijah White, March 3, 1841, Judson Papers, OHS.
69. Elijah White to Jason Lee, [August or September, 1841], UPS.

three years." [70] Like Beers and Willson, Judson was one of the men whose behavior led Gary to say that "Bro. Lee has had a difficult set to deal with." [71]

Alanson Beers was a member of the three-man executive committee elected on July 5, 1843. With Newell, he favored a weak government on May 2.[72] As a member of the Island Milling Company he looked forward to the validation of mission claims at the Falls and to the extension of American laws to Oregon. Like Josiah Parrish and George Abernethy, he engaged in speculation.[73] He was avid in the pursuit and care of money, once threatening to sue the mission for allegedly cheating him of a few dollars worth of scrap iron, a development that astonished even George Gary.[74] In March 1838 Beers joined Henry Perkins, W. H. Willson, Elijah White, and David Leslie in presenting Lee with a memorial claiming he was incompetent and should resign.[75] Beers's independence of mind was accompanied by an uncomplicated desire to please others and a willingness to follow the lead of stronger men. In 1843 the course of least resistance was compromise. A weak provisional government met the needs of Beers perfectly. As a quiet man and a hard worker he won the respect of his fellows,[76] and all groups spoke well of him. Jason Lee thought Beers "as good a man to work as you will find." [77] Gray called Beers "a good, honest, faithful, and intelligent Christian man, acting with heart and soul with the interests of the settlement and the American cause," [78] a brand

70. L. H. Judson, [Certificate], Willamette, November 27, 1843, UPS.

71. Gary, "Diary," p. 271.

72. Newell to Evans, August 8, 1867, Evans Papers.

73. In 1846 Beers, Abernethy, and John Force bought all the stock in the Island Milling Company. On July 11, 1844, Beers bought the mission farm. Because of his large family—wife and six children—Beers received almost $800 a year in salary plus table expense, and Gary deducted $1,000 from the price of the farm in compensation for what would have been the Missionary Society's expense for returning Beers and his family to the United States. Gary, "Diary," p. 96. Beers also speculated in horses. HBS, VI, 147.

74. Gary, "Diary," p. 159.

75. Elijah White to [Jason Lee], July 31, 1840, UPS. Lee did not deny that the memorial existed or that it was signed by Beers, Perkins, Willson, White, and Leslie. He said only that the memorial was returned to those who presented it. Jason Lee to [Elijah White], Mission House, August 14, 1840, UPS.

76. The same cannot be said of any other important figure in Willamette Valley affairs in the spring of 1843.

77. Cornelius J. Brosnan, "Transcript," *Jason Lee: Prophet of the New Oregon* (New York, 1932), p. 254.

78. William H. Gray, *A History of Oregon, 1792–1849* (Portland, 1870), p. 337.

of description Gray reserved for children and dead men, suggesting that Beers was receptive to persuasion. Newell approved of the ways Beers voted in the meetings of the legislature in May and June 1843—against Gray and with Newell.[79] Beers's success in pleasing everyone revealed him to be a pleasant gentlemen of limited analytical abilities who could detect only the sharpest of differences. The difference between the Shortess petition and the Champoeg meeting for Beers, a resident at the Old Mission, was clear only in the degree that the mission favored American jurisdiction or tolerated the most limited of local governments.

The inclusion of Josiah L. Parrish, blacksmith and local preacher, in group 2 is uncertain. His testimony, taken by Hubert Howe Bancroft's researchers in 1878, is confused and contradictory. Although he signed the Shortess petition he did not remember that the Hudson's Bay Company was anything but the settlers' friend in 1843.[80] And, while he said the members of the legislative committee of nine chosen on May 2 boarded at his house when they met in May and June, implying that he attended the meetings, he also stated flatly that "the first Champoeg meeting was about six months after the wolf meeting in 1843. I was at Clatsop at the time." [81] If Parrish was in the Willamette Valley at the time of the Champoeg meeting, which is not unlikely, there is nonetheless no sure evidence that he actually did attend it. More evidence than is presently at hand is required to determine his activities in this period.[82]

The mission's strength in 1843 and its relation to the proposed government were the result, oddly enough, of its physical division.[83] When the great reinforcement arrived in June 1840, the mission began filtering out of the Champoeg area, moving north to the Falls and south to Chemeketa. Mission growth, though meeting the needs of Methodism in the wilderness by separating secular and spiritual enterprises, left a middle region, Champoeg and contiguous settlements, without a source of employment for local residents. Along with being a major employer the mission was also a supplier. The Old Mission in the upper settlements of Champoeg provided certain services to settlers which only a larger corporation of in-

79. Newell to Evans, August 8, 1867, Evans Papers.
80. J. L. Parrish, *Anecdotes,* microfilm, reel 9, Bancroft Library.
81. *Ibid.,* frame 100.
82. Parrish was reported at Clatsop in August 1843. Lee to corresponding secretary, Fort George, August 12, 1843, UPS.
83. That is, the mission's separation of spiritual and temporal functions. See chapter 5.

dividuals could offer. The services included not only the provision of supplies but assistance in the areas of transportation, trade, and credit.[84] When the mission left Champoeg in mid-1841 the settlers were thrown back upon their original dependence on the Hudson's Bay Company. In time Champoeg would diminish in significance despite its agricultural population and its desirable situation as a shipping point and entrepôt, but for the next few years settlers thought its importance would continue to be substantial. Efforts to capitalize on that importance before Champoeg was overshadowed by the towns of Salem and Oregon City were made by various groups and individuals after the mission left.

The Hudson's Bay Company, Ewing Young, and the provisional government, specifically as Newell conceived it, were all attempts to fill the mission's old place in Champoeg. By mid-1841 the mission was committed to its secular establishment at the Falls and the spiritual program at Chemeketa, for which supplies from the East and credit in London were essential. From 1841 to 1843 Champoeg was, in the minds of Oregonians at the time, an unclaimed "empire" awaiting its emperor. In the story of the formation of the provisional government, wheat and geography are fundamental factors.

From the time of William Slacum's visit in 1837, Willamette Valley farmers, French Canadians among them, had grumbled about the price the Hudson's Bay Comapny paid for wheat. As the only buyer, McLoughlin was free to set the prices for grain. Characteristically combining generosity and self-interest, he set a liberal price for produce but paid only half of it in cash or in script redeemable at the company's store at Fort Vancouver. The other half was paid in the form of a 50 percent discount on goods purchased at the same company store. Thus McLoughlin managed to pay more for wheat than anyone else—about $1.10 a bushel—while receiving a rebate in the assured sale of supplies to his payees. As Lieutenant Wilkes pointed out, McLoughlin was paying a good price, for the company retailed wheat at $1.50 a bushel to the Russian American Company. The farmers, however, found McLoughlin's methods "difficult to understand," as Wilkes put it, and were "by no means satisfied with the rate." [85]

84. The importance of the mission was admitted by all. As 1843 opened Robert Newell commented in his diary that, except "for this mission . . . this colony would do badly." Dorothy Johansen, ed., *Robert Newell's Memoranda* (Portland, 1959), p. 40.

85. Wilkes, *Exploring Tour*, IV, 365.

McLoughlin's arrangement with the farmers hurt the mission store at the Falls, where supplies were limited to begin with. Methodist milling prospects and, with them, mission hopes for an export trade would suffer if the mission could not buy wheat. Moreover, since the company's policy was not to fight competition but to overwhelm it, the Chief Factor bought all the wheat he could to keep potential competitors away.[86] The Shortess petition was directed specifically to these issues: "Every means will be made use of by them [the Hudson's Bay Company] to break down every thing that will draw trade to this country or enable persons to get goods at any other place than their store. . . . All the Wheat raised in Oregon, they are anxious to get, as they ship it to the Russians on the North West Coast." [87]

Before the intrusive question of independence forced the mission to rely on a device like the Shortess petition, Methodists had gained a degree of economic distance from Fort Vancouver. Although the Chief Factor sold goods to the missionaries at a discount of 50 percent, the mission was selling its supplies "at fifteen per cent, on all wholesale prices" paid in New York.[88] At that rate, the corresponding secretary of the Missionary Society sardonically commented, goods "were disposed of at less than prime cost . . . which certainly was not the design of the arrangement." [89] Prices had become more reasonable by 1842, but Lee extended liberal credit, a policy for which he was later roundly criticized by the board. George Gary, beginning the arduous task of putting the mission's

---

86. James Douglas to governor and committee, October 18, 1838, HBS, IV, 241 (E. E. Rich, ed., *The Letters of John McLoughlin from Fort Vancouver to the Governor and Committee*, 1st ser. [Toronto, 1941]). "Grain is, now, the only export, of the Colony: the surplus produce of 1836 was 100 Bus. [a very small number indicating how important small numbers were in the life of the settlement]. Wheat, which we purchased, and I am now buying up the crop of this season, to clear the market and leave nothing in store for casual visiters, a policy that ought not to be neglected."

87. Duniway and Riggs, "Archives," p. 232. These assertions were true of course. As early as 1838 James Douglas had predicted these developments, as Lee had done in his petition of the same year to the United States Congress. Douglas pointed out that "when the introduction of foreign capital terminates this dependence [i.e., the dependence of settlers' on the company] . . . our general influence will decline as the wants of the Settlement find a provision in other sources." Douglas to governor and committee, October 18, 1838, HBS, IV, 242. See also HBS, VII, 253–54.

88. Lee to corresponding secretary, Mission House, March 15, 1841, UPS.

89. *Minutes, B.M.*, IV, 91.

accounts in order in 1844, said that there "never should have been such an amount trusted out to almost everybody in this territory." [90]

While Gary was condemning Lee's policies in Oregon, Lee was justifying them to the board in New York. He argued that the purpose and the effect of his efforts had been to save the settlers "from succumbing to the H.B. Co." [91] Nevertheless, even two years before Lee returned east, the mission had been seriously in debt. Lee's credit policies, along with his unpaid debts at Fort Vancouver, explain many of the mission's difficulties. In August 1843 the mission accountant, George Abernethy, promised the board he was going to ask 100 to 150 percent advance on the invoice cost of Methodist goods, and he would refuse "to give credit." He would "endeavor to get in what is due the mission," a feat he accomplished only when the mission's debts were bought by his own Island Milling Company in 1846.[92] The importance of wheat and the crucial connection between the Falls site and export trade had been recognized by Methodists from the beginning. The Falls, Alvan Waller wrote his brother, was "destined to be, the great emporium of the interior of this country. Its water power for manufacturing purposes is probably not rivaled in the States: at least, few and far between are the privileges which equal or excel it." [93]

An export market was the most essential requirement of Oregonians in 1840, as it would be for some years to come. Oregon missionaries were consistently on the lookout for opportunities to establish an export trade. Waller chafed at the restraints imposed by Oregon's isolation and the powers of the Hudson's Bay Company. Writing to a Presbyterian friend in the Sandwich Islands, where Jason Lee had already been investigating the possibilities for trade, Waller said that

> there probably have not been less than twenty thousand bushels of wheat and other grain raised in Oregon if not thirty thousand in all. Our Mission could forward salmon sufficient to purchase our groceries had we an opportunity to send, fifty or a hundred bushels might have been provided but

90. Gary, "Diary," p. 181.

91. Brosnan, "Transcript," *Lee,* p. 252.

92. George Abernethy to corresponding secretary, Willamette [Falls], August 3, 1843, UPS.

93. Alvan Waller to his brother, Willamette Falls, April 6, 1842, in *Ohio Statesman,* March 10, 1843, *OHQ* 4 (1905): 178.

there was no vessel that we could get them on board of. The HB Co., has probably taken 10,000 or 12,000 bushel of wheat this fall. If navigation opens suitably, much grain or flour may be exported from here to the Islands in a few years, but the Company seems determined to monopolize the whole of this business.[94]

Here then, just as the Island Milling Company was being formed, were the germs of the Shortess petition. Only the threat of independence was lacking. Lee's views about trade, wheat, and export were the same as Waller's. Explaining the conflict between the mission and the Hudson's Bay Company to board members in 1844, Lee told them that "the history of . . . [this] matter . . . [began when the] settlers became convinced that the H.B. Co., wished to monopolize the commerce. This injured the settlers and the Mission. They believed they could build a Mill at the Falls that would bring in other vessels besides the H.B. Co's." [95] And if the relation of trade to milling was explicit in the letters of Lee and Waller, plans to develop both were fully invested with evangelical content.

Daniel Lee, for example, charted a grand design for exploiting the connection between wheat and evangelism. In his view, which in modified form became the actual practice of the Missionary Society, a commercial establishment was basic to the health of the mission. His plan was for the society to buy a ship (Fisk, it will be recalled, approved the objective but not the ship) [96] to trade in the Pacific and "on the Spanish Main." Wheat from Oregon, Daniel believed, could be sold on the northern coast of South America for six times its cost. Trade in the same commodity with the Russians in Alaska would also come within the scope of mission commerce. There beaver could be taken in trade and sold in Canton. Daniel was rethinking the plans of John Ledyard, fulfilled by American traders three decades earlier, but his thoughts were directed to the future. He believed the society could expect profits of not less than "$66,000 per year: . . . a vessel . . . [could] be wholly employed in the work, the Mission . . . can hardly fail of success. And the missionary spirit will not only be awakened by it; but the whole work will feel the impulse, not only in Ourgon but throughout the world, an impulse, that hell cannot withstand and by which the salvation of the world will be hastened [by]

94. Waller to Amos Cooke, November 30, 1841, OHS.
95. Brosnan, "Transcript," *Lee*, p. 268.
96. Willbur Fisk to F. P. Tracy, November 10, 1838, *Oregonian and Indian's Advocate* 2 (1838): 78.

centuries." [97] If Daniel Lee could think that a vast speculative venture in trade and shipping was a way to touch off a missionary revival and hasten the salvation of the world by centuries, it is not difficult to understand how Jason Lee and Willbur Fisk might suppose that the Island Milling Company would materially aid missionary work in Oregon.

While the mission strove to find ways to break the company's monopoly, the French Canadians began, in their own way, to strive for better treatment from the company. By 1840 they realized that their leverage with the Chief Factor had increased as a consequence of his dependence on Willamette wheat to meet the Hudson's Bay Company's contract with the Russian American Fur Company. Accordingly, in July, French-Canadian wheat growers in Champoeg asked McLoughlin to build a warehouse to save them the trouble of delivering their wheat to Fort Vancouver or to any other point. [98] If the farmers were testing their power, they were also demonstrating the expansion of the wheat industry in Oregon. Times were changing. The simple and easy days of tenant farmer and patriarch were coming to a close. McLoughlin agreed to build the warehouse, but he did not build it. When William F. Tolmie came to pick up the fall harvest of 1840 for the company, the settlers were slow to bring the wheat to him. McLoughlin advised Tolmie to threaten that the company might not come for the wheat at all if the settlers remained balky. The wheat was important to the company, however, and McLoughlin assured Tolmie that "between you and me we will do all we can" [99] to get it. Calculating that Champoeg, not the Falls, would be the center of an American Oregon, McLoughlin thought that a mill might be more appropriate than a warehouse in 1840.

Until the mid-1830s there was no mill at all in the Champoeg area for either the upper or the lower settlements. Webley Hauxhurst of the Ewing Young party built the first mill in the Willamette Valley in 1835. Years later Daniel Lee wrote that Hauxhurst's mill "greatly added to the comfort of the inhabitants, who had previously, some of them, to pound their wheat in mortars. At the mission we have a small cast-iron corn-

97. Daniel Lee to corresponding secretary, Wascopam, April 30, 1838, UPS.
98. See Hussey, *Champoeg*, pp. 108–10. The situation of the French-Canadian farmers may be likened in several respects to that of the American farmers in the Ohio and Mississippi valleys in 1796 when a Federalist administration offered to trade away the farmers' right of deposit at New Orleans to the Spanish.
99. Hussey, *Champoeg*, p. 109.

cracker, in which we ground wheat after a fashion, and a large wooden mortar, holding a bushell, in which was pounded off the hull of the barley used in soup." [100] In 1839, the year the company signed its contract with the Russians and began farming operations at Puget Sound, Thomas McKay, McLoughlin's stepson, built a gristmill on Champoeg Creek. Although McKay was considered a wealthy man, the two-story mill he erected in 1839–40 almost surely cost more than any one individual in the country could afford—except John McLoughlin. Once again McLoughlin was mixing his personal affairs with those of the company, and this time he added parental concern to the mixture. There is only circumstantial evidence that McLoughlin backed McKay's mill financially, but his desire to keep settlers south of the Columbia and his visions of Champoeg's future made building a mill an attractive project.

In 1839 McLoughlin was wiser than he and Simpson had been in 1828 in the matter of claiming lands. McLoughlin learned a lesson from the growing confusion over the claim at Willamette Falls. Instead of claiming the Champoeg mill site in his own name, he had McKay claim it for him. McLoughlin was also "convinced that the settlers would burn any building erected . . . by the Company in its own name." [101] McKay continued to maintain his huge farm on the Columbia at Scappoose while operating the mill and another good-sized farm in the Willamette Valley. It does not appear that McKay owned the mill after 1844 or that he operated it personally during the time of his putative ownership. [102]

In February 1843 a flood in the Willamette Valley put McKay's mill out of operation until the fall and destroyed a considerable amount of

100. Daniel Lee and John Frost, *Ten Years in Oregon* (New York, 1844), p. 134. I am most grateful to John A. Hussey for pointing Lee's comment out to me.

101. This view was also held by Douglas. He said that the company must either furnish "them with supplies on the security they can offer, or incur . . . the greater risk of exciting them to crime and plunder." James Douglas to governor and committee, Fort Vancouver, October 14, 1839, HBS, VI, 225.

102. This account follows Hussey, *Champoeg*, pp. 92–99, although Hussey does not suggest McLoughlin's possible ownership. The published facts concerning McKay's investments are contradictory in several respects. William Sampson, ed., *John McLoughlin's Business Correspondence, 1847–1848* (Seattle and London, 1973), p. 71, believes the mill was in fact McKay's, although McKay evidently did not pay taxes on it in 1844. At his death in 1849 or 1850 McKay was said to own a gristmill and a sawmill valued at $5,500, although Hussey, *Champoeg*, p. 99, doubts that these were the mills built in 1839. Much of our information comes from an early article by Annie Laurie Bird, who points out that McKay and McLoughlin had engaged in the building of Fort Boise in a manner quite like the one described here. See Annie Laurie Bird, "Thomas McKay," *OHQ* 40 (1939): 5.

stored wheat. The warehouse requested in 1840 by French-Canadian settlers had still not been built, and only the mills at Fort Vancouver and the Falls were available in the emergency. It was these serious economic factors that led to McLoughlin's decision to build his long-promised warehouse.[103] Robert Newell's rediscovery of an interest in Champoeg was likewise induced by the questions of wheat and trade. Newell, never much of a farmer, came back to Champoeg in 1843 with dreams of becoming a capitalist. His newly purchased home site was on poor farming land, but it included the lower course of Champoeg Creek, the area that had attracted Webley Hauxhurst and Thomas McKay to Champoeg.[104]

Champoeg had neither a store nor a warehouse, and it also lacked a supplier. McKay's mill, even when it was functioning, did not serve as a bank or a trading center for wheat grown by the farmers of French Prairie and Tualatin Plains. Instead, the mills and the stores at Fort Vancouver and the Falls provided banking services. Either wheat had to be shipped to one or the other of those places or a store had to be built at Champoeg. In fact, both would probably be necessary. McLoughlin built the store and Newell looked after the shipping. If McLoughlin's warehouse did not join the McKay mill in creating a mill-store-warehouse complex like those at the Falls and at Fort Vancouver, then wheat would have to be shipped downriver. If, on the other hand, McLoughlin made Champoeg into another Fort Vancouver for the sake of the farmers, then supplies would have to be shipped from Fort Vancouver. Either way it seemed that Newell could not go wrong. Nor could the farmers, whom both Newell and McLoughlin hoped to serve and to profit from. In the spring of 1843 French-Canadian farmers, instead of confronting conspiring partisans eager for their votes on May 2, enjoyed a surprising array of alternatives for the disposal of their wheat.[105] Naturally they would oppose any move to diminish those alternatives and would resent political proposals tending to cut McLoughlin and the company out of the wheat business.

103. Hussey, *Champoeg*, pp. 108–10. The date of McLoughlin's decision and the date of the actual building of the warehouse are not known precisely.

104. *Ibid.*, p. 195.

105. One of the most awkward facts confronting the theory of international rivalry as the genesis of the provisional government is that no concerted effort was made to organize for or against the objectives of the May 2 meeting. Gray says the French Canadians were drilled to vote in the negative on all questions, but there is no hint of this in other sources. Gray, *History*, p. 279.

McLoughlin and Newell were simply repeating in 1843 what Ewing Young and the mission had done, or had attempted to do, a few years earlier. Although the death of Ewing Young in 1841 is associated with the beginnings of provisional government, what has been overlooked is Young's second scheme for independence from the company (his first was the distillery), the building of mills to handle the wheat of French Prairie farmers. Young, never a man to go halfway, even tried to learn French.[106] His death and the mission's departure from the Champoeg area for Salem and the Falls left the gap that McLoughlin and Newell were attempting to close in 1843. Certainly it would have been suicidal for French Canadians to support an effort to put the company outside the boundaries of a new government, for they would then have only one market. The inevitable clash of interests on May 2 stemmed from the French Canadians' disagreement with the swing group, whose members wanted to diminish the company's influence or exclude it from the area altogether. Thus it was an economic conflict, not an international or an ethnic one, which led many later writers to see a contest of patriots on May 2, 1843. Moreover, it is possible to show that the French Canadians did not go to the May 2 meeting with the purpose of defeating the government.

Evidence that the French-Canadian position was not one of opposition comes from a McLoughlin letter frequently cited as proof of the contrary. His comments to his superiors in London have been interpreted to fit the view that the May 2 meeting at Champoeg was basically a struggle of French Canadians against Americans. In reporting to the governor and committee, McLoughlin did not say that French Canadians were directly involved in the meeting. Since it had been his idea originally to allow retired company employees to settle in the Willamette, he might well have been loath to picture them as unhappy. His position was doubly awkward inasmuch as he was deeply implicated in Willamette business life. What McLoughlin did report was that the "American population of the Wallamette had a political meeting last May and invited the Canadians to unite with them in organizing themselves into a community, the Canadians who are fully as many as the others, told them they would positively take no part in their plans of organization and government." [107] This state-

106. F. G. Young, "Ewing Young and His Estate," *OHQ* 21 (1920): 196, 210.
107. John McLoughlin to governor and committee, November 15, 1843, HBS, VI, 130. McLoughlin did not alter the sense of his earlier communication of March 1843 when

ment has been wrongly used as evidence of French-Canadian opposition to organization of a government. At least eight French Canadians did go to the meeting and did vote for organization. Second, McLoughlin said, not that the French Canadians voted against American plans, but that they did not participate in those plans. Since French-Canadian opposition in the form of votes, if it had actually developed, would have put McLoughlin in a better light, his failure to say specifically that the French Canadians voted down an American effort is significant.[108]

No doubt a number of French Canadians did attend the meeting and some of them certainly voted against organization. It will come as no surprise to find that the confusion concerning how many people voted is traceable to William Gray.[109] His assertion in 1870 that the vote on May 2 was 52-50 "for government" sent antiquaries in search of fifty French names to set against fifty-two Anglo-Saxon ones. But even if fifty French Canadians really did attend the meeting, not all of them voted against organization. What they opposed was the big-government wing, not organization per se. And there were some Americans, Sidney Smith and "others of his kind," who "opposed us most bitterly." [110] Smith was a friend of Hines's and Hines was the most outspoken antagonist of the three-man executive committee.[111]

It was the issue of the governor's office, and not international or ethnic conflict, which was the immediate cause of dispute on May 2. The issue

---

he told Simpson that the French Canadians were not "inclined to join" with Americans. McLoughlin to Simpson, March 20, 1843, in Robert C. Clark, *History of the Willamette Valley* (3 vols.; Chicago, 1927), I, 793.

108. By this time, November 1843, McLoughlin and Simpson were on very unfriendly terms. Any effort by McLoughlin to water down unfavorable developments is not surprising in view of the increasing precariousness of his position. McLoughlin's annual financial report for 1843 was computed in such a way as to show profits for 1842 and 1843 when in fact those years brought deficits. Although McLoughlin does not appear to have been at fault in the compilation, he must have known as well as anyone that the figures were not meaningful or valid. See W. Kaye Lamb, "Introduction," HBS, VII, lvi–lvii.

109. Gray, *History*, p. 279. Gray first made the assertions, later published in his history, in the *Astoria Marine Gazette*. An interesting account of the literature of the May 2 vote is Russell B. Thomas, "Truth and Fiction of Champoeg Meeting," *OHQ* 30 (1929): 218–37. Lists of French Canadians said to have attended are found in Frederick V. Holman, "A Brief History of the Oregon Provisional Government and What Caused Its Formation," *OHQ* 13 (1912): 114–16; F. X. Matthieu, "Reminiscences," *OHQ* 1 (1900): 91.

110. Newell to Evans, August 8, 1867, Evans Papers.

111. Gray, *History*, pp. 348–49; Newell to Evans, August 8, 1867, Evans Papers.

was crucial in May, although it had not been so at the mid-March meeting.[112] Now that evidence of the "report of a previous meeting" mentioned at the May 2 meeting is available, it is possible to distinguish two separate votes on May 2 and not, as traditionally thought, two counts of the same vote.[113] The first vote was on the report of the mid-March meeting referred to in Newell's letter of March 18, 1843, to Henry Brewer. This report outlined a hierarchy of officers for the provisional government already agreed to in mid-March. It was common knowledge in 1843 that the top official was to be a governor. As early as April 1843, in a letter to the wife of the Reverend Elkanah Walker, who served under the American Board of Commissioners for Foreign Missions, Elvira Perkins, wife of Henry Perkins, wrote from The Dalles that "they are doing great things in the Willamette, making laws, *electing Governor* and other officers, laying out Oregon city," and otherwise changing things so that "you will perhaps, think yourself in the United States." [114]

Newell remembered well that the first vote on May 2 was negative and that opposition to the plan of a government with a governor was the reason. The "first vote taken," he wrote, was "that we have no Governor to defeat the wolf bummers." [115] Gray, twenty years later, and historians after him, accepted the second vote recorded in the May 2 minutes as a recount of the first. The second vote was, says Gray, "for the report of the committee and an organization." [116] Gray was in error, as seen by Newell's testimony and the minutes of the meeting, which report that after the second vote for or against "the objects of this meeting," that is, in

112. See chapter 7.

113. These two votes are explicit in the minutes. Thus, once the motion to accept the report was lost, a second vote, the famous "division" on the question of "the objects of this meeting," was taken. Duniway and Riggs, "Archives," pp. 236–37. The division is Joe Meek's "call for a division."

114. Elvira Perkins to Mrs. Mary Richardson Walker, Wascopam, April 11, 1843, Perkins's Letters: 1838–1844, Beinecke.

115. Robert Newell's personal copy of *Oregon Archives*, p. 14. "Bummers" might also be "business."

116. Gray, *History*, p. 279. That is, the second vote was not, as Gray states, for both the organization and the report but only for the organization. Gray makes a good deal of the fact that the French Canadians could not speak English well, if they could speak it at all. His purpose was to suggest that the French Canadians were instructed to vote like sheep. In fact, the French Canadians were opposed to a governor and not to the idea of government. The second vote, the vote for "organization," was very likely the one in which language played a part; many people may not have known what was really going on, including the secretary who recorded the events.

favor of "organization," it was moved "that the report of the committee be taken up, and disposed of article by article." [117] All the articles taken up are specified, but no governor's position is mentioned. The only possible inference is that once the meeting had decided not to have a governor, the majority did vote to approve the organization as agreed upon in mid-March.[118]

Clearly the group opposed to organization with a governor was made up of French Canadians and, as Newell said, of those who opposed the "wolf bummers." Although this conclusion is implicit in the minutes of the May 2 meeting, the gathering on July 5 at Champoeg, "where nearly all the Americans in the country, and many of the French and English assembled," leaves no doubt in the matter.[119] On that day the Reverend Gustavus Hines, whom Newell, with some justice, called a "political bilk," [120] addressed the assemblage at length, loudly condemning the three-man executive as a "hydra-headed monster." [121] Had Hines attended the May 2 meeting he would have realized, as Newell did, that the three-man executive, like the provision forbidding taxation, grew out of a compromise among groups that consented to the provisional government.

If, as Newell said, all would fall to the ground unless Hines "changed his tune," [122] there must have been a group on July 5, as there had been on May 2, powerful enough to reject the idea of having a governor. Gray contends, and he is undoubtedly correct, that Lee favored the three-man executive committee in preference to a governor.[123] Everything known about Lee, particularly his opposition to a local government, supports this view. But the mission's toleration of the provisional government was won by giving in exchange the famous proviso to the land laws. The people Hines was alienating, Newell realized, were the French Canadians. Their attitude toward the provisional government was tied to the question of a governor, which in turn reflected the factors of wheat and geography.

Just as French-Canadian farmers were worried lest McLoughlin's influence in the settlements be curtailed, thus weakening their competitive

117. Duniway and Riggs, "Archives," p. 237.
118. *Ibid.*
119. Gustavus Hines, *A Voyage Round the World: With a History of Oregon Mission* (Buffalo, 1850), p. 425.
120. Newell to Evans, August 8, 1867, Evans Papers.
121. Gray, *History,* p. 350. Also see p. 164, above.
122. Newell to Evans, August 8, 1867, Evans Papers.
123. Gray, *History,* p. 348.

position, so Blanchet and the French Canadians were bound from the beginning to reject executive leadership as a threat to the powers of McLoughlin. In fact, Blanchet referred to McLoughlin as the "governor." [124] In a remonstrance presented to the May 2 meeting, the French Canadians expressed willingness to abide by "either the mode of senate or council, to judge the difficulties, punish the crimes . . . and make the regulations suitable for the people . . . [with] a president of said council." [125] This remonstrance, or one like it, said Newell, "was intended to be submitted as a code of laws for the time being," not as a rejection of government or a refusal to "unite" with the Americans, as McLoughlin later claimed.[126]

Symbolically, and to some degree in fact, the provisional government had something for everyone. The new government had gifts for those who opposed it and promises for its friends, an arrangement suggesting that the enemies were fairly powerful and the friends were less than completely enthusiastic. The remarkable thing about the provisional government, created in what has recently been called a "solemn conclave of democracy," [127] is that it was a nongovernment or even an antigovernment. Based upon the counterrevolutionary principle of representation without taxation, the provisional government pledged itself to provide services and to guarantee land claims while asking neither taxes nor allegiance in return. In a word, the provisional government was utopia. In a time when it seemed that all Americans were searching for the promised land of harmony and peace, Oregon settlers had stumbled onto the true article by inadvertence.

124. Blanchet to Demers, February 11, 1841, PAA, in Lyons, *Blanchet,* p. 93.
125. Frein, "Address," p. 339. See n. 21, above.
126. Newell to Evans, August 8, 1867, Evans Papers.
127. Johansen and Gates, *Empire of the Columbia,* p. 189.

CHAPTER 9

Equality on the Oregon Frontier

> Only the learned read old books and we have now so
> dealt with the learned that they are of all men the least
> likely to acquire wisdom by doing so. We have done
> this by inculcating the Historical Point of View . . .
> [which] means that when a learned man is presented
> with any statement in an ancient author, the one ques-
> tion he never asks is whether it is true. He asks who in-
> fluenced the . . . writer, and how far the statement is
> consistent with what he said in other books, and what
> phase in the writer's development, or in the general his-
> tory of thought, it illustrates, and how it affected later
> writers, and how often it has been misunderstood . . .
> and what the general course of criticism on it has been
> for the last ten years. . . . [T]hanks to . . . the His-
> torical Point of View, great scholars are now as little
> nourished by the past as the most ignorant mechanic
> who holds that "history is bunk."
> —C. S. LEWIS, *The Screwtape Letters:*
> *Letters from a Senior to a Junior Devil*

EW indeed would fail to accord the author of *Democracy in America* a high place among those who have written about the Jacksonian era and about American equality. Nevertheless, Alexis de Tocqueville has been accused of reducing all American life to egalitarian terms while failing at the same time to define equality adequately or to show its precise causal properties. In fact, however, Tocqueville's shortcomings are at least partly explained by the inherently paradoxical character of the idea he hoped to divine. Tocqueville was among the first and most insightful of those who sensed what American historians from George Bancroft to Henry Adams and Carl Becker have also sensed about the United States. The national past, they all agree, was somehow about democracy, that is, about equality. Harry V. Jaffa has fleshed out this intuition. "American politics," writes Jaffa, "is unprecedented and unique in that in it alone all disagreements have ultimately been disagreements concerning the true import and meaning of equality." American

[229]

history has been a continuing clash of what he calls "the antinomies contained within the idea of equality," [1] most often conceived as logical opposites: liberty-equality, public-private, conservative-liberal. Jaffa explains that these pairings are intrinsic to equality. While models of equilibrium, reciprocity, and the dialectic are the usual instruments employed by egalitarian theorists to promote the recollection of the antinomies, Jaffa suggests a more profound view of the matter. For example, the principle of equal rights for which Lincoln contended in 1858 was an appropriate inference from the Declaration of Independence, but so too was the principle of consent of the governed which Douglas argued against Lincoln. But while Jaffa suggests that Lincoln resolved the conflict, thereby rescuing the egalitarian ideal as well as the Union, one may with perhaps greater justice draw the opposite conclusion. The episodes described in this book, no less than the larger matters surrounding the Civil War with which Jaffa deals, seem to indicate that the antinomies of egalitarianism are implacably irreconcilable, and that the idea and the suppositions upon which it rests are at the very best simply false. The profound and tragic failure of federalism is a remarkable instance of the historic transformation of the egalitarian ideal. The story of Jason Lee and the Oregon mission, though less startling, is paradigmatic. Tocqueville's analysis is germane to that story, for he detected an ineradicable flaw in the American democratic setting. [2]

1. Harry V. Jaffa, *Liberty and Equality* (New York, 1965), p. 128. Also his *Crisis of the House Divided: An Interpretation of the Issues in the Lincoln-Douglas Debates* (Seattle, 1973). Detection of a certain duality or contrariety in American democratic history is a familiar theme. Examples are George Sabine, "Two Democratic Traditions," *Philosophical Review* 52 (1946), and Carl Degler, "The Two Cultures and the Civil War," in Stanley Coben and Lorman Ratner, eds., *The Development of an American Culture* (Englewood Cliffs, 1970), pp. 92–119.

More recent, and perhaps somewhat polemical, are studies such as Michael Kammen, *People of Paradox: An Inquiry Concerning the Origins of American Civilization* (New York: Knopf, 1972). Etienne Gilson, considering these same antinomies at the most critical philosophical and historical levels, has written, in an essay of surpassing sweep and brilliance: "Modern society . . . , in so far as it attempts to reform itself on the model of its own doctrines [naturalistic monism and conceptual dualism], is condemned to oscillate perpetually between anarchism and collectivism, or to live empirically by a shameful compromise which is without justification." "Concerning Christian Philosophy: The Distinctiveness of the Philosophic Order," in Raymond Klibansky and H. J. Paton, eds., *Philosophy and History: Essays Presented to Ernst Cassirer* (New York: Harper & Row, 1963), I, 68.

2. Alexis de Tocqueville, *Democracy in America,* ed. Phillips Bradley (2 vols.; New

Tocqueville suggests that equality among individuals, or what has been called "ethical individualism," would at length erode all bonds between individuals, presumably even severing the umbilical linkage itself.[3] In time each soul, standing totally free in a world of other totally free individuals, must turn to the state as the source of authority and identification. Statism is what Tocqueville believed to be the promise of American life. Americans, of course, had thrashed out these issues in theoretical form before Tocqueville arrived to document the practical consequences. In what were unquestionably the most rarefied and metaphysical months in modern history, the delegates to the Constitutional Convention of 1787 debated the advantages and the disadvantages of modernity. It was Alexander Hamilton who was the seer and the modernist. Calling for the central government to act directly upon the citizens in the manner of Rousseau, and scorning those who would retain the obtrusive mediation of the states with all their local prejudices, Hamilton was a man ahead of his time. The sage Madison, who saw "no fatal consequence . . . in the tendency in the General Government to absorb the State Governments," appears only quaint even from the perspective of the 1830s, when the Hamiltonian vision of a "distinction between State Governments and the people" was already becoming a reality.[4] Robert Nisbet has refined and clarified Tocqueville's insights in their twentieth-century setting with great acuity.[5] But while the antebellum portrait of equality as suggested by the historical account in these pages is not misconceived by the terms of Tocquevillian analysis, or by Jaffa's insights, more is required. The focus is still not adequate.

York: Vintage Books, 1945), I, 73–74, 99, 193, 264n; II, 99, 101, 113, 116–18, 147, 310–20.

3. Cecelia M. Kenyon, "Alexander Hamilton: Rousseau of the Right," in Sidney Fine and Gerald S. Brown, eds., *The American Past* (2d ed.; 2 vols.; New York, 1965), I, 227–40.

4. James Madison, *Notes of Debates in the Federal Convention of 1787* (Athens, Ohio, 1966), pp. 166, 173.

5. Nisbet's excellent study, *The Quest for Community* (London, 1969), is a critique of Enlightenment consequences, that is, of anomie, alienation, and so on. But Nisbet, like the socialist Sidney Hook and the pluralist Ernest Van den Haag, has retained a commitment to Enlightenment values. Holding views that might be called conservative, Nisbet seems nonetheless to hold them for pragmatic reasons, not because he believes they are intrinsically, or even absolutely, good or virtuous. For the views of a social historian in these matters see John Higham, "Hanging Together: Divergent Unities in American History," *JAH* 61 (1974): 5–28.

The suggestion that American politics has been about disagreements within the idea of equality is fascinating, but the disagreement has actually centered on the lengths to which the egalitarian principle should be carried. The antinomies of group versus individual, liberty versus equality, or property versus the collective are only parts of a larger question: Should the egalitarian principle apply to politics alone, or to economics, society, the cosmos? Where in fact does it end? The discovery, of course, has been that a thoroughgoing egalitarianism does not end. It becomes the quest, or the dream, or simply change, and in addition equality is transformed as it is extended. Moreover, there is an ultimate connection between this view of democracy and the historiographical modes sketched in chapter 3, that is, between the Enlightenment perspective and modern democracy. It has been suggested that the social scientists, having necessarily brought about "the reduction of the political to the sub-political, . . . are compelled to speak sooner or later of such things as 'the open society' which is their definition of the good society." [6] America, not Tocqueville, had begun the reduction of all life to egalitarian terms. The dangers Tocqueville sensed in the democratic idea were not the classical ones of anarchy, leveling, mediocrity, and so on, but the more significant dangers divined by Leo Strauss. What Tocqueville appears to have grasped was that equality, a political principle, must ultimately create philosophical anarchy—a cosmological reduction of everything to everything else. Methodists, like all others, resisted. It is their resistance that historians of the modern democratic faith have disapproved, as resistance to openness, experimentation, change, and the rest. The history of Jason Lee's mission is, above all, one of democratization, suggesting that when Methodism could no longer resist the disintegrating strain of its own self-inflicted demos, the church transposed the base of its values from theological to Enlightenment referents. Methodists in Oregon resisted, as if by instinct, the egalitarianization of theology and the total homogenization of all differences even while they pursued both goals. Their resistance and their pursuit make the Methodists especially significant and fascinating.

6. Leo Strauss, *Liberalism Ancient and Modern* (New York, 1968), p. 219. Of course, "democracy" may simply designate operations or structures devoted to specific egalitarian goals. The best typology continues to be that of Aristotle. See Ernest Barker, ed. and trans., *The Politics of Aristotle* (New York: Oxford University Press, 1962), pp. 160–88, 263–69. Equality is used here, however, following Tocqueville, to mean the consequences of democratization, just as democracy is considered the end-product of egalitarianization.

Their failure to make the Indians into Methodists was not merely a consequence of the fact, if it was a fact, that Methodism was a culture-bound sect. The failure was essential to group survival. Methodists resisted the temptation, for some years after the Civil War, to turn the gospel of salvation into a social gospel. In their resistance they were deeply motivated by a desire to retain fidelity to suprarational objectives, specifically the plausibility of seeking knowledge of God. For precisely this reason Jason Lee struggled to preserve the priority of Christianization before civilization. Although saving the Indians would have vindicated the universality of Methodism and its doctrines, it was imperative to reserve group distinctiveness against the danger of assimilation. The failure to convert the Indians and thereby justify treasured doctrine was the means of preventing group disintegration. The Methodist dilemma was the inherent conflict between the noble objective of converting the Indians to Christianity and the pragmatic desire to preserve the group intact. From the perspective of Enlightenment values and the categories of social science, the dilemma appears either mechanical or perverse, because the notion of absolutes is a priori untenable and retrograde.[7] A new or at least a different ontological context is required to absorb the poignant, perhaps even tragic, sense of the dilemma. Disengagement from the boundlessness of Enlightenment values would seem to be the first step.

The obvious second step must be a reassessment of Weber's views of Calvin and Calvinism. This leads in two directions. First, it leads in the direction of a return to questions that rationalism has reduced to "perennial" matters, questions about God, the soul, virtue. Second, it leads to the simple question whether Methodist doctrine is tenable.

The question of group survival, which arose in the midst of the mission's dilemma, took interesting forms. As the survey of old and new evidence has indicated, the dilemma was the central theme of the Oregon mission under Jason Lee. His efforts to Christianize the Indians inspired the formulation of systems that uniformly tended to civilize the heathen

---

7. "The most important example of . . . dogmatism . . . is supplied by the treatment of religion. . . . The new science uses sociological or psychological theories regarding religion which exclude, without considering it, the possibility that religion rests ultimately on God's revealing himself to man. . . . The New science rests on a dogmatic atheism which presents itself as merely methodological or hypothetical" (*ibid.*, p. 218). Compare, for example, John Y. Fenton, "Reductionism in the Study of Religions," *Soundings* 53 (Spring 1970): 61–76.

rather than convert them. The systems in turn transformed the dilemma even while appearing to solve it in the eyes of missionaries such as Jason and Daniel Lee. Methodists were particularly susceptible to the lure of system. Unreflective where first principles were concerned, they often looked to system as the cause of failure or success. In this respect the Oregon mission was no different from other Methodist missions. The spirit of the Gospel was served, and indeed rescued, by the spirit of system which included reliance upon a methodical use of marriage and upon the physical divisions between teaching and preaching missions, in which adult Indians were separated from children. Still, no system could be found which would ensure the conversion of the Indians. Nevertheless, the systems devised for converting the heathen were not without effect: they converted the mission.

Lee's impulsive program of reinforcement and marriage submerged the mission and replaced it with a community that resembled Kentucky or upper New York State in the early 1800s.[8] The process of dividing and subdividing Indians in the Willamette Valley eventually squeezed most of them out of white settlements into segregated enclaves, where they had no opportunity to emulate the piety and the industry of white couples recruited to serve as models. By 1843 there was no mission in Oregon at all; there was only a replica of frontier Methodism complete with itinerants and a church. As David Leslie, evidently unaware of irony, said in 1845, "Our mission and our work in this country [are now] . . . purely spiritual in . . . character."[9] The purely spiritual character of the mission

8. These areas were especially responsive to religious enthusiasm. See Whitney R. Cross, *The Burned Over District* (New York, 1950); Bernard Weisberger, *They Gathered at the River* (Boston, 1958); Peter Cartwright, *Autobiography* (Nashville, Tenn., 1956); C. C. Cole, *The Social Ideals of the Northern Evangelists, 1826–1860* (New York, 1954). Robert Peters, a vigorous student of Oregon Methodism, has very generously shared his findings with me. His doctoral study covers the Oregon Methodists from 1844 (the end of the mission period) to the Civil War, with emphasis on the relations between Methodist theology and techniques. He has found "a fascinating move from churchly vision in the mission period, to a much more narrow sectarian view in the next few years, with a gradual trend back toward the world. The conflict was recognized by the Methodists themselves, but it is almost as though they were caught in an inevitable attraction to the customs and affairs of the world" (Robert Peters to author, December 20, 1971). Peters's conclusions are all the more fascinating because of their remarkable similarity to my own conclusions, though what Peters calls "the inevitable attraction to . . . the world" is here considered an inevitable attraction to group survival.

9. David Leslie to corresponding secretary, Willamette, January 1, 1845, UPS.

was what Lee had striven so hard to create. Now that there was no real effort being made to convert Indians and hence no need for what Lee had called "all the . . . helps of a civilized colony" [10] (specifically a moral influence in place of the Hudson's Bay Company), Methodist ministers had little difficulty in returning to their strictly spiritual functions.

Ten years in Oregon had produced no converts to Methodism, yet the Oregon experience had evoked no real questioning of Methodist goals. Only Alvan Waller, among the missionaries who had not given up, had apparently given serious consideration to the unwelcome possibility that Indians were incapable of becoming Christians. He feared that perhaps it was not "unprincipled white men and Romanists" after all who were the toughest obstacles to the conversion of Indians; maybe it was the Indians themselves. His Indian charges at the mission at The Dalles were free of Romanists and white men, but he was having no better luck with them than with the Indians at Willamette Falls. The red men, he observed, do not reject the Gospel; they simply do "not . . . embrace it. . . . When told of present enjoyments of the operations of the Holy Spirit upon the heart of a peaceful or triumphant death and glorious resurrection after death . . . they do not seem to understand." [11] Lee had no such doubts. He was contemptuous of John Richmond [12] who, thinking the Indians were utterly doomed, left Oregon in disgust. Lee did not mince words in his denunciation of Richmond:

> To know, that there is, in the M.E. Church, a conference Preacher, who could enter the Missionary field, with the express stipulation, that he should remain *ten* years, at *least,* and before he had labored *one,* determine to abandon it, fills my heart with *grief;* and I am ready to cry out, where is justice? Where is conscience? Where is *Methodism?* How are the mighty fallen? What will the veteran Fathers who traversed the wilds and clambered over the rugged mountains of N.E. say to such conduct? What will the Pioneer of the West, who followed the early settler to that land of labour and sickness think of such Missionaries? What will the Catholics who singly, are penetrating this whole region to make proselytes to their dogmas, think of such *Methodists?* I am ashamed, I am grieved, I am perplexed. . . . And I am ready to turn to all around and enquire, *will ye also go away?* [13]

10. Lee to Cushing, January 17, 1839, House Doc. no. 101, 25th Cong., 3d sess., Vol. I, January 4, 1839, p. 3.
11. Alvan Waller to George Gary, Wascopam, February 3, 1847, UPS.
12. On Richmond, see chapter 4.
13. Lee to corresponding secretary, March 15, 1841, UPS.

Certainly Lee did not go. He clung fast to the old ways and to the hopes that had inspired Fisk and, before him, Bishops McKendree and Asbury and John Wesley as well.[14]

Repeated failure, combined with his own tenacity, made Jason Lee a much more mystical missionary in 1843 than he had been in 1834. Writing Daniel Lee in the late summer of 1843, he admitted that "the prospect of final *success* among the *Indians* seemed enshrouded in . . . a cloud of *impenitrable* darkness." But, he asked his nephew rhetorically, am I to say "with semi-infidels and '*I pray-thee-have-me-excused*'—professors . . . 'The Indians are a doomed race'?" [15] He would not say that, but he did say that the conversion of Indians must surely be a miraculous affair, something he would not have said in the first six or eight years of his ministry. He had become "more and more convinced," he wrote the board in January 1843, "that all depends on the *unction* . . . , without the special annointing of the Holy Ghost, we labour in vain, and spend our strength for naught." [16] The record of conversions suggested his strength might indeed have been expended for naught. There had to be some explanation.

By 1843 there was no longer a mission to perform the work of converting the heathen; if the job was to be done at all, "the unction" or some other means would have to be found. The divisions fashioned for Indian salvation succeeded only in fragmenting missionary activities and personnel. The missionary institutions in Oregon had been supplanted by the institutions of Methodism, just as whites had replaced Indians in the Willamette Valley. The transformation was as complete as it was silent and guileless. For Jason Lee, who measured all changes in the numbers of sin-

---

14. Francis Asbury was the first Methodist bishop in America and William McKendree became the first native-born bishop in 1808. It was McKendree who revised the motto of the church in 1816, changing it, as pointed out earlier, from reforming the continent *and* spreading scriptural holiness to reforming it *by* spreading scriptural holiness. See Sidney Mead, "The Rise of the Evangelical Conception of the Ministry in America, 1607–1850," in H. Richard Niebuhr and Daniel D. Williams, eds., *The Ministry in Historical Perspective* (New York, 1956), pp. 207–49.

15. Jason Lee to Daniel Lee, August 1, 1843, Willamette University.

16. Lee to corresponding secretary, March 27, 1843, UPS. Unction or holiness was Methodist doctrine. Lee's conception of it here, however, as a means to the Indian's salvation underlines his resistance to other means, specifically, his resistance to reversing or merging the order of Christianization and civilization.

ners brought to Christ, the transition went unnoticed, hidden from view by plans and systems. The transformation of the Oregon mission had been going on from the beginning, but its direction and its magnitude first became visible in 1843 when Jason Lee began to daydream about "native Elisha's" who would wander the hills of Oregon, searching out their red brethren and exhorting them in English to become Christians. The original mission plan, it will be remembered, called for Jason and Daniel Lee to "throw themselves into the nation [of Indians], learn their language and preach Christ to them." [17]

The most astonishing and illuminating transformations affected the two basic systems Lee had implemented in Oregon for missionary work: marriage and physical division. The plan to convert Indians by getting them to imitate white exemplars did not work because the separation of spiritual from temporal functions put Indians beyond the reach of their white preceptors. Nor were Indians Christianized by missionaries who used the mixed marriages of Indians and whites to gain entrée into Indian precincts. Marriage as a missionary method did not produce Christians but it did help to resolve the missionary dilemma by producing children who were not Indians. Half-breeds and amalgamation, Lee was happy to report to the Missionary Society in 1844, were the wave of the future. If Lee knew that the Democrats in Washington—of all politicians, the least respected by Methodists—who were urging the annexation of Mexico, promoted miscegenation as a policy for conquest, he was evidently not embarrassed by the fact. [18] In 1844 he prophesied that "there will be more Indian blood through amalgamation, running in the veins of white men a hundred years hence than would have been running in the veins of the Indians, if they had been left to themselves. The Missionaries have performed many such marriages among them." [19] The Methodist community in Oregon was prepared for the arrival of half-breeds. When the Oregon Institute wrote its constitution in March 1842, Article III proclaimed that although the "primary object of this institution is to educate the children of white men . . . no person shall be excluded on account of

17. Fisk to editors, *Christian Advocate and Journal,* March 22, 1833, p. 118.

18. See Frederick Merk, *Manifest Destiny and Mission in American History* (New York, 1963), pp. 120–24, 160–65.

19. Cornelius J. Brosnan, "Transcript,"*Jason Lee: Prophet of the New Oregon* (New York, 1932), p. 258.

color if he has good moral character and can read, write and speak the English language intelligibly." [20]

The Oregon Institute is significant because it was not obviously inspired by evangelical ideas but by the equally basic impulse to survive as a distinctive group. No sooner did the idea of a school for white children show signs of materializing than it captured the enthusiastic support of most elements in the community; its boosters included such case-hardened enemies as Alvan Waller and Elijah White. David Leslie was apparently the first missionary to give serious thought to the possibility of a "literary institution" in Oregon.[21] On the eve of Jason Lee's departure for the United States in March 1838, Leslie wrote Willbur Fisk about his idea. "We are all unanimous in desireing a teacher to instruct our children," he told Fisk, offering to pay the teacher's salary and passage to Oregon. Since he knew that the Missionary Society would not look with favor on his plan, he made an attempt to disarm his eastern critics:

> I can anticipate some of your objections. You are ready to inquire; is there no school at the Mission;—cannot your children be instructed at the Mission schools—Is not one important object in sending families with children to heathen lands, the advantage which heathen children will derive by the exple and conversation of the children who come among them;—
>
> I surely thout so once;—I thought so when I arived at the Sandwish Islands; But I noticed that the missionaries there were most scrupuolously avoided all conversation or intercourse between their children & the native or halfbreed children. I did not at first approve this policy;—But observation & experience have convinced me that I had something to lear[n] on this subject;—and that any person unacquainted with the moral and physical contamination of the heathen of every sex and age as it is found throughout this country cannot at all appreciate the reasons why our children may not associate with the natives;—But, reasons there are in this and every other heathen land of which I have any knowledge; in this and every other native school which I have seen;—Yes; reasons there are; which I forbare to name; and such to[o] as in the eye of reason & propriety fix a great and impasable gulph between children whose manners morals and conversation have been guarded in the most scrupulous manner;—and children who were born heathens surrounded with heathen customs and examples; who are dayly being

20. This constitution appears in several published sources. Read Bain prints the article quoted in "Methodist Educational Effort in Oregon to 1860," *OHQ* 21 (1920): 79.

21. Leslie and others described the school in this way before it was named.

gathered in from Indian lodges, who tho; in infantile years are skill'd & practiced in the most revolting vices of maturer age.[22]

The immediate cause of Leslie's interest in a school was his concern for the safety and welfare of his young daughters. But at a time when Indian children were "dayly being gatherd in from Indian lodges" and when Jason Lee was planning to bring in large numbers of exemplary laymen from the East, the idea of a separate school for white children was inappropriate and contradictory. It cut directly across mission strategy. Leslie did not say, and may not even have thought, that the "impasable gulph" implied inherent differences between Indians and whites. He certainly had no objection to nonwhite Methodists, and he was perfectly willing that his daughters should meet in a love feast with Hawaiians and half-breed men who showed signs of becoming "respectable [members of] . . . this community."[23] What Leslie's logic implied, and what the Oregon Institute later demonstrated, was not only that Christianization would have to follow civilization if Indians were to become Methodists, but that Leslie and all the others "unanimous in desireing" a school wanted it for the purpose of protecting and perpetuating their own kind. Oregon Methodists did not see their planned institute as in any way ideologically distinct from the evangelical work to which they were all dedicated. Nor did they recognize the implication for the missionary ideal even as it was changing in their midst. The institute was symptomatic of the change from Christianizing the Indians to the time when the civilization of the Indians would become the work of missionaries in Oregon and elsewhere.[24] Article III of the institute's constitution looked forward to the day when the native Elishas, turned civilized, would start enrolling in the school as full-fledged Methodists. The purpose, as Indians learned to their sorrow and as Methodists remember with guilt, was never realized.

Jason Lee knew, as did all Methodists, that men differed "egregiously,"[25] but he prayed for better days. In the meantime he could

22. David Leslie to Willbur Fisk, Willamette, March 24, 1838, UPS.

23. *Ibid.*

24. Assimilation and the reservation idea were made official United States policy in the 1850s, and missionaries were given a lion's share of the responsibility for carrying out the policy. This process has been recently elaborated by Robert Trennert, *Alternative to Extinction: Federal Indian Policy and the Beginnings of the Reservation System, 1846–1851* (Philadelphia, 1975).

25. Lee used this language in his letter to the corresponding secretary, March 30,

only wonder why God had seen fit to make men so different from horses. "O that like the faithful beast man might answer the end for which he was created," he sighed as he plodded from conversion to conversion, from backslider to backslider.[26]

The Oregon Institute was pivotal in the transformation of the mission. Its actual beginnings gave substance to the alteration. In 1844 the Indian Manual Labor School at Chemeketa, with only thirty Indian pupils enrolled, sold its buildings to the trustees of the Oregon Institute. These were the most elaborate and costly structures in Oregon below the Columbia. So the missionaries returned, as Leslie said, to the "spiritual work." Prospects for the export of piety from Oregon looked at least as good in 1843 as the promise of Indian converts in Oregon had looked to easterners in 1834. Writing to Superintendent Gary in February 1847, Alvan Waller confided his hopes for Mexico:

> I am praying God that our national trouble with Mexico may be so overruled that the Gospel untramelled by popery may be introduced into that country and the Church have opened before her another vast field for Missionary labor and the time might not be far distant when we shall have Conferences in Mexico; and that the final result will be nothing less than evangelization of this entire western world even down to Cape-Horn. To this end, may the Lord go forth with our armies! [27]

The Methodists had come to Oregon so that they might expand their sect abroad as they invigorated their brethren at home. Eventually they succeeded. Oregon came to feel the impact of Methodism deeply, and the church, despite the major schism of 1844 and other minor schisms, grew apace. Waller gave expression to a sense of continuation, suggesting either that he did not believe Methodism had failed to convert the Indians or that he wished to think of other matters. There is certainly no way of knowing what was in his mind, but he had been the one to broach, if only haltingly, the possibility that Leslie's "impasable gulph" did exist between Christian Methodists and the Indians. The church could not long continue to employ methods that failed to bring desired results. Methodists could not simultaneously believe that Indians were inherently dif-

---

1843, UPS. Lee also provides an insight into his approach to human conflict in a soliloquy on marriage in his diary (Lee, "Diary," *OHQ* 17 [1916]: 406–7).

26. *Ibid.,* p. 249.

27. Waller to Gary, February 3, 1847, UPS.

ferent from whites, where salvation was concerned, and work for the goal of world evangelization. The church chose to keep the doctrine of evangelization and to modify its visions of deity. Eventually a far-reaching egalitarianism would come to bridge the gap between Methodists and Indians. Whether Methodism was saved thereby or whether it was devoured to meet the seemingly insatiable requirements of egalitarian logic and practice are questions we should now in some measure be prepared to discuss.

Bibliography

BIBLIOGRAPHICAL GUIDES AND INDEXES

Ahlstrom, S. "A Bibliography of American Religious History." *American Studies* (Autumn 1972).

Barry, J. Neilson. "First Local Government, 1841 Index to Primary Sources." *OHQ* 41 (June 1940):195–202.

Barry, J. Neilson, ed. "Documents: Primary Sources to Early Government [in Oregon]." *WHQ* (April 1934): 139–47.

Bromberg, Erik. "A Bibliography of Theses and Dissertations Concerning the Pacific Northwest and Alaska." *PNQ* 40 (July 1949); 42 (April 1951); *OHQ* 59 (March 1958); 65 (December 1964).

Burr, Nelson. *Critical Bibliography of Religion in America.* 2 vols. Princeton: Princeton University Press, 1961.

Checklist of United States Public Documents 1789–1909. 3d ed. Washington, 1911.

Child, Sargent B., and Dorothy P. Holmes. *Checklist of Historical Records Survey Publications: Bibliography of Research Projects Reports.* W.P.A. Technical Series Research and Records Bibliography no. 7. Rev. April 1943. Baltimore: Genealogical Publishing Company, 1969.

Christensen, M. E., comp. "Sources and Literature for Western American History: A List of Dissertations." *Western Historical Quarterly* (July 1972).

Hale, Richard W., Jr., ed. *Guide to Photocopied Historical Materials in the United States and Canada.* Ithaca, N.Y.: Cornell University Press, 1961.

Historical Records Survey. *Guide to Depositions of Manuscript Collections in the United States.* Oregon and Washington. Portland: Oregon Historical Records Survey Project, 1940.

———. *Guide to the Manuscript Collections of the Oregon Historical Society.* Portland: Oregon Historical Records Survey Project, 1940.

———. *Inventory of the County Archives of Oregon.* Vols. 2, 4, 26. Portland: Oregon Historical Records Survey Project, 1940–42.

History of the Pacific Northwest and Canadian Northwest Available on Microfilm and Xerox Duopage. New Haven, Conn.: Research Publications, n.d.

Jenkins, William S., and Lillian A. Hamrick, eds. *A Guide to the Microfilm Collection of Early State Records Prepared by the Library of Congress in Association with the University of North Carolina.* Washington: Library of Congress, 1950.

Jonas, Frank. "Bibliography of Western Politics." *WPQ* (December 1958), Supplement.

Bibliography

Judson, Katherine B. *Subject Index to the History of the Pacific Northwest, Alaska, As Found in U.S. Government Documents . . . , 1789–1881*. Olympia, Wash.: F. M. Lamborn, 1913.

Mode, Peter G. *Source Book and Bibliographical Guide for American Church History*. Menosha, Wisc.: George Banta Publishing Co., 1921.

Oregon Historical Society. *Guide to the Manuscripts of the Oregon Hitorical Society*. Portland: Oregon Historical Society, 1972.

Phillips, P. C., ed. *Sources of Northwest History*. Vols. 1–29. Missoula, Mont.: State University of Montana, 1928–39.

Rockwell, E. R. *Books of the Pacific Northwest for Small Libraries*. New York: H. W. Wilson Co., 1923.

Rockwood, Eleanor Ruth. *Oregon State Documents: A Checklist, 1843–1925*. Portland: Oregon Historical Society, 1947.

Smith, Charles Wesley. *Pacific Northwest Americana*. 2d ed. rev. New York: H. W. Wilson Co., 1921.

Sweet, William W., Shirley J. Case, J. J. McNeill, W. Pauck, and M. Spinka. *A Bibliographical Guide to the History of Christianity*. Chicago: University of Chicago Press, 1931.

Winton, Harry N. M. "A Pacific Northwest Bibliography, 1940, 1941." *PNQ* 32 (1941): 203–14; 33 (1942): 187–203.

GOVERNMENT DOCUMENTS

Abridgement of Debates of Congress. Vols. 13–14. New York, 1860.

American State Papers. 1832–61.

Manning, W. R., ed. *Diplomatic Correspondence of the United States: Canadian Relations, 1784–1860*. Washington, 1940–45.

Poore, B. P., ed. *The Federal State Constitutions, Colonial Charters and Other Organic Laws of the United States*. Washington, 1877.

Register of All Officers and Agents . . . in the Service of the United States. Washington, 1816–88.

Statutes at Large. Vol. V. 1841.

U.S. Congress. House.

Doc. 101, 25th Cong., 3d sess. Vol. I. January 4, 1839 (Serial 213).

Doc. 142, 27th Cong., 3d sess. Vol. IV. January 26, 1843 (Serial 421).

Doc. 157, 27th Cong., 3d sess. Vol. II. February 9,1843 (Serial 427).

Doc. 133, 28th Cong., 1st sess. Vol. IV. January 13, 1844 (Serial 442).

Doc. 308, 28th Cong., 1st sess. Vol. I. March 12, 1844 (Serial 445).

Doc. 56, 28th Cong., 2d sess. Vol. II. January 9, 1845 (Serial 464).

Doc. 56, 33d Cong., 2d sess. Vol. I. January 30, 1855 (Serial 808).

Exec. Doc. 13, 20th Cong., 2d sess. Vol. I. December 10, 1828 (Serial 184).

————. Senate.

Doc. 255, 25th Cong., 2d sess. Vol. III. March 16, 1838 (Serial 316).

Doc. 470, 25th Cong., 2d sess. Vol. IV. January 12, 1846 (Serial 473).

Doc. 266, 25th Cong., 3d sess. Vol. IV. January 20, 1839 (Serial 341).

Doc. 237, 25th Cong., 3d sess. Vol. III. January 31, 1839 (Serial 340).

Doc. 25, 26th Cong., 1st sess. Vol. II. December 30, 1839 (Serial 355).

Doc. 40, 26th Cong., 1st sess. Vol. II. January 6, 1840 (Serial 344).

Doc. 172, 26th Cong., 1st sess. Vol. IV. February 10, 1840 (Serial 357).

Doc. 244, 26th Cong., 1st sess. Vol. V. March 4, 1840 (Serial 358).

Doc. 514, 26th Cong., 1st sess. Vol. VII. June 4, 1840 (Serial 360).

Doc. 84, 27th Cong., 1st sess. Vol. V. August 2, 1841 (Serial 390).

Doc. 102, 27th Cong., 3d sess. Vol. III. January 23, 1843 (Serial 415).

Doc. 158, 27th Cong., 3d sess. Vol. III. February 10, 1843 (Serial 415).

Doc. 159, 27th Cong., 3d sess. Vol. III. February 10, 1843 (Serial 415).

Doc. 175, 27th Cong., 3d sess. Vol. III. February 15, 1843 (Serial 415).

Doc. 105, 28th Cong., 1st sess. Vol. III. February 7, 1844 (Serial 433).

Doc. 8, 29th Cong., 1st sess. Vol. III. June 8, 1845 (Serial 472).

Doc. 54, 29th Cong., 1st sess. Vol. IV. January 12, 1846 (Serial 473).

Exec., Doc. 37, 41st Cong., 3d sess. Vol. I. February 9, 1871 (Serial 1440).

————. Congressional Legislation Concerning Oregon.

S. 52, 25th Cong., 3d sess. December 11, 1838.

S. 206, 25th Cong. 2d sess. February 7, 1838.

S. 7, 26th Cong., 1st sess. March 31, 1840.

S. 191, 26th Cong. 2d sess. January 8, 1841.

S. 331, 26th Cong., 1st sess. April 28, 1840.

S. 58, 27th Cong., 2d sess. December 16, 1841.

S. 23, 28th Cong., 1st sess. December 21, 1843.

H.R. 21, 28th Cong., 1st sess. January 4, 1844.

S. 45, 28th Cong., 2d sess. December 19, 1844.

MANUSCRIPTS

Bancroft Library

Abernethy, Anne. The Mission Family.

Applegate, Jesse. Views of Oregon History.

Bacon, J. M. Oregon City Mercantile Life.

Bancroft, H. H. Miscellaneous Correspondence Concerning Oregon. 11 folders.

Blanchet, F. N. Catholic Missionaries of Oregon.

Brown, Joseph H. Autobiography.

————. Oregon Miscellanies.

————. Willamette Valley.

Buck, W. W. Oregon City Enterprises.

Burnett, P. H. Recollections of the Past. 2 vols.

Crawford, Medorem. Missionaries and Their Work.

Deady, Matthew P. Oregon History and Progress.

Ebberts, George. Trapper's Life in the Rocky Mountains and Oregon from
    1829 to 1839.

Edwards, Philip L. Diary of 1837.

————. Sketches of Oregon.

Ekin, Richard. Sailor and Saddle Maker.

Geer, R. C. Blooded Cattle in Oregon.

Gibbs, Addison C. Notes on Oregon History.

Grim, J. U. Emigrant Anecdotes.

Grover, LaFayette. Notable Things in a Public Life in Oregon.

Holman, Joseph. The Peoria Party.

Lovejoy, A. L. Founding of Portland.

Matthieu, F. X. Refugee, Trapper, Settler.

Minto, John. Early Days in Oregon.

Moss, Sydney W. Pioneer Times.

Nesmith, J. Reminiscences.

Parrish, J. L. Anecdotes of Oregon.

Pettygrove, Francis. Oregon in 1842.

Roberts, George B. Recollections.

Shaw, William. Pioneer Life.

Strong, William. History of Oregon.

Thornton, J. Quinn. Autobiography.

Victor, Frances Auretta Fuller. Correspondence and Notes Concerning
    Oregon.

Waldo, Daniel. Critiques.

Watt, W. A. First Things in Oregon.

White, Elijah. Early Government of Oregon.

Pacific University, Forest Grove, Oregon

John Smith Griffin Papers.

Oregon Historical Society, Portland

George Abernethy Letters.

Burt Brown Barker Collection.

Peter Burnett Papers.

Levi Chamberlain Papers.

Amos Cook Papers.

Caleb Cushing Papers.

Matthew Deady Collection.

Eva E. Dye Collection.

William H. Gray Papers.

Edwin O. Hall Letters.

Lewis Judson Papers.

George LeBreton Letters.

Anna Maria Pittman Lee Letters. Oregon Government File 36.

Daniel Lee Papers.

Jason Lee Papers.

Robert Newell Papers.

Petitions of French-Canadian Settlers to Bishop of Juliopolis. Typewritten.

Provisional and Territorial Governments Papers, 1841–1849 (indexed). 26 reels microfilm.

Cyrus Shepard Letters.

Robert Shortess Papers.

Frances Fuller Victor Papers, 1866–1902. Microfilm.

Alvan Waller Papers.

Washington State Historical Society, Tacoma

Canse Collections of Henry B. Brewer Papers and H. K. W. Perkins Papers.

Willamette University Archives, Salem, Oregon

Robert M. Gatke Papers.

Jason Lee Letters

George Roberts Papers.

Chloe Clark Willson Diary.

University of Puget Sound Archives, Puget Sound, Washington

George Abernethy Papers.

Alanson Beers Letters.

John Frost Papers.

George Gary Papers.

Gustavus Hines Letters.

Jason Lee Letters.

David Leslie Letters.

Letters to Corresponding Secretary from Missionary Applicants.

Miscellaneous Letters and Documents.

Oregon Committee to Board of Managers, Missionary Society of Methodist Episcopal Church. Minutes, September 7–October 15, 1839.

H. K. W. Perkins Papers.

William H. Raymond Papers.

John Richmond Letters.

S. Doc. 22, 27th Cong., 3d sess., January 1843. Copy.

Beverly Waugh Letters.

Elijah White Papers.

Bibliography

Wesleyan University, Middletown, Connecticut
Nathan Bangs Letters.
William Capers Letters.
Willbur Fisk Papers.

University of Oregon, Eugene
Calbreath Collection (including Sydney Smith's Account Book).
Almira David Raymond Letters.
Frances Fuller Victor Papers.

Oregon State Archives, Salem
Barry, J. Neilson. Champoeg File. Microfilm.
Brewer, H. B. Day Book, 1839–43.
Brewer, Louise. Biographical sketch of her father, H. B. Brewer.
Lewis Judson Papers.
Adelia Judson Turkington Olley Leslie Papers.
David Leslie Papers.
Letters from Albert Tozier to J. Neilson Barry. Microfilm.
Letters received by Office of Indian Affairs, 1842–81, on Oregon Superintendency, 1842–80 and 1842–52. National Archives Microcopy 234.
Provisional Government Documents:
 1367. Public Meeting at Oregon Institute, February 2, 1843.
 1523. Address of Canadian Citizens, March 4, 1843.
 341, 421, 431. Public Meeting at home of J. Gervais, March 6, 1843.
 Public Meeting at Champoeg, May 2, 1843.
 72, 73, 76. Meetings of Legislative Committee, May 16–19, June 27–28, 1843.
 74. Rules of Legislative Assembly, May 16–June 28, 1843.
 75. Meeting of Committee of the Whole, May 17–19, 1843.
 422, 423, 425, 426, 430. Public Meeting at Champoeg, July 5, 1843.
 4936. Committee Report on Redistricting.
 273, 427, 428, 429, 1582, 4244, 4374, 4376. Judiciary Committee Reports.
 5043. Report of Committee on Land Claims.
 424. Militia Committee Report.
 Report of Ways and Means Committee.
Washington County Court Records, 1837–1893. 3 reels microfilm.

Board of Missions, New York
Board of Managers, Missionary Society. Minutes. Vols. II–IV.
Estimating Committee, Board of Managers, Missionary Society. Minutes, May 8–September 17, 1839.
General and Annual Conference Minutes to 1844.

Missionary Record Book, Willamette Station, 1834–[December 30, 1838].
Oregon Committee, Board of Managers, Missionary Society. Minutes, June
21, 1842–April 19, 1853.

Beinecke Library, Western Americana Collection, Yale University
George Abernethy Letters.
Jesse Applegate Letters.
John and Kate Blaine Papers.
Henry Ellsworth Letters.
Elwood Evans Papers.
William Gray Letters.
John Smith Griffin Papers.
Letters of H. K. W. Perkins and wife.
Journal of Cyrus Shepard.
William Fraser Tolmie Papers.
Elijah White Letters.

Reed College Library, Portland, Oregon
Walls, Florence, ed. "Bush-Deady Correspondence." B.A. honors thesis,
1941.

Archdiocesan Archives, Portland, Oregon
Francis N. Blanchet Letters.
Modest Demers Letters.
Jason Lee Letters.

Rosenbach Foundation Museum, Philadelphia
Anna Maria Pittman Lee letter.
Jason Lee Letters.

NEWSPAPERS AND BULLETINS

Christian Advocate and Journal
Himes, George H. "Organization of Oregon Provisional Government." *Oregon
Blue Book, 1915–1916* (Salem, 1916): 14–16.
Oregonian and Indian's Advocate. Vols. I–III.
Pacific Christian Advocate
*Souvenir of the Seventy-Seventh Anniversary of the Organization of the First American
Civil Government West of the Rocky Mountains and the Nineteenth Celebration of the
Same, at old Champoeg . . . on the East Bank of the Willamette River, Saturday,
May First, Nineteen Hundred Twenty.* Portland, [1920].
The Dalles Times Mountaineer
Western Christian Advocate
Youngson, William W. "Why Jason Lee Father of American Oregon Should be
one of the Two Historical Figures to be Allotted a Statue in the Statuary Hall in

Bibliography

Our National Capital." *Diamond Jubilee of Methodism of the Pacific*. Seattle, Wash., n.d.

Zion's Herald

CONTEMPORARY PERIODICALS

Hunt's Merchants' Magazine
Methodist Preacher
Methodist Quarterly Review
Missionary Notices
Niles Register
North American Review

PUBLISHED PRIMARY SOURCES

Books

Allen, A. J., comp. *Ten Years in Oregon: Travels and Adventures of Doctor E. White and Lady*. Ithaca, N.Y.: Andrus, Gauntlett, 1850.

American Board of Commissioners for Foreign Missions. *Twenty-sixth Annual Report*. New York: Crocker, 1835.

Applegate, Jesse. *Recollections of My Boyhood*. Roseburg, Ore.: Review Publishing Co., 1914.

Arfwedson, Carl D. *The United States and Canada in 1832–1833, 1834*. 2 vols. London: R. Bentley, 1834.

Bacon, L. W. *A History of American Christianity*. New York: Christian Literature Co., 1897.

Bailey, Margaret Jewett. *The Grains, or Passages in the Life of Ruth Rover*. 2 vols. Portland: Carter & Austin Printers, 1854.

Baird, Robert. *Religion in America, or, An Account of the Origin and Progress, Relation to the State, and Present Condition of the Evangelical Churches of the United States, with Notices of the Unevangelical Denominations*. Repr. New York: Harpers, 1841.

Ball, John. *Autobiography*. Comp. Kate Ball Powers *et al*. Grand Rapids, Mich.: Dean-Hicks, 1925.

Bangs, Nathan. *An Authentic History of the Missions under the Care of the Missionary Society of the Methodist Episcopal Church*. New York: Emory and Waugh, 1832.

———. *A History of the Methodist Episcopal Church*. 4 vols. New York: Mason & Lane, 1839.

Barker, Burt B., ed. *Letters of Dr. John McLoughlin Written at Fort Vancouver, 1829–1832*. Portland: Binfords and Mort, 1948.

———. *The Financial Papers of John McLoughlin*. Portland: Binfords and Mort, 1949.

Chittenden, Hiram M., and Alfred T. Richardson, eds. *Life, Letters and Travels of Father Pierre-Jean De Smet, S.J.* 4 vols. New York: F. P. Harper, 1905.

Combe, George. *Elements of Phrenology.* 4th American ed. Boston: Marsh, Capen & Lyon, 1835.

————. *Notes on the United States of America during a Phrenological Visit in 1838–1840.* Philadelphia: Carey & Hart, 1841.

DeSmet, Pierre J. *Oregon Missions and Travels over the Rocky Mountains, in 1845–46.* New York, 1847. Vol. 19 of *Early Western Travels, 1748–1846.* Ed. Reuben G. Thwaites.

Edwards, Philip L. *Sketch of the Oregon Territory.* Liberty, Mo.: "Herald" Office, 1842.

————. *The Diary of Philip Leget Edwards.* San Francisco: Granhorn Press, 1932.

Farnham, T. J. *Travels in the Great Western Prairies, the Anahuac and Rocky Mountains, and in the Oregon Territory.* Poughkeepsie: Killey and Lossing, 1841.

Fleming, Harvey R., ed. *Minutes of Council Northern Department of Rupert's Land, 1821–31.* HBS. Vol. III. Toronto: Champlain Society, 1940. London: Hudson's Bay Record Society, 1940.

Fowler, O. S. *Synopsis of Phrenology.* New York: Fowlers & Wells, 1852.

Fremont, John C. *Report of the Exploring Expedition to the Rocky Mountains in the Year 1842, and to Oregon and North California in the Years 1843–44.* Washington: Blair and Rives, 1845.

Gay, Theressa. *Life and Letters of Mrs. Jason Lee.* Portland: Metropolitan Press, 1936.

Gray, William H. *A History of Oregon, 1792–1849.* Portland: Harris and Holman, 1870.

Grover, LaFayette. *Oregon Archives.* Salem: Asabel Bush, 1853.

Grund, Francis J. *The Americans.* [London, 1837.] New York: Johnson Reprint Corp., 1968.

Hafen, LeRoy R., ed. *The Mountain Men and the Fur Trade of the Far West.* 10 vols. Glendale, Calif.: A. H. Clark, 1965–72.

Hastings, Lansford W. *The Emigrants' Guide to Oregon and California.* Ed. Charles H. Carey. Princeton: Princeton University Press, 1932.

Henning, W. W., ed. *The Statutes at Large of All the Laws of Virginia.* Vol. X. Richmond: Thomas Ritchie, 1811.

Hines, Gustavus. *A Voyage Round the World: With a History of Oregon Mission.* Buffalo: G. H. Derby, 1850.

Johansen, Dorothy O., ed. *Robert Newell's Memoranda.* Portland: Binfords and Mort, 1959.

Lee, Daniel, and John Frost. *Ten Years in Oregon.* New York: Privately printed, 1844.

Merk, Frederick. *Fur Trade and Empire: George Simpson's Journal.* Rev. ed. Cambridge: Belknap Press, 1968.

Mofras, Duflot, Eugene. *Travels on the Pacific Coast.* Trans. Marguerite Eyer Wilbur. 2 vols. Santa Ana, Calif. Fine Art Press, 1937.

Newcomb, Harvey. *Cyclopedia of Missions.* New York: Scribner, 1860.

Parker, Samuel. *Journal of a Tour.* Ithaca: Privately printed, 1838.

Reed, Andrew, and James Matheson. *A Narrative of a Visit to the American Churches by the Deputation from the Congregational Union of England and Wales.* 2 vols. N.p., n.d.

Rich, E. E., ed. *Simpson's 1828 Journey to the Columbia: Part of Dispatch from George Simpson, Esqr., Governor of Rupert's Land, to the Governor and Committee of the Hudson's Bay Company, London, March 1, 1829, Continued and Completed March 24 and June 5, 1829.* HBS. Vol. X. Toronto: Hudson's Bay Record Society, 1947.

————. *The Letters of John McLoughlin from Fort Vancouver to the Governor and Committee.* 1st, 2d, 3d ser. HBS. Vols. V–VII. Toronto: Hudson's Bay Record Society, 1941–44.

Richardson, James I., ed. *A Compilation of the Messages and Papers of the Presidents.* 10 vols. Washington: Government Printing Office, 1896.

Sampson, William R., ed. *John McLoughlin's Business Correspondence, 1847–1848.* Seattle and London: University of Washington Press, 1973.

The Correspondence and Journals of Captain Nathaniel J. Wyeth, 1831–1836. Sources of the History of Oregon. Eugene: University Press, 1899.

Tyron, Warren, ed. *A Mirror for Americans: Life and Manners in the United States, 1790–1870, as Recorded by American Travelers.* 3 vols. Chicago: University of Chicago Press, 1952.

White, Elijah. *A Concise View of Oregon Territory. . . .* Washington: T. Barnard, 1846.

————. *Testimonials and Records.* [Washington, 1861.]

Wilkes, Charles. *Narrative of the United States Exploring Expedition during the Years 1838, 1839, 1840, 1841, 1842.* 5 vols. Philadelphia: Lea & Blanchard, 1849.

Williams, Glyndwr. *London Correspondence from Sir George Simpson, 1841–42.* London: Hudson's Bay Record Society, 1973.

Williams, Joseph. *Narrative of a Tour from the State of Indiana to the Oregon Territory in the Years 1841–2.* New York: Cadmus Book Shop, 1921.

Wyeth, John B. *A Short History of a Long Journey.* Cleveland: A. H. Clark, 1905. Vol. 21 of *Early Western Travels, 1748–1846.* Ed. Reuben G. Thwaites.

Articles

Applegate, Jesse. "A Day with the Cow Column." *OHQ* 1 (1900): 371–83.

Barker, Burt B. "John McLoughlin's Proprietary Account with the Hudson's Bay Company." *OHQ* 45 (1944): 1–4.

———. "The Estate of Dr. John McLoughlin." *OHQ* 50 (1949): 155–85.

Bird, Annie Laurie. "Will of Thomas McKay." *OHQ* 40 (1939): 15–18.

Brown, J. Henry. "Sketches of Salem from 1851–1869." *MCH* 3 (1957): 18–20.

Canse, John M. "The Diary of Henry Bridgman Brewer, Being a Log of the Lausanne and the Time Book of the Dalles Mission." *OHQ* 29 (1928): 189–208, 288–309, 347–62; 30 (1929): 53–62, 111–19.

Carey, Charles H. "Methodist Annual Reports Relating to the Willamette Mission (1834–1848)." *OHQ* 23 (1922): 301–64.

Carey, Charles H., ed. "Diary of Reverend George Gary." *OHQ* 24 (1923): 68–105, 152–85, 269–333.

———. "The Mission Record Book of the Methodist Episcopal Church, Willamette Settlement, Oregon Territory, North America, Commenced 1834." *OHQ* 23 (1922): 230–66.

Crawford, Medorem. "Journal of 1842." In *Sources of the History of Oregon*. Vol. I. Salem, 1899.

"David Leslie's Report on the Oregon Mission, 1843. . . ." *MCH* 3 (1957): 15–18.

"Diary of Asahel Munger." *OHQ* 8 (1907): 387–405.

"Document: Letter, Jesse Applegate to W. H. Rees, Secretary Oregon Pioneer Association [Yoncalla, Oregon, December 25, 1874]." *OHQ* 20 (1919): 397–99.

"Document: Letter from J. M. Peck [concerning Jesse Applegate]." *OHQ* 15 (1914): 217–18.

"Document: Peter Burnett's Letters to the New York Herald." *OHQ* 2 (1901): 405.

"Document: Slacum's Report on Oregon 1836–1837." *OHQ* 13 (1912): 175–224.

"Documents." *OHQ* 3 (1902): 390–93.

"Documents." *OHQ* 4 (1903): 176–80, 278–301.

"Documents." *OHQ* 13 (1912): 381.

Duniway, David C., and Neil R. Riggs, eds. "The Oregon Archives, 1841–1843." *OHQ* 60 (1959): 211–80.

Frein, P. J., trans. "Address (By the Canadian settlers of the Willamette Valley to the American settlers on proposed political organization)." *OHQ* 13 (1912): 338–41.

Bibliography

Gatke, Robert M. "A Document of Mission History, 1833–1843." *OHQ* 36 (1935): 71–181.

———. "The Letters of the Rev. William M. Roberts, 3d Superintendent of the Oregon Mission." *OHQ* 21 (1920): 33–48, 225–51.

Gray, William. "Journal." *Whitman College Quarterly* 16 (June 1913): 11–13.

———. "Journal of William H. Gray." In *Gray, Kamm and Allied Families*. New York, n.d.

[Hastings, Lansford W.] "Letter in the Saint Louis New Era, March 25, 1844." *OHQ* 2 (1901): 202.

Judson, Katherine B., ed. "Documentary: Letter, Doctor John McLoughlin to Sir George Simpson, March 20, 1844." *OHQ* 17 (1916): 215–39.

Lee, Jason. "Diary." *OHQ* 17 (1916): 116–46, 240–66, 397–430.

Lyman, H. S., ed. "Reminiscences of F. X. Matthieu." *OHQ* 1 (1900): 73–104.

McLoughlin, John. "Copy of a Document Found among the Private Papers of the Late Dr. John McLoughlin." *TOPA* 1880 (Salem, 1881): 46–55.

Meany, Edmund S., ed. "Diary of Wilkes in the Northwest." *WHQ* 16 (1925): 49–61, 137–45, 206–24, 290–301; 17 (1926): 43–65, 129–44, 223–29.

"Oregon Tax Roll, 1844." *OHQ* 31 (1930): 11–24.

Phillips, Paul C., and W. S. Lewis, eds. "The Oregon Missions as Shown in the Walker Letters, 1839–1851." *Frontier* 11 (1930): 74–89.

Pipes, Nellie B., ed. "Journal of John H. Frost, 1840–43." *OHQ* 35 (1934): 50–73, 139–67, 235–62, 348–75.

"Reminiscences of O. Barlow." *OHQ* 13 (1912): 240–86.

"Report of Lt. Neil M. Howison on Oregon, 1846." *OHQ* 14 (1913): 1–60.

Roberts, George B. "The Round Hand of George Roberts." *OHQ* 63 (1962): 101–236.

Robertson, James R. "Reminiscences of Alanson Hinman." *OHQ* 2 (1901): 266–86.

Schafer, Joseph, ed. "Documents Relative to Warre and Vavasour's Military Reconnaissance in Oregon, 1845–46." *OHQ* 10 (1909): 1–99.

———. "Letters of Sir George Simpson, 1841–43." *AHR* 14 (1908): 70–94.

Scott, Leslie M., ed. "First Taxes in Oregon." *OHQ* 31 (1930): 1–10.

———. "Report of Lieutenant Peel on Oregon in 1845–46." *OHQ* 29 (1928): 51–76.

Shortess, Robert. "First Emigrants to Oregon." *TOPA* 1897 (Portland, 1898).

Strong, William. "Narrative." *OHQ* 62 (1961): 57–87.

Waller, Alvan. "Letter Printed in Ohio Statesman, March 10, 1843." *OHQ* 6 (1905): 178.

Young, F. G. "Ewing Young and His Estate." *OHQ* 21 (1920): 196–210.

THE METHODISTS AND OREGON

Books

Ambler, Charles H. *Life and Diary of John Floyd*. Richmond, Va.: Richmond Press, 1918.

Anderson, W. K., ed. *Methodism*. Cincinnati: Methodist Publishing House, 1947.

Atwood, Albert. *The Conquerors: Historical Sketches of the American Settlement of the Oregon Country Embracing Facts in the Life and Work of Jason Lee the Pioneer and Founder of American Institutions on the Western Coast of North America*. Cincinnati: Jennings and Graham, 1907.

Bagley, Clarence B. *The Acquisition and Pioneering of Old Oregon*. Seattle: Argus Printing, 1924.

Bancroft, H. H. *History of Oregon*. Vols. XXIX and XXX of *Works*. San Francisco: History Company, 1886–88.

Barclay, W. C. *History of Methodist Missions*. 3 vols. New York: Board of Missions of the Methodist Church, 1949–57.

Barker, Burt B., ed. *The McLoughlin Empire and Its Rulers*. Glendale, Calif.: A. H. Clark, 1959.

Barrows, William. *Oregon: The Struggle for Possession*. 7th ed. Boston: Houghton Mifflin, 1892.

Barry, J. Neilson. *The French Canadian Pioneers of the Willamette Valley*. Portland: Sentinel Printery, 1933.

Bashford, J. W. *The Oregon Missions: The Story of How the Line Was Run between Canada and the United States*. New York: Abingdon Press, 1918.

Bishoff, William N. *The Jesuits in Old Oregon*. Caldwell, Idaho: Caxton Printers, 1945.

Blanchet, Francis N. *Historical Sketches of the Catholic Church in Oregon*. Portland: Catholic Sentinel, 1878.

Brosnan, Cornelius J. *Jason Lee: Prophet of the New Oregon*. New York: Macmillan, 1932.

Brown, James H. *Political History of Oregon*. Portland: W. B. Allen, 1892.

Bucke, Emory S., ed. *The History of American Methodism*. 3 vols. New York: Abingdon Press, 1964.

Burns, Robert Ignatius. *The Jesuits and the Indian Wars of the Northwest*. New Haven: Yale University Press, 1966.

Burrell, Orin Kay. *Gold in the Woodpile: An Informal History of Banking in Oregon*. Eugene: University of Oregon Press, 1967.

Cameron, Richard M. *Methodism and Society in Historical Perspective*. New York: Abingdon Press, 1961.

————. *The Rise of Methodism: A Source Book.* New York: Philosophical Library, 1954.

Cannon, Elizabeth. *Methodist Trail Blazer: Philip Gatch, 1751–1834.* Cincinnati: Creative Publishers, 1970.

Carey, Charles H. *A General History of Oregon Prior to 1861.* 2 vols. Portland: Metropolitan Press, 1935.

Chapman, Charles H. *The Story of Oregon and Its People.* Chicago: O. P. Barnes, 1912.

Chiles, Robert. *Theological Transition in American Methodism 1790–1935.* New York: Abingdon Press, 1965.

Clark, Robert C. *History of the Willamette Valley.* 2 vols. Chicago: S. J. Clarke, 1927.

Clarke, S. A. *Pioneer Days of Oregon History.* 2 vols. Portland: J. K. Gill, 1905.

Corning, Howard M., ed. *Dictionary of Oregon History.* Portland: Binfords & Mort, 1956.

————. *Willamette Landings.* Portland: Binfords & Mort, 1944.

Dicken, Samuel N. *Oregon Geography.* 3d ed. Ann Arbor: Edwards Bros., 1959.

Dobbs, Caroline C. *Men of Champoeg.* Portland: Metropolitan Press, 1932.

Drinkhouse, E. J. *History of Methodist Reform.* Baltimore: Board of Publication of the Methodist Protestant Church, 1899.

Drucker, Philip. *Cultures of the North Pacific Coast.* San Francisco: Chandler Publication Co., 1965.

Drury, Clifford M. *Henry Harmon Spalding, Pioneer of Old Oregon.* Caldwell, Idaho: Caxton Printers, 1936.

————. *Marcus and Narcissa Whitman and the Opening of Old Oregon.* 2 vols. Glendale, Calif.: A. H. Clark, 1973.

————. *Marcus Whitman, M.D., Pioneer and Martyr.* Caldwell, Idaho: Caxton Printers, 1937.

Dryden, Cecil P. *Give All to Oregon! Pioneers of the Far West.* New York: Hastings House, 1968.

Dunne, Peter M. *Pioneer Black Robes on the West Coast.* Berkeley: University of California Press, 1940.

Eayrs, George, W. J. Townsend, and H. B. Workman, eds. *A New History of Methodism.* 2 vols. London, 1909.

Eells, Myron. *History of Indian Missions on the Pacific Coast, Oregon, Washington and Idaho.* New York: American Sunday School Union, 1882.

Elliot-Binns, L. E. *The Early Evangelicals.* London: Butterworth Press, 1953.

Elsbree, Oliver W. *Rise of the Missionary Spirit in America, 1790–1815.* Williamsport, Pa., 1928.

Evans, Elwood. *History of the Pacific Northwest.* 2 vols. Portland: North Pacific History Co., 1889.

Farmer, Judith, *et al. An Historical Atlas of Early Oregon.* Portland: Historical Cartographic Publications, 1973.

Federal Writers' Project. *Oregon, End of the Trail.* Rev. ed. Portland: Binfords & Mort, 1951.

———. *Oregon Oddities.* Portland: Binfords & Mort, n.d.

Findlay, G. G., and W. W. Holdsworth. *The History of the Wesleyan Methodist Missionary Society.* 5 vols. London, 1921.

Fuller, George W. *A History of the Pacific Northwest.* 2d rev. ed. New York: Knopf, 1947.

Galbraith, John S. *The Hudson's Bay Company as an Imperial Factor, 1821–1869.* Berkeley and Los Angeles: University of California Press, 1957.

Gaston, Joseph. *The Centennial History of Oregon.* 4 vols. Chicago: Harper & Row, 1962.

Gates, Charles M., ed. *Readings in Pacific Northwest History, 1790–1865.* Seattle: University Bookstore, 1941.

Gausted, E. S. *Historical Atlas of Religion in America.* New York: Harper & Row, 1962.

Gilbert, J. H. *Trade and Currency in Early Oregon.* New York: Columbia University Press, 1907.

Graebner, Norman A. *Empire of the Pacific.* New York: Ronald Press, 1955.

Hafen, LeRoy R., and Ann W. Hafen, eds. *To the Rockies and Oregon, 1839–42.* Glendale, Calif.: A. H. Clark, 1955.

Harmon, N. B. *The Organization of the Methodist Church.* 2d rev. ed. Nashville: Methodist Publishing House, 1962.

Hewitt, Ethel Erford. *Into the Unknown.* New York: Pageant Press, 1957.

Hines, Harvey K. *Missonary History of the Pacific Northwest Containing the Wonderful History of Jason Lee.* Portland: H. K. Hines, 1899.

Holbrook, Stewart H. *The Columbia.* New York: Rinehart, 1956.

Holdich, Joseph. *Life of Fisk.* New York: Harper, 1856.

Holman, Frederick V. *Dr. John McLoughlin: The Father of Oregon.* Cleveland: A. H. Clark, 1907.

Holmes, Kenneth L. *Ewing Young, Master Trapper.* Portland: Binfords & Mort, 1967.

Horner, John B. *Oregon, Her History, Her Great Men. . . .* Portland: J. K. Gill, 1921.

Howard, Joseph K. *Strange Empire: A Narrative of the Northwest.* New York: Morrow, 1952.

Hussey, John A. *Champoeg: Place of Transition.* Portland: Oregon Historical Society, 1967.

Jacobs, Melvin C. *Winning Oregon: A Study of an Expansionist Movement.* Caldwell, Idaho: Caxton Printers, 1938.

Jessett, T. E., ed. *Reports and Letters of Herbert Beaver, 1836–1838, Chaplain to the Hudson's Bay Company and Missionary to the Indians at Fort Vancouver.* Portland: Champoeg Press, 1959.

Johannsen, Robert W. *Frontier Politics and the Sectional Conflict: The Pacific Northwest on the Eve of the Civil War.* Seattle: University of Washington Press, 1955.

Johansen, Dorothy O., and Charles M. Gates. *Empire of the Columbia.* 2d ed. New York: Harper & Row, 1967.

Johnson, Olga W. *Flathead and Kootenay.* Glendale, Calif.: A. H. Clark, 1969.

Johnson, Robert C. *John McLoughlin, Patriarch of the Northwest.* Portland: Metropolitan Press, 1935.

Josephy, Alvin M., Jr. *The Nez Perce Indians and the Opening of the Northwest.* New Haven: Yale University Press, 1965.

Landerholm, Carl, ed. and trans. *Notices of Voyages of the Famed Quebec Mission to the Pacific Northwest.* Portland: Champoeg Press, 1956.

Lang, H. O., ed. *History of the Willamette Valley.* Portland: Himes and Lang, 1885.

Latourette, K. S. *Christianity in a Revolutionary Age.* New York: Harper, 1958.

Lavender, David. *Westward Vision: The Story of the Oregon Trail.* New York: McGraw-Hill, 1963.

Lednum, J. *A History of the Rise of Methodism in America.* Philadelphia: Privately printed, 1859.

Lee, Humphrey. *The Historical Backgrounds of Early Methodist Enthusiasm.* New York: Columbia Studies in History, 1931.

Luccock, H. E., and Paul Hutchinson. *The Story of Methodism.* New York: Abingdon Press, 1949.

Lyman, Horace S. *History of Oregon.* 4 vols. New York: North Pacific Publishing Society, 1903.

Lyons, L. M. *Francis Norbert Blanchet and the Founding of the Oregon Missions, 1838–1848.* Washington: Catholic University of America Press, 1940.

McCulloh, G. O., ed. *The Ministry in the Methodist Heritage.* Nashville: Department of Ministerial Education, 1960.

Mathews, Donald G. *Slavery and Methodism: A Chapter in American Morality, 1780–1845.* Princeton: Princeton University Press, 1965.

Merk, Frederick. *Albert Gallatin and the Oregon Problem.* Cambridge: Harvard University Press, 1950.

———. *Fruits of Propaganda in the Tyler Administration.* Cambridge: Harvard University Press, 1971.

———. *The Oregon Question.* Cambridge: Belknap Press, 1967.

Moede, G. F. *The Office of the Bishop in Methodism.* New York: Abingdon Press, 1965.

Montgomery, Richard G. *The White Headed Eagle.* New York: Macmillan, 1934.

Moores, Charles B. *Oregon Pioneer Wa-wa: A Compilation of Addresses Relating to Oregon Pioneer History*. Portland [?], 1923.

Morgan, Dale. *Jedediah Smith and the Opening of the West*. Indianapolis: Bobbs-Merrill, 1953.

Morton, Arthur S. *Sir George Simpson, Overseas Governor of the Hudson's Bay Company: A Pen Picture of a Man of Action*. Toronto: J. M. Dent & Sons, 1944.

Mudge, Z. A. *Sketches of Mission Life among the Indians of Oregon*. New York: Carlton & Phillips, 1854.

————. *The Missonary Teacher: A Memoir of Cyrus Shepard*. New York: Lane & Tippett, 1848.

Nichols, Marie Leona. *The Mantle of Elias: The Story of Fathers Blanchet and Demers in Early Oregon*. Portland: Binfords & Mort, 1941.

Norwood, John N. *Church Membership in the Methodist Tradition*. Nashville: Methodist Publishing House, 1958.

————. *The Schism in the Methodist Episcopal Church, 1844–1846*. Alfred, N.Y.: Alfred Press, 1923.

Nottingham, Elizabeth K. *Methodism and the Frontier: Indiana Proving Grounds*. New York: AMS Press, 1966.

O'Hara, E. V. *Pioneer Catholic History of Oregon*. Paterson, N.J.: St. Anthony Guild Press, 1939.

Olin, Stephen. *The Life and Letters of Stephen Olin*. 2 vols. New York: Harper, 1854.

Oregon Historical Society. *Proceedings, 1899–1905*. Salem, 1900–1906.

Oregon Native Son, The. Vols. I–II. Portland: Native Son Publishing Co., 1899–1901.

Oregon Pioneer Association. *Transactions, 1873–1928*. Vols. 1–56. Portland, 1875–1933.

Palladino, L. B. *Indian and White in the Northwest*. 2d ed. Lancaster, Pa.: Wickersham Publishing Co., 1922.

Parsons, John. *Beside the Beautiful Willamette*. Portland: Metropolitan Press, 1924.

Pilkington, J. P. *The Methodist Publishing House*. New York: Abingdon, 1968.

Playter, George. *The History of Methodism in Canada*. Toronto, 1869.

Pletcher, David M. *The Diplomacy of Annexation: Texas, Oregon, and the Mexican War*. Columbia: University of Missouri Press, 1973.

Pollard, Lancaster. *Oregon and the Pacific Northwest*. Portland: Binfords & Mort, 1946.

Powell, Fred. *Hall Jackson Kelley: Prophet of Oregon*. Portland: Ivy Press, 1917.

————. *Hall Jackson Kelley on Oregon*. Princeton: Princeton University Press, 1932.

Powers, Alfred. *History of Oregon Literature*. Portland: Metropolitan Press, 1935.

Reid, J. M. *Missionaries and the Missionary Society of the Methodist Episcopal Church.* 2 vols. New York, 1895–96.

Rich, E. E. *Hudson's Bay Company, 1670–1870.* 3 vols. New York: Macmillan, 1961.

Scott, Harvey W. *History of the Oregon Country.* 6 vols. Cambridge: Riverside Press, 1924.

Scudder, M. L. *American Methodism.* Chicago: O. F. Gibbs, 1867.

Seaman, Samuel. *Annals of New York Methodism.* New York: Hunt & Eaton, 1892.

Semmel, Bernard. *The Methodist Revolution.* New York: Basic Books, 1973.

Simpson, M., ed. *Cyclopedia of Methodism.* Philadelphia: Louis Everts, 1881.

Smith, George. *Polity of Wesleyan Methodism.* London, 1851.

Strickland, W. P. *History of the Missions of the Methodist Episcopal Church.* Cincinnati: Methodist Book Concern, 1849.

Strickland, W. P., and James Finley. *Sketches of Western Methodism.* Cincinnati: Methodist Book Concern, 1855.

Sweet, William W. *Methodism in American History.* New York: Abingdon Press, 1961.

Sweet, William W., ed. *Men of Zeal: The Romance of American Methodist Beginnings.* New York: Abingdon Press, 1935.

———. *The Methodists: A Collection of Source Materials.* Chicago: University of Chicago Press, 1946.

Throckmorton, Arthur. *Oregon Argonauts: Merchant Adventurers on the Western Frontier.* Portland: Oregon Historical Society, 1961.

Tipple, E. W., ed. *The Heart of Francis Asbury's Journal.* New York: Eaton L. Mains, 1904.

Tobie, Harvey E. *No Man Like Joe.* Portland: Binfords & Mort, 1949.

Tyler, David B. *The Wilkes Expedition: The First United States Exploring Expedition, 1838–1842.* Philadelphia: American Philosophical Society, 1968.

Vestal, Stanley. *Joe Meek.* Caldwell, Idaho: Caxton Printers, 1952.

Victor, Frances Auretta. *All Over Oregon and Washington.* San Francisco: J. H. Carmany, 1872.

———. *River of the West.* Hartford, Conn.: Long's College Book Company, 1870.

Warren, Sidney. *Farthest Frontier: The Pacific Northwest.* New York: Macmillan, 1949.

Wesley, John. *The Letters of John Wesley.* Ed. John Telford. 8 vols. London, 1931.

Wheat, Carl I. *Mapping the Trans-Mississippi West, 1540–1861.* 5 vols. San Francisco: Institute of Historical Cartography, 1957–63.

Winther, Oscar O. *The Great Northwest.* New York: Knopf, 1947.

————. *The Old Oregon Country: A History of Frontier Trade, Transportation and Travel.* New York and Stanford: Stanford University Press, 1950.

Woodward, Walter C. *The Rise and Early History of Political Parties in Oregon, 1843–1868.* Portland: J. K. Gill, 1913.

Articles

Ambler, Charles H. "The Oregon Country, 1810–1830: A Chapter in Territorial Expansion." *MVHR* 30 (1943): 3–24.

Bain, Read. "Educational Plans and Efforts by Methodists in Oregon to 1860." *OHQ* 23 (1922): 63–94.

Barry, J. Neilson. "Site of the Historic Granary of the Methodist Mission." *OHQ* 43 (1942): 286–91.

————. "The Champoeg Meeting of March 4, 1844." *OHQ* 38 (1937): 425–32.

Beidleman, Richard G. "Nathaniel Wyeth's Fort Hall." *OHQ* 58 (1957): 197–250.

Blue, G. V. "Green's Missionary Report on Oregon." *OHQ* 30 (1929): 259–71.

Bradley, Marie Merriman. "Political Beginnings in Oregon: The Period of the Provisional Government." *OHQ* 9 (1908): 42–72.

Bright, Verne. "The Folklore and History of the 'Oregon Fever.' " *OHQ* 52 (1951): 241–53.

Brosnan, C. J. "The Signers of the Oregon Memorial of 1838." *WHQ* 24 (1933): 174–89.

Canse, John M. "The Oregon Mission: Its Transition." *WHQ* 25 (1934): 203–9.

Carey, Charles H. "British Side of the Oregon Question, 1846." *OHQ* 36 (1935): 263–94.

————. "Lee, Waller and McLoughlin." *OHQ* 33 (1932): 187–213.

Cartwright, Charlotte M. "Glimpses of Early Days in Oregon." *OHQ* 4 (1903): 55–69.

"Champoeg Legend, The." *Bancroftiana* 20 (April 1959): 8.

Cheney, Charles B. "Political Movements in the Northwest." *Review of Reviews* 21 (1905): 337–41.

Clark, D. W. "Life and Times of Elijah Hedding." *Methodist Quarterly Review* 35 (1853): 234–56.

Clark, Ella E. "The Mythology of the Indians in the Pacific Northwest." *OHQ* 54 (1953): 163–89.

Clark, Robert C. "Hawaiians in Early Oregon." *OHQ* 35 (1934): 22–31.

————. "How British and American Subjects Unite in a Common Government: Oregon Territory in 1844." *OHQ* 16 (1915): 313–29.

Commager, Henry S. "England and the Oregon Treaty of 1846." *OHQ* 28 (1927): 13–38.

Cramer, Richard S. "British Maps and the Oregon Question." *PHR* 32 (1963): 369–82.

D'Arcy, Peter H. "Historical Review: Champoeg, the Plymouth Rock of the Northwest." *OHQ* 29 (1928): 217–24.

Eaton, W. Clement. "Nathaniel Wyeth's Oregon Expeditions." *PHR* 4 (1935): 101–13.

Edgerton, R. P. "Government Comes to Oregon." *Pacific Northwesterner* (Winter 1958): 28–36.

Elliot, T. C. " 'Doctor' Robert Newell: Pioneer." *OHQ* 9 (1908): 103–26.

———. "Religion among the Flatheads." *OHQ* 37 (1936): 1–8.

Frost, O. W. "Margaret J. Bailey, Oregon Pioneer Author." *MCH* 5 (1959): 64–65.

Galbraith, John S. "The Early History of the Puget Sound Agricultural Company, 1838–43." *OHQ* 55 (1954): 234–59.

Georges, Maurice O. "A Suggested Revision of the Role of a Pioneer Political Scientist [William Gilpin]." *Reed College Bulletin* (April 1947).

Graebner, Norman A. "Maritime Factors in the Oregon Compromise." In *American History: Recent Interpretations. Book 1: To 1877*. Ed. Abraham S. Eisenstadt. 2d ed. New York: Crowell, 1969. Pp. 374–86.

———. "Politics and the Oregon Compromise." *PNQ* 52 (1961): 7–14.

Haines, Francis. "Pioneer Portraits: Robert Newell." *Idaho Yesterdays* 60 (Spring 1965): 2–9.

Hansen, William A. "Thomas Hart Benton and the Oregon Question." *Missouri Historical Review* 58 (July 1969): 489–97.

Herriott, F. L. "Transplanting Iowa's Laws to Oregon." *OHQ* 5 (1904): 138–51.

Hicks, C. R. "Champoeg." *OHQ* 40 (1939): 343–44.

Holman, Frederick V. "A Brief History of the Oregon Provisional Government and What Caused Its Formation." *OHQ* 13 (1912): 89–139.

Howe, D. W. "The Mississippi Valley in the Movement for Fifty-four Forty or Fight." *Mississippi Valley Historical Association Proceedings* 5 (1912): 99–116.

Hull, Dorothy. "The Movement in Oregon for the Establishment of a Pacific Coast Republic." *OHQ* 17 (1916): 177–200.

Idleman, L. H. "Long Continued Influences of Methodism in Oregon." *OHQ* 43 (1942): 210–14.

Judson, Lewis. "Reverend Lewis Hubbel Judson." *MCH* 4 (1958): 21–25.

Kaplan, Mirth T. "Courts, Counselors and Cases: The Judiciary of Oregon's Provisional Government." *OHQ* 62 (1961): 117–63.

Knuth, Priscilla. "Nativism in Oregon." *Reed College Bulletin* (January 1946).

Kroll, Helen B. "The Books That Enlightened the Emigrants." *OHQ* 45 (1944): 103–20.

Lomax, Alan L. "History of Pioneer Sheep Husbandry in Oregon." *OHQ* 29 (1928): 99–143.

Long, S. A. "Mrs. Jesse Applegate." *OHQ* 9 (1908): 179–83.

McCabe, James O. "Arbitration and the Oregon Question." *CHR* 41 (1960): 308–27.

MacEachern, John. "Elwood Evans, Lawyer-Historian." *PNQ* 52 (1961): 15–23.

Mallett, Edmond. "The Origin of the Flathead Mission in the Rocky Mountains." *Records of the American Catholic Historical Society of Philadelphia* 2 (1889): 174–205.

Mathews, Donald G. "The Methodist Schism of 1844 and the Popularization of Anti-Slavery Sentiments." *Mid-America* 51 (January 1969): 3–23.

Merk, Frederick. "British Government Propaganda and the Oregon Treaty." *AHR* 40 (1934): 38–62.

———. "British Party Politics and the Oregon Treaty." *AHR* 37 (1932): 653–77.

———. "Oregon Pioneers and the Boundary." *AHR* 29 (1924): 681–99.

———. "The British Corn Crisis of 1845–64 and the Oregon Treaty." *Agricultural History* 8 (July 1934): 95–123.

———. "The Oregon Question in the Webster-Ashburton Negotiations." *MVHR* 43 (1956): 379–404.

Minto, John. "Antecedents of the Oregon Pioneers and the Light These Throw on Their Motives." *OHQ* 5 (1904): 38–63.

———. "Champoeg, Marion County, the First Grain Market in Oregon." *OHQ* 15 (1914): 283–84.

———. "The Number and Condition of the Native Races in Oregon When First Seen by White Men." *OHQ* 1 (1900): 296–315.

———. "What I Know of Dr. McLoughlin and How I Know It." *OHQ* 11 (1910): 177–200.

Morton, W. L. "The Significance of Site in the Settlement of the American and Canadian Wests." *Agricultural History* 25 (July 1951): 97–104.

Munnick, Harriet D. "The Transition Decades on French Prairie, 1830–1850." *MCH* 4 (1958): 35–42.

Murray, Keith A. "The Role of the Hudson's Bay Company in the Pacific Northwest." *PNQ* 9 (1961): 24–30.

———. "The Transfer of Hudson's Bay Headquarters from Fort Vancouver to Fort Victoria." *CCH* 8 (1967).

Nesmith, J. W. "Annual Address." *TOPA* 1880 (Portland, 1881): 8–27.

O'Callaghan, Jerry A. "Extinguishing Indian Titles on the Oregon Coast." *OHQ* 52 (1951): 139–44.

Odgers, Charlotte. "Jesse Applegate: Study of a Pioneer Politician." *Reed College Bulletin* (January 1945).

Oliphant, J. Orin. "George Simpson and Oregon Mission." *PHR* 6 (1937): 213–48.

———. "Robert Moore in Oregon History." *WHQ* 15 (1924): 163–86.

———. "Some Neglected Aspects of the History of the Pacific Northwest." *PNQ* 61 (1970): 1–9.

Overmeyer, Philip H. "Members of First Wyeth Expedition." *OHQ* 36 (1935): 95–101.

Perrine, Fred S. "Early Days on the Willamette." *OHQ* 25 (1924): 295–312.

Pike, C. J. "Petitions of Oregon Settlers, 1838–48." *OHQ* 34 (1933): 216–35.

Pollard, Lancaster. "The Pacific Northwest." In *Regionalism in America.* Ed. Merrill Jensen. Madison, Wisc., 1965. Pp. 187–214.

Porter, Kenneth W. "Roll of Overland Astorians, 1810–1812." *OHQ* 34 (1933): 103–12.

Reed, Henry E. "Lovejoy's Pioneer Narrative." *OHQ* 30 (1929): 237–60.

———. "William Johnson." *OHQ* 34 (1933): 314–23.

Rich, E. E. "Mr. Beaver Objects." *The Beaver,* Outfit 272 (September 1941): 21–30.

Robertson, James Rood. "The Genesis of Political Authority and of a Commonwealth Government in Oregon." *OHQ* 1 (1900): 3–59.

Schafer, Joseph. "Jesse Applegate: Pioneer Statesman and Philosopher." *WHQ* 1 (1907): 212–33.

———. "The British Attitude toward the Oregon Question, 1815–1846." *AHR* 16 (1911): 273–99.

Scott, Harvey W. "Jason Lee's Place in History." *WHQ* 1 (1907): 21–33.

———. "The Formation and Administration of the Provisional Government of Oregon." *OHQ* 2 (1901): 95–118.

Scott, Leslie M. "Indian Diseases as Aids to Pacific Northwest Settlement." *OHQ* 29 (1928): 144–61.

———. "Modern Fallacies of Champoeg." *OHQ* 32 (1931): 213–16.

Taylor, Herbert C., Jr., and Lester L. Hoaglin, Jr. "The 'Intermittent Fever' Epidemic of the 1830's on the Lower Columbia River." *Ethnohistory* 9 (1962): 160–78.

Thomas, Russell. "Truth and Fiction of the Champoeg Meeting." *OHQ* 30 (1929): 218–37.

Vaughan, Thomas, ed. *The Western Shore: Oregon Country Essays in Honor of the American Revolution.* Portland: Durham and Downey, 1975.

Wardell, M. L. "Oregon Immigration Prior to 1846." *OHQ* 27 (1926): 41–64.

Welch, Richard E. "Caleb Cushing's Chinese Mission and the Treaty of Wanghia: A Review." *OHQ* 59 (1958): 327–57.

Winch, Martin, and Thomas Vaughan. "Joseph Gervais: A Familiar Mystery Man." *OHQ* 66 (1965): 331–62.

Winther, Oscar O. "The British in the Oregon Country: A Triptych View." *PNQ* 58 (1967): 179–87.

Young, F. G. "The Financial History of the State of Oregon." *OHQ* 10 (1909): 263–95.

Zorn, Henry. "Robert Newell and Newell House." *MCH* 8 (1962–1964): 39–42.

Theses

Bailey, A. K. "The Strategy of Sheldon Jackson in Opening the West for National Missions: 1860–1880." Ph.D. thesis. Yale University, 1948.

Barnhart, K. E. "The Evolution of the Social Consciousness in Methodism." Ph.D. thesis. University of Chicago, 1924.

Cobb, J. L. "The Establishment of Civil Government in Oregon, 1837–1845." M.A. thesis. University of California, Berkeley, 1917.

Crane, Fred A. "The Noble Savage in America, 1815–1860: Concepts of the Indian with Special Reference to the Writers of the Northeast." Ph.D. thesis. Yale University, 1952.

Decker, Robert J. "Jason Lee, Missionary to Oregon: A Re-evaluation." Ph.D. thesis. Indiana University, 1961.

Delamarter, George G. "The Career of Robert Newell." M.A. thesis. University of Oregon, 1924.

Fariss, Jessie. "Ewing Young: Western Pioneer." M.A. thesis. University of California, Berkeley, 1928.

Guest, Anna Lee. "The Historical Development of Southern Oregon, 1825–1852." M.A. thesis. Oklahoma College for Women, 1924.

Jordan, Rush. "Oregon, 1834–1844, with Special Reference to the Influence of the Methodist Mission in Its Non-Ecclesiastical Aspects." M.A. thesis. University of Idaho, 1929.

Martha, Edward. "Government Patronage of Indian Missions, 1789–1832." Ph.D. thesis. University of Wisconsin, 1916.

Nichols, C. A. "Moral Education among North American Indians." Ph.D. thesis. Teachers College, Columbia University, 1930.

Shaefer, Ruth E. "The Influence of Methodism in Early Oregon History." M.A. thesis. University of Oregon, 1929.

Bibliography

GENERAL WORKS

(Items in this section are highly selective. Many of the important subjects treated in this book, especially democracy, historicism, and the Jacksonian era, have an extensive literature. No effort is made here to do anything more than indicate which books I have consulted most frequently. I have excluded the most familiar along with the more specialized volumes.)

Books

Ahlstrom, Sydney E., ed. *A Religious History of the American People.* New Haven: Yale University Press, 1972.

Anshen, Ruth N., ed. *Freedom: Its Meaning.* New York: Harcourt Brace, 1940.

Arieli, Yehoshua. *Individualism and Nationalism in American Ideology.* Cambridge: Harvard University Press, 1964.

Bailyn, Bernard. *The Ideological Origins of the American Revolution.* Cambridge: Belknap Press, 1967.

————. *The Origins of American Policies.* New York: Knopf, 1968.

Banton, Michael, ed. *Anthropological Approaches to the Study of Religion.* New York: Praeger, 1966.

Bassett, John Spencer, and J. Franklin Jameson, eds. *Correspondence of Andrew Jackson.* Vol. III. Washington: Carnegie Institution, 1928.

Bates, Ernest S. *American Faith: Its Religious, Political and Economic Foundations.* New York: Norton, 1940.

Beaver, Robert P. *Church, State and the American Indians: Two and a Half Centuries of Partnership in Missions between Churches and Government.* Saint Louis: Concordia Publishing House, 1966.

————. *Missionary Motivation through Three Centuries.* Chicago: University of Chicago Press, 1968.

Bemis, Samuel Flagg. *John Quincy Adams and the Foundations of American Foreign Policy.* New York: Knopf, 1949.

Benedict, Ruth. *Race, Science and Politics.* Rev. ed. New York: Viking, 1962.

Berger, Peter L. *A Rumor of Angels: Modern Society and the Rediscovery of the Supernatural.* Garden City: Doubleday, 1969.

Berger, Peter L., and Thomas Luckmann. *The Social Construction of Reality.* Garden City: Doubleday, 1967.

Berkhofer, Robert F., Jr. *Salvation and the Savage: An Analysis of Protestant Missions and American Indian Response, 1787–1862.* New York: Atheneum, 1972.

Berlin, Isaiah. *Two Concepts of Liberty.* Oxford: Clarendon Press, 1958.

Berthoff, Rowland B. *An Unsettled People: Social Order and Disorder in American History.* New York: Harper and Row, 1971.

[265]

Billington, Ray A., ed. *Frontier and Section: Selected Essays of Frederick Jackson Turner.* Englewood Cliffs: Prentice-Hall, 1961.

Bingham, Edwin, and Robert B. Hine, eds. *The Frontier Experience.* Belmont, Calif.: Wadsworth Publishing Co., 1963.

Bodo, John F. *The Protestant Clergy and Public Issues, 1812–1848.* Princeton: Princeton University Press, 1954.

Boles, J. B. *The Great Revival, 1787–1805: The Origins of the Southern Evangelical Men.* Lexington: University of Kentucky Press, 1972.

Boller, Paul F., Jr. *American Thought in Transition: The Impact of Evolutionary Nationalism, 1865–1896.* Chicago: Rand McNally, 1969.

Boorstin, Daniel. *The Genius of American Politics.* Chicago: University of Chicago Press, 1953.

Boren, Carter E. *Religion on the Texas Frontier.* San Antonio: Naylor Co., 1968.

Boyd, Julian P. *The Declaration of Independence: The Evolution of the Text as Shown in Facsimiles of Various Drafts by Its Author.* Princeton: Princeton University Press, 1945.

Brock, William R. *The Evolution of American Democracy.* New York: Dial Press, 1970.

Burns, E. M. *The American Idea of Mission.* New Brunswick: Rutgers University Press, 1957.

Clark, John G., ed. *The Frontier Challenge: Responses to the Trans-Mississippi West.* Lawrence: University of Kansas Press, 1971.

Clebsch, William A. *From Sacred to Profane America: The Role of Religion in American History.* New York: Harper and Row, 1968.

Cole, C. C., Jr. *The Social Ideals of the Northern Evangelists, 1826–1860.* New York: Columbia University Press, 1954.

Collier, John. *Indians of the Americas.* New York: New American Library, 1964.

Davies, John D. *Phrenology, Fad and Science: A 19th Century American Crusade.* New Haven: Yale University Press, 1955.

Davis, David B. *The Problem of Slavery in the Age of Revolution, 1770–1823.* Ithaca: Cornell University Press, 1975.

Dealey, J. J. *Growth of American State Constitutions.* New York: Ginn, 1915.

DeVoto, Bernard. *Across the Wide Missouri.* Boston: Houghton Mifflin, 1947.

———. *The Course of Empire.* Boston: Houghton Mifflin, 1952.

———. *The Year of Decision, 1846.* Boston: Little Brown, 1943.

Diamond, Martin, and Morton J. Frish, eds. *Seminars on the American Political Tradition.* De Kalb: Northern Illinois University Press, 1968.

Diamond, Sigmund, ed. *The Creation of Society in the New World.* Chicago: Rand McNally, 1963.

Bibliography

Durkheim, Emile. *The Elementary Forms of the Religious Life.* Trans. Joseph Ward Swain. New York: Collier Books, 1961.

Eccles, W. J. *The Canadian Frontier, 1534–1760.* New York: Holt, Rinehart and Winston, 1969.

Eckstein, Harry. *A Theory of Stable Democracy.* Research Monograph no. 10. Center of International Studies. Princeton: University of Princeton Press, 1961.

Ekirch, Arthur A., Jr. *The Idea of Progress in America, 1815–1860.* New York: P. Smith, 1951.

Ellis, David M., ed. *The Frontier in American Development.* Ithaca: Cornell University Press, 1969.

Fairchild, Hoxie Neale. *The Noble Savage: A Study in Romantic Naturalism.* New York: Russell & Russell, 1961.

Ferguson, Charles W. *Organizing to Beat the Devil: Methodists and the Making of America.* Garden City: Doubleday, 1971.

Foster, Charles I. *An Errand of Mercy: The Evangelical United Front, 1790–1837.* Chapel Hill: University of North Carolina Press, 1960.

Fried, Morton. *The Evolution of Political Society: An Essay in Political Anthropology.* New York: Random House, 1967.

Frisch, M. H. *Town into City: Springfield, Massachusetts, and the Meaning of Community, 1840–1880.* Cambridge: Harvard University Press, 1972.

Gay, Peter. *The Enlightenment: An Interpretation: The Rise of Modern Paganism.* New York: Vintage, 1968.

———. *The Party of Humanity: Essays in the French Enlightenment.* New York: Knopf, 1964.

Gilson, Etienne. "Concerning Christian Philosophy: The Distinctiveness of the Philosophic Order." In Raymond Klibansky and H. J. Paton, eds., *Philosophy and History: Essays Presented to Ernst Cassirer.* New York: Harper and Row, 1963.

Goodykoontz, Colin B. *Home Missions on the American Frontier.* Caldwell, Idaho: Caxton Printers, 1939.

Gordon, Milton. *Assimilation in American Life.* New York: Oxford University Press, 1964.

Gossett, Thomas. *Race: The History of an Idea in America.* Dallas: Southern Methodist University Press, 1963.

Gough, J. W. *The Social Contract: A Critical Study of Its Development.* 2d ed. Oxford: Oxford University Press, 1957.

Griffin, Clifford. *The Ferment of Reform, 1830–1860.* New York: Crowell, 1967.

———. *Their Brother's Keeper: Moral Stewardship in the United States, 1800–1865.* New Brunswick: Rutgers University Press, 1960.

Gusfield, Joseph R. *Symbolic Crusade: Status Politics and the American Temperance Movement.* Urbana: University of Illinois Press, 1963.

Gustafson, James M. *Treasure in Earthen Vessels: The Church as a Human Community.* New York: Harper, 1961.

Hagen, William T. *American Indians.* 2 vols. Chicago: University of Chicago Press, 1961.

Handy, Robert. *A Christian America: Protestant Hopes and Historical Realities.* New York: Oxford University Press, 1971.

Haraszti, Zoltan. *John Adams and the Prophets of Progress.* Cambridge: Harvard University Press, 1952.

Harrod, Howard L. *Mission among the Blackfeet.* Norman: Oklahoma University Press, 1971.

Hartshorne, Thomas L. *The Distorted Image: Changing Conceptions of the American Character since Turner.* Cleveland: Press of Case Western Reserve University, 1968.

Hartz, Louis. *Economic Policy and Democratic Thought: Pennsylvania Politics, 1776–1860.* Cambridge: Harvard University Press, 1948.

———. *The Founding of New Societies.* New York: Harcourt, Brace & World, 1964.

———. *The Liberal Tradition in America: An Interpretation of American Political Thought since the Revolution.* New York: Harcourt, Brace, 1955.

Heimert, Alan. *Religion and the American Mind: From the Great Awakening to the Revolution.* Cambridge: Harvard University Press, 1966.

Hentoff, Nat. *The New Equality.* New York: Viking, 1965.

Herring, E. Pendleton. *The Politics of Democracy: American Parties in Action.* New York: Norton, 1965.

Hibberd, Benjamin H. *A History of Public Land Policy.* New York, 1924.

Hine, Robert V. *California's Utopian Communities.* New Haven: Yale University Press, 1966.

———. *The American West: An Interpretive History.* Boston: Little Brown, 1973.

Hofstadter, Richard. *Anti-Intellectualism in American Life.* New York: Knopf, 1964.

———. *The Paranoid Style in American Politics, and Other Essays.* New York: Vintage Books, 1967.

Hudson, Winthrop. *Religion in America.* 2d ed. New York: Scribner, 1973.

———. *The Great Tradition of the American Churches.* New York: Harper, 1953.

Humphrees, Edward F. *Nationalism and Religion in America, 1774–1784.* Boston, 1924.

Jaffa, Harry V. *Crisis of the House Divided: An Interpretation of the Issues in the Lincoln-Douglas Debates.* Garden City: Doubleday, 1959.

Bibliography

————. *Liberty and Equality: Theory and Practice in American Politics.* New York: Oxford University Press, 1965.

Jones, Howard M. *O Strange New World.* New York: Viking Press, 1964.

Jordan, Winthrop. *White over Black: American Attitudes toward the Negro, 1550–1812.* Chapel Hill: University of North Carolina Press, 1968.

Kallen, Horace M. *Cultural Pluralism and the American Idea: An Essay in Social Philosophy.* Philadelphia: University of Pennsylvania Press, 1956.

Kammen, Michael. *People of Paradox: An Inquiry Concerning the Origins of American Civilization.* New York: Knopf, 1972.

Karnes, Thomas L. *William Gilpin, Western Naturalist.* Austin: University of Texas Press, 1970.

Keiser, Albert. *The Indian in American Literature.* New York: Oxford University Press, 1933.

Kendall, Willmore, and George Carey. *The Basic Symbols of the American Political Tradition.* Baton Rouge: Louisiana State University Press, 1970.

Kerber, Linda K. *Federalists in Dissent: Imagery and Ideology in Jeffersonian America.* Ithaca: Cornell University Press, 1970.

Key, V. O. *Politics, Parties and Pressure Groups.* 5th ed. New York: Crowell, 1964.

Kristol, Irving. *On the Democratic Idea in America.* New York: Harper and Row, 1972.

Kroeber, Clifton B., ed. *The Frontier in Perspective.* Madison: University of Wisconsin Press, 1957.

Lakoff, Sanford A. *Equality in Political Philosophy.* Boston: Beacon Press, 1968.

Leder, Lawrence H. *Liberty and Authority: Early American Political Ideology, 1689–1763.* Chicago: Quadrangle Books, 1968.

Lee, Robert, and Martin E. Marty, eds. *Religion and Social Conflict.* New York: Oxford University Press, 1964.

Lewis, R. W. B. *The American Adam: Innocence, Tragedy, and Tradition in the Nineteenth Century.* Chicago: University of Chicago Press, 1955.

Linton, Ralph. *Acculturation in Seven American Indian Tribes.* New York: Appleton-Century, 1940.

Lipset, Seymour M. *Political Man.* Garden City: Doubleday, 1960.

Löwith, Karl. *Meaning in History.* Chicago: University of Chicago Press, 1949.

Lyons, E. J. *Isaac McCoy: His Plan for Indian Colonization.* Topeka: Kansas State Printing Plant, 1945.

McLoughlin, William G. *New England Dissent, 1630–1833.* Cambridge: Harvard University Press, 1971.

McLoughlin, William G., and Robert N. Bellah, eds. *Religion in America.* Boston: Houghton Mifflin, 1968.

Mardock, Robert W. *The Reformer and the American Indian*. Columbia: University of Missouri Press, 1971.

Marty, Martin E. *Righteous Empire: The Protestant Experience in America*. New York: Dial Press, 1970.

Mason, L. A. *Frontiersmen of the Faith: A History of Baptist Pioneer Work in Texas, 1865–1888*. New York: Naylor, 1970.

Mathews, Lois K. *The Expansion of New England*. New York: Russell & Russell, 1962.

Mead, Sidney E. *The Lively Experiment: The Shaping of Christianity in America*. New York: Harper and Row, 1963.

Merk, Frederick. *Manifest Destiny and Mission in American History*. New York: Knopf, 1963.

Merk, Frederick, with collaboration of Lois Bannister Merk. *The Monroe Doctrine and American Expansionism, 1843–1849*. New York: Knopf, 1966.

Merritt, Richard L. *Symbols of Community in America, 1735–1775*. New Haven: Yale University Press, 1966.

Miller, Perry. *Life of the Mind in America from the Revolution to the Civil War*. New York: Harcourt Brace and World, 1965.

Mimar, David. *Ideas and Politics: The American Experience*. Homewood, Ill.: Dorsey Press, 1964.

Miyakawa, T. Scott. *Protestants and Pioneers: Individualism and Conformity on the American Frontier*. Chicago: University of Chicago Press, 1964.

Mode, Peter G. *The Frontier Spirit in American Christianity*. New York: Macmillan, 1923.

Moore, Arthur K. *The Frontier Mind: A Cultural Analysis of the Kentucky Frontiersman*. Lexington: University of Kentucky Press, 1957.

Myrdal, Gunnar. *An American Dilemma: The Negro Problem and American Democracy*. New York: Harper and Row, 1962.

Olmstead, Clifton E. *History of Religion in the United States*. Englewood Cliffs: Prentice-Hall, 1960.

Ostrander, Gilman. *The Rights of Man in America, 1606–1861*. Columbia: University of Missouri Press, 1969.

Ostrogorski, Mosei. *Democracy and the Organization of Political Parties*. Trans. Frederick Clarke. 2 vols. Chicago: Quadrangle Books, 1964.

Nagle, Paul. *One Nation Indivisible: The Union in American Thought, 1776–1861*. New York: Oxford University Press, 1964.

Nash, Roderick. *Wilderness and the American Mind*. New Haven: Yale University Press, 1967.

Nichols, Roy F. *Religion and American Democracy*. Baton Rouge: Louisiana State University Press, 1959.

Bibliography

Nichols, Roy F., Roscoe Pound, and Charles H. McIlwain. *Federalism as a Democratic Process.* New Brunswick: Rutgers University Press, 1942.

Niebuhr, H. Richard. *The Kingdom of God in America.* New York: Harper and Row, 1959.

———. *The Social Sources of Denominationalism.* New York: Henry Holt, 1929.

Nozick, Robert. *Anarchy, State and Utopia.* New York: Basic Books, 1974.

Parsons, Talcott. *Structure and Process in Modern Society.* Glencoe: Free Press, 1960.

Pearce, Roy Harvey. *Historicism Once More.* Princeton: Princeton University Press, 1969.

———. *Savagism and Civilization.* Baltimore: Johns Hopkins Press, 1965.

Perry, Ralph B. *Puritanism and Democracy.* New York: Vanguard Press, 1944.

Philbrick, Francis S. *The Rise of the West, 1754–1830.* New York: Harper and Row, 1965.

Phillips, Clifton J. *Protestant America and the Pagan World.* Cambridge: Harvard University Press, 1969.

Pierson, George. *Tocqueville and Beaumont in America.* New York: Oxford University Press, 1938.

Prucha, Francis P. *American Indian Policy in the Formative Years: The Indian Trade and Intercourse Acts, 1790–1834.* Cambridge: Harvard University Press, 1962.

Prucha, Francis P., William T. Hagen, and Alvin M. Josephy, Jr. *American Indian Policy.* Indianapolis: Indiana Historical Society, 1971.

Rawls, John. *A Theory of Justice.* Cambridge: Belknap Press, 1971.

Robbins, Roy M. *Our Landed Heritage.* Princeton: Princeton University Press, 1942.

Rossiter, Clinton. *The American Quest 1790–1860.* New York: Harcourt Brace Jovanovich, 1971.

Sandeen, Ernest R. *The Roots of Fundamentalism: British and American Millennarianism, 1800–1930.* Chicago: University of Chicago Press, 1970.

Sanford, Charles L. *The Quest for Paradise: Europe and the American Moral Imagination.* Urbana: University of Illinois Press, 1961.

Saum, Lewis O. *The Fur Trade and the Indian.* Seattle: University of Washington Press, 1965.

Schaff, Philip. *America: A Sketch of Its Political, Social and Religious Character.* Ed. Perry Miller. Cambridge: Belknap Press, 1961.

Schattschneider, E. E. *Party Government.* New York: Rinehart, 1942.

———. *The Semi-Sovereign People.* New York: Holt, Rinehart and Winston, 1961.

Schlesinger, A. M. *The American as Reformer.* Cambridge: Harvard University Press, 1968.

Schumpeter, Joseph. *Capitalism, Socialism and Democracy.* 3d ed. New York: Harper, 1950.

Sellers, Charles G. *James K. Polk.* 3 vols. Princeton: Princeton University Press, 1957–66.

Semple, Ellen C. *American History and Its Geographic Conditions.* Boston: Houghton Mifflin, 1933.

Smith, Chard P. *Yankees and God.* New York: Hermitage House, 1954.

Smith, Henry N. *Virgin Land: The American West as Symbol and Myth.* New York: Vintage Books, 1957.

Smith, James Ward, and A. Leland Jamison, eds. *Religion in American Life.* 4 vols. Princeton: Princeton University Press, 1961.

Somkin, Fred. *Unquiet Eagle: Memory and Desire in the Idea of American Freedom, 1815–1860.* Ithaca: Cornell University Press, 1967.

Spicer, E. H. *Cycles of Conquest.* Tucson: University of Arizona Press, 1962.

Sweet, William W. *Religion in the Development of American Culture, 1765–1840.* New York: Scribner, 1952.

———. *Revivalism in America.* New York: Scribner, 1944.

Tawney, R. H. *Equality.* New York: Barnes & Noble, 1964.

Thernstrom, Stephan. *Poverty and Progress: Social Mobility in a Nineteenth Century City.* Cambridge: Harvard University Press, 1964.

Trennert, Robert. *Alternative to Extinction: Federal Indian Policy and the Beginnings of the Reservation System, 1846–1851.* Philadelphia: Temple University Press, 1975.

Tuveson, Ernest Lee. *Millennium and Utopia: A Study in the Background of the Idea of Progress.* Berkeley: University of California Press, 1949.

———. *Redeemer Nation: The Idea of America's Millennial Role.* Chicago: University of Chicago Press, 1968.

Stein, Maurice. *The Eclipse of Community.* Princeton: Princeton University Press, 1972.

Stephenson, George M. *The Political History of the Public Lands from 1840 to 1862.* Boston: R. G. Badger, 1917.

Strauss, Leo. *Liberalism Ancient and Modern.* New York: Basic Books, 1968.

———. *Natural Right and History.* Chicago: University of Chicago Press, 1953.

VanZandt, Roland. *The Metaphysical Foundations of American History.* The Hague: Mouton, 1959.

Voegeli, V. Jacque. *Free but Not Equal.* Chicago: University of Chicago Press, 1967.

Ward, John W. *Red, White and Blue: Men, Books, and Ideas in American Culture.* New York: Oxford University Press, 1969.

Washburn, Wilcomb E. *Red Man's Land—White Man's Law.* New York: Scribner, 1971.

Bibliography

Weber, Max. *The Protestant Ethic and the Spirit of Capitalism.* Trans. Talcott Parsons. New York: Scribner, 1958.

—————. *The Sociology of Religion.* Trans. Ephraim Fischoff. Boston: Beacon Press, 1963.

Weinberg, Albert K. *Manifest Destiny: A Study of Nationalist Expansion in American History.* Baltimore: Johns Hopkins Press, 1953.

Weisberger, Bernard. *They Gathered at the River.* Boston: Little Brown, 1958.

Wellington, Raynor G. *Political and Sectional Influence of Public Lands, 1828–1842.* N.p., 1924.

Wiebe, Robert. *The Search for Order.* New York: Hill and Wang, 1967.

Wolfe, Don M. *The Image of Man in America.* 2d ed. New York: Crowell, 1970.

Articles

Abel, Annie H. "Proposals for an Indian State, 1778–1878." *American Historical Association, Annual Report for the Year 1907* 1 (1908): 87–104.

Ahlstrom, Sydney E. "The Problem of the History of Religion in America." *CH* 39 (1970): 224–25.

Bell, Susan Groag. "Johan Eberlin Von Gunzburg's *Welfaria:* The First Protestant Utopia." *CH* 36 (1967): 122–39.

Bestor, Arthur, Jr. "Patent-Office Models of the Good Society: Some Relationships between Social Reform and Westward Expansion." In *American History: Recent Interpretations. Book I: To 1877.* Ed. Abraham S. Eisenstadt. 2d ed. 2 vols. New York: Crowell, 1969. I, 412–30.

—————. "State Sovereignty and Slavery: A Reinterpretation of Proslavery Constitutional Doctrine, 1846–1860." *Journal of the Illinois State Historical Society* 54 (1961): 117–80.

Brauer, Jerald C. "Images of Religion in America." *CH* 30 (1961): 3–18.

Buel, Richard, Jr. "Democracy and the American Revolution: A Frame of Reference." *WMQ* 21 (1964): 165.

Burns, Robert I. Review of *Salvation and the Savage,* by Robert F. Berkhofer, Jr. *OHQ* 70 (1969): 336–37.

Clebsch, William A. "A New Historiography of American Religion." *HMPEC* 32 (1963): 224–57.

Curti, Merle. "The Great Mr. Locke: America's Philosopher, 1783–1861." *Huntington Library Bulletin* 11 (April 1937): 107–51.

Drury, Clifford M. "The Oregonian and Indian's Advocate." *PNQ* 56 (1965): 159–67.

Formisano, Ronald, P. "Political Character of Anti-Partyism, and the Second Party System." *AMQ* 21 (Winter 1970): 683–709.

Bibliography

Gabriel, Ralph H. "Evangelical Religion and Popular Romanticism in Early 19th Century." In *American History: Recent Interpretations. Book I: To 1877*. Ed. Abraham S. Eisenstadt. 1st ed. New York, 1962. Pp. 427–42.

Goodwin, Gerald J. "Christianity, Civilization and the Savage: The Anglican Mission to the American Indian. *HMPEC* 42 (1973): 93–110.

Goodwin, Mary F. "Christianizing and Educating the Negro in Colonial Virginia." *HMPEC* 1 (1932): 143–52.

Hansen, K. "The Millennium, the West, and Race in the Ante-Bellum American Mind." *Western Historical Quarterly* (October 1972): 373–90.

Harding, F. A. J. "The Social Impact of the Evangelical Revival." *HMPEC* 15 (1946): 256–84.

Heimert, Alan. "Puritanism, the Wilderness, and the Frontier." In *Puritanism and the American Experience*. Ed. Michael McGiffert. Reading, Mass., 1969. Pp. 163–80.

Heise, David R. "Prefatory Findings in the Sociology of Missions." *Journal for the Scientific Study of Religion* 6 (April 1967): 49–58.

Higham, John. "Hanging Together: Divergent Unities in American History." *JAH* 51 (1974): 5–28.

Hudson, Winthrop H. "Theological Convictions and Democratic Government." *Theology Today* 10 (1953): 235–47.

Johansen, Dorothy O. "A Working Hypothesis for the Study of Migrations." *PHR* 36 (1967): 1–12.

Johnson, C. A. "Frontier Camp Meeting: Contemporary and Historical Appraisals, 1805–1840." *MVHR* 37 (1950): 91–110.

Kushner, H. I. "The Oregon Question Is . . . a Massachusetts Question." *OHQ* 75 (1974): 317–35.

Loewenberg, Robert J. "Elijah White vs. Jason Lee: A Tale of Hard Times." *Journal of the West* 11 (1972): 636–62.

Lovejoy, A. O., and George Boas. "Primitivism and Related Ideas in Antiquity." In *A Documentary History of Primitivism and Related Ideas*. Ed. A. O. Lovejoy *et al*. Vol. I. Baltimore, 1935.

McLoughlin, W. G. "Pietism and the American Character." *American Quarterly* 17 (1965): 163–85.

Marshall, Lynn. "The Strange Stillbirth of the Whig Party." *AHR* 72 (1967): 445–68.

Masland, John W. "Missionary Influence upon American Far Eastern Policy." *PHR* 10 (1941): 279–96.

Mathews, Donald G. "Methodist Mission to the Slaves." *JAH* 51 (1965): 615–31.

May, Henry F. "The Recovery of American Church History." *AHR* 70 (1964): 79–92.

Bibliography

Mead, Sidney E. "Church History Explained." *CH* 32 (1963): 17–31.

———. "The American People: Their Space, Time and Religion." *Journal of Religion* 34 (1954): 244–55.

Moats, F. I. "The Rise of Methodism in the Midwest." *MVHR* 15 (1928): 68–88.

Morison, Samuel E. "American Strategy in the Pacific Ocean." *OHQ* 62 (1961): 5–56.

Norwood, Frederick A. "The Shaping of Methodist Ministry." *Religion in Life* 43 (1974): 337–51.

Opie, John, Jr. "James McGready: Theology of Frontier Revivalism." *CH* 34 (1965): 445–54.

Outler, Allen C. "Theodosius' Horse: Reflections on the Predicament of Church History." *CH* 34 (1965): 251–61.

Paluden, Phillip S. "The American Civil War Considered as a Crisis in Law and Order." *AHR* 77 (1972): 1013–34.

Pomeroy, Earl S. "Towards a Reorientation of Western History." *MVHR* 41 (1955): 579–600.

Posey, W. B. "The Advance of Methodism in the Lower Southwest." *JSH* 2 (1936): 439–52.

Robbins, Roy M. "Preemption—A Frontier Triumph." *MVHR* 17 (1931): 331–49.

Sandeed, Ernest R. "Toward a Historical Interpretation of the Origins of Fundamentalism." *CH* 36 (1967): 66–83.

Sheehan, Bernard W. "Indian White Relations in Early America: A Review Essay." *WMQ* 26 (1969).

Smith, T. L. "Religious Denominations as Ethnic Communities: A Case Study." *CH* 35 (1966): 207–26.

Thomas, John L. "Romantic Reform in America, 1815–1865." *AMQ* 17 (Winter 1965): 656–81.

Washburn, Wilcomb. "The Writing of American Indian History." *PHR* 40 (1971): 261–82.

Welter, Rush. "The Frontier West as the Image of American Society, 1776–1860." *PNQ* 52 (1961): 1–6.

———. "The Idea of Progress in America: An Essay in Ideas and Method." *Journal of the History of Ideas* 16 (1955): 401–15.

Wilson, Major L. "Paradox Lost: Order and Progress in Evangelical Thought of Nineteenth-Century America." *Church History* 44 (1975): 352–66.

Wyatt-Brown, Bertram. "Abolitionism: Its Meaning for Contemporary American Reform." *MWQ* 8 (Autumn 1966): 45–48.

———. "Elkins' Anti-Slavery Interpretation Reexamined." *American Quarterly* 25 (May 1973): 154–76.

Index

identity of preacher with missionary, 49, 50; as missionary church, 49, 94, 95; and dilemma, 50, 53, 233; Fisk on, 62; and Indians, 83, 95, 106, 167, 233, 239, 240; Wesley on, 92, 112; devotion to system, 114, 234; antipartyism of, 168, 169; and Oregon Institute, 239; mentioned, 47, 49, 50, 52, 61, 96, 108, 111, 124, 125, 131, 145, 234, 239

Methodistica: collections at University of Puget Sound and the Washington State Historical Society, 106

Methodist missionaries: in Oregon, 4, 6, 35, 50, 97, 100, 103-4, 106, 109, 110, 113, 114, 116, 130, 134, 135, 142, 146, 149, 169, 180, 201, 211, 216, 236; Victor on, 9, 201; and Catholics, 95-96, 97, 146, 148, 149, 150, 165; and Indians, 96, 98, 105, 124; secular activities of, 109, 166, 169, 179, 185, 200, 208, 218; applicants to become, 109-10, 124, 125-27; and marriage, 113, 129; accused by Griffin, 134, 135; and government, 141, 145, 149, 163, 166, 196, 201, 209, 211, 212, 218; and French Canadians, 146; and Hudson's Bay Co., 151, 199; Gray on, 157; and Falls claim controversy, 188, 204, 219

Mexico, 240

Mid-March meeting: and Champoeg meeting, 141, 161, 226; and independence, 161, 164-66, 201; and governor's office, 227; mentioned, 44, 140, 196

Miller, Perry, 52

Minutes: of wolf meetings, 153, 157-58; of Champoeg meeting, 160-61, 226-27

Missionaries, English, 25

Missionary methods, 100. *See also* Methodist Episcopal Church; Methodist missionaries

Missionary Society. *See* Board of Managers

Mission party, 18

Mission school, 65

Mission steward, 118, 136

Mission store, 66, 137, 218

Monism, 10

Monroe, James, 57

Moore, Robert, 210

Morison, J. L., 210

Murray, Sir George, 28, 32

Murrin, John M., 44*n*16

Nass River, 23-24

Naturalism, 10

Negotiators: American and British in 1846, 202-3

Negroes: Methodist views of, 52

Newburyport, Mass., 171

Newell, Robert: as witness, 153, 154, 156, 162, 208, 210; in Champoeg, 155, 165, 166, 217, 223; and Gray, 155, 165; on provisional government, 161, 164, 165, 198, 207, 209, 226; letter to Brewer, 161, 162, 226; on executive committee, 163; and independence, 164, 199; and Hines, 164, 227; supporters of, 197, 198; on Hudson's Bay Co. views of independence, 199; factors of group led by, 210; entrepreneurs in group, 210; wheat production of group, 210; and Young compared, 224; mentioned, 63, 154, 155, 165, 215, 216

New England, 210

New England Conference: bill of objections against Lee, 184 and *n*38

New York City: mail from, 183, 187; mentioned, 5, 138, 193

New York Evening Post, 55

New York State: and Oregon, compared, 234

Nez Percé Indians, 7, 78*n*1

Nisbet, Robert, 40, 231 and *n*5

Nisqually mission, 65

North West Company, 17

Noyes, John Humphrey, 53

Ogden, Peter Skene: expedition of, 25

Old Mission, 216-17

Olin, Stephen: quoted on Methodism, 49

Olley, James: hired as carpenter, 127, 129; marriage of, 128, 132-33; mentioned, 197

Olley, Mrs. James. *See* Judson, Adelia Turkington Olley Leslie

O'Neil, James, 154, 212

Order of Exercises: and Olley's marriage, 131, 132

Index

ereignty, 140; commentaries on, 140, 141, 150, 151, 157, 197, 198; Victor's view of, 141; and "organization," 142; steps toward, 142, 143, 198; functions of, 143, 147, 157, 163, 195, 207, 217, 227, 228; and Young's death, 143, 224; Gray's theories of, 157; and wolf meetings, 160; and Shortess petition, 206; not ethnic contest, 207; and wheat growers, 209; agreed to, 226; proviso in land laws, 227; mentioned, 8, 9, 134, 140, 195, 196, 211, 215

Proviso, in Organic Laws. See Falls claim controversy

Puget Sound, 222

Puget Sound, University of, 9

Puget Sound Agricultural Company, 175

Purcell, Edward A., Jr., 39n7

Puritans: and Methodism, 37

Racism, 52

Raymond, William W.: claims Oregon Institute, 133; mentioned, 133, 214

Reductions. See Jesuits

Reformers: American, 47, 53

Relativism: and naturalism, 12; mentioned, 43

Religious historians: sect and church typology, 48

Revisionism, 9

Revolution, American: and Methodism, 5

Richmond, John P.: on Indians, 90-91, 235; at Nisqually, 90; and Lee, 91

Riesman, David, 52

Rocky Mountains, 8

Rousseau, Jean Jacques: and Hamilton, 231; mentioned, 12

Rover, Ruth. See Bailey, Margaret Jewett

Rupert's Land, 25

Russia, 23

Russian American Fur Company, 23, 174, 217, 221

Russians, 220

Salem, Ore.: and Oregon Institute, 184; and Champoeg, 208, 217; mentioned, 224. See also Chemeketa

Salmon, 7

Salvation: Methodists' view of, 4-5

Sands, Hodgson, Turner and Co., 182, 193

Sandwich Islands: and mission supplies, 182; mentioned, 187

Sargeant, Mary, 134

Sauvies Island, 148

Scappoose, 222

Schism of 1844: and slavery, 50; and Christianization, 104; mentioned, 50, 240

Second reinforcement, 70

Semmel, Bernard: on John Wesley, 48

Seys, John: on Christianization, 104

Shepard, Cyrus: as first mission teacher, 65, 80, 81; and Jason Lee, 81, 98, 122

Shortess, Robert: and Organic Laws, 64; and Peoria party, 147; Newell on, 154; and Gray, 164; mentioned, 163, 165, 197, 212

Shortess petition: and Farnham petition, 147; Methodist purposes reflected by, 194, 201, 204, 218; and Champoeg meeting, 195, 205, 206, 209, 213; and Hudson's Bay Co., 202, 206; and Distribution-Preemption law, 205; non-Methodist signers of, 206-7; Victor quoted on, 211; and petition of 1840, 212; and wheat, 218; mentioned, 145, 188, 204, 205, 214, 220

Sierra Leone, 104

Simpson, Sir George: and Falls claim controversy, 18, 189, 202; and McLoughlin, 20, 27, 34-35, 174, 203; and Oregon question, 21-24, 25, 28, 30, 33, 35; views change concerning Oregon, 21; and negotiations of 1827, 26, 28-29, 30; fears U.S., 29-30; and Benton, 31; mentioned, 17, 19, 20, 23, 24, 29, 33, 34, 222

Slacum, William: and Young, 170; mentioned, 217

Slavery: and Methodism, 5, 6

Smith, Jedediah: and Simpson, 30

Smith, Margaret Jewett Bailey. See Bailey, Margaret Jewett

Smith, Sidney, 63, 225

Smith, Solomon, 210

Smith, William: writes Simpson, 32

[285]